Geraint Jones and Mary Sheeran (Eds.)

Designing Correct Circuits

Workshop jointly organised by the
Universities of Oxford and Glasgow
26–28 September 1990, Oxford

Published in collaboration with the
British Computer Society

BCS

Springer-Verlag
London Berlin Heidelberg New York
Paris Tokyo Hong Kong

Geraint Jones
Oxford University Computing Laboratory
11 Keble Road
Oxford, OX1 3QD, England

Mary Sheeran
Department of Computing Science
University of Glasgow
Glasgow, G12 8QQ, Scotland

ISBN 3–540–19659–5 Springer-Verlag Berlin Heidelberg New York
ISBN 0–387–19659–5 Springer-Verlag New York Berlin Heidelberg

British Library Cataloguing in Publication Data
Designing correct circuits
  1. Computers. Circuits
  I. Jones, Geraint *1957–* II. Sheeran, Mary *1959–* III. British Computer
Society IV. Series
621.395
ISBN 3–540–19659–5

C.I.P. Data available

34/3830–543210 Printed on acid-free paper

WORKSHOPS IN COMPUTING

Series edited by C. J. van Rijsbergen

Also in this series

AI and Cognitive Science '89, Dublin City University, Eire,
14–15 September 1989
A. F. Smeaton and G. McDermott (Eds.)

Specification and Verification of Concurrent Systems, University of
Stirling, Scotland, 6–8 July 1988
C. Rattray (Ed.)

Semantics for Concurrency, Proceedings of the International
BCS-FACS Workshop, Sponsored by Logic for IT (S.E.R.C.), University
of Leicester, UK, 23–25 July 1990
M. Z. Kwiatkowska, M. W. Shields and R. M. Thomas (Eds.)

Functional Programming, Proceedings of the 1989 Glasgow
Workshop, Fraserburgh, Scotland, 21–23 August 1989
K. Davis and J. Hughes (Eds.)

Persistent Object Systems, Proceedings of the Third International
Workshop, Newcastle, Australia, 10–13 January 1989
J. Rosenberg and D. Koch (Eds.)

Z User Workshop, Proceedings of the Fourth Annual Z User Meeting,
Oxford, 15 December 1989
J. E. Nicholls (Ed.)

Formal Methods for Trustworthy Computer Systems (FM89), Halifax,
Canada, 23–27 July 1989
Dan Craigen (Editor) and Karen Summerskill (Assistant Editor)

Security and Persistence, Proceedings of the International Workshop
on Computer Architectures to Support Security and Persistence of
Information, Bremen, West Germany, 8–11 May 1990
John Rosenberg and J. Leslie Keedy (Eds.)

Women into Computing: Selected Papers 1988–1990
Gillian Lovegrove and Barbara Segal (Eds.)

3rd Refinement Workshop, Proceedings of the 3rd Refinement
Workshop (organised by BCS-FACS, and sponsored by IBM UK
Laboratories, Hursley Park and the Programming Research Group,
University of Oxford) 9–11 January 1990, Hursley Park
Carroll Morgan and J. C. P. Woodcock (Eds.)

Functional Programming, Glasgow 1990, Proceedings of the 1990
Glasgow Workshop on Functional Programming, 13–15 August 1990,
Ullapool, Scotland
Simon L. Peyton Jones, Graham Hutton and Carsten Kehler Holst
(Eds.)

Preface

These proceedings contain the papers presented at a workshop on Designing Correct Circuits, jointly organised by the Universities of Oxford and Glasgow, and held in Oxford on 26–28 September 1990. There is a growing interest in the application to hardware design of the techniques of software engineering. As the complexity of hardware systems grows, and as the cost both in money and time of making design errors becomes more apparent, so there is an eagerness to build on the success of mathematical techniques in program development. The harsher constraints on hardware designers mean both that there is a greater need for good abstractions and rigorous assurances of the trustworthyness of designs, and also that there is greater reason to expect that these benefits can be realised. The papers presented at this workshop consider the application of mathematics to hardware design at several different levels of abstraction.

At the lowest level of this spectrum, Zhou and Hoare show how to describe and reason about synchronous switching circuits using UNITY, a formalism that was developed for reasoning about parallel programs. Aagaard and Leeser use standard mathematical techniques to prove correct their implementation of an algorithm for Boolean simplification. The circuits generated by their formal synthesis system are thus correct by construction. Thuau and Pilaud show how the declarative language LUSTRE, which was designed for programming real-time systems, can be used to specify synchronous circuits. They also present a tool for the automatic verification of circuit correctness. Collavizza and Borrione also use a functional formalism: they specify the micro-program parallelism of von Neumann style microprocessors. Luk shows how to optimise array-based designs by systematically rearranging components and interconnections. Delgado Kloos and Dosch show that it is possible to derive both asynchronous and synchronous implementations from a single specification. Zhu and Johnson consider data abstraction in an algebraic framework, and by now we are almost at the other extreme of the spectrum.

The topical area of the design of delay-insensitive circuits is represented by two papers. Josephs and Udding present an algebra in which expressions specify delay-insensitive circuits; they illustrate their method by designing a delay-insensitive stack. Brown shows how to compile programs written in a subset of occam* into delay-insensitive circuits. He demonstrates that it is possible to build interesting and purely delay-insensitive circuits using only a small set of building blocks. Akella and Gopalakrishnan also use a process algebra to describe hardware: they consider the problem of high-level test generation.

The idea of building a logic for hardware design on top of a theorem prover is also a hot topic in the field. Mendler builds a logic for design with constraints using the LEGO theorem prover. The Isabelle theorem prover provides the basis for Suk's constructive type theory for hardware synthesis and for Rossen's implementation of the algebra of the relational hardware design language Ruby. Busch shows how to do correctness-preserving circuit transformations using the LAMBDA system. Camurati, Margaria and Prinetto report on their experiences in using a First Order Logic theorem prover (OTTER) to verify the correctness of combinational logic. Joyce advocates the use of generic, that is parametrised, specifications and shows how they fit well in the context of Higher Order Logic (HOL). His paper also provides a good introduction to formal verification using the HOL system. Eker, Stavridou and Tucker use OBJ3 as a theorem proving tool for the verification of synchronous concurrent algorithms.

The papers present a good cross section of current work developing and applying formal methods in circuit design.

The papers in this volume were refereed before being selected for presentation, and have been revised in the light of the discussion at the workshop. We would like to thank the following referees and members of the program committee: Raymond Boute, Shiu-Kai Chin, John O'Donnell, Mike Fourman, Damir Jamsek, Steve Johnson, Wayne Luk, Tom Melham, Christian D. Nielsen, Donna E. Peterson, Jan van de Snepscheut, Edward P. Stabler, and Jørgen Staunstrup.

5th November 1990   Geraint Jones
                                                          Mary Sheeran

---

*occam is a trade mark of INMOS Limited

Contents

Constrained Proofs: A Logic for Dealing with Behavioural
Constraints in Formal Hardware Verification
Michael Mendler 1

Hardware Synthesis in Constructive Type Theory
Dany Suk 29

An Algebraic Framework for Data Abstraction in Hardware
Description
Zheng Zhu and Steven D. Johnson 50

Generic Specification of Digital Hardware
Jeffrey J. Joyce 68

Sampling and Proof: A Half-case Study *(Invited evening lecture)*
John Hughes 92

High Level Test Generation via Process Composition
Venkatesh Akella and Ganesh Gopalakrishnan 99

Towards Truly Delay-insensitive Circuit Realizations of Process
Algebras
Geoffrey M. Brown 120

The Design of a Delay-insensitive Stack
Mark B. Josephs and Jan Tijmen Udding 132

Specifying the Micro-program Parallelism for Microprocessors
of the von Neumann Style
Hélène Collavizza and Dominique Borrione 153

The Implementation and Proof of a Boolean Simplification System
Mark Aagaard and Miriam Leeser 171

A Model for Synchronous Switching Circuits and its Theory of
Correctness
Zhou Chaochen and C. A. R. Hoare 196

Efficient Circuits as Implementations of Non-strict Functions
Carlos Delgado Kloos and Walter Dosch 212

Verification of Synchronous Concurrent Algorithms using OBJ3:
A Case Study of the Pixel-planes Architecture
S. M. Eker, V. Stavridou and J. V. Tucker 231

Use of the OTTER Theorem Prover for the Formal Verification of
Hardware
Paolo Camurati, Tiziana Margaria and Paolo Prinetto 253

Proof-based Transformation of Formal Hardware Models
Holger Busch 271

Ruby Algebra
Lars Rossen 297

Using the Declarative Language LUSTRE for Circuit Verification
Ghislaine Thuau and Daniel Pilaud 313

Optimising Designs by Transposition
Wayne Luk 332

Author Index 355

Constrained Proofs:
A Logic for Dealing with Behavioural Constraints
in Formal Hardware Verification*

Michael Mendler[†]
Department of Computer Science
University of Edinburgh

Abstract

The application of formal methods to the design of correct computer hardware depends crucially on the use of abstraction mechanisms to partition the synthesis and verification task into tractable pieces. Unfortunately however, behavioural abstractions are genuine mathematical abstractions only up to behavioural *constraints*, i.e. under certain restrictions imposed on the device's environment. Timing constraints on input signals form an important class of such restrictions. Hardware components that behave properly only under such constraints satisfy their abstract specifications only approximately.

This is an impediment to the naive approach to formal verification since the question of how to apply a theorem prover when one only knows *approximately* what formula to prove has not as yet been dealt with.

In this paper we propose a notion of *constrained proof* and *constrained proposition* which provides for 'approximate' verification of abstract specifications and yet does not compromise the rigour of the argument. It is based on the idea of removing the constraints from the specification and making them part of its proof. Thereby the abstract verification is separated from constraint analysis which in turn may be delayed arbitrarily. We have implemented the logic on the interactive theorem prover LEGO and verified simple examples. The presentation in this paper uses one of these examples for explaining the problem and demonstrating the use of the logic.

---

*This work was supported by the *Studienstiftung des deutschen Volkes* and SERC grant No.GR/F 35890 "Formal System Design"

[†]Now at University of Erlangen-Nürnberg, Institute for Computer Aided Circuit Design, email *mendler@faui77.informatik.uni-erlangen.de* or *mm@lfcs.ed.ac.uk*

1   Introduction

Quite a lot of work has been done to make hardware verification practicable at a non-academic scale [5,4,19,20,25]. What still seriously limits its success is the almost insurmountable complexity from which verification of non-trivial hardware designs suffers. First steps are being undertaken by various researchers to exploit structuring concepts such as *modularisation* and *abstraction* in the design of hardware to break up the verification task into a series of smaller chores, each of which can be dealt with independently [5,4,26,18,35,32,10]. The question arises how this approach should best be implemented in modern interactive theorem provers.

1.1   The Problem of Constraints

A typical phenomenon one encounters with the implementation of even conceptually simple abstraction steps which are standard practice in hardware engineering is that they cannot be formalised without introducing *constraints*. Constraints are assumptions about the device's environment under which the particular abstraction (of its behaviour) at hand is actually valid.

An example is the passage from a sequential circuit, built according to the synchronous design paradigm, to its abstract description in terms of an input-output automaton. Here the abstraction is only valid as long as the environment (among other things) obeys a *timing constraint* which says that all input lines of the sequential circuit must be kept stable during a certain well-defined phase of the clock. Clearly, the necessity for imposing timing constraints is a general phenomenon, not restricted to the synchronous case. It is an even more important issue in asynchronous designs. [17,34,31].

The interaction between abstraction and constraints poses a tangled problem. Constraints interfere with the essential idea of reasoning about a behaviour in *abstract* terms which is to avoid details specific to the implementation at the more *concrete* level. For it is impossible to work with the device's abstract behaviour without at the same time having to deal with the concrete-level constraints on which it depends. To verify, for instance, that the behaviour of a composite device meets its abstract specification it does not suffice simply to compose the abstract specifications of its components. The verification also has to show that at the concrete level the composition does not violate the constraints of each component. This, in general, will make it necessary to impose constraints again on the environment of the composite device.

Thus, constraints defeat the idea of top-down refinement, which is first to decompose a system into components at the abstract level and then independently to implement each component at the concrete level; Verifying constraints requires knowledge both of the overall structure of the system (the environment of a component) from the abstract level *and* of the implementation (the constraints of a component) at the lower level. In short, the general situation in the modeling of hardware seems to be that of incomplete abstractions, i.e. abstractions *modulo constraints*. The constraints on which the abstraction depends embody residual aspects of the concrete level that impinge on the subsequent design and cannot be abstracted away once and forall.

1.2   A Possible Solution

The best one can expect here is to find means by which *reasoning about abstract behaviour* and *constraint analysis* fall into two separate verification passes rather than having them intertwined as the straight-forward approach suggests. The goal of this paper is to introduce and justify a logic in which the main verification of an abstract behaviour is truly an abstract verification in that it does not have to be concerned with constraints. It proceeds by assuming a successful constraint analysis wherever it depends on constraints. In the course of this main verification information about the constraints is accumulated as a proof obligation to be filled in at a later stage. Ideally, the remaining verification task corresponding to constraint analysis would then be handed over to a specialised tool. In some cases it could be done automatically, for instance extracting the minimal clock period for a synchronous system. In other cases, where the logic is undecidable, it has to be done manually. An example of this would be proving that the output of a certain integer function lies within a given finite range.

The idea leading to the proposed logic presented in this paper is not new. It reflects good engineering practice: In a first approximation one tries to establish the feasability of a design. Only then is it worthwhile to attempt a complete validation in a second step. New however, is the attempt to formalise this engineering principle mathematically and to implement it at the root of a theorem prover.

We have implemented an experimental prototype of the logic with the help of the mechanical proof checker LEGO [29]. LEGO provides a bed for encoding natural deduction style logics in the type theory of the Logical Framework (LF) [16] or the Calculus of Constructions (CC) [6,7] plus some extensions. We have used an extension of CC [22] which, as the most prominent feature, provides Σ-types, i.e. a generalisation of ordinary pairing where the *type* of the second component in a pair may depend on the *value* of the first component (ordinary pairing is the special case in which the types of both components are independent from their respective values). The following will show that it is in fact the Σ-types that make it possible to cut out and delay constraint analysis, so that the main proof can be performed without looking at or even manipulating constraints. It merely records necessary information about what has to be proved later, when one turns to analysing the constraints.

It is outside the scope of this paper to give an introduction to LEGO and to present the implementation in detail. Instead, we will use an informal mathematical language which, as we hope, will serve to explain the underlying idea in a compact and lucid way. We would like to stress that everything presented in this paper actually can be done interactively, modulo syntax, with the LEGO system even where we do not mention it explicitly.

2   Constraints and Synchronous Hardware Design

We are going to explain the implemented logic by means of a simple example that is just complex enough to convey the basic idea. As the area of hardware design where the example is taken from we have chosen the particular form of temporal abstraction that is fundamental to the design of synchronous hardware. Let us first briefly explain the general situation (Section 2.1) and then turn to a concrete example (Section 2.2).

4

2.1 Synchronous Circuits

A typical synchronous circuit is built up from *latches* (such as D-type flipflops) and *combinational circuits* (such as nand gates, inverters, and nets thereof). In a slightly simplified view[1] one can summarise the essence of the synchronous design paradigm in the following *design rules*:

C1 All latches are triggered by a common clock signal

C2 There is at least one latch in every feedback loop

C3 The clock period is long enough to allow for signal changes caused by any clock event to settle throughout the circuit before the next clock event

C4 The inputs to the circuit have to be stable long enough prior to any clock event for signals to have become stable by the clock event.

In a broad sense all of these design rules can be interpreted as constraints, more precisely, C1-C2 as *structural* constraints and C3-C4 as *behavioural* constraints. From a verification point of view the structural constraints C1-C2 are essentially reflections of internal behavioural constraints, i.e. they are conditions necessary for verifying that no behavioural constraints are violated by components within the circuit.

Much of the success of the synchronous design style is due to the fact that under the design rules C1-C4 one does not need to consider propagation delays when reasoning about the circuit's behaviour. If one is interested in the state of the circuit only at every clock event (or during a certain interval around it) and records the evolution of input and output values at these points, then the descriptive effort can be drastically reduced:

A1 Latches behave like unit delays

A2 Combinatorial circuits behave like delay free boolean functions

A3 The complete synchronous circuit reduces to a finite automaton and the automaton's behaviour can be derived by composing unit delays and delay-free boolean functions. More precisely, every unit delay gives rise to one state variable and the state transition function is determined by the interconnection of state variables through boolean functions.

Thus, relativising the synchronous circuit's behaviour to the *abstract time* given by the succession of clock events abstracts from propagation delays. Note, that the restriction on clock events can also be viewed as part of the design rules and as a constraint on the usage of the circuit which is characteristic to synchronous abstraction.

Although, either implicitly or explicitly, *timing abstraction* has always been used in the design of synchronous systems [36,3,8,23], it seems that first attempts to formalise it for the purpose of verification have only recently been made [26,18]. The separation of design rule checking (C1–C4) from reasoning in abstract terms (A1–A3) is crucial for practical applications, but there seems to be no satisfactory implementation of this separation on an interactive theorem prover. For instance, Herbert's methodology [18], implemented on

---

[1]We ignore here, among other things, for the sake of simplicity set-up and hold times of latches or the possibility to use multiple clocks. This does not, however, affect the point.

5

Figure 1: xor-gate and level triggered latch

the proof checker HOL [11,12], though it conceptually distinguishes between statements about timing and abstract behaviour, leaves both aspects intertwined at the level of proofs. This basically means that design rule checking and reasoning in abstract terms have to go together in a single proof. The logic presented in this paper provides a way to separate these concerns within a single logical inference system.

2.2 A Simple Circuit Design

Let us turn to a specific example. Take the simple case of a combinational circuit such as a 'xor' gate and a level triggered latch (Figure 1) which, as in [18], are to be considered as components of a synchronous system; i.e. they are put into an environment with a global clock, relative to which certain conditions on the stability of inputs can be imposed as *timing constraints* to allow timing abstraction.

Their behaviour can be described by predicates over input and output signals. For simplicity we take signals to be functions from integers to booleans, i.e.

$$signal = int \rightarrow bool$$

Assuming that both gates have constant propagation delays $\delta_{xor} > 0$ and $\delta_{latch} > 0$, their behaviour may be defined by the following axioms:

$$xor\,(x, y, z) \stackrel{df}{=} \forall t : int.\ z(t + \delta_{xor}) = xt + yt$$
$$latch\,(d, c, q) \stackrel{df}{=} \forall t : int.\ (ct = 1 \supset q(t + \delta_{latch}) = dt)\ \wedge$$
$$(ct = 0 \supset q(t + \delta_{latch}) = q(t + \delta_{latch} - 1))$$

Note, that we are using the operator $+$ both for addition over *int* as well as for modulo-2 sum over *bool*. According to the axioms the xor-gate performs the modulo-2 sum of its inputs x, y at every time step and outputs them with a delay δ_{xor} on output z. The latch is enabled to pass data from input d to output q with a delay δ_{latch} by positive levels of the clock input c, and it is locked when $ct = 0$.

For the purpose of this paper these simple axioms are assumed to be the low-level, most detailed, description available for the components *xor* and *latch*. Clearly, they are already an abstraction of real devices' behaviours. A more realistic description would have to account for variable gate delays as well as setup and hold times for the latch; it would perhaps assume continuous rather than discrete time and signal values, require maximal signal rise and fall times, and so on. Since for describing our logic it is of no importance how detailed a model of behaviour one actually starts from we have taken the simplest axioms possible.

The reader is referred to [2,14] for a discussion of more sophisticated axiomatizations of elementary digital circuits.

The important thing to note is that *xor* and *latch* contain both timing (delays) and functional aspects (operations on booleans) intertwined. In a synchronous design context, however, where one takes advantage of the design rules, one expects not having to care about delays. More precisely, the xor-gate should behave like a delay-free boolean function and the latch like an one-unit delay (A1-A2). Therefore, in place of *xor* and *latch* one would rather work with axioms like

$$xor\_syn\,(x,y,z) \overset{df}{=} \quad \forall t : int.\ zt = xt + yt \tag{1}$$

$$latch\_syn\,(d,q) \overset{df}{=} \quad \forall t_1, t_2 : int.\ next\,(t_1\,,\,t_2) \supset q(t_2) = d(t_1) \tag{2}$$

where $next\,(t_1\,,\,t_2)$ is a predicate expressing that t_1 and t_2 are two consecutive points in time. It is defined abstractly[2] by

$$next\,(t_1\,,\,t_2) \overset{df}{=} \quad t_1 < t_2 \wedge \forall t : int.\ t_1 < t \supset t_2 \leq t$$

In this abstract view the clock does no longer appear as an input to the latch. For in a synchronous circuit the latch's clock input is always connected to the global clock signal and consequently no longer available as an input. Thus, assume a clock signal

$$clk : signal$$

which is globally defined throughout the system. As a result *clk* may be used within formulae without it being mentioned explicitly as a parameter.

Obviously, *xor_syn*, *latch_syn* cannot be proved from *xor* and *latch* right away since the delays cannot be wiped out. What can be proved, however, by introducing constraints are certain approximations thereof. Before we can state them we need some predicates for formulating constraints. We first assume that clock ticks are marked by rising edges of *clk* and define a corresponding predicate

$$tick\ t \overset{df}{=} clk(t-1) = 0 \wedge clk(t) = 1$$

which obtains true if there is a clock tick at time t. Given this predicate one may define what it means that a signal x is stable in all intervals of length δ pri͟ ͟ɔ clock events:

$$stable\ x\ \delta \overset{df}{=} \quad \forall t_1, t_2 : int.\ (tick\ t_1 \ \wedge\ t_1 - \delta \leq t_2 \leq t_1) \supset x(t_1) = x(t_2)$$

Finally, for constraining the clock we have two other predicates, the first expressing that the 1-phase of the clock lasts exactly one time step, and the second imposing a minimal distance δ on two consecutive clock ticks:

$$one\_shot \overset{df}{=} \quad \forall t : int.\ clk(t) = 1 \supset (clk(t-1) = 0 \wedge clk(t+1) = 0)$$

$$min\_sep\ \delta \overset{df}{=} \quad \forall t_1, t_2 : int.\ (t_1 < t_2 \ \wedge\ tick\ t_1 \wedge tick\ t_2) \supset t_2 \geq t_1 + \delta$$

---

[2] One might want to turn the predicate *next* into a function which for time t yields the successive time step $next(t)$ and is undefined otherwise. In a logic with partial terms this could be done using the so-called ι-operator which we do not have available in LEGO.

With these predicates put into place the promised approximations of xor_syn and $latch\_syn$ can be formulated:

$$xor\_abs\,(x,y,z) \;\overset{df}{=}\; \textbf{stable } x\, \boldsymbol{\delta_{xor}} \wedge \textbf{stable } y\, \boldsymbol{\delta_{xor}}$$
$$\supset \forall t : int.\; \textbf{tick } t \supset zt = xt + yt$$

$$latch\_abs\,(d,q) \;\overset{df}{=}\; (\textbf{one\_shot} \wedge \textbf{min\_sep } \boldsymbol{\delta_{latch}}) \supset \forall t_1, t_2 : int.(\textbf{tick } t_1 \wedge \textbf{tick } t_2$$
$$\supset (next\_abs(t_1,t_2) \supset q(t_2) = d(t_1)))$$

where $next\_abs$ is the following approximation of $next$:

$$next\_abs(t_1,t_2) \;\overset{df}{=}\; t_1 < t_2 \wedge \forall t : int.\; \textbf{tick } t \supset (t_1 < t \supset t_2 \leq t)$$

The bold-faced parts indicate the offset of the approximations from the ideal versions xor_syn and $latch\_syn$. This offset explicitly reflects the design rules (C3-C4): timing constraints on inputs, on the clock signal, and the sampling at clock events. In contrast to xor_syn, $latch\_syn$ these approximations now can be derived from axioms xor and $latch$, i.e. we have

$$xor\,(x,y,z) \;\vdash\; xor\_abs\,(x,y,z)$$
$$latch\,(d,clk,q) \;\vdash\; latch\_abs\,(d,q)$$

We state this without proof here. The gap will be filled later when we have introduced the logic. Note, that due to the simplification of the latch's behaviour (i.e. no set-up and hold conditions) $latch\_abs$ does not require stability of data input d relative to the clock.

The observation that stability constraints essentially work to squeeze out delays of the behavioural description and thereby separate timing behaviour from functional behaviour is already employed in [18,26]). Here we push this idea further so as to also encompass constraints on time points, i.e. $tick\ t$. Being restrictions which also reflect the design rules, constraints on time points should be subjected to the same treatment as are stability constraints on signals. In fact, our logic will also deal with this type of constraints.

Now suppose as a simple design task, we wanted to build a stoppable $modulo$-2 counter. It is to have one input and one output, and to produce a stream of alternating 0s and 1s as long as the input is at 1 and stop at the current output value when the input switches to 0. More formally, its behaviour is specified by the following logical formula:

$$cnt\_spec\,(x,y) \;\overset{df}{=}\; \forall t_1, t_2 : int.\; next\_abs\,(t_1,t_2) \supset y(t_2) = x(t_2) + y(t_1)$$

From this input-output specification one derives easily a Moore automaton or equivalently an implementation consisting of an exclusive-or function and a one-unit delay as depicted in Figure 2. Given, that xor_syn (1) describes the behaviour of the exclusive-or and $latch\_syn$ (2) that of the one-unit delay, the behaviour of the implementation is given by

$$cnt\_syn\,(x,y,z) \;\overset{df}{=}\; xor\_syn\,(x,z,y) \wedge latch\_syn\,(y,z) \tag{3}$$

which employs logical *conjunction* $\wedge$ of predicates to express *composition* or *superposition* of two behaviours. Another important operation on behaviours is *hiding* of internal wires which logically is achieved by *existential quantification*. Since in the example the specification of the counter describes a circuit with one input and one output we have to consider signal z as internal in the implementation (3), i.e. x and y are the required input and output

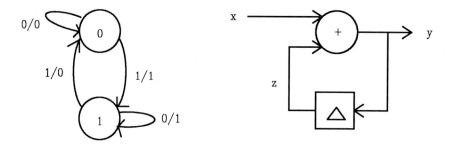

Figure 2: Implementation of the *modulo*-2 counter

signals visible to the environment. Verifying that the implementation is correct would now amount to proving that after hiding of the internal signal z the implementation (3) entails the specification, i.e.

$$\exists z : signal.\; cnt\_syn\,(x, y, z) \;\vdash\; cnt\_spec\,(x, y) \qquad (4)$$

This would be an easy exercise invoking the rules of ordinary first-order logic. Unfortunately, applying synchronous abstraction to *xor* and *latch* does not provide an ideal exclusive-or or an ideal one-unit delay satisfying *xor_syn* and *latch_syn* but merely approximations *xor_abs* and *latch_abs*. Therefore the implementation we are actually able to get is

$$cnt\_abs\,(x, y, z) \;\overset{df}{=}\; xor\_abs\,(x, z, y) \;\wedge\; latch\_abs\,(y, z)$$

Of course there is no reason to expect that $\exists z : signal.\; cnt\_abs\,(x, y, z)$ entails $cnt\_spec\,(x, y)$. Rather, in place of the original *cnt_spec*, we will again only achieve an approximation, perhaps something of the form

$$
\begin{aligned}
cnt\_appr\,(x, y) \;\overset{df}{=}\; & (\boldsymbol{C_0} \wedge \boldsymbol{C_1(x, y)}) \supset (\forall t_1, t_2 : int.\; \boldsymbol{C_2(t_1, t_2)} \\
& \supset (next\_abs\,(t_1, t_2) \supset y(t_2) = x(t_2) + y(t_1)))
\end{aligned}
$$

where C_0, C_1, and C_2 are constraints that have to be imposed on the composite circuit to allow the envisaged derivation

$$\exists z : signal.\; cnt\_abs\,(x, y, z) \;\vdash\; cnt\_appr\,(x, y) \qquad (5)$$

Here we are facing the question of how to go about finding the constraints C_0, C_1, C_2 and thus the modified specification *cnt_appr*. The straightforward approach, as employed for instance in [14], is attempting a derivation of *cnt_spec* (from *cnt_abs*), finding out where it fails, and at each such dead end identifying assumptions that would make it work if they were available in the first place. This information can then be used for determining the constraints C_0, C_1, C_2 and the place where they have to go to weaken the specification appropriately. This is however not quite satisfactory since it means going through the verification proof twice, once for finding the constraints and a second time after pasting them into the specification for completing the proof. Furthermore, and more importantly, the proof has to intermingle timing constraints with abstracted properties; it aims to prove the abstract specification *cnt_spec* while at the same time having to deal with the constraints inside the propositions *xor_abs*, *latch_abs*, *next_abs*, and *cnt_appr*.

As argued before, this is not what one really would like to do. Rather, one would like first to perform the abstract verification (4) *without* consideration of constraints. This establishes the feasibility of the design at the abstract level. The constraints, which are dependent on a particular implementation mechanism -here the implementation as a synchronous circuit-, are not determined before the implementation of the abstract components is chosen. In the example, this leads to the approximations *xor_abs*, *latch_abs*. Finally, a constraint analysis should be able to use the abstract proof (4) together with the knowledge of the constraints contained in *xor_abs* and *latch_abs* for extracting the constraints in *cnt_appr*.

In the following we will show how to achieve this goal by reformulating the notions of proof and proposition so as to 'hide' constraints within them and set up a rudimentary calculus of derivations to deal with this *constrained* logic.

3 Logic of Constrained Proofs

The logic will consist of a suitable base logic in which to express both the constraints and the abstraction properties of the verification example. For the purpose of our particular example it is sufficient to assume a formal system for typed first order logic. It is not really essential what the base logic looks like as long as it fulfills certain minimal requirements which we set out below. This base logic will then be extended by a new syntactic operator [.] for 'hiding' constraints. The described logic of constrained proofs therefore need not be seen as a particular and fixed logic but rather as a method for extending ones favourite logic for accomodating constraints.

In the following we assume some familiarity with natural deduction style logics and the lambda calculus (with explicit pairing) as a simple functional programming language.

3.1 Base Logic

Of the base logic we will require logical connectives for conjunction $\phi \wedge \psi$, implication $\phi \supset \psi$, universal and existential quantification $\forall x : A.\phi$, $\exists x : A.\phi$ together with the usual natural deduction rules

$$\wedge I : \frac{\phi \wedge \psi}{\phi \quad \psi} \qquad \wedge E_l : \frac{\phi}{\phi \wedge \psi} \qquad \wedge E_r : \frac{\psi}{\phi \wedge \psi} \qquad \supset E : \frac{\psi}{\phi \supset \psi \quad \phi} \qquad \supset I : \begin{array}{c} \dfrac{\phi \supset \psi}{\psi} \\ \vdots \\ \phi \\ \hline \sqrt{} \end{array}$$

$$\forall E_t : \frac{\phi\{t/x\}}{\forall x : A.\phi} \qquad \forall I_x : \frac{\forall x : A.\phi}{\phi} \qquad \exists I_t : \frac{\exists x : A.\phi}{\phi\{t/x\}} \qquad \exists E_x : \begin{array}{c} \dfrac{\psi}{\exists x : A.\phi \quad \psi} \\ \vdots \\ \phi \\ \hline \sqrt{} \end{array}$$

Here $\phi\{t/x\}$ denotes the substitution of term t for variable x in ϕ. Additionally, the logic comprises negation $\neg\phi$, disjunction $\phi \vee \psi$, the propositional constants $\top$ for *true* and $\bot$ for *contradiction* with rules

$$\vee I_l : \frac{\phi \vee \psi}{\phi} \qquad \vee I_r : \frac{\phi \vee \psi}{\psi} \qquad \vee E : \frac{\psi}{\phi_1 \vee \phi_2 \quad \psi \quad \psi} \\ \vdots \quad \vdots \\ \frac{\phi_1 \quad \phi_2}{\sqrt{\quad} \quad \sqrt{\quad}}$$

$$\neg I : \begin{array}{c} \frac{\neg\phi}{\bot} \\ \vdots \\ \frac{\phi}{\sqrt{\quad}} \end{array} \qquad \neg E : \frac{\bot}{\phi \ \neg\phi} \qquad \bot E : \frac{\phi}{\bot} \qquad \top I : \frac{\top}{\phi}$$

These rules are to be understood in the usual way in what regards free and bound variables, substitution of a term for a free variable and the variable restrictions associated with rules $\forall I_x$ and $\exists E_x$. In $\forall I_x$, x must not occur in any assumption on which ϕ depends, and in $\exists E_x$, x must not occur in ψ or in any other assumption save ϕ on which the lower occurrence of ψ depends. The letter I in the name of a rule stands for 'introduction' and E for 'elimination'.

For (refinement) proofs these rules are read top-down, i.e. they reduce proving the proposition above the rule bar to proving the propositions below it. In what follows all rules are written in this top-down way. It is useful to have *syntactic definition* available in the logic as a means for abbreviating a complex formula by some user-defined name possibly with syntactic parameters. Definitions also have their introduction and elimination rules, e.g. a definition $\phi' \overset{df}{=} \phi$ is acompanied by rules

$$dfI : \frac{\phi'}{\phi} \qquad\qquad dfE : \frac{\phi}{\phi'}$$

For the logic of constrained proofs we will not only have to treat propositions but also proofs as mathematical entities which are manipulated by the inference system. All modern interactive theorem provers, like HOL, VERITAS, LAMBDA, IPE [30], ELF [13], or LEGO are based on this principle as they are essentially programming systems for manipulating proofs. A formula is identified with the set of its proofs and a rule is implemented by a program which transforms proofs of the rule's hypotheses into proofs of its conclusion. In this spirit we associate with each of the above rules a program which implements the rule bottom-up, i.e. it can be applied to proofs of the propositions below the bar to yield a proof for the proposition above it. The name of each rule will be taken to denote its associated program on proofs. Consider the rules $\wedge I$, $\wedge E_l$ and $\wedge E_r$. The introduction rule $\wedge I$ describes how to build proofs of a formula $\phi \wedge \psi$ from proofs of its components ϕ and ψ; it serves to *introduce* the junctor $\wedge$. Rules $\wedge E_l$, $\wedge E_r$ say that from a proof of $\phi \wedge \psi$ proofs of the components ϕ and ψ can be extracted; it serves to *eliminate* the junctor $\wedge$.

To be more precise, as we are dealing with rule schemata rather than single rules we would have to instantiate each rule name with the actual propositions to denote a particular program on proofs. For instance, we would write $\wedge I(\phi,\psi)$ for the function which takes pairs of proofs of ϕ and ψ to a proof of $\phi\wedge\psi$. However, since it is clear from the proofs to which $\wedge$-introduction is applied which instance of the schemata is meant we may simply write $\wedge I$. The same applies to the other rules. A nice feature of LEGO is that it supports this style of *polymorphism*. It knows to infer the type of a function from the type of the arguments to which it is applied (or, more generally, from the context in which it is used).

We do not need to know what the basic programs implementing the rules look like nor what exactly a proof is. All we want is compose them to form derived rules or *derivations* and assume that they satisfy certain natural equations guaranteeing that they interact in a coherent way. Of such equations only those are given below which are used in the sequel.

First some notation: The language chosen to compose and reason about derivations is essentially a typed lambda calculus with explicit pairing. To denote that p is a proof of ϕ we write $p:\phi$ and for f a derivation of ψ from ϕ we write $f:\phi\to\psi$.[3] So, for instance, the (basic) derivation $\wedge I(\phi,\psi):\phi\times\psi\to\phi\wedge\psi$ may be applied to proofs $p:\phi$ and $q:\psi$ to yield a proof $\wedge I(\phi,\psi)(p,q):\phi\wedge\psi$. As remarked above this is more simply written $\wedge I(p,q):\phi\wedge\psi$. λ-abstraction is written as usual, and $\circ$ stands for the sequential composition of derivations in reversed order (which matches with the bottom-up notation of proof trees). The operator $\circ$ is an abbreviation definable in terms of λ-abstraction; for instance

$$\wedge E_l\circ\wedge I \;=\; \lambda x:\phi\times\psi.\,\wedge E_l(\wedge I(x)) \;:\phi\times\psi\to\phi$$

The equations required to hold between the basic rules all state that an introduction rule can be cancelled by subsequent application of the corresponding elimination rule.

$$\wedge E_l\circ\wedge I(p:\phi,q:\psi) \;=\; p \tag{6}$$
$$\wedge E_r\circ\wedge I(p:\phi,q:\psi) \;=\; q \tag{7}$$
$$\supset E(\supset I(f:\phi\to\psi),p:\phi) \;=\; f(p) \tag{8}$$
$$\exists E_x(\exists I_t(p:\phi\{t/x\}),f:\phi\to\psi) \;=\; f\{t/x\}(p) \tag{9}$$
$$\forall E_t\circ\forall I_x(p:\phi) \;=\; p\{t/x\} \tag{10}$$
$$dfE\circ dfI(p:\phi) \;=\; p \tag{11}$$

3.2   Extending the Base Logic

On top of this b·   we encode the idea of a *constrained proposition* proofs of which, also called *constrained proofs*, are allowed to have hidden assumptions. In the example hidden assumptions will be behavioural constraints. To introduce the general concept, we begin with the central definition.

Definition 1 *(Motivation) Let ϕ be a proposition. A* constrained proof *of ϕ is a pair $c=(\gamma,p_\gamma)$ consisting of a proposition γ and a proof of $\gamma\supset\phi$. The set of constrained proofs of ϕ will be denoted by $[\phi]$ and referred to as a* constrained proposition.

The motivation for this definition in view of the envisaged application for handling constraints is the following: Constructing a proof $c=(\gamma,p_\gamma)$ of a specification of the form $[\phi]$ amounts to proving ϕ under *some* assumption γ, for instance a timing constraint. The

[3]Note the difference between $p:\phi\supset\psi$ and $f:\phi\to\psi$; in the former p is a *proof*, in the latter f is a *derivation* (a program on proofs).

assumption is determined by the proof c and recorded as its first component. Given such a constrained proof $c : [\phi]$, one can extract both the hidden constraint $\pi_1(c)$ and the proof

$$\pi_2(c) : \pi_1(c) \supset \phi$$

that this constraint implies ϕ (π_1 and π_2 denote first and second projection, respectively). The constraint $\pi_1(c)$ may be subjected to constraint analysis and from the second component $\pi_2(c)$ one may build proof of ϕ for any proof of the constraint $\pi_1(c)$ via the $\supset E$ rule.

Definition 1 suggests to extend the base logic by a new syntactic operator $[.]$ which for any proposition ϕ forms the constrained proposition $[\phi]$. This operator as we shall see should work for all propositions, not just for those of the base logic. More precisely, we want to build propositions like

$$[\forall t : A.[\phi]],$$

i.e. we want to iterate the operator. As to the associated rules for $[.]$, the discussion above yields

$$[I]: \quad \begin{array}{c} \dfrac{[\phi]}{\phi} \\ \vdots \\ \dfrac{\gamma}{\sqrt{}} \end{array} \qquad\qquad [E]: \dfrac{\phi}{p : [\phi] \quad \downarrow(p)}$$

The introduction rule $[I]$ says that in order to prove $[\phi]$ we may prove ϕ under some assumption γ, which we are free to choose[4]. Read bottom-up, $[I]$ says that if a proposition ϕ can be derived from some assumption γ then there is a proof of $[\phi]$ which no longer depends on γ. The assumption γ effectively is discharged in favour of the $[.]$ construct which only indicates its presence. Note that even though the assumption γ to be hidden by an application of $[I]$ may be inferred (in LEGO) directly from the argument derivation $f : \gamma \rightarrow \phi$, we will supply it as an explicit argument, i.e. we write $[I](\gamma, f : \gamma \rightarrow \phi)$ rather than $[I](f : \gamma \rightarrow \phi)$.

The elimination rule is stated with the help of an operator $\downarrow$ which is meant to project out the assumption hidden in a proof of $[\phi]$. It represents the first projection π_1 from above. $[E]$ proves ϕ from a proof p of $[\phi]$ if also a proof of the assumption $\downarrow(p)$ hidden in p is given. The interaction of $[I], [E]$, and $\downarrow$ is governed by the equations

$$\downarrow \circ [I](\gamma, f : \gamma \rightarrow \phi) \;=\; \gamma \tag{12}$$
$$[E]([I](\gamma, f : \gamma \rightarrow \phi), c : \gamma) \;=\; f(c) \tag{13}$$

which state that $\downarrow$ indeed yields the assumption hidden by $[I]$ and the elimination rule $[E]$ recovers the proof hidden by $[I]$. Note, that (13) makes implicit use of (12). The reader might find it useful to compare rules $[I]$ and $[E]$ with $\supset I$ and $\supset E$ for implication.

---

[4] For practiacl applications it does not seem to be a restriction to confine application of $[I]$ to propositions γ of the base logic. Since it is technically advantageous our implementation imposes this restriction.

Two examples of rules which can be derived from the rules introduced are 'lifting' $[L]$ and 'constrained $\wedge$-introduction' $[\wedge I]$:

$$[L]: \begin{array}{c} [\psi] \\ \hline \psi \quad [\phi] \\ : \\ \phi \\ \hline \checkmark \end{array} \qquad\qquad [\wedge I]: \frac{[\phi \wedge \psi]}{[\phi] \quad [\psi]}$$

Rule $[L]$ lifts an unconstrained derivation $f : \phi \to \psi$ to a constrained one, namely if ϕ is provable under some (hidden) assumption then the conclusion ψ is provable under the same (hidden) assumption. Rule $[\wedge I]$ is the $\wedge$ introduction for constrained propositions melting the hidden assumptions of $[\phi]$ and $[\psi]$ into a single hidden assumption for their conjunction. This interpretation of $[L]$ and $[\wedge I]$ is captured by the equations

$$\downarrow \circ [L](f : \phi \to \psi, \, p : [\phi]) \;=\; \downarrow(p) \tag{14}$$
$$\downarrow \circ [\wedge I](p : [\phi], \, q : [\psi]) \;=\; \downarrow(p) \wedge \downarrow(q) \tag{15}$$

That $[L]$ and $[\wedge I]$ are derived rules is shown by the derivation trees in Figure 3. The derivations translate into the following 'programs' implementing the two rules:

$$[L](f : \phi \to \psi, \, p : [\phi]) \;\overset{df}{=}\; [I](\downarrow(p), \, \lambda x : \downarrow(p). \supset E(\supset I(f), \, [E](p,x)))$$
$$[\wedge I](p : [\phi], \, q : [\psi]) \;\overset{df}{=}\; [I](\downarrow(p) \wedge \downarrow(q), \, \lambda x : \downarrow(p) \wedge \downarrow(q).$$
$$\wedge I([E](p, \wedge E_l(x)), \, [E](q, \wedge E_r(x))))$$

for which the equations (14) and (15) immediately follow from (12) above. Let us take $[L]$ as an example to explain how the program is constructed. The arguments to the $[L]$ rule is a derivation $f : \phi \to \psi$ and a proof $p : [\phi]$. The derivation tree for $[L]$ (upper tree) in Figure 3 describes which rules have to be composed in which order to transform these two arguments into a proof of $[\psi]$. The term given above for defining $[L]$ is exactly this composition. The top rule $[I]$ is applied to a pair consisting of an assumption (to be hidden in $[\psi]$), in this case $\downarrow(p)$, and a derivation of ψ from this assumption. This derivation $g : \downarrow(p) \to \psi$ is given by the subtree with 'input' $x : \downarrow(p)$ and 'output' ψ. The associated subterm for g is the λ-term $g = \lambda x : \downarrow(p). \supset E(\supset I(f), \, [E](p,x))$. The λ-abstraction corresponds to the discharging of the assumption $x : \downarrow(p)$ by $[I]$.

We should perhaps remark at this point that in the the real proof session all of the proof terms are automatically constructed and manipulated by LEGO. The user only develops the proof tree top-down in an interactive way and does not have to be concerned with the underlying proof terms. This also applies to the equations which in LEGO are built-in automatic reductions. Thus, whenever proof terms are explicitly spelled out in the rest of the paper it is to show the mathematical mechanism of handling constraints as parts of proofs. All of this, however, is done by LEGO and need not bother the user.

Let us end this section with some remarks concerning the LEGO implementation of the logic. In the LEGO implementation the base logic is a higher order intuitionistic calculus encoded in the type theory of the Calculus of Constructions, or more precisely in Luo's extension ΣCC_C[22] of it. An introduction on using type theories as logical calculi can be found in [21]. The following papers present examples of encoding particular logics in

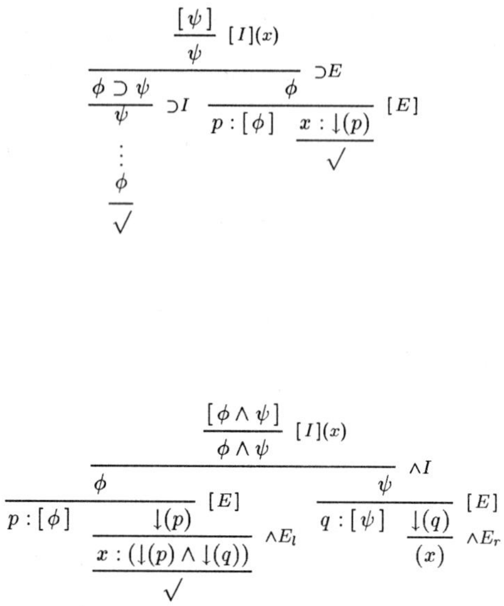

$$\cfrac{\cfrac{[\psi]}{\psi}\;[I](x)}{}\quad \supset E$$

$$\cfrac{\phi \supset \psi}{\psi}\;\supset I \quad \cfrac{\phi}{p:[\phi]\quad x:{\downarrow}(p)}\;[E]$$

$$\vdots$$

$$\cfrac{\phi}{\checkmark}$$

$$\cfrac{\cfrac{[\phi \wedge \psi]}{\phi \wedge \psi}\;[I](x)}{}\;\wedge I$$

$$\cfrac{\phi}{p:[\phi]\quad \cfrac{{\downarrow}(p)}{x:({\downarrow}(p)\wedge{\downarrow}(q))}\;[E]}\;\wedge E_l \qquad \cfrac{\psi}{q:[\psi]\quad \cfrac{{\downarrow}(q)}{(x)}\;[E]}\;\wedge E_r$$

$$\checkmark$$

Figure 3: The derived rules $[L]$ and $[\wedge I]$

the type theory of LF [24,1], CC [6], or Martin-Löf [27,28]. For implementating the $[.]$ operator it suffices to assumes a type universe $Type$ which is closed under the formation of simple function types $A \to B$, dependent function types $\Pi x : A.M$, and strong sum types $\Sigma x : A.M$. Further, there is a type $Prop$, the type of all propositions of the base logic which is embedded in $Type$ both as a type (the type of propositions) and as a subuniverse (each proposition is the type of its proofs), in symbols

$$Prop : Type \quad \text{and} \quad Prop \subset Type.$$

All this is provided by the type theory ΣCC_C.

If $\phi : Prop$ and $\psi : Prop$ are propositions then the proposition $\phi \supset \psi : Prop$ is encoded as the function type $\phi \to \psi$, i.e. a proof of $\phi \supset \psi$ is a function that maps proofs of ϕ to proofs of ψ[5]. This is all what is needed for encoding Definition 1, on which the logic of constrained propositions is based, as a particular type of proofs. Definition 1 is represented by the following Σ-type:

$$[\phi] \stackrel{df}{=} \Sigma \gamma : Prop.\, \gamma \supset \phi.$$

A Σ-type $\Sigma a : A.B(a)$ is the type of all pairs (a,b) where a is of type A and b is of type $B(a)$. The crucial feature of a Σ-type is that the type of the second component (here $B(a)$) may depend on the value of the first (here a). This is the feature needed to express $[\phi]$ as a type: the type of pairs where the second component is a proof of a proposition $(\gamma \supset \phi)$ which

---

[5]Thus, in our LEGO implementation of the logic derivations $f : \phi \to \psi$ and proofs $p : \phi \supset \psi$ are actually the same

depends on the first component (the assumption γ). This is why the implementation resides on the fact that LEGO provides Σ-types[6]. The properties of constrained propositions then follow from the properties of Σ types within the LEGO type system.

Now, having available a logic for dealing with constrained propositions, we turn back to the example and demonstrate its use.

4 Verification of the Example

To keep explanations reasonably short we will not mention all details that have to be presented in the actual (complete) LEGO implementation. Among those are for instance all definitions to do with basic data types such as integers and booleans. We simply assume a LEGO context in which the usual mathematical properties regarding these data types are available in the base logic. We may then focus on those parts of the verification that are done using the constrained logic introduced in the previous section. The example presented has been completely formalised and verified in LEGO.

The task, set up in Section 2.2, is to find a derivation for

$$\exists z : signal.\ cnt\_abs\,(x,y,z) \vdash cnt\_appr\,(x,y) \tag{16}$$

where

$$
\begin{aligned}
xor\_abs\,(x,y,z) &= (stable\,x\,\delta_{xor} \wedge stable\,y\,\delta_{xor}) \\
&\qquad \supset \forall t : int.\ tick\ t \supset zt = xt + yt \\
latch\_abs\,(d,q) &= (one\_shot \wedge min\_sep\,\delta_{latch}) \supset \forall t_1, t_2 : int. \\
&\qquad (tick\ t_1 \wedge tick\ t_2) \supset (next\_abs(t_1,t_2) \supset q(t_2) = d(t_1)) \\
cnt\_abs\,(x,y,z) &= xor\_abs\,(x,z,y) \wedge latch\_abs\,(y,z) \\
cnt\_appr\,(x,y) &= (C_0 \wedge C_1(x,y)) \supset (\forall t_1, t_2 : int.\ C_2(t_1,t_2) \\
&\qquad \supset (next\_abs\,(t_1,t_2) \supset y(t_2) = x(t_2) + y(t_1)))
\end{aligned}
$$

which is split into a main proof, free of constraints, and a successive constraint analysis to establish constraints C_0, C_1, C_2 for the composite device. The first goal is achieved by reformulating xor_abs, $latch\_abs$, cnt_abs, and cnt_appr as constrained propositions:

$$
\begin{aligned}
xor\_abs'\,(x,y,z) &\stackrel{df}{=} [\,\forall t : int.[\,zt = xt + yt\,]\,] \\
latch\_abs'\,(d,q) &\stackrel{df}{=} [\,\forall t_1, t_2 : int.[\,next\_abs\,(t_1,t_2) \supset q(t_2) = q(t_1)\,]\,] \\
cnt\_abs'\,(x,y,z) &\stackrel{df}{=} xor\_abs'\,(x,z,y) \wedge latch\_abs'\,(y,z) \\
cnt\_appr'\,(x,y) &\stackrel{df}{=} [\,\forall t_1, t_2 : int.[\,next\_abs\,(t_1,t_2) \supset y(t_2) = x(t_2) + y(t_1)\,]\,]
\end{aligned}
$$

Syntactically speaking, all constraints are now removed from the formulae and replaced by the [ ] construct. Semantically speaking, and this is the crucial idea, a constraint now is no longer part of the proposition but of the proof. For instance,

$$[\,\forall t : int.[\,zt = xt + yt\,]\,] \tag{17}$$

---

[6]The current implementation also makes use of LEGO's type universes and the built-in synthesis of universe levels, also called "typical ambiguity".

does not give any more information regarding constraints than indicating that there *may be* hidden assumptions, namely one for each instance of the [ ]-operator. It is the proof of (17) that actually determines these constraints. In fact, the constraints depend on from which low-level axioms about the exclusive-or gate the abstracted proposition (17) is derived, and by which abstraction process. Here *xor* is used but one might take a more detailed description of the gate, e.g. with variable delays, and then of course some other constraints would result. Also, there may me more than one way to verify an abstract behaviour of a composite device from properties about its components and each may result in a different constraint.

4.1 Abstract Verification of Modulo-2 Counter

As the 'constraint-free' version of (16) we now demonstrate a derivation of

$$\exists z : signal. \; cnt\_abs'(x, y, z) \vdash cnt\_appr'(x, y) \tag{18}$$

It differs from the ideal derivation (4) only in the presence of the [.]-construct.

First note that we can dispense with the existential quantifier since (18) is logically equivalent to a derivation

$$cnt\_abs'(x, y, z) \vdash cnt\_appr'(x, y) \tag{19}$$

i.e. every proof of (18) gives rise to a proof of (19) and vice versa. Thus it does not really matter whether we hide internal signals in the implementation (left hand side of the turnstile) in the first place or not; they are always eventually 'opened' when verified against a specification (right hand side). Consequently, we decide to take (19) as the verification goal right away.

Now let us introduce the following syntactic abbreviations:

$$\theta \stackrel{df}{\equiv} next\_abs(t_1, t_2)$$

$$\epsilon \stackrel{df}{\equiv} y(t_2) = x(t_2) + y(t_1)$$

$$\phi \stackrel{df}{\equiv} yt = xt + zt$$

$$\psi \stackrel{df}{\equiv} z(t_2) = y(t_1)$$

where x, y, z are, from now on, fixed variables of type *signal* and t_1, t_2 fixed variables of type *int*. With these abbreviations (19) essentially amounts to finding a derivation

$$\frac{[\forall t_1, t_2 : int.[\theta \supset \epsilon]]}{[\forall t : int.[\phi]] \wedge [\forall t_1, t_2 : int.[\theta \supset \psi]]}$$

This will depend on a derivation

$$\mathbf{Q} \; : \; (\phi\{t_2/t\} \wedge \psi) \to \epsilon$$

which shall be assumed given.

Figure 4 shows the complete natural deduction tree for (19), using **Q** and applying the rules of Section 3, where all typing information is removed to improve legibility. The refinement mechanism in LEGO allows constructing the derivation and the corresponding

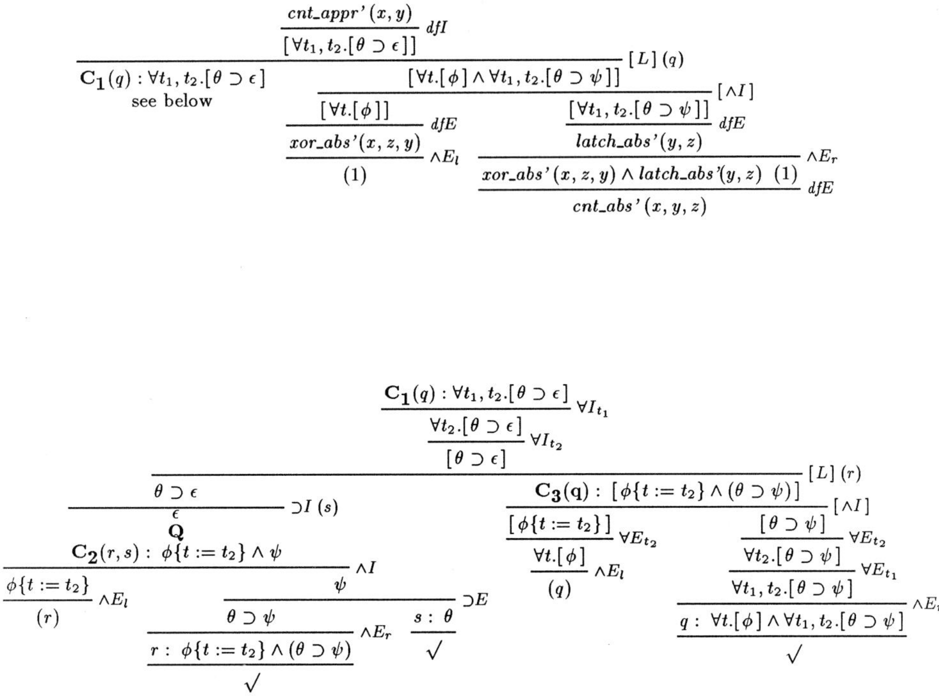

$$\dfrac{\dfrac{cnt\_appr'(x,y)}{[\forall t_1,t_2.[\theta \supset \epsilon]]}\,dfI}{\begin{array}{c}\mathbf{C_1}(q):\forall t_1,t_2.[\theta \supset \epsilon]\\ \text{see below}\end{array}}$$

$$\dfrac{\dfrac{[\forall t_1,t_2.[\theta \supset \epsilon]]}{[\forall t.[\phi] \wedge \forall t_1,t_2.[\theta \supset \psi]]}\,[L]\,(q)}{\dfrac{[\forall t.[\phi]]}{xor\_abs'(x,z,y)}\,dfE \quad \dfrac{[\forall t_1,t_2.[\theta \supset \psi]]}{latch\_abs'(y,z)}\,dfE}\,\wedge I$$

$$\dfrac{\dfrac{[\forall t.[\phi]]}{xor\_abs'(x,z,y)}\,dfE \quad \dfrac{\dfrac{[\forall t_1,t_2.[\theta \supset \psi]]}{latch\_abs'(y,z)}\,dfE}{}}{\dfrac{xor\_abs'(x,z,y) \wedge latch\_abs'(y,z)\ \ (1)}{cnt\_abs'(x,y,z)}\,dfE}$$

$$\dfrac{\dfrac{\dfrac{\mathbf{C_1}(q):\forall t_1,t_2.[\theta \supset \epsilon]}{\forall t_2.[\theta \supset \epsilon]}\,\forall I_{t_1}}{[\theta \supset \epsilon]}\,\forall I_{t_2}}{}$$

$$\dfrac{\theta \supset \epsilon}{\dfrac{\epsilon}{\mathbf{Q}}}\,\supset I\ (s)$$

$$\dfrac{\dfrac{\phi\{t:=t_2\}}{(r)}\,\wedge E_l \qquad \dfrac{\mathbf{C_2}(r,s):\ \phi\{t:=t_2\} \wedge \psi}{\dfrac{\psi}{\dfrac{\theta \supset \psi}{r:\ \phi\{t:=t_2\} \wedge (\theta \supset \psi)}\,\wedge E_r}}\,\wedge I \quad \dfrac{s:\theta}{\sqrt{}}}{\supset E}$$

$$\dfrac{\dfrac{\mathbf{C_3}(\mathbf{q}):\ [\phi\{t:=t_2\} \wedge (\theta \supset \psi)]}{\dfrac{[\phi\{t:=t_2\}]}{\dfrac{\forall t.[\phi]}{(q)}\,\wedge E_l}\,\forall E_{t_2} \qquad \dfrac{[\theta \supset \psi]}{\dfrac{\forall t_2.[\theta \supset \psi]}{\forall t_1,t_2.[\theta \supset \psi]}\,\forall E_{t_1}}\,\forall E_{t_2}}\,[L]\,(r)}{\dfrac{q:\ \forall t.[\phi] \wedge \forall t_1,t_2.[\theta \supset \psi]}{\sqrt{}}}\,\wedge E_r$$

Figure 4: Verification of correctness for *modulo*-2 counter

proof term interactively in a top-down fashion. The proof term collects together the rules in the order in which they are applied. In this case the proof tree of Figure 4 defines the proof function

$$\mathbf{C} : cnt\_abs'(x, y, z) \rightarrow cnt\_appr'(x, y)$$

which (if typing information is again supressed) reads:

$$
\begin{aligned}
\mathbf{C}(p_C) &= \quad dfI \circ [L](\lambda q.\mathbf{C_1}(q)\,,\, [\wedge I](dfE \circ \wedge E_l \circ dfE(p_C)\,,\, dfE \circ \wedge E_r \circ dfE(p_C))) \\
\mathbf{C_1}(q) &= \quad \forall I_{t_1} \circ \forall I_{t_2} \circ [L](\lambda r.\, \supset I(\lambda s.\mathbf{Q} \circ \mathbf{C_2}(r, s))\,,\, \mathbf{C_3}(q)) \\
\mathbf{C_2}(r, s) &= \quad \wedge I(\wedge E_l(r)\,,\, \supset E(\wedge E_r(r)\,,\, s)) \\
\mathbf{C_3}(q) &= \quad [\wedge I](\forall E_{t_2} \circ \wedge E_l(q)\,,\, \forall E_{t_2} \circ \forall E_{t_1} \circ \wedge E_r(q))
\end{aligned}
$$

This derivation provides a solution to the first part of the task: It corresponds to the main proof that composing a delay-free *modulo*-2 sum and an one-unit delay as in Figure 2 yields a stoppable *modulo*-2 counter. The only steps in the above derivation that would not arise in an ideal proof, i.e. one which does not consider constraints at all, are the two occurrences of the $[L]$ rule. This rule is necessary to lift a proof from the base logic, for instance $\mathbf{Q}$, to a constrained proof.

The derivation can be called abstract since it is performed without looking at or even manipulating explicit constraints. Remember that *cnt_abs'* and the other formulae do not actually carry constraints. The square brackets only indicate where constraints are to be expected and so intuitively serve as a *place-holder* for constraints. In manipulating the place-holder instead of real constraints the (abstract) derivation $\mathbf{C}$ is independent of constraints and yet retains enough information for extracting the constraints inside $\mathbf{C}(p_C)$: *cnt_appr'* (x, y) out of those in p_C : *cnt_abs'* (x, y, z), which can now be done in a completely separate phase: in the *constraint analysis*.

Before we can demonstrate this we need to give proofs

$$
\begin{aligned}
\mathbf{X} \quad &: \quad xor\,(x, z, y) \rightarrow xor\_abs'(x, z, y) \\
\mathbf{L} \quad &: \quad latch\,(y, clk, z) \rightarrow latch\_abs'(y, z)
\end{aligned}
$$

and thus establish *that* and *how* the exclusive-or and latch are implementations of the abstract components. In these proofs the actual constraints for the place-holders inside *xor_abs'* and *latch_abs'* and consequently inside

$$cnt\_abs'(x, y, z) = xor\_abs'(x, z, y) \,\wedge\, latch\_abs'(y, z)$$

will be determined.

4.2 Synchronous Abstraction of Exclusive-Or and Latch

We begin with the derivation $\mathbf{X}$. The main means for introducing constraints of course is the $[I]$ rule which will be used twice, namely for hiding the constraints *stable* $x\,\delta_{xor}$ $\wedge$ *stable* $z\,\delta_{xor}$ and *tick* t. The derivation will also have to assume $\delta_{xor} \geq 0$, use substitution rules –all abbreviated as 'subst'–, and the following facts about *int*:

$$Inv : \frac{\forall t, u : int.\ t - u + u = t}{\top} \qquad Refl : \frac{\forall t : int.\ t \leq t}{\top} \qquad Sub : \frac{\forall t, u : int.\ u \geq 0 \supset t - u \leq t}{\top}$$

$$\dfrac{xor\_abs'\,(x,z,y)}{\dfrac{[\forall t.[yt = xt + zt]]}{\dfrac{\forall t.[yt = xt + zt]}{\dfrac{[yt = xt + zt]}{yt = xt + zt}\,[I]\,(q)}\,\forall I_t}\,[I]\,(p)}\,dfI$$

$$\dfrac{\dfrac{yt = x(t - \delta_{xor}) + zt \qquad \dfrac{}{\mathbf{X_2}(p,q):xt = x(t - \delta_{xor})}\,subst}{\mathbf{X_1}(p,q):yt = x(t - \delta_{xor}) + z(t - \delta_{xor}) \qquad \mathbf{X_4}(p,q):zt = z(t - \delta_{xor})}\,subst}$$

$$\dfrac{\dfrac{}{\dfrac{y(t - \delta_{xor} + \delta_{xor}) = yt}{\dfrac{t - \delta_{xor} + \delta_{xor} = t}{\dfrac{\forall u.\,t - u + u = t}{\dfrac{\forall t, u.\,t - u + u = t}{\top}\,Inv}\,\forall E_t}\,\forall E_{\delta_{xor}}}\,subst} \qquad \dfrac{\dfrac{\mathbf{X_1}(p,q):yt = x(t - \delta_{xor}) + z(t - \delta_{xor})}{y(t - \delta_{xor} + \delta_{xor}) = x(t - \delta_{xor}) + z(t - \delta_{xor})}\,subst}{\dfrac{\forall t.\,y(t + \delta_{xor}) = xt + zt}{xor\,(x,z,y)}\,dfE}\,\forall E_{t - \delta_{xor}}}{}$$

$$\dfrac{\dfrac{\mathbf{X_2}(p,q):\ xt = x(t - \delta_{xor}) \qquad \mathbf{X_3}(q):tick\,t \wedge t - \delta_{xor} \leq t - \delta_{xor} \leq t}{(tick\,t \wedge t - \delta_{xor} \leq t - \delta_{xor} \leq t) \supset xt = x(t - \delta_{xor})}\,\supset E}{\dfrac{\forall t_2.(tick\,t \wedge t - \delta_{xor} \leq t_2 \leq t) \supset xt = x(t_2)}{\dfrac{\forall t_1, t_2.(tick\,t_1 \wedge t_1 - \delta_{xor} \leq t_2 \leq t_1) \supset x(t_1) = x(t_2)}{\dfrac{stable\,x\,\delta_{xor}}{\dfrac{p:\ stable\,x\,\delta_{xor} \wedge stable\,z\,\delta_{xor}}{\surd}\,\wedge E_r}\,dfE}\,\forall E_t}\,\forall E_{t - \delta_{xor}}}$$

$$\dfrac{\mathbf{X_3}(q):tick\,t \wedge t - \delta_{xor} \leq t - \delta_{xor} \leq t}{}$$

$$\dfrac{q:\ tick\,t}{\surd} \qquad \dfrac{\dfrac{t - \delta_{xor} \leq t - \delta_{xor} \leq t}{t - \delta_{xor} \leq t - \delta_{xor} \wedge t - \delta_{xor} \leq t}\,dfI}{}\,\wedge I$$

$$\dfrac{\dfrac{t - \delta_{xor} \leq t - \delta_{xor}}{\dfrac{\forall t.\,t \leq t}{\top}\,Refl}\,\forall E_{t - \delta_{xor}} \qquad \dfrac{\dfrac{t - \delta_{xor} \leq t}{\dfrac{\delta_{xor} \geq 0 \supset t - \delta_{xor} \leq t}{\dfrac{\forall u.\,u \geq 0 \supset t - u \leq t}{\dfrac{\forall t, u.\,u \geq 0 \supset t - u \leq t}{\top}\,Sub}\,\forall E_t}\,\forall E_{\delta_{xor}}} \qquad \delta_{xor} \geq 0}{}\,\supset E}{}\,\wedge I$$

Figure 5: Derivation for abstracting *xor* as a synchronous device

Figure 5 presents the proof tree, again split into several parts. The subtree named $\mathbf{X_4}(p,q)$ is not given as it is identical to the subtree $\mathbf{X_2}(p,q)$ with variable x is replaced by z and the $\wedge E_l$ rule instead of $\wedge E_r$.

The two constraints built into the proof term by the introduction rule $[\,I\,]$ can be extracted by applying the $\downarrow$ function to the proof term $\mathbf{X}$ in the appropriate places. To this end let p_X be a proof of $xor\,(x,z,y)$ and consider the proof term $\mathbf{X}(p_X)$ of $xor\_abs'\,(x,z,y)$:

$$
\begin{aligned}
\mathbf{X}(p_X) \;=\;& dfI \circ [\,I\,](stable\,x\,\delta_{xor} \;\wedge\; stable\,z\,\delta_{xor}\,, \\
& \lambda p.\forall I_t \circ [\,I\,](tick\,t\,,\;\lambda q.subst(subst(\mathbf{X_1}(p,q)(p_X)\,,\;\mathbf{X_4}(p,q))\,,\;\mathbf{X_2}(p,q)))) \\
\mathbf{X_1}(p,q)(p_X) \;=\;& subst(subst \circ \forall E_{\delta_{xor}} \circ \forall E_t \circ Inv\,,\;\forall E_{t-\delta_{xor}} \circ dfE(p_X)) \\
\mathbf{X_2}(p,q) \;=\;& \supset E(\forall E_{t-\delta_{xor}} \circ \forall E_t \circ dfE \circ \wedge E_r(p)\,,\;\mathbf{X_3}(q)) \\
\mathbf{X_4}(p,q) \;=\;& \supset E(\forall E_{t-\delta_{xor}} \circ \forall E_t \circ dfE \circ \wedge E_l(p)\,,\;\mathbf{X_3}(q)) \\
\mathbf{X_3}(q) \;=\;& \wedge I(q\,,\;dfI \circ \wedge I(\forall E_{t-\delta_{xor}} \circ Refl\,,\;\forall E_{\delta_{xor}} \circ \forall E_t \circ Sub))
\end{aligned}
$$

Now from

$$
dfE \circ \mathbf{X}(p_X) : [\,\forall t.[\,yt = xt + zt\,]\,]
$$

we can regain the constraint hidden by the outer ocurrence of the square brackets by computing

$$
\begin{aligned}
CX_{outer}(x,z,y) \;\overset{df}{=}\;& \downarrow \circ dfE \circ \mathbf{X}(p_X) \\
=\;& \downarrow \circ dfE \circ dfI \circ [\,I\,](stable\,x\,\delta_{xor} \,\wedge\, stable\,z\,\delta_{xor}\,,\;\lambda p.\cdots) \\
\text{by (11)} \quad =\;& \downarrow \circ [\,I\,](stable\,x\,\delta_{xor} \,\wedge\, stable\,z\,\delta_{xor}\,,\;\lambda p.\cdots) \\
\text{by (12)} \quad =\;& stable\,x\,\delta_{xor} \,\wedge\, stable\,z\,\delta_{xor}
\end{aligned}
$$

In order to get to the constraint hidden by the inner occurrence of $[\,.\,]$ we have to assume a proof $p : stable\,x\,\delta_{xor} \,\wedge\, stable\,z\,\delta_{xor}$ of the outer constraint and a variable t to instantiate the universal quantifier with. Then,

$$
\forall E_t \circ [\,E\,](dfE \circ \mathbf{X}(p_X)\,,\;p) : [\,yt = xt + zt\,]
$$

and

$$
\begin{aligned}
CX_{inner}(x,z,y;t) \;\overset{df}{=}\;& \downarrow \circ \forall E_t \circ [\,E\,](dfE \circ \mathbf{X}(p_X)\,,\;p) \\
=\;& \downarrow \circ \forall E_t \circ [\,E\,](dfE \circ dfI \circ [\,I\,](stable\,x\,\delta_{xor} \,\wedge\, stable\,z\,\delta_{xor}\,,\;\lambda p.\cdots)\,,\;p) \\
\text{by (11)} \quad =\;& \downarrow \circ \forall E_t \circ [\,E\,]([\,I\,](stable\,x\,\delta_{xor} \,\wedge\, stable\,z\,\delta_{xor}\,,\;\lambda p.\cdots)\,,\;p) \\
\text{by (13)} \quad =\;& \downarrow \circ \forall E_t \circ \lambda p.\cdots\,(p) \\
=\;& \downarrow \circ \forall E_t(\cdots) \\
=\;& \downarrow \circ \forall E_t(\forall I_t([\,I\,](tick\,t\,,\;\lambda q.\cdots))) \\
=\;& \downarrow \circ \forall E_t \circ \forall I_t([\,I\,](tick\,t\,,\;\lambda q.\cdots)) \\
\text{by (10)} \quad =\;& \downarrow \circ [\,I\,](tick\,t\,,\;\lambda q.\cdots)) \\
\text{by (12)} \quad =\;& tick\,t
\end{aligned}
$$

These computations show that, modulo renaming of variables,

$$
\mathbf{X} : xor\,(x,z,y) \rightarrow xor\_abs'\,(x,z,y)
$$

indeed captures the derivation

$$xor\,(x,y,z) \vdash xor\_abs\,(x,y,z)$$

with the difference that the constaints do not show up in the proposition xor_abs' of abstract behaviour but in the proof $\mathbf{X}$. Similarly, there is a derivation

$$\mathbf{L}: latch\,(y,clk,z) \to latch\_abs'\,(y,z)$$

for the latch swallowing the constraints in $latch\_abs$, which can also be constructed interactively in LEGO. It is slightly more involved than $\mathbf{X}$ for it has to utilize bounded induction on int. We do not present the derivation here and content ourselves with stating that it contains the expected constraints. More precisely, if p_L is a proof of $latch\,(y,clk,z)$ then

$$dfE \circ \mathbf{L}(p_L)\ :\ [\,\forall t_1,t_2 : int.[\,next\_abs\,(t_1\,,\,t_2)\ \supset\ q(t_2)=q(t_1)\,]\,]$$

and we have

$$CL_{outer}(y,z)\ \stackrel{df}{=}\ \downarrow \circ\, dfE \circ \mathbf{L}(p_L)$$
$$=\ one\_shot\ \wedge\ min\_sep\ \delta_{latch}$$

and for q a proof of $one\_shot \wedge min\_sep\ \delta_{latch}$, and t_1, t_2 variables of type int

$$CL_{inner}(y,z;t_1,t_2)\ \stackrel{df}{=}\ \downarrow \circ\, \forall E_{t_2} \circ \forall E_{t_1} \circ [\,E\,](dfE \circ \mathbf{L}(p_L)\,,\,q)$$
$$=\ tick\,t_1\ \wedge\ tick\,t_2$$

4.3 Constraint Analysis

Section 4.1 has shown that composition of delay-free $modulo$-2 sum and one-unit delay satisfies the specification of a $modulo$-2 counter. The verification is summed up in the derivation

$$\mathbf{C}: cnt\_abs'\,(x,y,z) \to cnt\_appr'\,(x,y) \tag{20}$$

In the previous section we gave proofs

$$\mathbf{X}\ :\ xor\,(x,z,y) \to xor\_abs'\,(x,z,y) \tag{21}$$
$$\mathbf{L}\ :\ latch\,(y,clk,z) \to latch\_abs'\,(y,z) \tag{22}$$

witnessing that in a synchronous environment xor and $latch$ may be regarded as implementations of the corresponding abstract components delay-free $modulo$-2 sum and one-unit delay. Residing inside $\mathbf{X}$ and $\mathbf{L}$ are certain behavioural constraints which record assumptions about the environment of the components under which this abstraction is possible. Now we may put pieces together and prove that in a synchronous environment the composition of xor and $latch$ can be regarded as an implementation of the abstract $modulo$-2 counter. This comes down to a derivation

$$\mathbf{I}: xor\,(x,z,y)\ \wedge\ latch\,(y,clk,z)\ \to\ cnt\_appr'\,(x,y)$$

from the data (20), (21), and (22).

$$
\dfrac{
\dfrac{
\dfrac{
\dfrac{\begin{array}{c} cnt\_appr'(x,y) \\ \mathbf{C} \end{array}}{cnt\_abs'(x,y,z)}
}{
\dfrac{xor\_abs'(x,z,y) \;\wedge\; latch\_abs'(y,z)}{\begin{array}{c}\dfrac{xor\_abs'(x,z,y)}{\begin{array}{c}\mathbf{X}\\ xor\,(x,z,y)\end{array}} \end{array}} \;dfI
}
}{}
}{}
$$

Figure 6: Low-level implementation of *modulo*-2 counter

As an aside note that again all applications of existential quantification for hiding internal signals are dropped. This is done without loss of generality since it can be shown that taking explicit account of hiding would reduce to the case considered here anyway. A more detailed discussion of hiding in the context of the proposed logic is outside the scope of this paper but we believe that hiding of signals via existential quantification does not introduce any intrinsic complications. After all, hiding seems to be eliminable for all practical examples.

Constraint analysis consists in examining the constraints residing in $\mathbf{I}$ which, as they are synthesised from the constraints in $\mathbf{X}$ and $\mathbf{L}$, will embody the weakest constraint for the composite circuit which guarantees that the constraints of its components are met. Figure 6 shows the derivation tree for $\mathbf{I}$. The corresponding proof term reads as follows:

$$
\begin{aligned}
\mathbf{I}(p_I) &= \mathbf{C} \circ dfI \circ \mathbf{I_1}(p_I) \\
\mathbf{I_1}(p_I) &= \wedge I(\mathbf{X} \circ \wedge E_l(p_I),\; \mathbf{L} \circ \wedge E_r(p_I))
\end{aligned}
$$

where p_I is a proof of $xor\,(x,z,y) \wedge latch\,(y,clk,z)$. From

$$
dfE \circ \mathbf{I}(p_I) : [\,\forall t_1, t_2.[\,next\_abs\,(t_1,\,t_2) \supset y(t_2) = x(t_2) + y(t_1)\,]\,]
$$

we may then extract constraints for both occurrences of [ ]. The most important of these is the outer one:

$$
\begin{aligned}
CI_{outer}(x,y,z) \;&\stackrel{df}{=}\; \downarrow \circ\, dfE \circ \mathbf{I}(p_I) \\
&= \downarrow \circ\, dfE \circ \mathbf{C} \circ dfI \circ \mathbf{I_1}(p_I) \\
&= \downarrow \circ\, dfE \circ dfI \circ [\,L\,](\lambda q.\,\mathbf{C_1}(q),\\
&\qquad [\wedge I\,](dfE \circ \wedge E_l \circ dfE \circ dfI \circ \mathbf{I_1}(p_I),\; dfE \circ \wedge E_r \circ dfE \circ dfI \circ \mathbf{I_1}(p_I))) \\
\text{by (11)} \quad &= \downarrow \circ [\,L\,](\lambda q.\,\mathbf{C_1}(q),\; [\wedge I\,](dfE \circ \wedge E_l \circ \mathbf{I_1}(p_I),\; dfE \circ \wedge E_r \circ \mathbf{I_1}(p_I))) \\
\text{by (14)} \quad &= \downarrow \circ [\wedge I\,](dfE \circ \wedge E_l \circ \mathbf{I_1}(p_I),\; dfE \circ \wedge E_r \circ \mathbf{I_1}(p_I)) \\
\text{by (15)} \quad &= \downarrow \circ\, dfE \circ \wedge E_l \circ \mathbf{I_1}(p_I) \;\wedge\; \downarrow \circ\, dfE \circ \wedge E_r \circ \mathbf{I_1}(p_I) \\
&= \downarrow \circ\, dfE \circ \wedge E_l \circ \wedge I(\mathbf{X} \circ \wedge E_l(p_I),\; \mathbf{L} \circ \wedge E_r(p_I)) \\
&\qquad \wedge\; \downarrow \circ\, dfE \circ \wedge E_r \circ \wedge I(\mathbf{X} \circ \wedge E_l(p_I),\; \mathbf{L} \circ \wedge E_r(p_I)) \\
&= \downarrow \circ\, dfE \circ \mathbf{X} \circ \wedge E_l(p_I) \;\wedge\; \downarrow \circ\, dfE \circ \mathbf{L} \circ \wedge E_r(p_I) \\
&= stable\; x\; \delta_{xor} \;\wedge\; stable\; z\; \delta_{xor} \;\wedge\; one\_shot \;\wedge\; min\_sep\; \delta_{latch}
\end{aligned}
$$

The inner constraint on time points recorded within $dfE \circ \mathbf{I}(p_I)$ can be computed as

$$
CI_{inner}(x,y,z;t_1,t_2) = tick\; t_2 \;\wedge\; tick\; t_1 \;\wedge\; tick\; t_2
$$

This shows that the derivation **I** has in fact collected together the constraints for *xor* and *latch*.

Constraint analysis in this framework is *proof analysis*: 'analyse the constraint hidden in a constrained proof and replace it by a simpler proposition'. Consider the general situation of a derivation $f : \phi \to [\psi]$, of which **I** is a special instance. f constructs for each proof p of ϕ essentially a pair consisting of a hidden assumption γ and a proof of $\gamma \supset \psi$.[7] Performing a constraint analysis on f means replacing γ by a *simpler* or *weaker* assumption γ'. The condition under which this is possible is that

$$\phi \wedge \gamma' \vdash \gamma$$

holds, i.e. γ' together with ϕ is stronger than γ. (Note, this means γ can always be replaced by a *stronger* assumption $\gamma' \vdash \gamma$). In the extreme case where γ' is to be the weakest possible assumption, namely $\gamma' = \top$, this amounts to proving γ from ϕ. Given that the hidden assumption γ is an input constraint of a hardware device this will only be possible if ϕ contains complete information about the environment of the device and then amount to proving that the environment satisfies the input constraints. The typical case, however, is that ϕ (as in **I**) merely describes parts of a complete circuit in which case only 'parts' of γ will follow from ϕ while other 'parts' have to be retained in γ'. Formally, constraint analysis may be summarised by the following

Proposition 1 *Let $f : \phi \to [\psi]$ be a derivation in the logic of constrained proofs and γ the constraint constructed by f, i.e. γ is a proposition of the base logic with $\downarrow \circ f(p) = \gamma$ for all $p : \phi$. Then for all propositions γ' of the base logic such that $\phi \wedge \gamma' \vdash \gamma$ there is a derivation $f' : \phi \to [\psi]$ with $\downarrow \circ f'(p) = \gamma'$ for all $p : \phi$.*

Back to the example: Since we regard signal z as internal to the composite circuit we want to replace $CI_{outer}(x, y, z)$ by a constraint of the form $C_0 \wedge C_1(x, y)$ which does not have z as a free variable and thus embodies a constraint on the environment of the *modulo*-2 counter. In view of the above discussion on constraint analysis we are lead to search for a proof of

$$xor\,(x, z, y) \wedge latch\,(y, clk, z) \wedge C_0 \wedge C_1(x, y) \vdash CI_{outer}(x, y, z)$$

It is not difficult to see that this is equivalent to a derivation

$$C_0 \wedge C_1(x, y) \vdash \forall z.\,(xor\,(x, z, y) \wedge latch\,(y, clk, z)) \supset CI_{outer}(x, y, z)$$

or equivalently

$$
\begin{aligned}
C_0 \wedge C_1(x, y) \vdash\ & one\_shot \wedge min\_sep\ \delta_{latch} \\
& \wedge \forall z.\,(xor\,(x, z, y) \wedge latch\,(y, clk, z)) \supset (stable\ x\ \delta_{xor} \wedge stable\ z\ \delta_{xor})
\end{aligned}
\tag{23}
$$

A simple way to arrive at constraints C_0 and C_1 that satisfy this property is simply to use the right hand side of the derivation as their definition, i.e.

$$C_0 \overset{df}{=} one\_shot \wedge min\_sep\ \delta_{latch}$$

$$C_1(x, y) \overset{df}{=} \forall z.\,(xor\,(x, z, y) \wedge latch\,(y, clk, z)) \supset (stable\ x\ \delta_{xor} \wedge stable\ z\ \delta_{xor})$$

---

[7] γ may in general depend on the proof p. However, it is a property of the logic that if ϕ is a proposition of the base logic then $\downarrow \circ f(p)$ must be independent of p, i.e. $\downarrow \circ f(p) = \gamma$ for some fixed proposition γ of the base logic. In particular this is the case for our example **I** as the computation above confirmed.

$C_1(x, y)$ says that no matter what internal signal z is produced by the circuit for given observable signals x, y the stability constraints for *xor* and *latch* are satisfied. C_0 is the restriction on the clock originating from *latch*. This choice of C_0 and C_1 corresponds to the weakest restriction on the *environment* of the composite circuit for which the constraints of all components are met.

Alternatively, a more intelligent constraint analysis could take advantage of knowledge about the type of constraints and the behaviour of the components involved and try to simplify C_0 and C_1. For instance, the stability constraint *stable* $z\,\delta_{xor}$ on signal z can be traded against the clock period since z is the output of the latch and the characteristic feature of the latch is to keep the output stable as long as it is not triggered by clock ticks. More precisely, we have

$$min\_sep\,(\delta_{latch} + \delta_{xor}) \wedge latch\,(y, clk, z) \;\vdash\; stable\,z\,\delta_{xor} \tag{24}$$

which suggests to define the constraints as follows

$$C_0 \;\overset{df}{=}\; one\_shot \wedge min\_sep\,(\delta_{latch} + \delta_{xor})$$

$$C_1(x, y) \;\overset{df}{=}\; stable\,x\,\delta_{xor}$$

The constraint analysis now consist in formally verifying (23). This simple proof, which we do not give here, makes reference to fact (24) and may, according to Proposition 1, be used for building a new derivation

$$\mathbf{I}' : xor\,(x, z, y) \wedge latch\,(y, clk, z) \;\rightarrow\; cnt\_appr'\,(x, y)$$

such that $\downarrow \circ\, dfE \circ \mathbf{I}'(p_I) = C_0 \wedge C_1(x, y)$.

5 Conclusion and Future Work

As has been hinted at in the beginning, the global aim of our work is investigating the application of abstraction mechanisms in hardware verification. This paper focused on a particular problem arising from such an undertaking, namely the problem of constraint handling. Recognising the special rôle of constraints in the design process we are proposing to distinguish at the level of the logical inference system between propositions pertaining to specifications and those pertaining to constraints. To this end a logic of constrained proofs has been introduced that, roughly speaking, provides a mechanism to move parts of a proposition into the proof. We have demonstrated by means of a simple example from synchronous circuit design that this mechanism, when used to take constraints out of specifications of abstracted behaviour, acommodates for uncoupling the verification of abstracted behaviour from the analysis of constraints without giving up the rigour of a complete formal verification. Moreover, the logic does not prejudice the type of constraints, so that its application is not limited to the usual input constraints of hardware components but also encompasses constraints on sampling times and any other type which need not be related to input signals. Also, it does not prejudice the way components are modelled, i.e. it is applicable for both the "components as functions" and the "components as predicates" paradigm.

The logic has been implemented on the interactive proof editor LEGO. First verification examples, one of which was described in the paper indicate that at least for the special case of timing abstraction in synchronous hardware design the implemented scheme of a constrained logic works up to the expectations. The examples are however still too simple to judge practical utility for 'real' verification problems. Also we did not as yet systematically explore the analysis of constraints within the logic and the possibility for automating parts of it in special cases like synchronous abstraction. A lot of work is left to be done here.

LEGO has proven to be a convenient and flexible environment for experimenting with a prototype logic. The scheme is implemented using $\Sigma CC_{\sqsubseteq}$ and type universes, a rather powerful type theory supported by LEGO. Since the goal is to arrive at a logic that knows to differenciate between constraints and abstract properties it was important for the first experiments that LEGO does not enforce the use of any particular logic. It is basically a tool for implementing mathematics and therefore allows to experiment with various logics and to translate very directly mathematical definitions into an executable formal system. An implementation on other verification systems which are tailored to the needs of hardware design and provide the necessary infrastructure to run larger examples is planned. In particular LAMBDA [9] and VERITAS [15] seem promising candidates. LAMBDA, for instance, because its logic kernel is a higher order proof system, i.e. it manipulates rules rather than propositions, has already built-in the flexibility to introduce constraints at any time in the design process and arbitrarily to defer their analysis. The possibility of programming complex refinement tactics will allow automating large portions of constraint analysis and verification for specific circuit design styles like synchronous or speed independent circuits.

The main characteristic of the proposed logic for handling constraints is that it considers constraints as part of the proof and consequently constraint analysis as proof analysis. Although this is intuitively appealing and seems to encode the idea of decoupling abstract reasoning and constraint analysis quite well from a pragmatic point of wiew, it has to be further justified through both practical examples and mathematical analysis. The implementation in its current form is mathematically not yet completely satisfactory. For example, among all constrained proofs of a proposition $[\phi]$ there are also worthless ones, like

$$(\mathit{false}\,,\ \mathit{ex\text{-}falso\text{-}quodlibet}(\phi))$$

or

$$(\phi\,,\ \supset E(\lambda a : \phi.\ a)).$$

and no built-in measures have been taken to prevent these from being introduced in a proof. So far the only way to avoid this loss of information, is to restrict proofs to chose from only a well-defined set of elementary proof rules, which are known to be nicely behaved in this respect.

We consider the logic of constrained proofs an intermediate stage towards abstraction which means reasoning on (two ore more) different levels: on a concrete and an abstract level, connected via an abstraction function or relation. The example used in this paper lives at the concrete level only. For example, there is only a single notion of time, i.e. no distinction between abstract synchronous time and concrete level time. Eventually we want to combine constrained logic with abstraction mappings and reason about hardware at several levels of abstraction within one verification framework. It could be investigated in LEGO using Σ-type which provide a mechanism for theory abstraction [33] allowing to identify and keep apart the corresponding levels of theories. This was yet another reason for chosing LEGO.

6   Acknowledgements

The development of our work has been strongly influenced by discussions with Rod Burstall. We would also like to thank Mike Fourman for his encouraging support, Terry Stroup and the anonymous referees for valuable comments on a draft of this paper, and Julian Bradfield for his help with type-setting and for supplying TEX-macros for proof trees.

References

[1] A. Avron, F. Honsell, and I. Mason. Using typed lambda calculus to implement formal systems on a machine. Technical Report ECS-LFCS-87-31, Edinburgh Univ., Dept. of Comp. Sci., June 1987.

[2] J. C. Barros and B. W. Johnson. Equivalence of the arbiter, the synchronizer, the latch, and the inertial delay. *IEEE Trans. on Comp.*, C-32(7):603–614, July 1983.

[3] Y. Brzozowsky. *Digital Networks*. Prentice-Hall, 1976.

[4] A. Cohn. Correctness properties of the VIPER block model: The second level. Technical Report 134, University of Cambridge, Computer Laboratory, May 1988.

[5] A. Cohn. A proof of correctness of the VIPER microprocessor: the first level. In P. Subrahmanyam G. Birtwistle, editor, *VLSI specification, verification, and synthesis*, pages 27–72. Workshop on hardware verification, Kluwer Academic Publishers, 1988.

[6] Th. Coquand and G. Huet. Constructions: A higher order proof system for mechanizing mathematics. In B. Buchberger, editor, *Proceedings EUROCAL'85*, pages 151–184, LNCS 203, 1985. Springer Verlag.

[7] Th. Coquand and G. Huet. The Calculus of Constructions. *Information and Computation*, 76:95–120, 1988.

[8] W. I. Fletcher. *An engineering approach to digital design*. Prentice-Hall, Englewood Cliffs, N.J., 1980.

[9] M. Fourman and E. M. Mayger. Formally based system design - Interactive hardware scheduling. In G. Musgrave and U. Lauther, editors, *Proceedings of the IFIP TC 10/WG 10.5 International Conference on VLSI, Munich, Aug. 16-18, 1989*, pages 101–112, 1989.

[10] Ganesh C. Gopalakrishnan, M. K. Srivas, and David R. Smith. From algebraic specifications to correct VLSI circuits. In D. Borrione, editor, *From HDL descriptions to guaranteed correct circuit designs*, pages 197–225. IFIP, North Holland, 1987.

[11] M. J. C. Gordon. HOL: A machine oriented formulation of higher order logic. Technical Report 68, University of Cambridge, Computer Laboratory, July 1985.

[12] M. J. C. Gordon. HOL: A proof generating system for higher-order logic. In G. Birtwistle and P. Subrahmanyam, editors, *VLSI Specification, Verification, and Synthesis*, pages 73–128. Workshop on Hardware Verification, Kluwer Academic Publishers, 1988.

[13] T. G. Griffin. An environment for formal systems. Technical Report ECS-LFCS-87-34, Edinburgh Univ., Dept. of Comp. Sci., August 1987.

[14] F. K. Hanna and N. Daeche. Specification and verification using higher order logic: A case study. In G. M. Milne and P. A. Subrahmanyam, editors, *Formal Aspects of VLSI design, Proc. of the 1985 Edinburgh conf. on VLSI*, pages 179–213. North-Holland, 1986.

[15] F. K. Hanna, N. Daeche, and M. Longley. VERITAS+:a specification language based on type theory. In *Proc. Conf. on Hardware Specification, Verification and Synthesis, Cornell University*, July 1989.

[16] R. Harper, F. Honsell, and G. Plotkin. A framework for defining logics. In *Proceedings LICS'87*, pages 194–204, Ithaca, New York, June 1987.

[17] J. Herbert. Formal verification of basic memory devices. Technical Report 124, University of Cambridge, Computer Laboratory, February 1988.

[18] John Herbert. Temporal abstraction of digital design. In G. Milne, editor, *The fusion of hardware design and verification*, pages 1–25, University of Strathclyde, Glasgow, Scotland, July 1988. IFIP WG 10.2.

[19] W. A. Hunt, Jr. The mechanical verification of a microprocessor design. In D. Borrione, editor, *From HDL descriptions to guaranteed correct circuit designs*, pages 89–196. IFIP, North Holland, 1987.

[20] J. Joyce. Formal specification and verification of microprocessor systems. In S. Winter and H. Schumny, editors, *EUROMICRO'88*. North Holland, 1988.

[21] J. Lambek and P. J. Scott. *Introduction to higher order categorical logic*. Cambridge University Press, 1986.

[22] Zhaohui Luo. A higher order calculus and theory abstraction. Technical Report ECS-LFCS-88-57, Edinburgh Univ., Dept. of Comp. Sci., July 1988.

[23] L. R. Marino. *Principles of computer design*. Computer Science Press, Rockwell, 1986.

[24] I. Mason. Hoare's logic in the LF. Technical Report ECS-LFCS-87-32, Edinburgh Univ., Dept. of Comp. Sci., June 1987.

[25] D. May and D. Shepherd. Formal verification of the IMS T800 microprocessor. Internal report INMOS Limited, 1987.

[26] Thomas F. Melham. Abstraction mechanisms for hardware verification. In G. Birtwistle and P. Subrahmanyam, editors, *VLSI Specification, Verification, and Synthesis*, pages 267–292. Workshop on Hardware Verification, Kluwer Academic Publishers, 1988.

[27] B. Nordström. Martin-Löf's type theory as a programming logic. Technical Report 27, Chalmers University of Technology and University of Göteborg, September 1986.

[28] B. Nordström, K. Petersson, and J. M. Smith. *Programming in Martin-Löf's type theory. An introduction*. To be published by Oxford University Press, 1989.

[29] Randy Pollack. The theory of LEGO. Draft report, LFCS, Univ. of Edinburgh, October 1988.

[30] Brian Ritchie. *The Design and implementation of an interactive proof editor.* PhD thesis, Edinburgh Univ., Dept. of Comp. Sci., 1989.

[31] P. A. Subrahmanyam. Contextual constraints, temporal abstraction, and observational equivalence. In G. Milne, editor, *The fusion of hardware design and verification*, pages 156–182, University of Strathclyde, Glasgow, Scotland, July 1988. IFIP WG 10.2.

[32] P. A. Subrahmanyam. Towards a framework for dealing with system timing in very high level silicon compilers. In P. Subrahmanyam G. Birtwistle, editor, *VLSI specification, verification, and synthesis*, pages 159–215. Workshop on hardware verification, Kluwer Academic Publishers, 1988.

[33] P. Taylor and Z. Luo. Theories, mathematical structures, and strong sums. Preliminary notes, December 1988.

[34] S. H. Unger. *Asynchronous sequential switching circuits.* Wiley-Interscience, New York, 1969.

[35] D. W. Weise. *Formal multilevel hierarchical verification of synchronous MOS VLSI.* PhD thesis, Massachusetts Institute of Technology, 1986.

[36] S. Wendt. *Entwurf komplexer Schaltwerke.* Springer Verlag, Berlin, 1974.

Hardware synthesis in constructive type theory

Dany Suk*

Introduction

Methods and techniques for verifying digital circuits are well established [2, 1]. It is often argued that verifying digital circuits is a very tedious business. According to several researches the remedy is formal synthesis. The work presented in this paper was inspired by the work of F K Hanna [3]. Hanna argues that it is preferable to synthesize the circuits directly by a formal design process. It is then possible to discover major design flaws before the entire circuit design is completed. That is due to the fact that some erroneous design decisions can be detected in the early stages of the synthesis. The errors are discovered by partial correctness proofs.

The synthesis method presented in this paper will hopefully support design of efficient circuits. It attempts to mimic the intuitive way of design that experienced engineers are accustomed with.

The system is based on Martin-Löf's type theory [4, 5] and its implementation called Isabelle [6, 7]. Specifications of the circuits are given as types in type theory and implementations are objects (functions) of the specification types – see [8]. Type theory is constructive, e.i. it supports formal synthesis. The hardware functions are synthesized during the proof of specification types (which are viewed as propositions). The derived hardware is represented by functions, which are executable. This is an important point as this allows simulations, which are easier then formal proofs. The drawback of this functional approach is that bidirectional structures can not be represented in this formalism.

When presented with a specification the designer inspects it and identifies segments of the specification, which can be implemented with predefined library circuits. The design is then split into a number of subdesigns. The designer determines the specifications (types) of the subdesigns and thereafter instantiates the subdesigns into library circuits, which satisfy the subspecifications. The last step is the actual proof of the circuit correctness. An example of a small circuit design is given.

Hardware type theory

Our system to reason about the hardware is called the **hardware type theory**. It consists of several layers of theories. These are:

- The interactive Isabelle generic theorem prover, which supports variety of object logics (for more information see [6, 7]).

*Chalmers University of Technology, Department of Computer Engineering, S-412 96 Gothenburg, Sweden; *dany@ce.chalmers.se*

- CTT (Constructive Type Theory) – an object logic implemented in Isabelle.

- Switch level – a theory on top of CTT, which defines the transistor level of circuit structures.

- Gate level – a theory on top of the switch level, which defines the combinatorial TTL components.

- Register Transfer Level – a theory on top of the gate level, which deals with the synchronous systems.

Constructive type theory

The Martin-Löf's constructive type theory is a typed lazy functional language with powerful inference mechanism for reasoning about its programs and its types. The proof rules can be used to verify and to construct correct programs.

The types in type theory are far more expressive the those present in other typed languages. When viewed as sets, the types can be interpreted as propositions. The proofs of the propositions are objects (functions, programs) of the types (sets). The types **specify** these objects. For example an implication proposition can be explained by:

- $A \supset B$ is identified with $A \rightarrow B$, the type of functions from A to B.

- The elements of the type $A \rightarrow B$ are proof objects of the implication proposition and are functions of the form $\lambda x.b(x)$.

Type theory includes types which interpret all logical constants of the predicate logic. Further details can be found in [5].

As in the case when dealing with programs, properties of a hardware structure can be specified as a type - e.g. **Specif_type**. Possible implementations of the specification **Specif_type** are objects (e.g. **implem_obj**) in the specification type (set). If the implementation is known then its correctness can be verified by proving in type theory that

$$\mathbf{implem\_obj} \in \mathbf{Specif\_type}$$

is true, i.e. that the **implem_obj** is an element in type (set) **Specif_type**. If only type **Specif_type** is known, i.e. the specification proposition of the hardware, it is then possible to synthesize one of the potential hardware implementations during the process of proving that the proposition **Specif_type** is true i.e. (the type – the set – is non empty).

The syntax of CTT is similar to that used at the University of Gothenburg (see the appendix). For example expression

$$(\Pi x \in A)(\Pi y \in B)\{z \in C \mid \mathbf{Eq}(C, z, e(x,y))\}$$

can be expressed as

```
PROD x:A. PROD y:B. SUB z:C. Eq(C, z, e(x,y))
```

or as

```
Prod(A, %(x)Prod(B, %(y)Sub(C, %(z)Eq(z, e(x,y), C))))
```

When dealing with circuits, this type is interpreted as the following proposition (specification):

- For all input values **x** of type A and for all values **y** of type B there is an output value **z** of type C such that **z** is equal to the expression **e(x,y)** and both **z** and **e(x,y)** are of type C. This specifies a circuit with two inputs **x** and **y**, output **z** and the expression **z = e(x,y)**.

Prod is type constructing function for the cartesian product of family of types. It corresponds to ∀ quantifier. **Sub** is type constructing function for the subset type and **Eq** is type constructing function for the equality types. **%** stands for abstraction. The other types implemented in Isabelle are:

- → – the function type

- **Sum** (Σ) – the disjoint union of family of types

- **N** – the type of natural numbers

- **List** – the list type

- **F** – the empty type

- **T** – the one-element type

Again, for additional information see [5]. The formation, introduction, elimination and computation rules for the various types are implemented as meta-theorems in Isabelle's meta-logic. For example the elimination rule for the product type

$$\frac{f \in \mathrm{II}(A,B) \quad a \in A}{\mathbf{apply}(f,a) \in B(a)}$$

(called **Prod_elim** in Isabelle) is the meta-theorem:

[| p: Prod(A,B) |] ==> [| a: A |] ==> [| p ' a: B(a) |]

where **'** is the infix apply operator. Expressions of type theory are translated to the meta-logic by enclosing them in [| ... |] parenthesis. ==> is the implication on the meta-logic level. The theorems in Isabelle are resolved by backwards proofs – e.i. by inverting the rules (which are then called tactics). So for example in the case of product elimination, in order to proof that application of a function p to its argument a (e.i. – p ' a) is an object of type B(a) you have to show that p is an object of type Prod(A,B) (same as PROD x: A. B(x)) and that a is an object of type A.

The CTT implementation includes also variety of powerful tactics to speed up obvious proofs.

Switch level theory

The hardware is traditionally divided into several abstraction levels. Our reasoning mechanism has to cope with all of them. The switch level is the lowest abstraction level. It handles the transistor structures of the integrated circuits. We assumed that the circuits are implemented in the **CMOS** technology. In our implementation transistors are viewed as functions and not as bidirectional devices in HOL. This level, its associated type (**Signal**), its canonical elements **hi, lo, zz, err** and the inference rules are described in [8].

Gate level theory

The gate level, which is the level this paper is concerned with deals basically with such hardware components as various gates (and, nand, or, nor, xor ...) and other combinatorial components (multiplexers, decoders, adders,...). This theory consists of two parts. The first one defines types **Bit** and **Bus** with their canonical and noncanonical elements and their inference rules. The second part is a library of theorems concerning various components (so called TTL library).

Gate level types

- **Bus** type (to describe hardware buses) is defined as subset type of natural numbers:

  - Bus(n) == SUB m:N. Eq(Bool,true,m<(2^n)))

The objects of n-bits wide bus are natural numbers m such that m<(2^n).

- **Bit** type is defined as:

  - Bit == Bus(1)

It is one-bit wide bus. There are two canonical elements describing the logical "one" and the logical "zero". They are defined in terms of natural numbers as:

  - hi == succ(0)

  - lo == 0

There is also one noncanonical selector **ifg**. The computation rule for this selector states that the value of ifg(a,b,c) is b if a computes to the canonical element hi and c if a computes to lo. The various derived rules for this level are described in the appendix.

TTL library

This data base includes various facts (stored as theorems) about the components of this level. For example an adder with two four bit busses, one bit carry input and with one five bit bus output (to include carry out bit) is stored as theorem:

```
        lam a.   lam b.   lam cin.   adder_four(a,b,cin) :
   PROD a:  Bus(4).   PROD b:  Bus(4) .   PROD cin:  Bit.
       SUB sum :   Bus(5).   Eq(Bus(5),sum,(a+b+cin))
```

lam a.   lam b.   lam cin.   adder_four(a,b,cin) is adder implementation function. adder_four(a,b,cin) is an expression defined in terms of gates (component 7483 in TTL Data Book). a, b and c are bound variables and lam is the constant λ from λ-calculus. The specification type states that the output sum is equal to the sum a+b+cin.

See the appendix for the library entries of several basic gates (together with their associated rules).

Register transfer level theory

This level enables us to reason about synchronous systems. The RTL level introduces the notion of time. It defines new type Time and its associated inference rules. It also introduces new noncanonical constant **stmach**, which defines an abstract finite state machine. Expressions for Moore and Mealy abstract machines were defined in terms of **stmach** constant. More can be found in [8].

Gate level synthesis

The main goal of this work was to investigate methods for guided formal synthesis based on type theory. To start with the gate level was studied. The following section outlines the studied methodology.

Synthesis principles

When presented with a specification (by a type) the designer inspects it and identifies those segments which can be directly implemented with predefined **library** circuits (or with other previously completed designs). Such circuits are typically various gates, decoders, multiplexers, adders and etc. This library is called in hardware jargon the TTL Data Book. Some of the TTL components are stored as theorems in our system.

The top down formal synthesis process can be summarized by the following four steps:

1. To start with, identify those segments in the circuit specification (type), which can be realized directly by off-shelf components stored in the TTL library.

2. **Split** the design into templates, which serve as placeholders for those components. Each such template is has structure (?a:?A). Templates are unknown objects (?a) of unknown types (?A) (question mark in Isabelle stands for unknown instances).

3. Define (instantiate) the **subspecification** types (?A types of the templates – so we get new templates of the form ?a:Spec).

4. Call the tactic **library** to check if the TTL data base includes proven circuit theorems for the typed (specified) templates. Such theorems are of form (circuit:Spec). If found, the tactics instantiate the objects (?a) of the templates with library objects (circuit). In case of failure proceed to step 1 and split further the failing templates.

5. Prove the correctness of the synthesized circuit.

It is our belief, that such methods reflect the manner in which designers construct their circuits. The basic design tactics we implemented are:

- **split** tactic, which is basically an inverted product elimination rule:

    [| p: Prod(A,B) |] ==> [| a: A |] ==> [| p ' a: B(a) |]

    For example, if applied to a subgoal

    [| ?obj : B(arg) |]

where an identified object ?obj is of a type B(arg) (type B and object **arg** are defined), the tactic splits the object ?obj into two new subobjects. ?func (a function) and **arg** (an argument) so that (?func ' arg : B(arg)). The designer is then presented with two new subgoals, which have to be proved:

1. [| ?func: Prod(A,B) |]

2. [| arg: A |]

There is also a variant of the split tactic, which applies the product elimination rule n times in order to split an object into n subcomponents.

- **subspecification** tactic, which instantiates an undefined type of a subobject (template). This is basically an assumption tactic.

- **library** tactic, which tries to resolve a subgoal by unifying it with theorems stored in the TTL library.

Synthesis example

The following example illustrates the process of formal design. This example is very limited in its scope, but still it requires all crucial design steps which would be employed even in larger constructions. The goal of this example is to design a combinatorial circuit, which would selectively add two numbers (z or y) to a third number x. The numbers are input on four bit busses and the output o is delivered on five bits bus (the fifth bit is carry out bit). The type theoretical specification of such a circuit is given by the type:

$$(\Pi x \in \mathbf{Bus}(4))(\Pi y \in \mathbf{Bus}(4))(\Pi z \in \mathbf{Bus}(4))(\Pi sel \in \mathbf{Bit})$$
$$\{o \in \mathbf{Bus}(5) \mid \mathrm{Eq}(\mathbf{Bus}(5), o, \mathrm{ifg}(sel, x+z, x+y))\}$$

So the goal is to design a hardware function f, which is an object in this specification type such that:

$$f \in (\Pi x \in \mathbf{Bus}(4))(\Pi y \in \mathbf{Bus}(4))(\Pi z \in \mathbf{Bus}(4))(\Pi sel \in \mathbf{Bit})$$
$$\{o \in \mathbf{Bus}(5) \mid \mathrm{Eq}(\mathbf{Bus}(5), o, \mathrm{ifg}(sel, x+z, x+y))\}$$

The following goal statement is input into Isabelle CTT system:

```
[| ?f : PROD x:Bus(4).  PROD y:Bus(4).  PROD z:Bus(4).  PROD sel:Bit.
        SUB o:Bus(5).  Eq(Bus(5), o, ifg(sel, x+z, x+y)) |]
```

---

where ?f is an uninstantiated variable to be synthesized during the proof. After parsing the goal, the following is displayed by the Isabelle system:

```
[| ?f : PROD x:Bus(4).  PROD y:Bus(4).  PROD z:Bus(4).  PROD sel:Bit.
         SUB o:Bus(5).  Eq(Bus(5), o, ifg(sel, x+z, x+y)) |]
 1. [| ?f : PROD x:Bus(4).  PROD y:Bus(4).  PROD z:Bus(4).  PROD sel:Bit.
          SUB o:Bus(5).  Eq(Bus(5), o, ifg(sel, x+z, x+y)) |]
```

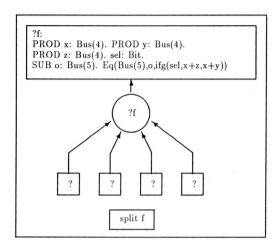

Figure 1: **Initial situation**

There is only one subgoal, which is the entire proof. This situation could be presented graphically to the designer as shown on figure 1. It would depict the entire goal – ?f with its four inputs (still to be named). In the upper part of the figure the specification (type) and its object (the implementation) of the whole design would be presented. In the following figures this object is successively synthesized. The lower part of the figure shows the next tactic to be applied (**split** in this case).

As mentioned before, the synthesis is guided by the designer and is not fully automatic. Due to the experience and the intuition of the designer this would lead hopefully to an efficient implementation. In this particular case, the designer guesses immediately, that the circuit can be implemented by an adder and a multiplexer. So, guided by his/her intuition, the designer splits **f** into two subobjects (templates) by calling tactic "**split f**". This results in a new proof tree as displayed by Isabelle (only subgoal 6 is shown here):

```
[| lam ka. lam kb. lam kc. lam kd.  ?p6(ka, kb, kc, kd) '
              ?a6(ka, kb, kc, kd) :
   PROD x:Bus(4).  PROD y:Bus(4).  PROD z:Bus(4).  PROD sel:Bit.
      SUB o:Bus(5).  Eq(Bus(5), o, ifg(sel, x+z, x+y)) |]
            *
 6. !(ka)[| ka : Bus(4) |] ==> !(kb)[| kb : Bus(4) |] ==>
            !(kc)[| kc : Bus(4) |] ==> !(kd)[| kd : Bit |] ==>
            [| ?a6(ka, kb, kc, kd) : ?A6(ka, kb, kc, kd) |]
            *
```

Subgoal 6 can be read as :

- For all **ka** of type **Bus(4)** (same as saying that under an assumption that **ka** is of type **Bus(4)**) and for all **kb** of type **Bus(4)** and for .... there is an undefined object **a6**, which can be a function of `ka,kb,kc` and `kd` and is of an undefined type `A6`, which can be also a function of `ka,kb,kc` and `kd`.

The `?f` object is partially synthesized by this step to a lambda expression:

- `lam ka. lam kb. lam kc. lam kd. ?p6(ka, kb, kc, kd) '`
  `?a6(ka, kb, kc, kd)`

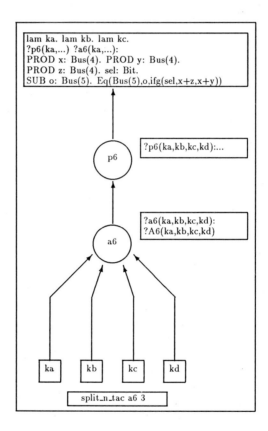

Figure 2: **Design state after "split f"**

Figure 2 depicts this new situation (see the uninstantiated type of unknown object `a6` and the graphical representation of function application of `?p6` to its argument `?a6`).

The designer desires to implement `a6` as multiplexer. A multiplexer has two inputs (`x, y`) and one select signal (`sel`). We now, that the multiplexer is implemented by a function taking three arguments. This requires to split `a6` further three more times (by tactic "`split_n_tac a6 3`" as shown on figure 2).

The new undefined object `p11` (see figure 3) is the template object for the intended multiplexer function and `a11, a8` and `a7` are its arguments. Isabelle display this new situation (see bellow). The partially synthesized implementation consists now of unknown function

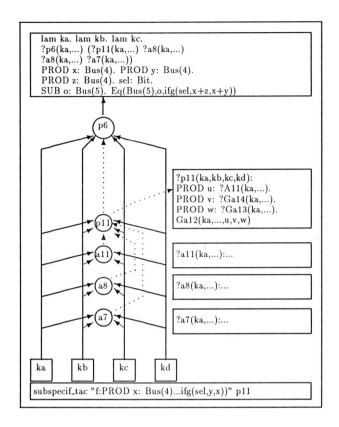

Figure 3: **Design state after "split 3x a6"**

objects **p6**, **p11** and of unknown argument objects **a7**, **a8**, **a11**. The type of the function **p6** in subgoal 6 is partially structured – there are three PROD type constructors (subgoal 6):

```
[| lam ka. lam kb. lam kc. lam kd.  ?p6(ka, kb, kc, kd) '
     (?p11(ka, kb, kc, kd) ' ?a11(ka, kb, kc, kd) '
       ?a8(ka, kb, kc, kd) ' ?a7(ka, kb, kc, kd)) :
   PROD x:Bus(4).  PROD y:Bus(4).  PROD z:Bus(4).  PROD sel:Bit.
     SUB o:Bus(5).  Eq(Bus(5), o, ifg(sel, x+z, x+y)) |]
                 *
                 *
                 *
```

```
6. !(ka)[| ka : Bus(4) |] ==> !(kb)[| kb : Bus(4) |] ==>
         !(kc)[| kc : Bus(4) |] ==> !(kd)[| kd : Bit |] ==>
                        [| ?p11(ka, kb, kc, kd) :
                        PROD u:?A11(ka, kb, kc, kd).
                        PROD v:?Ga14(ka, kb, kc, kd, u).
                        PROD w:?Ga13(ka, kb, kc, kd, u, v).
                        ?Ga12(ka, kb, kc, kd, u, v, w) |]

                    *
```

In this rather trivial design case it would be apparent to instantiate **p11** directly to the multiplexer function. However, we want to show here what would happen if a more complicated circuit was synthesized. In that case the designer would specify **p11** by instantiating its type and then try to find its implementation in the TTL data library or in other data base of correct designs. The type instantiating is executed by calling the tactic **subspecific_tac** with two arguments (the type specification and the search object):

```
subspecif_tac "PROD x:Bus(4).  PROD y:Bus(4).  PROD sel:Bit.  SUB o:Bus(4).
          Eq(Bus(4), o, ifg(sel, y, x))" p11.
```

Isabelle displays the result (see the instantiated type of **p11** in subgoal 6):

```
[| lam ka. lam kb. lam kc. lam kd.   ?p6(ka, kb, kc, kd) '
      (?p11(ka, kb, kc, kd) ' ?a11(ka, kb, kc, kd) ' ?a8(ka, kb, kc, kd) '
        ?a7(ka, kb, kc, kd)) :
   PROD x:Bus(4).  PROD y:Bus(4).  PROD z:Bus(4).  PROD sel:Bit.
      SUB o:Bus(5).  Eq(Bus(5), o, ifg(sel, x+z, x+y)) |]
                  *
6. !(ka)[| ka : Bus(4) |] ==> !(kb)[| kb : Bus(4) |] ==>
         !(kc)[| kc : Bus(4) |] ==> !(kd)[| kd : Bit |] ==>
                        [| ?p11(ka, kb, kc, kd) :
                        PROD x:Bus(4).  PROD y:Bus(4).
                        PROD sel:Bit.  SUB o:Bus(4).
                        Eq(Bus(4), o, ifg(sel, y, x)) |]

                    *
```

See also figure 4 for graphical representation (with the type of **p11** properly instantiated). The designer then tries to instantiate **p11** by calling tactic "library p11" which attempts to unify proven theorems in the TTL library with the subgoal 6. If this tactic fails, (there is no appropriate theorem in the data base) then **p11** has to be split further into new subcomponents (templates). However, in this particular case it succeeds and that with "**mux_two_fourb**" theorem (two input multiplexer with four bits wide busses). This theorem states that

```
                lam x. lam y. lam sel. mux_two_fourb(x, y, sel)
```

is an object in the type

```
        PROD x:Bus(4). PROD y:Bus(4). PROD sel:Bit. SUB o:Bus(4).
                Eq(Bus(4), o, ifg(sel, y, x))
```

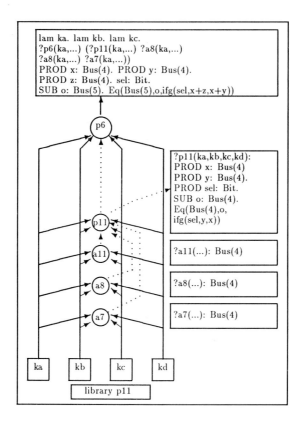

Figure 4: **Design state after the subspecification of p11**

It can be read as:

- For all inputs x of type B(4) and for all inputs y of type B(4) and for all inputs sel of type Bit there is an output o such that o = ifg(sel, y, x) and both o and ifg(sel, y, x) are of type Bus(4).

The result of the library tactic application is (see the partially synthesized goal object, which includes the multiplexer):

```
[| lam ka. lam kb. lam kc. lam kd.  ?p6(ka, kb, kc, kd) '
    ((lam x. lam y. lam sel.  mux_two_fourb(x, y, sel)) '
     ?a11(ka, kb, kc, kd) ' ?a8(ka, kb, kc, kd) ' ?a7(ka, kb, kc, kd)) :
  PROD x:Bus(4).  PROD y:Bus(4).  PROD z:Bus(4).  PROD sel:Bit.
    SUB o:Bus(5).  Eq(Bus(5), o, ifg(sel, x+z, x+y)) |]
                          *
                          *
```

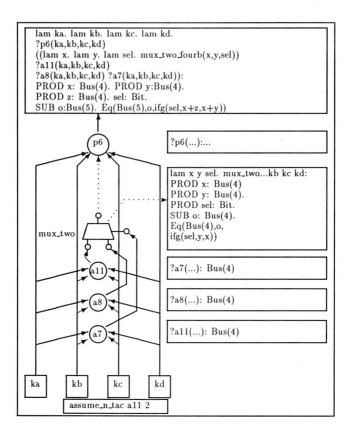

Figure 5: **Design state after the implementation of p11 by a mux**

```
6. !(ka)[| ka : Bus(4) |] ==> !(kb)[| kb : Bus(4) |] ==>
        !(kc)[| kc : Bus(4) |] ==> !(kd)[| kd : Bit |] ==>
                              [| ?a11(ka, kb, kc, kd) : Bus(4) |]
                *
```

See also figure 5, which includes now the introduced multiplexer component.

The multiplexer function takes three arguments – a11, a8 and a7. These have to be instantiated. a11 is instantiated to the bound variable kb (which is the second input argument to the whole circuit) by applying tactic "assume_n_tac a11 2". This tactic resolves the subgoal 6 (see above) by unifying it with its second assumption (kb – by an assumption rule).

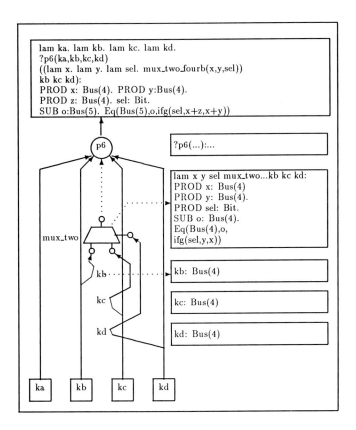

Figure 6: **Design state after the complete implementation of the mux subpart**

Isabelle displays is:

```
[| lam ka. lam kb. lam kc. lam kd.  ?p6(ka, kb, kc, kd) '
     ((lam x. lam y. lam sel. mux_two_fourb(x, y, sel)) '
         kb ' ?a8(ka, kb, kc, kd) ' ?a7(ka, kb, kc, kd)) :
   PROD x:Bus(4).  PROD y:Bus(4).  PROD z:Bus(4).  PROD sel:Bit.
      SUB o:Bus(5).  Eq(Bus(5), o, ifg(sel, x+z, x+y)) |]
              *
              *
```

Subgoal 6 disappeared as ?a11 in that goal is unified with bound variable kb. a8 and a7 are instantiated in the same way as a11. The complete multiplexer design with its arguments properly instantiated is depicted on figure 6.

The adder design is accomplished in similar fashion. p6 is split into p23, a23, a20 and a18 as shown on figure 7. p23 is instantiated to the adder implementation function with

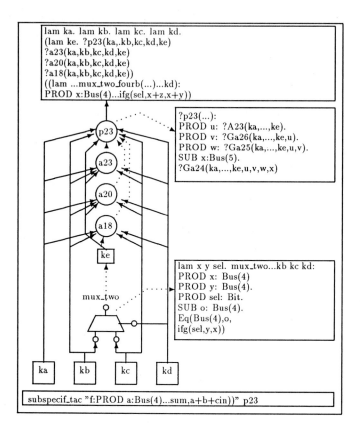

```
lam ka. lam kb. lam kc. lam kd.
(lam ke. ?p23(ka,.kb,kc,kd,ke)
?a23(ka,kb,kc,kd,ke)
?a20(ka,kb,kc,kd,ke)
?a18(ka,kb,kc,kd,ke))
((lam ...mux_two_fourb(...)...kd):
PROD x:Bus(4)...ifg(sel,x+z,x+y))
```

```
?p23(...):
PROD u: ?A23(ka,...,ke).
PROD v: ?Ga26(ka,...,ke,u).
PROD w: ?Ga25(ka,...,ke,u,v).
SUB x:Bus(5).
?Ga24(ka,...,ke,u,v,w,x)
```

```
lam x y sel. mux_two...kb kc kd:
PROD x: Bus(4)
PROD y: Bus(4).
PROD sel: Bit.
SUB o: Bus(4).
Eq(Bus(4),o,
ifg(sel,y,x))
```

```
subspecif_tac "f:PROD a:Bus(4)...sum,a+b+cin))" p23
```

Figure 7: **Design state after the split of adder part**

its carry input grounded (lo = logical zero). The complete design (with arguments of the adder properly instantiated) is depicted on figure 8. Isabelle display is then:

```
[| lam ka. lam kb. lam kc. lam kd.
  (lam ke. (lam a. lam b. lam cin.  adder_four(a, b, cin))
                                      ' ka ' ke ' lo) '
    ((lam x. lam y. lam sel.  mux_two_fourb(x, y, sel)) ' kb ' kc ' kd) :
  PROD x:Bus(4).  PROD y:Bus(4).  PROD z:Bus(4).  PROD sel:Bit.
    SUB o:Bus(5).  Eq(Bus(5), o, ifg(sel, x+z, x+y)) |]
                *
        **  several other subgoals **
```

That concludes the guided synthesis phase of the proof. f is instantiated and now it has to be shown that it is object in the specification type of the circuit. In this particular case the proof is rather simple. In one of the remaining subgoals it has to be shown that:

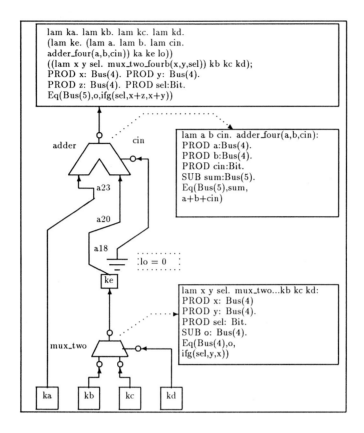

Figure 8: **Final result**

```
!(ka)[| ka : Bus(4) |] ==>
        !(kb)[| kb : Bus(4) |] ==>
            !(kc)[| kc : Bus(4) |] ==>
                !(kd)[| kd : Bit |] ==>
  adder_fourb(ka, mux_two(kb, kc, kd), lo) = ifg(kd, ka+kc, ka+kb): Bus(4)
```

---

where `adder_fourb(ka, mux_two(kb, kc, kd), lo)` stands for the implementation and
`ifg(kd, ka+kc, ka+kb)` is the specification. The adder and the mux are defined as:

- `adder_fourb(a, b, cin) == a + b + cin`

- `mux_two_fourb(a, b, sel) == ifg(sel, b, a)`

By substitution we get:

```
!(ka)[| ka : Bus(4) |] ==>
      !(kb)[| kb : Bus(4) |] ==>
            !(kc)[| kc : Bus(4) |] ==>
                  !(kd)[| kd : Bit |] ==>
                  ka + ifg(kd, kc, kb) + lo = ifg(kd, ka+kc, ka+kb): Bus(4)
```

---

which is quite easy to show to be true.

Conclusions

We have presented a formal system for hardware design based on Martin-Löf's type theory. Type theory is a fundamentally new kind, providing a single integrated framework for programs and proofs.

The main advantage of our system is that it integrates :

synthesis process – and that due to the constructive nature of proofs in type theory. The synthesis presented in this paper is done in top down fashion. It is however possible to incorporate in this framework bottom up design. In that case the designer starts from the bottom by synthesizing subdesigns, which can be then used in higher design levels.

verification process – if a hardware function already exists, it can be verified by proof as in synthesis case.

simulations process – as the derived hardware structures are functions. Simulations are important in order to alleviate obvious mistakes before any tedious formal proofs are attempted. An unusual property of those functions is that they all always terminate.

In this work we developed a method for synthesis of circuits in type theory, which mimics the design fashion of experienced designers. This should lead to efficient implementations. It allows partial proofs of crucial parts of the design (similarly to the *prudent* design fashion introduced by F K Hanna). It also allows for incremental development of theorem data base of proven designs. The drawbacks of the system are:

- The system is undecidable (due to the dependent types) - fully automatic synthesis is not possible (This applies to Veritas+ and to all other higher-order systems as well).

- The structures are functions e.i. bidirectional circuits can not be modeled as in case of Veritas+. However the basic approach in such a modern silicon design language as Model is unidirectional.

- The objects (programs) of the type theory do not include general recursion, which means, that some of the hardware structures probably could not be expressed in it. However most of these cases could be covered by using high order functions.

- The type theory lacks constructors for integers and it lacks real numbers as well. It includes however a basic arithmetic theory.

- There is no efficient implementation of the type theory language for simulation purposes. However it could be easily translated to LML functional language with its type control deactivated.

The long term goal of this project is to create an expert system for hardware design based on the type theory. Such a system will consist of a rich collection of library circuit theorems. It will also include powerful set of tactics, which will enable to do fast semiautomatic proofs of hardware structures. What is needed in short run:

- To synthesize more complicated examples.

- To expand the library.

- To develop a compiler from type theory expressions to Model language which can be further compiled to silicon by Solo 1400 system (done by F K Hanna in his Veritas+ system).

- To develop an user friendly graphical interface understandable to an design engineer (so called schematic capture). There is one to one correspondence between actions undertaken while using the schematic capture (as in Solo 1400 for example) and the split, subspecification and the library tactics.

References

[1] Albert Camilleri, Mike Gordon, and Tom Melham. Hardware verification using higher-order logic. In *From H.D.L. Descriptions to Guaranteed Correct Circuit Designs, IFIP International Working Conference*, Grenoble, France, September 9-11 1986.

[2] M.J.C. Gordon. Why high-order logic is a good formalism for specifying and verifying hardware. In G.J. Milne and North-Holland Publishing P.A. Subrahmanyam, eds., editors, *Formal Aspects of VLSI design:Proc. 1985 Edinburgh Conf. VLSI*, pages 153–177, Amsterdam, Holland, 1986.

[3] F K Hanna, M Longley, and N Daeche. Formal synthesis of digital systems. In Dr. Luc Cleasen, editor, *Proceedings of the IMEC-IFIP International Workshop on Applied Formal Methods For Correct VLSI Design*, pages 535–548, Leuven Belgium, November 1989.

[4] Per Martin-Löf. Constructive mathematics and computer proframming. In North-Holland Publishing, editor, *Logic, Methodology and Philosophy of Science, VI, 1979*, pages 153–175, Grenoble, France, 1982.

[5] Bengt Nordström, Kent Petersson, and Jan Smith. *An Introduction to Martin-Löf's Type Theory*. Programming Methodology Group, Dep. of Comp. Science, Göteborg, Chalmers University of Technology, S-412 96 Göteborg, Sweden, 1986.

[6] Lawrence C. Paulson. The foundation of a generic theorem prover. Technical Report 130, Computer Laboratory, Cambridge, England, March 1988.

[7] Lawrence C. Paulson. A preliminary user's manual for isabelle. Technical Report 133, Computer Laboratory, Cambridge, England, May 1988.

[8] D. Suk. Formal verification and synthesis of hardware in the framework of martin-löf's intuitionistic type theory. Technical Report 82, Department of Computer Engineering, Chalmers University of Technology, Göteborg, Sweden, December 1989.

Appendix

Syntax of CTT

symbol	meta-type	description
'	$[term, term] \rightarrow term$	function application
*	$[type, type] \rightarrow type$	product of two types
+	$[type, type] \rightarrow type$	sum of two types
-->	$[type, type] \rightarrow type$	function type

INFIXES

Isabelle notation	Isabelle internal	Chalmers notation
A type	$\text{Type}(A)$	the judgment A type
$A = B$	$\text{Eqtype}(A, B)$	the judgment $A = B$ type
$a : A$	$\text{Elem}(a, A)$	the judgment $a \in A$
$a = b : A$	$\text{Eq}(a, b, A)$	the judgment $a = b \in A$
PROD $x : A . B$	$\text{Prod}(A, \lambda x.B)$	the product $(\Pi x \in A)B$
A --> B	$\text{Prod}(A, \lambda x.B)$	the function $A \rightarrow B$
SUM $x : A . B$	$\text{Sum}(A, \lambda x.B)$	the sum $(\Sigma x \in A)B$
A * B	$\text{Sum}(A, \lambda x.B)$	the cartesian product $A \times B$
lam $x . b$	$\text{lambda}(\lambda x.b)$	the abstraction $(\lambda x)b$
$\langle a, b \rangle$	$\text{pair}(a, b)$	the pair $\langle a, b \rangle$

TRANSLATIONS

$$
\begin{aligned}
judgment \quad = \quad & type \ \textbf{type} \\
| \quad & type \ \texttt{=} \ type \\
| \quad & term \ \texttt{:} \ type \\
| \quad & term \ \texttt{=} \ term \ \texttt{:} \ type \\
type \quad = \quad & \texttt{PROD} \ var \ \texttt{:} \ type \ \texttt{.} \ type \\
| \quad & \texttt{SUM} \ var \ \texttt{:} \ type \ \texttt{.} \ type \\
| \quad & others \ldots \\
term \quad = \quad & \texttt{lam} \ var \ \texttt{.} \ term \\
| \quad & \texttt{<} \ term \ \texttt{,} \ term \ \texttt{>} \\
| \quad & others \ldots
\end{aligned}
$$

GRAMMAR

48

Formation, introduction, elimination and computation rules for the bit type

Bit_form:

```
[| Bit type |]
```

Bit_intr_hi:

```
[| hi : Bit |]
```

Bit_intr_lo:

```
[| lo : Bit |]
```

Bit_elim:

```
[| p : Bit |]   ==> [| a : C(hi) |]   ==>
[| b : C(lo) |]   ==> [| ifg(p,a,b) : C(p) |]
```

Bit_elim_long:

```
[| p = q : Bit |]   ==> [| a = b : C(hi) |]   ==>
[| c = d : C(lo) |]   ==> [| ifg(p,a,c) = ifg(q,b,d) : C(p) |]
```

Bit_comp_hi:

```
[| p = hi : Bit |]   ==> [| a : C(hi) |]   ==>
[| b : C(lo) |]   ==> [| ifg(p,a,b) = a : C(hi) |]
```

Bit_comp_lo:

```
[| p = lo : Bit |]   ==> [| a : C(hi) |]   ==>
[| b : C(lo) |]   ==> [| ifg(p,a,b) = b : C(lo) |]
```

Bit_comp_eq:

```
[| p : Bit |]   ==> [| ifg(p,hi,lo) = p : Bit |]
```

TTL library

Not gate

not_def:

```
not(a) == ifg(a,lo,hi)
```

not_impl:

```
lam i. not(i) :  PROD a: Sig. SUB o : Sig. Eq(Sig,o,neg(a))
```

not_comp_hi:

```
not(hi) = lo : Sig
```

not_comp_lo:

```
not(lo) = hi : Sig
```

And gate

and_def:

       `and(a,b) == ifg(a,ifg(b,hi,lo),lo)`

and_impl:

       `lam a. lam b. and(a,b) :`
       `PROD a: Sig. PROD b: Sig. SUB o : Sig. Eq(Sig,o,a & b)`

and_comp_lo_dc:

       `!(b)[| b : Sig |] ==> [| and(lo,b) = lo : Sig |]`

and_comp_dc_lo:

       `!(a)[| a : Sig |] ==> [| and(a,lo) = lo : Sig |]`

and_comp_hi_hi:

       `and(hi,hi) = hi : Sig`

Or gate

or_def:

       `or(a,b) == ifg(a,hi,ifg(b,hi,lo))`

or_impl:

       `lam a. lam b. or(a,b) :`
       `PROD a: Sig. PROD b: Sig. SUB o : Sig. Eq(Sig,o,a | b)`

or_comp_hi_dc:

       `!(b)[| b : Sig |] ==> [| or(hi,b) = hi : Sig`

or_comp_dc_hi:

       `!(a)[| a : Sig |] ==> [| or(a,hi) = hi : Sig |]`

or_comp_lo_lo:

       `or(lo,lo) = lo : Sig |]`

An Algebraic Framework for Data Abstraction in Hardware Description

Zheng Zhu[*]   Steven D. Johnson[†]

Abstract

The aim of this work is to extend a standard treatment of data types to a foundation for hardware synthesis. Hardware synthesis exposes several problems not typically considered in software oriented theories. These include architectural constraints in the use of type instances, parallelism in the use of multiple instances, and consolidation of distinct types in a common process. Since we are concerned with the question of incorporating (more) concrete implementations of (more) abstract types found in higher levels of specification, our foundation must address these aspects of description. The paper begins with a condensed example of a stack based processor operating on a standard memory. This specification is compared to a target description in which both the stack and the memory are implemented by a single memory process. The remainder of the paper formalizes issues raised in the example.

1   Introduction

If one tries to apply standard treatments of data abstraction to hardware design, a number of formal problems are exposed. For example, there is a need to describe architecture in a type formalization. There is a need to reformulate notions of implementation in the context of parallel control. There is a need to reflect a process oriented view of behavior. While these issues are obviously present in software, one can go a good distance without confronting them directly. However, they are the essence of many hardware design problems.

Our approach to formalizing design is based on function algebra. An abstract behavioral description is transformed to an architecture description by the function algebra [8, 9]. An implementation of this algebra has been used successfully to derived several working designs [2, 11]. However, this algebra manipulates descriptions at a fixed level of data abstraction. Consequently, specifications must be given in more detail than we would like.

We now turn to the question of translating specifications expressed over a higher level of data representation to implementations expressed at a lower level. Our goal is to lay a foundation for a general treatment of data abstraction in hardware description. We develop extensions to the algebraic characterization of data types which permit us to specify architectures. We give a corresponding characterization of control as recursive functions on the resulting structures. In this framework, we consider the question of implementing relatively abstract architectures by relatively concrete ones.

---

[*]Computer Science Department, Indiana University, Bloomington, IN 47405 USA
zhu@iuvax.cs.indiana.edu

[†]Computer Science Department, Indiana University, Bloomington, IN 47405 USA
sjohnson@iuvax.cs.indiana.edu

The algebra of translating specifications expressed over a higher level of data abstraction to implementations expressed at a lower level has much in common with process formalisms, such as those of Milne [16], and Gopalkrishnan [6]. A difference in emphasis is that this work is directed toward *derivation* (i.e. synthesis in an algebraic framework) rather than *verification*. In addition, we focus on the complex interaction between *functional* and *physical* decomposition under the thesis that a logical hierarchy does not always dictate the physical modularity of a design.

In high-level synthesis, methods exist to explore the balance of architecture and control—the problems of *scheduling, allocation, module matching,* and *control synthesis* [14]. However, these methods are typically restricted to some fixed ground type, and they are often tied to specific architecture classes. Our motive is to develop a treatment for these kinds of problems at arbitrary levels of data abstraction. Although the most urgent practical needs remain at lowest levels of representation, such a foundation is required if synthesis is to address system designs.

Mahmood, Mavaddat, Elmasry and Cheng propose using a DTOL language model to specify hardware architectures [13]. The data paths of an architecture are defined by a set of homomorphic functions and the control of hardware is defined by a sequence of applications of those functions. An algorithm for synthesizing control (microcodes) is presented. Although our framework is similar to theirs, there exist two basic differences between the two: First, our framework is designed for derivation of architecture as well as synthesis of hardware control. It addresses issues such as the incorporation of correct data representation. Second, the foundation described takes into account the underlying algebraic properties of the abstract data type structures involved. However, this degree of generality also leads to undecidability of problems.

In Section 2, we present a condensed example to motivate the formal development. The example illustrates issues that we have been forced to deal with in previous design exercises. These issues are neither "solved" by the formal development nor currently handled by our mechanized subset of it. However, we believe that they can be characterized in the framework developed here. Sections 3 reviews fundamentals of the theory of abstract data types. In Sections 4 and 5, we extend the standard definitions to account for hardware architecture. In Section 6, we consider the central question of implementing one extended abstract type by another. Section 7 discusses the issue of modeling hardware control and incorporating architecture implementation into hardware control.

We develop three results in this paper. Theorem 1 (Section 3) states a condition under which one equational theory is said to implement another. This theorem characterizes implementation in terms of equational rewriting which implies that the validity of implementation can be established with the help of a computer. Theorem 2 (Section 5.1) states conditions under which the extended notion of data type preserves the implementation relationship. Finally, Theorem 3 (Section 7) incorporates the functional representation of control into the implementation relationship.

2 Motivation

Consider the simple machine specification shown in Figure 1 using a PureLisp-like notation. The machine has arithmetic instructions, such as *add* and *sub*, a load-constant instruction *ldc*, and a branch instruction *goto*. The machine state has an instruction memory (M-i) and an operand stack (S). Each arithmetic operation takes two operands from the stack and returns its result to the stack. The *ldc* operation copies a constant from the instruction memory to the stack; and *goto* sets the memory address register (*a-i*) to the content of the next instruction cell. The standard abstract memory is used, with *wr* (write), *rd* (read) operations. The *dcr, inc* operations respectively decrement and increment memory addresses. A standard abstract stack is used with *push, pop,* and *top* operations.

One task in implementing this specification is to develop data paths and a finite-state control for it. The intermediate description in Figure 2 associates a hardware control-state with each function definition. Details of algebra to obtain this description from that in Figure 1 are omitted [2]. In this description, each state is constrained to operate at most once on the memory and at most once on the stack; binary arithmetic operations are encapsulated by an arithmetic unit (arith); and three registers, *op1, op2* and *I*, are introduced to hold intermediate results.

The target description in Figure 3 further constrains the design in two ways. The stack abstraction S is implemented by a pair consisting of a memory and an address register, (*M-s,a-s*); and two memory objects, *M-i* and *M-s*, are merged into a single memory object M. The resulting architecture operates at most once on M in any control state.

Ultimately, it is this merging of distinct functional entities "stack" and "memory" into a single object that interests us. However, in order to reach this problem, we must also address the following issues:

1. What constitutes a correct implementation of hardware components? In the example, we need to know that how the memory *can* be used to implement the stack.

2. How are *correct* implementations *correctly* incorporated in hardware descriptions. The transformations that do this must satisfy not only the functional properties of the implementation, but also the architecture constraints surrounding its use.

We regard (1) as an issue for verification and (2) as an issue for synthesis. Although the correctness of implementations is not the immediate subject of this research, it is necessary to adopt a criterion of correctness before accounting for architectures. Thus, the immediate concern of this paper is a characterization of what one does *with* a correct implementation; that is, how specifications are transformed to incorporate them.

3   Term Algebra and Equational Specification

In this section, we briefly review the concepts of equational specification and implementation in universal algebra. There are mainly two schools in the *algebraic semantics* of abstract data types, *i.e. initial* semantics (*e.g.* [5], [4], [15]) and *final* semantics (*e.g* [19], [12]). (See also [1] for a comparative introduction to both approaches.) In our presentation, we attempt to avoid an association with any particular approach to semantics by keeping the framework on syntactic level as much as possible although this preliminary work is influenced by the ADJ group's results [5, 15]. We start with the concepts of Σ-algebra and its special form, Σ term algebra, then the concept of equational specification. At the end, we introduce a definition of implementation for equational specifications and a characterization theorem for implementation.

Let S be a set of sorts. An S-sorted *signature* Σ is a set $\bigcup_{w \in S^*, s \in S} \Sigma_{w,s}$. Every element σ of set $\Sigma_{w,s}$ is a function symbol of *arity* w and of sort s. The arity of a function symbol expresses what sorts of data it expects to take as its inputs and in what order. The sort of a function symbol expresses the sort of data it returns. Constant symbols are considered as function symbols of *empty* arity. An S-sorted set of variables is $X = \bigcup_{s \in S} X_s$. Each

```
(define machine (M-s a-s S)
    (case (rd M-s a-s)
        ('add'  (machine M-s (dcr a-s) (push (+ (top S) (top (pop S))) (pop (pop S)))))
        ('sub'  (machine M-s (dcr a-s) (push (- (top S) (top (pop S))) (pop (pop S)))))
        ('mul'  (machine M-s (dcr a-s) (push (* (top S) (top (pop S))) (pop (pop S)))))
        ('div'  (machine M-s (dcr a-s) (push (/ (top S) (top (pop S))) (pop (pop S)))))
        ('eq?'  (machine M-s (dcr a-s) (push (= (top S) (top (pop S))) (pop (pop S)))))
        ('le?'  (machine M-s (dcr a-s) (push (< (top S) (top (pop S))) (pop (pop S)))))
        ('goto' (machine M-s (rd (M-s (dcr a-s))) S))
        ('ldc'  (machine M-s (dcr (dcr a-s)) (push (rd M-s (dcr a-s)) S)))
```

Figure 1: **Specification of the Machine**

```
(define machine (M-s a-s S op1 op2 I)
    (case I
        ('goto' (goto       M-s (rd M-s a-s) S op1 op2 I))
        ('ldc'  (ldc1       M-s (dcr a-s) S (rd M-s a-s) op2 I))
        (else   (arithmetic1 M-s a-s (pop S) (top S) op2 I))))

(define goto (M-s a-s S op1 op2 I)
    (machine M-s (dcr a-s) S op1 op2 (rd M-s a-s)))

(define ldc1 (M-s a-s S op1 op2 I)
    (machine M-s (dcr a-s) (push S op1) op1 op2 (rd M-s a-s)))

(define arithmetic1 (M-s a-s S op1 op2 I)
    (arithmetic2 M-s a-s (pop S) op1 (top S) I))

(define arithmetic2 (M-s a-s S op1 op2 I)
    (machine  M-s (dcr a-s) (push S (arith I op1 op2)) op1 op2 (rd M-s a-s)))
```

Figure 2: **Modified Specification of the Machine**

```
(define machine (M a-s a-i op1 op2 I)
    (case I
        ('goto' (goto    M (rd M a-s) a-i op1 op2 I))
        ('ldc'  (ldc1    M (dcr2 a-s) a-i (rd M a-s) op2 I))
        (else   (arithmetic1 M a-s (dcr2 a-i) (rd M-s a-i) op2 I))))

(define goto (M a-s a-i op1 op2 I)
    (machine M (dcr2 a-s) a-i op1 op2 (rd M a-s)))

(define ldc1 (M a-s a-i op1 op2 I)
    (ldc2 (wr M (inc2 a-i) op1) a-s (inc2 a-i) op1 op2 I))

(define ldc2 (M a-s a-i op1 op2 I)
    (machine M (dcr2 a-s) a-i op1 op2 (rd M a-s)))

(define arithmetic1 (M a-s a-i op1 op2 I)
    (arithmetic2 M a-s (dcr2 a-i) op1 (rd M a-i) I))

(define arithmetic2 (M a-s a-i op1 op2 I)
    (arithmetic3 (wr M a-i (arith I op1 op2)) a-s (inc2 a-i) op1 op2 I))

(define arithmetic2 (M a-s a-i op1 op2 I)
    (machine M (dcr2 a_s) a_i op1 op2 (rd M a-s)))
```

Figure 3: **Implementation of Machine With One Memory**

element of the set X_s is called a variable of sort s. Given Σ, the set of terms generated from Σ and X, denoted by $T_\Sigma(X)$ is inductively defined as:

1. If $x_s \in X_s$ for some $s \in S$ then $x_s \in T_{\Sigma_s}(X)$.

2. If $c \in \Sigma_{\lambda,s}$ for some $s \in S$ then $c \in T_{\Sigma_s}(X)$.

3. If $f \in \Sigma_{w,s}$ where $w = s_1 s_2 \ldots s_n$, and $t_i \in T_{\Sigma_{s_i}}(X)$ $1 \le i \le n$, then $f(t_1, t_2, \ldots, t_n) \in T_{\Sigma_s}(X)$.

4. $T_\Sigma(X) = \bigcup_{s \in S} T_{\Sigma_s}(X)$.

Traditionally, T_Σ is used to denote $T_\Sigma(\phi)$. Let Y be an S-sorted set of variables which is disjoint from X. A Y-equation of $T_\Sigma(X)$ is a tuple (l, r) where $l, r \in T_\Sigma(X \cup Y)$. We usually write (l, r) as "$l \equiv r$". The set Y is called a set of meta-specification variables. Let E be a set of Y-equations of $T_\Sigma(X)$, then E induces an equivalence relation on the set $T_\Sigma(X)$; hence we can define $T_\Sigma(X)/E$ as the set of equivalence classes of $T_\Sigma(X)$ under E.

Let Σ be an S-sorted signature. A Σ-*algebra* A consists of a family of carriers $<A_s \mid s \in S>$ together with a set of functions $F = \{f_\sigma \mid \sigma \in \Sigma\}$ such that $f_\sigma: A_{s_1} \times A_{s_2} \times \ldots A_{s_n} \to A_s$ for every $\sigma \in \Sigma_{w,s}$ where $w = s_1 s_2 \ldots s_n$.

A special type of Σ-algebra, which is also our major interest, is $T(\Sigma, X) = \langle T_\Sigma(X), \Sigma \rangle$, called *the term algebra generated from* Σ. If E is a set Y-equations of $T_\Sigma(X)$, then E is a congruence relation on $T(\Sigma, X)$. We use $T(\Sigma, X, E)$ to denote $T(\Sigma, X)$ modulo E. It is important to realize that though X and Y are sets of variables, they are different in a sense that X is a set of *program variables* and Y is a set of *assertion variables*. A detailed discussion of the difference can be found in [18].

An equational specification is $\langle \Sigma, X, E \rangle$. It has been shown (*e.g.* [4, 5]) that equational specifications can be used to specify abstract data types and the algebra $T(\Sigma, X, E)$ can be used as the meaning of the specification. We also show later how an extension of equational specification defines an abstract hardware architecture syntactically.

The following two definitions define the notion of implementing one equational specification by another. These definitions are slight variations of those in [5]. The difference is that they are not based on the initial algebra semantics. The motive for this treatment becomes clear in section 5 where we define architectural implementation independently of semantics.

In the definitions, $T_\Sigma^*(X)$ designates, informally, a set of term-vectors of finite length, and λT designates the set of combinators (*i.e.* closed lambda expressions) involving terms in T.

Definition 1. Let Σ and Ω be S_1-sorted and S_2-sorted operator domains respectively. A *derivor* $d: \Sigma \to \Omega$ is a pair of functions $\langle \xi, \kappa \rangle$ where $\xi : S_1 \to S_2^*$ and $\kappa : \Sigma \to \lambda(T_\Omega^*(X_2))$, such that for every $\sigma \in \Sigma_{w,s}$, $\kappa(\sigma)$ is a $\xi(s)$-sorted function symbol of arity $\xi(w)$. The d-derived algebra from $T(\Sigma, X_1, E_1)$, $dT(\Omega, X_2, E_2)$, is a Σ-algebra defined as $\langle T_\Omega(X_2)/E_2, d(\Sigma) \rangle$.

Definition 2. Let $P = \langle \Sigma, E_1 \rangle$ be a specification. An *implementation* of P is a triple $<B, d, E>$, where $B = \langle \Omega, E_2 \rangle$ is another equational specification, d is derivor from Σ to Ω, and E is a congruence relation of $T(\Omega, E_2)$, such that $T(\Sigma, E_1)$ is a subalgebra of $(dB)/E$.

Definition 3. Let E_1, E_2 and E_3 be definite sets of equations.

1. $E_1 \vdash E_2$ means that for every $(l, r) \in E_2$, there exist $(l_1, r_1), \ldots, (l_n, r_n) \in E_1$ such that $l_1 \equiv l$, $r_n \equiv r$ and for every $i = 1, \ldots, n-1$, $r_i \equiv l_{i+1}$;

2. $E_1/E_2 \vdash E_3$ means that for every $(l, r) \in E_3$, there exists t such that $E_1 \vdash (l, t)$ and $E_2 \vdash (t, r)$;

3. Let d be a derivor $\Sigma \to \Omega$ and E be a set of equations on T_Σ. Define $d(E) = \{ (d(l), d(r)) \mid (l, r) \in E \}$.

Theorem 1. Let $\langle \Sigma, E_1 \rangle$ and $\langle \Omega, E_2 \rangle$ be two equational specifications. Let $d : \Sigma \to \Omega$ be a 1-1 derivor and E be a set of equations of T_Ω. If $E_2/E \vdash d(E_1)$ then $\langle T_\Omega, d, E \rangle$ is an implementation of T_Σ; that is, $\langle T(\Sigma, E_1), \Sigma \rangle$ is a subalgebra of $\langle T(\Omega, E_2), d(\Sigma) \rangle / E$.

One thing to notice is that $d(E_1) \vdash E_2$ and $d(E_1) \vdash E$ if E can be written as a finite set of equations. The significance of the theorem is that it characterizes implementation in terms of an equational rewriting mechanism.

We simplify the proof by considering the case when $\xi \colon S_1 \to S_2$. In that case, κ becomes $\Sigma \to \lambda(T_\Omega(X_2))$. The proof for $T_\Omega^*(X_s)$ is a straightforward generalization.

Proof. d is obviously a mapping $T_\Sigma \to T_\Omega$ such that $d(\sigma(t_1, \ldots, t_n)) = d(\sigma)(d(t_1), \ldots, d(t_n))$. Since E is a congruence relation on T_{Ω, E_2}, we can assume h is the homomorphism

$$h \colon T(\Omega, E_2)/E \to T(\Omega, E_2)$$

We prove that $h \circ d$ is a 1-1 homomorphism $T(\Sigma, E_1) \to T(\Omega, E_2)/E$, i.e. $T(\Sigma, E_1)$ is a subalgebra of $T(\Omega, E_2)/E$.

1. For every $t_1, t_2 \in T(\Sigma)$, $t_1 \equiv_{E_1} t_2$ implies that $d(t_1) \equiv_{d(E_1)} d(t_2)$, which in turn implies that $d(t_1) \equiv_{E_2/E} d(t_2)$ because $E_2/E \vdash d(E_1)$. That h is a homomorphism defines E, therefore $t_1 \equiv_{E_1} t_2$ implies $h \circ d(t_1) \equiv_{E_2} h \circ d(t_2)$ which means that $h \circ d$ is a well defined.

2. By the definition of d, $d(\sigma(t_1, \ldots, t_n)) = d(\sigma)(d(t_1), \ldots, d(t_n))$. Since h is an homomorphism, $h \circ d(\sigma(t_1, \ldots, t_n)) = h \circ d(\sigma)(h \circ d(t_1), \ldots, h \circ d(t_n))$.

3. Let $t_1, t_2 \in T_\Omega$ and assume that $h \circ d(t_1) \equiv_{E_2} h \circ d(t_2)$. Then $h \circ d(t_1) \equiv_{E_2/E} h \circ d(t_2)$ which implies $d(t_1) \equiv_{d(E_1)} d(t_2)$. Since d is 1-1, $t_1 \equiv_{E_1} t_2$.

Therefore, the image of $h \circ d$ is a subalgebra of $T(\Omega, E_2)/E$ which is equivalent to saying that $T(\Sigma, E_1)$ is a subalgebra of $(dT(\Omega, E_2))/E$. $\square$

4 Equational Specification of Hardware Architecture

In this section, we use an extended form of equational specification to characterize *register transfer level (RTL)* hardware architecture. A register transfer level hardware description consists of at least 3 parts: an underlying abstract data description; a set of registers; and a set of data paths characterizing interconnections among registers and functional units. Our goal is to extend the definition of underlying abstract data description to include those of registers and data paths. The first observation is the that registers play the role of program

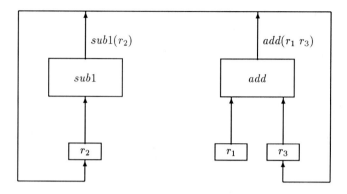

Figure 4: An Architecture

variables [18] in a hardware description. Thus, they are treated as an instantiation of the set X mentioned in equational specification.

Let $n \geq 0$ and $R = \{r_1, r_2, \ldots, r_n\}$ be a set of registers of some hardware architecture. Each r_i is associated with some sort s_i. Intuitively, the action of the circuit is to update each register by a value from the data path of the circuit. Therefore, it is natural to view data paths of the circuit as vectors of n-function (or n-value) where each function (or value) represents a new content for the designate register. In other words, a data path of a circuit with register set R is a function $h: R \rightarrow T_\Sigma(R)$. The interpretation of h has two parts:

1. h specifies n operations which can happen in one cycle;

2. For every $r \in R$, $h(r)$ is the value sent to the register r.

Thus, a set of data paths of a circuit architecture H specifies a set of *possible* basic operations the circuit can have. Call an element of H an R-datapath. For example, let $R = \{x, y\}$ and $c \in H$ be the function $c(x) = add(x, y)$ and $c(y) = y$. This c "connects" the output of an adder to the register x. Data transfers not explicitly mentioned in H are prohibited. As shown in the next section, H also characterizes all the possible computations in one cycle. It plays the role of Σ in equational specifications.

Let us consider an example (Figure 4) of specifying a hardware architecture over natural numbers, a system in which the basic data type is *natural-number*, possibly augmented with metatypes such as *boolean*. Assume R consists of three registers r_1, r_2, r_3 of type natural number, an *add* and a *sub1* which perform addition and decrement, respectively. Suppose the architecture can either add or decrement in one cycle, but not both. These requirements can be specified by a set of three functions $\{h_1, h_2, h_3\} \subseteq H$ where

$$h_1 = \{(r_1, r_1), (r_2, sub1(r_2)), (r_3, r_3)\}$$
$$h_2 = \{(r_1, r_1), (r_2, r_2), (r_3, add(r_1, r_3))\}$$
$$h_3 = \{(r_1, r_1), (r_2, r_2), (r_3, r_3)\}\}$$

the meaning of h_3 is "nothing happens in one cycle."

Given a set H, we would like to mimic the definition of $T_\Sigma(R)$ to define all the computations generated from H. Let $\mathcal{F}_{\Sigma,R}$ be the set of all functions $R \rightarrow T_\Sigma(R)$. The following two definitions classify two sets of possible computations derived from H.

Definition 4.

1. Let $f, g \in \mathcal{F}_{\Sigma, R}$. $h = f \circ g$ is an element of $\mathcal{F}_{\Sigma, R}$ such that for every $i : 1 \le i \le n$, $h(r_i) = f(r_i)[r_j \leftarrow g(r_j) : 1 \le j \le n] \in T_\Sigma(R)$ where $f(r_i)[r_j \leftarrow g(r_j) : 1 \le j \le n]$ denotes substituting every occurrence of r_j in $f(r_i)$ with $g(r_j)$ for all $j : 1 \le j \le n$. Define B_H be the transitive closure of H under $\circ$.

2. The set of *computation sequences derived from H*, denoted by D_H, is the transitive closure of H under concatenation. Concatenation of h and g is denoted by $h \, g$.

Each member of D_H is a sequence of computations allowed by the architecture while each element of B_H is a outcome of a computation sequence of the architecture. This suggests that every member of D_H designates an element of B_H as the *result or interpretation* of the computation sequence and every element of B_H is designated by an element of D_H. This observation is defined by a function $\mathcal{I}$:

Definition 5. Define function $\mathcal{I}: D_H \to \mathcal{F}_{\Sigma, R}$ as

1. $\mathcal{I}(f) = f$ if $f \in H$, and

2. $\mathcal{I}(f \, g) = f \circ g$ if $f, g \in \mathcal{F}_{\Sigma, R}$.

Since $\circ$ is associative, $\mathcal{I}$ is well defined. It is easy to show that $B_H = \mathcal{I}(D_H)$. As a matter of fact, B_H and D_H define different meanings of an architecture specification.

In equational specification, E is used to define corresponding properties of the function symbols in Σ. We would also like to have a set of equations to define properties of elements in H. Since elements of H are merely vectors of elements of Σ, the properties defined by E can be extended to relations on B_H and D_H, denoted by E_B and E_D and called R-extensions of E, respectively. Let $f, g \in B_H$ and $u_p \ldots u_2 u_1 \in D_H$, $v_q \ldots v_2 v_1 \in D_H$. $(f, g) \in E_B$ if and only if $(f(r_i), g(r_i)) \in E$ for all $1 \le i \le n$ and $(s, v) \in E_D$ if and only if $p = q$ and $(u_i, v_i) \in E$ for every $1 \le i \le p$. For simplicity, we usually drop the subscripts B and D when they are fixed by the context.

Furthermore, properties of H may need more equations than those extended from the equations of the underlying abstract data types as above. For example, in an implementation of stack by memory-address pair, $[m_1, 0] = [m_2, 0]$ is an equation but it can not be obtained from the extension of the equations concerning memory and address data types. However, the set of equations defining properties of H should contain the R-extension of E.

Definition 6. A specification of architecture is a quadruple $\langle A, R, \overline{E}, H \rangle$ where $A = \langle \Sigma, E \rangle$ is an equational specification, called *the underlying abstract data type specification*. $\overline{E}$ is a set of equations on B_H (D_H) which contains the R-extension of E. $H \subseteq \mathcal{F}_{\Sigma, R}$, which contains the identity function $id: r \to r$ for every $r \in R$.

5 Algebras for Hardware Architecture Specifications

In the last section, we defined hardware architecture as an extended form of equational specification. In this section, we define an H-algebra for the architecture specification $\langle A, R, \overline{E}, H \rangle$. This H-algebra serves as the meaning of the specification.

5.1   Architecture Algebra

Let $\langle A, R, \overline{E}, H \rangle$ be a specification of some architecture. The following lemmas state properties of D_H and B_H. The proofs are simple.

Lemma 1. Let $b \in B_H$, $d \in D_H$ and $f \in H$. If we define $f(b) = f \circ b$ and $f(d) = f\,d$ then both $\langle B_H, H \rangle$ and $\langle D_H, H \rangle$ are H-algebras.

Lemma 2. E_B and E_D are equivalence relations on B_H and D_H respectively.

Lemma 3. E_B and E_D are congruence relations on $\langle B_H, H \rangle$ and $\langle B_H, H \rangle$ respectively. Therefore, $\langle B_H, H \rangle / E_B$ and $\langle D_H, H \rangle / E_D$ are H-algebras.

We use $B(H, E_B)$ and $D(H, E_D)$ to denote $\langle B_H, H \rangle / E_B$ and $\langle D_H, H \rangle / E_D$ respectively. Both $B(H, E_B)$ and $D(H, E_D)$ are important in observing the behavior of a hardware architecture $P = \langle A, R, E, H \rangle$. The elements of $B(H, E_B)$ represent all the possible results which can be computed by P; this is P's behavioral aspect. The elements of $D(H, E)$ represent not only what results the architecture can obtain (through the interpretation $\mathcal{I}$), but also describe how those computations are performed. Therefore, $D(H, E_D)$ characterizes the operational aspect as well as behavioral aspect of P. It is a matter of emphasis to decide which aspect of P is used to characterize it.

Definition 7. Given an architecture specification $P = \langle A, R, E, H \rangle$. The behavior of P is defined as $B(H, E_B)$ and the computation of P is defined as $D(H, E_D)$.

5.2   Evaluation of Terms

We now discuss the evaluation of elements of $T_\Sigma(R)$. As mentioned previously, functions of D_H and B_H represent possible computations by the architecture. However, we did not mention the values of those computations.

Let S be a set of sorts and $\mathcal{A}$ be a S-sorted Σ-algebra. Let μ be a special *undefined* (or *unknown*) value present in every carrier. For every sort s, we extend A_s of some Σ-algebra to contain the value μ: $A_{s,\mu} \overset{\text{def}}{=} A_s \cup \{\mu\}$. An *interpretation* $\mathcal{V}$ of a specification $\langle A, R, E, H \rangle$ is a triple $\mathcal{V} = \langle \mathcal{A}, \mathcal{H}, \mathcal{O} \rangle$ where

$\mathcal{H}$: $\cup_{s \in S} \Sigma_{\lambda,s} \to \mathcal{A}$.

$\mathcal{O}$: interprets an $s_1 \ldots s_k$-sorted function symbol of Σ as a function of $A_{s_1,\mu} \times \cdots \times A_{s_k,\mu} \to A_{s,\mu}$. For every $\sigma \in \Sigma$, $\mathcal{O}(\sigma)$ is a function: if any one of the arguments of $\mathcal{O}(\sigma)$ is μ, then $\mathcal{O}(\sigma)$ returns μ.

Given $t \in T_\Sigma$, $\mathcal{V}(t)$ is defined as follows:

1. $\mathcal{V}(t) = \mathcal{H}(t)$ if $t \in \Sigma_{\lambda,s}$ for some $s \in S$.

2. $\mathcal{V}(t) = \mu$ if $t = r \in R$.

3. $\mathcal{V}(\mu) = \mu$.

4. $\mathcal{V}(t) = O(f)(\mathcal{V}(t_1), \mathcal{V}(t_2), \ldots, \mathcal{V}(t_n))$ if $t = f(t_1, t_2, \ldots, t_n)$.

This definition of $\mathcal{V}$ implies that all computations start with an undefined state, that is, all registers initially contain μ. However, it is also convenient to use the concept of *evaluation in an environment.* An environment e for an architecture $\langle A, R, E, H \rangle$ is an element of B_H. Let $t \in T_\Sigma$, the evaluation of t in the environment e, denoted as $\mathcal{V}_e(t)$, is defined as: $\mathcal{V}_e(t) = \mathcal{V}(t(e))$ where $t(e)$ is obtained by substituting every occurrence of r in t by $e(r)$ for all $r \in R$.

6 Implementation of Architectures

This section discusses the issue of implementation. The basic idea is to extend implementation of equational specifications to that of architecture specifications. It also explores the relationship between implementation of an architecture and its underlying abstract data type.

6.1 Implementation of Architectures

Definition 8 states a notion of architecture implementation. It merely reiterates the intuition stated in Definition 2 in a context of architecture specification.

Definition 8. Let $K_\Sigma = \langle A_\Sigma, R_\Sigma, E_\Sigma, H_\Sigma \rangle$ and $K_\Omega = \langle A_\Omega, R_\Omega, E_\Omega, H_\Omega \rangle$ be two architecture specifications. K_Ω is said to be an implementation (architecture) of K_Σ if there exists a derivor $d: H_\Sigma \rightarrow B_{H_\Omega}$ and an congruence relation E on $B(H_\Omega, E_\Omega)$ such that $B(H_\Sigma, E_\Sigma) \subseteq \langle B_{H_\Omega}/E_\Omega, d(H_\Sigma) \rangle / E$.

Let K_Σ be an architecture specification, let A_Σ be K_Σ's underlying type specification, and let $\langle A_\Omega, d, E \rangle$ be an implementation of A_Σ. We are interested in the derivation of an implementation architecture of K_Σ from d and E. Our approach is to extend d to a derivor function $H_\Sigma \rightarrow H_\Omega$ such that the extension is a derivor of the architecture implementation. We also discuss the condition under which we can "naturally extend" the implementation of the underlying type specification to derive an implementation of the corresponding architecture.

Let $d = \langle \xi, \kappa \rangle$ be a derivor from Σ to Ω. A first attempt at extending d to $\overline{d} = \langle \xi, \gamma, \hbar \rangle$ is to let:

1. $\xi : S_\Sigma \rightarrow S_\Omega^*$ be that of d;

2. $\gamma : R_\Sigma \rightarrow [R_\Omega]$ where $[R_\Omega]$ is a partition of R_Ω which satisfies the condition that for every $s \in S_\Sigma$, there exists a $[r] \in [R_\Omega]$ and there exists an vectorization for $[r]$ such that the resulting vector is $\xi(s)$ sorted;

Our goal for $\hbar$ is to extend κ to $\hbar: H_\Sigma \rightarrow H_\Omega$ according to γ. Since γ is a function from R_Σ to $[R_\Omega]$, a partition of R_Ω, $\hbar$ should be a function from H_Σ to $[R_\Omega] \rightarrow T_\Omega^*$. Fortunately, this does not cause any serious problem since we can always "flatten" elements of $[R_\Omega] \rightarrow T_\Omega^*$ to simulate functions of $R_\Omega \rightarrow T_\Omega$. Therefore, we ignore the difference between functions $[R_\Omega] \rightarrow T_\Omega^*$ and functions $R_\Omega \rightarrow T_\Omega$.

A natural way to achieve $\hbar$ from κ is that for every $c \in H_\Sigma$, $\hbar(c)$ is a function $[R_\Omega] \rightarrow T_\Omega^*$ defined as: for every $r \in R_\Sigma$,

$$\hbar(c)(\gamma(r)) = c(r)[\forall \sigma \in \Sigma. \ \sigma \leftarrow d(\sigma)]$$

That is, the result of substituting every occurrence of $\sigma \in \Sigma$ in $c(r)$ by $d(\sigma)$.

Unfortunately, this definition does have a problem when γ is not bijection. First, $\hbar(c)$ is *total* only if γ is onto. Second, if γ is not 1-1, that is, there are $r_1, r_2 \in R_\Sigma$ such that $r_1 \neq r_2$ but $\gamma(r_1) = \gamma(r_2)$, then $\hbar$ defined above is not well defined.

To solve the first problem, we add an assumption that γ is onto. It is important to realize that this assumption does not trivialize the result we are about to develop. As a matter of fact, we can define $\hbar(c)$ as: For every $c \in H_\Sigma$, $\hbar(c) \in B_\Omega$ such that for every $r \in R_\Sigma, \hbar(c)(\gamma(r)) = d(c(r))$. Although there are more than one such elements in B_H, it can be shown that the choice among those does not affect our result. To prove this requires additional notation which is largely irrelevant to our major purpose. Thus, we choose to impose the assumption that γ is onto.

We solve the second problem by introducing a *conflict-free* condition on the elements of H_Σ. It is intended to assure for every data transfer $h \in H$, at most one register from each partition of R_Σ by γ is updated. Assume that $R_r = \{ r' \in R_\Sigma \mid \gamma(r') = r \}$ for every $r \in R_\Omega$. Then

Definition 9. Let $r \in R$,

1. K_r is the set of all terms in $T_\Sigma(R)$ which have r as one of their subterms;

2. $B_r = \{ b(r) \mid b \in B_H \}$;

3. $T_r = K_r \cup B_r$;

4. $\Sigma_r = \{ \sigma \mid \sigma$ appears in an element of $T_r \}$.

Lemma 4. If $r \in R$, T_r, Σ_r as defined, then $\langle T_r, \Sigma_r \rangle$ is an algebra. $\langle T_r, \Sigma_r \rangle$ is called *the subalgebra of $\langle T_\Sigma, \Sigma \rangle$ associated with r.*

If $r_1 \neq r_2$ but $\gamma(r_1) = \gamma(r_2)$, it is necessary to have $\bar{d}(T_{r_1})$ distinct from $\bar{d}(T_{r_1})$. This consideration motives the following definition.

Definition 10. Let $\langle A, R, E, H \rangle$ be a specification of architecture and $\bar{d} = \langle \xi, \gamma, \hbar \rangle$. For $r \in R$, let $[r]_\gamma = \{ q \in R \mid \gamma(q) = \gamma(r) \}$. H is said *conflict-free with respect to $\bar{d}$* if

1. For every $f \in H$ and every $r \in R$, there is at most one $q \in [r]_\gamma$ such that $f(q) \neq q$;

2. For every $r \in R_\Omega$, all $r' \in [r]_\gamma$, $\bar{d}(T_{r'})$s are distinct from each other and are subalgebras of $T(\Omega, E_\Omega)$.

Now we can give a definition of the extension of d to $\bar{d}$: $H_\Sigma \to H_\Omega$ as follows:

Definition 11. Let $d = \langle \xi, \kappa \rangle$ be a derivor $\Sigma \to \Omega$, the extension of d to $H_\Sigma \to H_\Omega$ is $\bar{d} = \langle \xi, \gamma, \hbar \rangle$:

1. $\xi : S_\Sigma \to S_\Omega$ is ξ of d;

2. $\gamma : R_\Sigma \to [R_\Omega]$ is onto where $[R_\Omega]$ is a partition of R_Ω defined by γ;

3. $\hbar$ is a 1-1 function defined as: for every $c \in H_\Sigma$, $\hbar(c)$ is a function $\gamma(R_\Sigma) \to T_\Omega^*(R_\Omega)$ such that for $q \in [R_\Omega]$, $\hbar(f)(q) = d(f(r))$ such that $r \in R_q$ and $f(r) \neq r$.

$\overline{d}$ is said to be well defined if ξ, γ, and $\hbar$ are all functions.

The *conflict-free* condition is a sufficient condition under which the extension of d to $\overline{d}$ in Definition 11 preserves the implementation relationship:

Theorem 2. Let $K_\Sigma = \langle A_\Sigma, R_\Sigma, E_\Sigma, H_\Sigma \rangle$ be an architecture specification, $A_\Sigma = \langle A, E_\Sigma \rangle$, $A_\Omega = \langle \Omega, E_\Omega \rangle$, and $\langle A_\Omega, d, E \rangle$ be an implementation of A_Σ. Let $\overline{d} = \langle \xi, \gamma, \hbar \rangle$ be as defined by Definition 11. If H_Σ is conflict-free with respect to $\overline{d}$ then $\langle K_\Omega, \overline{d}, E \rangle$ is an implementation of K_Σ where $K_\Omega = \langle \Omega, \gamma(R_\Sigma), E_\Omega, \hbar(H_\Sigma) \rangle$ is called $\overline{d}$-generated architecture.

Proof. The only thing we need to prove is that there exists a 1-1 homomorphism $\overline{h}$ which maps $B(H_\Sigma, E_\Sigma)$ to $B(\hbar(H_\Sigma), E_\Omega)/\overline{E}$.

Let h be the 1-1 homomorphism which maps $T(\Sigma, E_\Sigma)$ to some subalgebra of $(dA_\Omega)/E$. We extend h to $\overline{h}: B(H_\Sigma, E_\Sigma) \to B(\hbar(H_\Omega), E_\Omega)/\overline{E}$ in the following way: for every $c \in H_\Sigma$, $f = \overline{h}(c)$ is a function such that for every $r \in \gamma(R_\Sigma)$, $f(r) = h(c(r'))$ where $r' \in R_r$ and $c(r') \neq r'$ or $f(r) = r$ if every $c(r') = r'$. Since there is only one such $r' \in R_r$ by the non-conflict condition and $R_r \neq \phi$ for every r, $f(r)$ is well defined thus so is $f = \overline{h}(c)$. Claim: $\overline{h}$ is a 1-1 homomorphism. We justify the claim by:

1. Let $b_1, b_2 \in B_{H_\Sigma}$,
$$b_1 \equiv_{E_\Sigma} b_2$$

is equivalent to
$$\forall r \in R_\Sigma.\ b_1(r) \equiv_{E_\Sigma} b_2(r)$$

implies
$$\forall r \in R_\Sigma.\ h(b_1)\gamma(r)) \equiv_{d(E_\Sigma)} h(b_2)\gamma(r))$$

implies
$$\forall r \in R_\Sigma.\ h(b_1)\gamma(r)) \equiv_{E_\Omega/E} h(b_2)\gamma(r))$$

is equivalent to
$$\overline{h}(b_1) \equiv_{E_\Omega/E} \overline{h}(b_2)$$

Therefore, $\overline{h}$ is well defined;

2. Let $b_1, b_2 \in B_{H_\Sigma}$, We consider the image of $\overline{h}(b_1 b_2)$. $b_1 b_2 = b_1[\forall r_i \in \gamma(R_\Sigma).\ r_i \leftarrow b_2(r_i)]$, therefore, for every $r \in \gamma(R_\Sigma)$

$$\overline{h}(b_1 b_2)(r) = \overline{h}(b_1[\forall r_i \in \gamma(R_\Sigma).\ r_i \leftarrow b_2(r_i)])(r)$$

$$= h(b_1(r')[\forall r_i \in R_\Sigma.\ r_i \leftarrow b_2(r_i)]) \qquad \text{The definition of } \overline{h} \text{ and } r' \in R_r$$

$$= h(b_1(r')[\forall r_i \in R_\Sigma.\ r_i \leftarrow h(b_2(r_i))]) \qquad h \text{ is homomorphism}$$

$$= h(b_1(r'))\overline{h}(b_2) \qquad \text{The definition of } \overline{h}$$

$$= \overline{h}(b_1)\overline{h}(b_2)(r)$$

Therefore, $\overline{h}(b_1 b_2) \equiv \overline{h}(b_1)\overline{h}(b_2)$ thus $\overline{h}$ is a homomorphism.

62

3. Let $b_1, b_2 \in B_{H_\Sigma}$ and assume that

$$\overline{h}(b_1) \equiv_{E_\Omega/E} \overline{h}(b_2)$$

which is equivalent to

$$\forall r \in \gamma(R_\Sigma).\ (\overline{h}(b_1))(r) \equiv_{E_\Omega/E} (\overline{h}(b_2))(r)$$

By the *conflict-free* condition of the theorem and the definition of $\overline{h}$, the above equation is equivalent to

$$\forall r \in \gamma(R_\Sigma).\ \forall r' \in R_r.\ h(b_1(r')) \equiv_{E_\Omega/E} h(b_2(r'))$$

which is equivalent to

$$\forall r \in R_\Sigma.\ h(b_1(r)) \equiv_{E_\Omega/E} h(b_2(r))$$

And since h is a 1-1 homomorphism thus

$$\forall r \in R_\Sigma.\ b_1(r) \equiv_{E_\Sigma} b_2(r)$$

and thus

$$b_1 \equiv_{E_\Sigma} b_2$$

which proves that $\overline{h}$ is 1-1.

This justifies the claim and concludes the proof. □

6.2 Serialization

In the previous discussion, the *conflict-free* condition of data paths is imposed as a necessary condition of implementation. The part of the problem to make a given set of data paths conflict-free with respect to γ, without changing the meaning of architecture, is called *serialization*. It is analogous to *allocation* and *scheduling* in high level synthesis (*e.g.* [3]), *register allocation* and *code generation* in program compilation, and *microcode generation* (*e.g.* [13]). What follows is a brief review of the material presented in [20].

Definition 12. Let $\langle \Sigma, R, E, H \rangle$ be a specification and $G \subset H$ be set of conflict-free data paths with respect to some γ. A *serialization problem* is: given a $h \in H - G$, find $c_n, c_{n-1}, \ldots c_1 \in G$ ($n \geq 2$) such that $h \equiv_E c_n \circ c_{n-1} \circ \cdots \circ c_1$. Such an h is said to be *serializable* by G.

If all elements of H are serializable by G, H can be replaced by G and $\langle A, R, E, G \rangle$ is an implementation of $\langle A, R, E, H \rangle$. Unfortunately, it is readily proved that the serialization problem is undecidable, in general [20]. Nevertheless, heuristic algorithms have been found to cope with similar problems (such as register allocation or microcode generation). [13] presents an algorithm to cope with microprogram generation which we believe can be employed to solve serialization problems where E is empty.

6.3 Research Direction

We discussed the implementation issue of architecture specification. We presented a derivational approach to construct an implementation of architecture from an implementation of an underlying type specification and an architecture specification. Although the method provides an insight to the relationship between implementation of architecture and its underlying type specification, it has the following limitations:

1. We are not able to find an effective decision procedure to test the *conflict-free* condition of the theorem and we suspect that it is not recursively decidable. This severely limits our chance of applying this theorem to any automated derivation system, which is one of the major goals of our research. Thus, a stronger characterization of implementation may be needed.

2. Theorem 2 only discusses behavioral implementation but does not consider timing issues. We would like to consider implementations which take multiple cycles where the more abstract type is intuitively combinational. That is, we would like to extend h to a function $H_\Sigma \to D_{R_\Omega, H_\Omega}$.

3. The theorem only addresses derivations whose γ function is onto, *i.e.* the derived architectures have register sets $\gamma(R_\Sigma)$ although it is not necessary by the definition. When a derived architecture's register set R is strictly contained in $\gamma(R_\Sigma)$, the registers in $R - \gamma(R_\Sigma)$ can be used as temporary registers. Because using temporary registers usually results in introducing new states of control, the framework has to have capability to address sequential properties of circuits.

7 Recursive Functions as Hardware Controls

The standard definition of recursive functions over the natural numbers can be generalized as that of recursive functions on abstract data types [7, 9, 18]. Tucker and Zucker present a theoretical treatment of recursive function over abstract data types [18]. Johnson shows that a recursive function of an abstract data type in certain form can be systematically transformed to a sequential circuit representation which segregates the control of circuit from its abstract basis [9], and examples of modeling digital circuits by recursive functions on abstract bases are shown in [7, 9]. We take a similar approach to hardware control here. As we have already shown that a hardware architecture can be modeled by extended abstract data types, we view a hardware system as a pair, consisting of an extended abstract data type and a recursive function on the extended abstract data type; the latter serves to control the circuit. This section also gives the meaning of such a circuit specification and discusses the concept of implementation of circuit specifications.

The set of recursive functions defined below directly corresponds to the primitive (course-of-value) recursive functions in the conventional theory of recursive functions, e.g. [17]. It is called *control functions* for circuit.

Definition 13. Let $A = \langle \Sigma, R, E, H \rangle$ be a specification of an architecture, e be a variable ranging over $B_{H,E}$, called an environment variable, and $\mathcal{V}$ be the evaluation function defined in Section 4. The set of control functions over A, $F(A)$, is defined as follows:

1. (Primitive Operators). If for every $f \in H$, $h(e) = f \circ e$, then $h \in F(A)$;

2. (Function Composition). If $f, g \in F(A)$, then $Com_{f,g} = f \cdot g(e) \in F(A)$ where $\cdot$ is the standard function composition;

3. (Definition by Cases). An n-case definition is $IF_{h,p,n}$ where $n > 0$ is a natural number, $h : \langle h_i \in F(A) \mid 0 \leq i < n \rangle$ and $p : \langle p_i \in T_\Sigma \mid 0 \leq i < n \rangle$.

$$IF_{h,p,n}(e) = \begin{cases} h_i(e) & \text{if } \mathcal{V}_e(p_i) = 1 \text{ for } 0 \leq i \leq n-1 \\ \bot & \text{Otherwise} \end{cases}$$

$IF_{h,p,n} \in F(A)$.

4. (Primitive Recursion). If $h_1, h_2, h_3 \in F(A)$, $p \in T_\Sigma$ and $PR_{h_1,h_2,h_3,p}$ is defined as:

$$PR_{h_1,h_2,h_3,p}(e) = \begin{cases} h_1(e) & \text{if } \mathcal{V}_e(p) = 0 \\ h_3 \cdot PR_{h_1,h_2,h_3,p} \cdot h_2(e) & \text{if } \mathcal{V}_e(p) > 1 \\ \bot & \text{Otherwise} \end{cases}$$

where $\mathcal{V}_{h_2(e)}(p) < \mathcal{V}_e(p)$ then $PR_{h_1,h_2,h_3,p} \in F(A)$.

Now, we can define a circuit specification as the combination of an architecture specification and a recursive function.

Definition 14. A specification of a circuit is a tuple $\langle A, f \rangle$ where A is a specification of an architecture and $f \in F(A)$.

In hardware designs, two hardware systems are said to be equivalent if these two systems produce the same outputs for the same inputs and the same initial states [3]. However, other criteria can be added. For example, a more restrictive condition is that two systems not only produce the same results but also take the same time (measured by cycles, for example) to produce the same results. We consider two hardware systems to be *equivalent* in the former sense. In our framework, input to a hardware system is included in those functions $f \in H$ such as $f(r) = c$ for some $r \in R$ and $c \in \Sigma_\lambda$[1]. In real designs, *equivalent values* does not necessarily mean identical values but values which are *equal with respect to some equivalence relation* or *equal with respect to some mapping*. For example, in a (natural number) modulo 2^n system, an element k may be thought of being equal to an n-bit binary string $b_{n-1} \ldots b_1 b_0$ if $k = h_n(b_{n-1} \ldots b_1 b_0)$ where $h_n(b_{n-1} \ldots b_1 b_0) = \Sigma_{0 \leq i \leq n-1} 2^i \times b_i$. Combining the discussion above with our definition of implementation of architecture, we have the following definition.

Definition 15. Let $\langle B_\Omega, d, E \rangle$ be an implementation of an architecture specification $B_\Sigma = \langle A, R, E_\Sigma, H_\Sigma \rangle$ and $f \in F(B_\Sigma)$. $d(f)$ is recursively defined as:

1. If $f = c \in H_\Sigma$ then $d(f) = \hbar(c)$;

2. If $f = Com_{f_1,f_2}$ then $d(f) = Com_{d(f_1),d(f_2)}$;

3. If $f = IF_{h,p,n}$, then

$$d(f)(e) = \begin{cases} d(h_i)(d(e)) & \text{if } \mathcal{V}_{d(e)}(d(p_i)) \equiv_E 1 \text{ for } 0 \leq i \leq n-1 \\ \bot & \text{Otherwise} \end{cases}$$

---

[1] We may extend this by allowing c be either some element of Σ_λ or some function which represents (part) of the environment in which the circuit is operating. Although this requires some minor changes in our definition of the constraint set H, it does not complicate the problem.

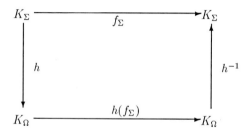

Figure 5: $f_\Sigma = h^{-1}\, h(f_\Sigma)\, h$

4. If $f = PR_{h_1,h_2,h_3,p}$ then

$$d(PR_{h_1,h_2,h_3,p})(e) = \begin{cases} d(h_1)(d(e)) & \text{if } \mathcal{V}_{d(e)}(d(p)) \equiv_E 0 \\ PR' & \text{if } \mathcal{V}_{d(e)}(d(p)) > 1 \\ \bot & \text{Otherwise} \end{cases}$$

where $PR' = d(h_3) \cdot PR_{d(h_1),d(h_2),(h_3),d(p)} \cdot d(h_2)(d(e))$.

Let $P_\Sigma = \langle K_\Sigma, f_\Sigma \rangle$ and $P_\Omega = \langle K_\Omega, f_\Omega \rangle$ are specifications of hardware systems.

Definition 16. If there exists a function $h : K_\Sigma \to K_\Omega$, a family of functions $h^{-1} = \langle h_r^{-1} : K_\Omega \to T_r \rangle_{r \in R_\Sigma}$ (for the definition of T_r, see Definition 10) and an equivalence relation E of K_Ω such that for every $a \in K_\Sigma$ and $r \in R_\Sigma$, $h_r^{-1}(f_\Omega(h(a))) \equiv_E f_\Sigma(a)(r)$, then $\langle P_\Omega, h, E \rangle$ is called an implementation of P_Σ.

The following theorem associates the implementation of systems to that of the architecture. It is analogous to the corollary of Theorem 2.

Theorem 3. If $P_\Sigma = \langle K_\Sigma, f_\Sigma \rangle$ is a circuit specification and $\langle K_\Omega, d, E \rangle$ is an implementation of K_Σ then $\langle P_\Omega, h, E \rangle$ is an implementation of P_Σ where $P_\Omega = \langle K_\Omega, d(f_\Sigma) \rangle$ and $h : K_\Sigma \to K_\Omega$ is defined as:

$$h(b)(r) = \begin{cases} d(b)(r) & \text{if } r \in \gamma(R_\Sigma) \\ r & \text{if } r \in R_\Omega - \gamma(R_\Sigma) \end{cases}$$

for every $b \in B_{R_\Sigma, H_\Sigma, E_\Sigma}$.

Since $\langle K_\Omega, d, E \rangle$ is an implementation of K_Σ, h^{-1} is actually implicitly defined by d. Figure 5 is a pictorial illustration of Theorem 3.

This theorem gives a derivational method of finding an implementation of a circuit specification through an implementation of its architecture. According to Theorem 2, we can go further to find an implementation through that of the underlying type specification.

8 Summary

This paper gives a formal approach to the description of hardware architecture systems based on the underlying abstract data types' specification. The semantics of architecture is given as universal algebras. We show that the implementation of a hardware system can be obtained from the implementation of the underlying abstract data types. The correctness of such an implementation is thus directly related to the correctness of the underlying abstract data type implementation.

This was done by extending the specification of an abstract data type to include a description of architecture, in the form of a set of permitted data transfers. A criterion for correct implementation of an underlying abstract data type was then adapted to the extension. Finally, a functional characterization of control was added and the notion of implementation was again extended to include control.

Theorem 1 states that the correctness of implementation, as defined in Definition 2, is equivalent to the provability of the implemented type's equations. Theorem 2 states that this form of correctness can be extended to conflict-free specifications of architectures. Theorem 3 states that control of the implementing architecture is derivable from that of the implemented architecture.

Acknowledgment

We are grateful to J. V. Tucker for his thoughtful comments on an early draft of this paper.

We are also grateful to National Science Foundation for its support, in part, of this research under the grants numbered MIP87-07067, DCR85-21947, and MIP89-21842.

References

[1] J. A. Bergstra and J. V. Tucker. Initial and final algebra semantics for data type specification: Two characterization theorems. *SIAM Journal of Computing*, Vol 12(No. 2):366–387, May 1983.

[2] C. David Boyer and Steven D. Johnson. Using the digital design derivation system: Case study of a VLSI garbage collector. In J. Darringer and F. Ramming, editors, *Proceedings of the IFIP WG 10.2 Ninth International Symposium on Computer Hardware Description Languages (CHDL)*, Amsterdam, 1989. Elsevier. Also published as Technical Report 274, Computer Science Department, Indiana University, April 1989.

[3] Raul Camposano. Behavior-preserving transformations for high-level synthesis. In M. Leeser and G. Brown, editors, *VLSI Specification, Verification and Synthesis: Mathematical Aspects*, New York, July 1989. Proceedings of Mathematical Sciences Institute Workshop, Cornell University, Springer-Verlag. Lecture Notes in Computer Science Vol-408.

[4] H. Ehrig and B. Mahr. *Fundamentals of Algebraic Specification 1; Equations and Initial Semantics*, volume 6 of *EATCS Monographs on Theoretical Computer Science*. Springer-Verlag, 1985.

[5] J. A. Goguen, J. W. Thatcher, and E. G. Wagner. An initial algebra approach to the specification, correctness and implementation of abstract data types. In R. Yeh, editor, *Current Trends in Programming Methodology*, chapter 5, pages 80–149. Prentice-Hall, Englewood Cliffs, N.J. 07632, 1978.

[6] G. Gopalkrishnan, R. M. Fujimoto, V. Akella, N. S. Mani, and K. N. Smith. Specification-driven design of custom architecture in HOP. In P.A. Subrahmanyam and G. Birtwistle, editors, *Current Trends in Hardware Verification and Automated Theorem Proving*, pages 128–170. Springer Verlag, 1989.

[7] K. M. Hobley, B. C Thompson, and J. V. Tucker. Specification and verification of synchronous concurrent algorithms: A case study of a convolution algorithm. In G. J. Milne, editor, *The Fusion of Hardware Design and Verification*, pages 347–374. Elsevier Science Publishers B.V., 1988.

[8] Steven D. Johnson. Applicative programming and digital design. In *Proceedings Eleventh Annual ACM SIGACT-SIGPLAN Symposium on Principles of Programming Languages*, pages 218–227, 1984.

[9] Steven D. Johnson. *Synthesis of Digital Designs from Recursion Equations*. The MIT Press, Cambridge, 1984.

[10] Steven D. Johnson. Manipulating logical organization with system factorizations. In G. Brown M. Leeser, editor, *Hardware Specification, Verification and Synthesis: Mathematical Aspects, Mathematical Sciences Institute Workshop*, pages 260–281. Cornell University, Ithaca, NY, USA, Springer Verlag, July, 1989. Lecture Notes in Computer Science Vol 408.

[11] Steven D. Johnson, Bhaskar Bose, and C. David Boyer. A tactical framework for digital design. In G. Birtwistle and P.A. Subrahmanyam, editors, *VLSI Specification, Verification and Synthesis*, pages 349–383. Kluwer Academic Publishers, Boston, 1988.

[12] S. Kamin. Final data types and their specification. *ACM Transaction of Programming Languages and Systems*, 5(1):97–123, January 1983.

[13] M. Mahmood, F. Mavaddat, M. I. Elmasry, and M. H. M. Cheng. A formal language model of local microcode synthesis. In Luc Claesen, editor, *Proceedings of The International Workshop on The Applied Formal Method for Correct VLSI Designs*, Leuven, Belgium, 1989. Elsevier Science Publishers B.V.

[14] M. C. McFarland, A. C. Parker, and R. Camposano. Tutorial on high-level synthesis. In *Proceedings of the 25th ACM/IEEE Design Automation Conference*, pages 330–336, Anaheim, CA, 1988. ACM/SIGDA.

[15] J. Meseguer and J.A. Goguen. Initiality, induction, and computability. In Maurice Nivat and John C. Reynolds, editors, *Algebraic Methods in Semantics*, pages 459–541. Cambridge University Press, 1985.

[16] G. J. Milne. CIRCAL and the representation of communication concurrency and time. *ACM Transactions on Programming Languages and Systems*, 7(2), 1985.

[17] Hartley Rogers. *Theory of Recursive Functions and Effective Computation*. McGraw-Hill Book Company, 1967.

[18] J. V. Tucker and J. I. Zucker. *Program Correctness over Abstract Data Types, with Error-State Semantics*. North-Holland, 1988.

[19] M. Wand. Final algebra semantics and data type extensions. *Journal of Computing System Science*, 19:27–44, 1979.

[20] Zheng Zhu and S. D. Johnson. An algebraic characterization of structural synthesis for hardware. In Luc Claesen, editor, *Proceedings of The international Workshop on The Applied Formal Methods for Correct VLSI Designs*. North Holland, 1989.

Generic Specification of Digital Hardware

Jeffrey J. Joyce
Department of Computer Science
University of British Columbia
Vancouver, B.C., CANADA V6T 1W5

phone: (604) 228-4327
e-mail: joyce@cs.ubc.ca

Abstract

This paper argues that generic description is a powerful concept in the context of formal verification, in particular, the formal verification of digital hardware. The paper also describes a technique for creating generic specifications in any language with (at least) the expressive power of higher-order logic. This technique is based on the use of higher-order predicates parameterized by function variables and type variables. We believe that this technique is a very direct (if not the most direct) way to specify hardware generically. Two examples of generic specification are given in the paper: a resettable counter and the programming level model of a very simple microprocessor.

Introduction

Generic description is already established as a powerful concept in many high-level programming languages. For instance, the 'generic mechanism' of Ada allows a subprogram or package to be parameterized by types and subprograms as well as values and objects. This feature supports modularity and abstraction and provides a convenient mechanism for the reliable re-use of software.

This paper argues that generic description is also a powerful concept in the context of formal verification. In addition to the well-known advantages of modularity, abstraction and re-usability, generic description can be used in a formal proof to filter out non-essential detail. The elimination of non-essential detail from a formal specification offers several potential benefits:

- it sharpens the distinction between what has and what has not been formally considered in a correctness proof.

- it supports a truly hierarchical approach to the formal verification of digital circuits where each level in a hierarchical specification is isolated from details only relevant to other levels.

- it reduces the amount of special-purpose infrastructure needed to reason about particular application areas, e.g., hardware-oriented data types.

It may be thought that the thesis of this paper - that formal specifications and correctness statements should be as general as possible - is inconvertible. But when one considers state-of-the-art examples such as the formal verifications of the Viper microprocessor [4, 5, 6] and the CLI 'verified stack' [1, 2, 15], it is easy to see that, in actual practice, formal specifications and correctness statements are not as general as possible. Instead, many examples of hardware verification are encumbered with non-essential details. These non-essential details are likely to obscure correctness results, interfere with the advantages of a hierarchical approach, and depend on the development of special-purpose infrastructure such as hardware-oriented data types.

The formal verification of the 'major state machine' of the Viper microprocessor [4] is an example of when specifications and correctness statements are not as general as possible. The Viper specification uses a number of special-purpose data types (e.g., `:word4`, `:word32`) and constants (e.g., `VAL4`, `WORD32`) for reasoning about hardware. However, the correctness results derived from these specifications are only concerned with the flow of control in the Viper state machine.[1] Cohn [5] writes:

> There was no computation of values at the major state level - that is, additions, comparisons, shifts, and so on - so the essential correctness of Viper was not really addressed; the proof did not require any analysis of the function representing the arithmetic-logic unit, at either level.

The use of special-purpose hardware-oriented data types and constants in the Viper specification was consistent with earlier work on hardware verification at Cambridge [3, 9]. However, building non-essential details into a computational model such as the formal specification of the Viper major state machine risks the false impression that these details have been formally considered in the correctness proof. Furthermore, correctness results for the Viper major state machine are not directly re-usable when low-level details are varied, e.g., different machine word sizes. Finally, the effort of building up a computational model 'from scratch' for non-essential details, e.g., defining arithmetic operations on Viper machine words, is wasted in the case of correctness results that do not depend on these details.

Another example of when specifications and correctness results are not as general as possible is the vertically verified computing system developed by Computational Logic Inc. (i.e., the CLI 'verified stack') [1, 2, 15]. For instance, Moore [15] observes that specifications and correctness results for the Piton assembler are "unnecessarily restricted" to a word size of 32 even though other word sizes are possible. It is also likely that the formal specification of the Piton assembler involves defined symbols whose actual definition are not needed to establish correctness results for the Piton assembler.

There are at least several reasons why non-essential details are built into formal specifications. One reason may simply be that this is common practice or at least common practice in software production. Another reason, suggested by Eveking [7], is the "the-more-detailed-the-better" attitude carried over from experience with multi-level simulation of digital hardware. Yet another reason is the absence of explicit mechanisms (analogous to the generic mechanism of Ada) in most hardware specification languages to support and encourage the creation of specifications which are as general as possible.

To avoid the disadvantages of building non-essential detail into formal specifications of digital hardware, we advocate the use of generic specifications. We also propose a technique for expressing genericity in any language with (at least) the expressive power of higher-order logic in a manner that avoids introduction of new constructs to explicitly support generic specifications. This technique is based on the use of higher-order predicates parameterized by function variables and type variables. We believe that this technique is a very direct (if not the most direct) way to specify hardware generically. Although the idea of parameterizing hardware specifications by functions variables has appeared previously [12, 16], singling

---

[1] While the first level of proof was only concerned with flow of control in the Viper major state machine, a second level of proof for the Viper microprocessor did take into account computational details [5].

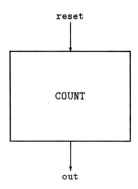

Figure 1: External View of the Resettable Counter

out a special technique (in particular, the use of 'representation variables') for expressing genericity is, to the best of our knowledge, a novel contribution of the research described in this paper.

We use the example of a resettable counter to describe a method for eliminating non-essential detail from a formal specification to eventually yield a generic specification. This example was used by Mike Gordon in an early discussion of hardware verification [9]. Although the resettable counter example is very simple, it is enough to illustrate the idea of using generic descriptions to formally specify digital hardware. Later in the paper, we give a more substantial example, namely, the generic specification of the programming level model of a simple microprocessor.

The Resettable Counter Example

The resettable counter is a sequential device which counts upwards until it is externally reset. Resetting the counter causes it to begin counting from zero. As shown in Figure 1, this device has a single input (the reset signal) and a single output (the current state of the counter).

This device can be implemented using a multiplexor, a register and an increment circuit. Figure 2 shows interconnection of these three components to implement the resettable counter.

Formal verification is a matter of showing that the interconnection of these three components yields a correct implementation of the resettable counter. This is not a guarantee of absolute correctness for a physical realization of the resettable counter. Formal verification only shows that models for the three components can be composed to yield a set of simultaneous constraints which satisfy the behavioural specification of the counter.

This paper focuses on writing formal specifications as a first step towards proving the correctness of a design. For the resettable counter, formal specifications need to be written for each of the three components together with a structural specification of the counter implementation, and finally, a behavioural specification of the counter.

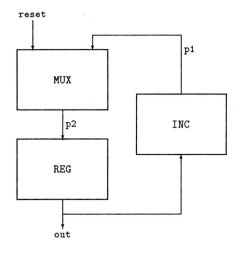

Figure 2: Internal View of the Resettable Counter

Basic Data Types and Primitive Operations

Translating an informal description into a formal specification is often the most interesting and creative aspect of using formal methods to verify hardware. A preliminary step is to decide upon a set of basic data types and a set of primitive operations involving these data types. For instance, in the formal specification of a microprocessor, this set of basic data types would probably include representations for bits, bytes and words. The corresponding set of primitive operations would probably include operations such as addition, subtraction, shift-left, and so on.

For the counter example, we need to decide upon basic data types for the reset signal and the internal state (which is also the output signal). We also need to decide upon a set of primitive operations to describe the functions performed by the multiplexor and the increment circuit.

It is reasonably easy to decide on a representation for values of the reset signal, namely, Boolean values, T and F. However, it is more difficult to decide upon a representation for the internal state of the counter.

A first attempt at a representation for the internal state of the counter is given in the next section: this is a very simple representation where the internal state of the counter is represented by a natural number. After identifying a problem with the accuracy of this simple (and idealized) representation - and how adding more detail is not an ideal solution - we describe several revisions to the counter specification which eventually lead to a generic specification of the resettable counter.

A First Attempt

In this first version of the counter specification, natural numbers are used to represent the internal state of the counter. The operation performed by the increment circuit is described in terms of natural number arithmetic, in particular, the 'plus one' function. Using the HOL formulation of higher-order logic [11], this version of the counter specification is given by the following set of predicate definitions.

```
⊢def MUX (reset,i,out) = ∀t. out t = (reset t ⇒ 0 | (i t))

⊢def REG (i,out) = ∀t. out (t+1) = i t

⊢def INC (i,out) = ∀t. out t = ((i t) + 1)

⊢def COUNT_IMP (reset,out) =
        ∃p1 p2.
          MUX (reset,p1,p2) ∧
          REG (p2,out) ∧
          INC (out,p1)

⊢def COUNT (reset,out) =
        ∀t. out (t+1) = (reset t ⇒ 0 | ((out t) + 1))
```

We digress briefly to describe how the above predicate definitions are used to formally describe hardware behaviour and structure.

Hardware is described either behaviourally or structurally by constraints on a set of signals. These signals represent the externally visible behaviour of the device. Because the resettable counter is a sequential device, signals are described by a sequence of values. It is convenient to represent this sequence of values by a function which maps discrete time (i.e. positions in the sequence) to signal values. For instance, the reset signal,

```
reset:time→bool
```

is modelled by a function which maps discrete time to Boolean values. Discrete time is a set of values denoted by the type :time which is isomorphic to the natural numbers.

Behavioural models for the three components of the implementation are formally specified by the definitions of MUX, REG and INC. For instance, the predicate INC specifies that, at all times, the current output of the increment circuit is the result of adding one to its current input value. The definition of MUX uses a conditional expression of the form b ⇒ t1 | t2 ("if b then t1 else t2") to select between the two data inputs. The predicate REG uses the current input and current output value to determine the next output value.

The predicate COUNT_IMP is a structural specification of the counter implementation. Interconnections are specified by common names, e.g., p2 is an internal connection between the multiplexor and the register. Logical conjunction is used to compose terms corresponding to each component of the implementation. Existential quantification is used to 'hide' the internal signals, namely, p1 and p2.

Finally, the predicate COUNT is a behavioural specification for the resettable counter. It is significant, in this particular example, that the 'plus one' function used in the definition of INC to denote the operation performed by increment circuit re-appears in the definition of COUNT when specifying the behaviour of the counter. (As we will see, this makes the resettable counter example a good candidate for generic specification.)

This style of using higher-order logic to specify the structure and behaviour of hardware is described more fully in a report by Gordon [10].

The essence of the verification problem, in this case, is to show that behavioural models of the three components of the counter implementation can be composed to satisfy the behavioural specification of the counter. From the above set of specifications, the following correctness result can be formally derived as a theorem of higher-order logic. This theorem states that the constraints imposed by COUNT_IMP (defined in terms of MUX, REG and INC) satisfy the constraints expressed by COUNT.

$\vdash_{thm}$ COUNT_IMP (reset,out) $\implies$ COUNT (reset,out)

Representing the internal state of the counter as a natural number is a very simple approach. But this approach has the disadvantage of being an idealized model of physically-realizable hardware. This idealized model of a counter will count continuously upwards until it is reset. However, in reality, the internal state of the counter will have a finite number of bits and therefore, it will eventually overflow unless it is reset at some point.

The next section of this paper considers the approach of adding more detail into the formal specification of the resettable counter to correct the problem of modelling overflow. However, we will eventually reject this approach in favour of the very opposite approach of eliminating non-essential detail.

The More Detailed, The Better ?

The following is a revised set of specifications for the resettable counter which uses modular arithmetic to model the finite limitations of physically-realizable hardware.

```
⊢_def MUX (n) (reset,i,out) = ∀t. out t = (reset t ⇒ 0 | (i t))

⊢_def REG (n) (i,out) = ∀t. out (t+1) = i t

⊢_def INC (n) (i,out) = ∀t. out t = (((i t) + 1) MOD 2ⁿ)

⊢_def COUNT_IMP (n) (reset,out) =
        ∃p1 p2.
          MUX (n) (reset,p1,p2) ∧
          REG (n) (p2,out) ∧
          INC (n) (out,p1)

⊢_def COUNT (n) (reset,out) =
        ∀t. out (t+1) = (reset t ⇒ 0 | (((out t) + 1) MOD 2ⁿ))
```

This revised set of specifications is a simple example of parameterized hardware description. Each predicate definition is parameterized by an additional variable, n, giving the number of bits used to represent the internal state of the counter. For reasons of (personal) style, this additional parameter is separated from the list of parameters representing the input and output signals of the counter. However, this separation has no logical significance. Technically speaking, this is an instance of a 'curried' function, that is, a function which can evaluate its arguments "one at a time".

Modular arithmetic models the fact that the counter will overflow when counting past the highest representable value, namely, $2^n - 1$. Undoubtedly, this revised set of specification is a more accurate model of physical hardware. One might think that a more accurate model entails a more comprehensive proof of correctness. But this is not necessarily true. In this case, proving a correctness result of the form,

$$\vdash_{thm} \text{COUNT\_IMP (n) (reset,out)} \implies \text{COUNT (n) (reset,out)}$$

does not involve any properties of either + or MOD. In fact, the above correctness result can be established even if + and MOD were replaced by undefined symbols in the formal specifications. Hence, + and MOD are no more than place-holders in this particular proof of correctness.

The fact than + and MOD are just place-holders underlines the difference between formal verification and conventional simulation. In the case of conventional simulation, + and MOD would have to be defined symbols to use this specification as input to a conventional simulator. But in the case of formal verification, a meaningful correctness result can be obtained without necessarily having to develop a full-scale model of the computation.

Eliminating Non-essential Detail

Because building more detail into the counter specification, in particular, the use of modular arithmetic, may give the false impression that a particular correctness result is more comprehensive than it really is, we argue in a favor of the very opposite approach. Instead of building more detail into the specification to remedy the inaccurate modelling of overflow in the original specification of the counter, we filter out details about the computation performed by the counter. Very importantly, this can be done without changing the essence of the verification problem.

The next few sections of this paper illustrate a method for eliminating non-essential detail by describing a series of incremental revisions to the original specification of the resettable counter. The first step involves parameterizing the formal specification by function variables. The second step involves parameterizing the formal specification by type variables. The third and final step is to 'package' function variables into a single 'representation variable'.

Parameterizing with Function Variables

The following set of specifications is obtained by replacing the 'plus one' operation in the original specification of the resettable counter by a function variable inc. Each of the specifications is parameterized by this function variable (and hence, they are higher-order predicates). For the sake of uniformity, the predicates MUX and REG are parameterized by inc even though they do not make use of this function.

```
⊢def MUX (inc) (reset,i,out) = ∀t. out t = (reset t ⇒ 0 | (i t))

⊢def REG (inc) (i,out) = ∀t. out (t+1) = i t

⊢def INC (inc) (i,out) = ∀t. out t = inc (i t)

⊢def COUNT_IMP (inc) (reset,out) =
        ∃p1 p2.
          MUX (inc) (reset,p1,p2) ∧
          REG (inc) (p2,out) ∧
          INC (inc) (out,p1)

⊢def COUNT (inc) (reset,out) =
        ∀t. out (t+1) = (reset t ⇒ 0 | (inc (out t)))
```

The parameterization of the above specifications by the function variable inc eliminates detail about the operation performed by the increment circuit which is not relevant to the verification problem. For this revised set of specifications, this verification problem is expressed by the following correctness result:

⊢thm COUNT_IMP (inc) (reset,out) ⟹ COUNT (inc) (reset,out)

Parameterizing with Type Variables

The next step is to revise the above specifications by using a type variable, namely, :*word, to represent the internal state of the counter. (In the HOL formulation of higher-order logic, a type variable always begins with an asterisk.)

In the previous set of specifications, the type associated with the function variable inc was a function from natural numbers to natural numbers. But now, the type of inc is a function from :*word to :*word.

Since we are now using the type variable :*word to replace natural numbers, we must also introduce a variable called zero to replace the natrual number constant 0. This variable stands for a value of type :*word (it is a function variable for a 0-place function). Each of the predicates in the revised specification of the counter, as shown below, will be parameterized by both inc and zero in addition to the input and output variables of the counter.

```
⊢def MUX (inc,zero) (reset,i,out) = ∀t. out t = (reset t ⇒ zero | (i t))

⊢def REG (inc,zero) (i,out) = ∀t. out (t+1) = i t

⊢def INC (inc,zero) (i,out) = ∀t. out t = inc (i t)

⊢def COUNT_IMP (inc,zero) (reset,out) =
        ∃p1 p2.
          MUX (inc,zero) (reset,p1,p2) ∧
          REG (inc,zero) (p2,out) ∧
          INC (inc,zero) (out,p1)

⊢def COUNT (inc,zero) (reset,out) =
        ∀t. out (t+1) = (reset t ⇒ zero | (inc (out t)))
```

These changes do not significantly alter the proof of correctness; likewise, the revised correctness result is not significantly different than before.

$$\vdash_{thm} \text{COUNT\_IMP (inc,zero) (reset,out)} \implies \text{COUNT (inc,zero) (reset,out)}$$

Representation Variables

Our approach to generic specification is based on the parameterization of formal specifications by function variables and type variables. Scaling this approach upwards for more complex specifications (with more function variables) could result in the unwieldy parameterization of predicates. However, this can be avoided by 'packaging' functions variables into a single representation variable.

```
⊢def inc rep = FST rep

⊢def zero rep = SND rep

⊢def MUX (rep) (reset,i,out) = ∀t. out t = (reset t ⇒ (zero rep) | (i t))

⊢def REG (rep) (i,out) = ∀t. out (t+1) = i t

⊢def INC (rep) (i,out) = ∀t. out t = (inc rep) (i t)

⊢def COUNT_IMP (rep) (reset,out) =
        ∃p1 p2.
          MUX (rep) (reset,p1,p2) ∧
          REG (rep) (p2,out) ∧
          INC (rep) (out,p1)

⊢def COUNT (rep) (reset,out) =
        ∀t. out (t+1) = (reset t ⇒ (zero rep) | ((inc rep) (out t)))
```

The above specifications are parameterized by a single representation variable called rep. This variable,

```
rep: ((*word→*word) × *word)
```

is a pair of values. The first element of this pair represents the function performed by the increment circuit. The second element of this pair is the representation of zero.

In this version of the counter specification, inc and zero are defined as 'selector functions' which extract the first and second elements of a representation. These two selectors functions are meaningful synonyms for the pre-defined selectors functions FST and SND. That is:

```
(inc rep)    - "the increment operation"
(zero rep)   - "the representation of zero"
```

Once again, the essence of the verification problem is unchanged from before. The following correctness result shows that behavioural models of the three components used to implement the resettable counter can be composed to satisfy the behavioural specification of the counter.

$$\vdash_{thm} \text{COUNT\_IMP (rep) (reset,out)} \implies \text{COUNT (rep) (reset,out)}$$

Re-usable Correctness Results

Eliminating detail from a specification does not result in a less comprehensive correctness proof. In fact, the opposite situation is true: a generic specification yields a correctness result which covers a wider range of possible implementation. The above correctness result (for the generic specification of the resettable counter) can be instantiated for various implementations, e.g., a 2-bit counter, an 8-bit counter, a 16-bit counter, etc. The correctness result is instantiated by assigning a particular representation to the representation variable rep.

For example, the original specification of the counter is described by the representation,[2]

```
REP_num = (λx. x + 1, 0)
```

where the 'plus one' function is used to represent the operation performed by the increment circuit and the natural number constant 0 is the representation of zero. Instantiating the generic correctness result for this particular value of the representation variable,

$$\vdash_{thm} \text{COUNT\_IMP (REP\_num) (reset,out)} \implies \text{COUNT (REP\_num) (reset,out)}$$

yields a correctness result which is logically equivalent to the first correctness result given for the counter specification.

Another example is based on the built-in HOL data types for bit strings and machine words used, for instance, in the formal verification of the Viper microprocessor. An 8-bit version of the resettable counter is described by the representation,

```
REP8 = (λx. WORD8 ((VAL8 x) + 1), WORD8 0)
```

where WORD8 is a pre-defined function for converting a natural number into a 8-bit word and VAL8 is a pre-defined function for converting a 8-bit word into a natural number. The corresponding correctness result is an instance of the generic correctness result:

$$\vdash_{thm} \text{COUNT\_IMP (REP8) (reset,out)} \implies \text{COUNT (REP8) (reset,out)}$$

Hierarchical Verification

Correctness proofs for digital hardware are typically organized into several levels. For instance, another level of verification could be used to verify that each of the three components used in the counter implementation is correctly implemented by logic gates. An even lower level of proof would establish that logic gates are correctly implemented by networks of transistors.

To sharpen the distinction between what has and what has not been considered at each level, we believe that a truly hierarchical approach to formal verification depends on the use of generic specifications to eliminate non-essential detail from each proof level. In other words, each level is a highly localized concern which should be isolated as much as possible from details relevant only to other levels. This is achieved by using generic specifications at higher levels parameterized by data types and functions which only need to be "fleshed out" at lower levels in the proof hierarchy. This contrasts with a 'closed-world approach' to formal verification where every data type and every operator is completely defined at each level. Eveking [7] elaborates on the distinction between an open (or interpreted) approach and a closed-world approach.

---

[2]The term λx. x + 1 is a lambda-expression which denotes the 'plus one' function.

Generic Specification of a Microprocessor

We have used the techniques described in this paper to write generic specifications for a very simple microprocessor called TAMARACK-3 [14]. A design for the register-transfer level implementation of this microprocessor has been proven correct with respect to a programming level model of its operation. These correctness results can be re-used for various realizations of the microprocessor, e.g., an 8-bit version, a 16-bit version, etc. Moreover, the generic specification of this microprocessor does not depend on any special-purpose infrastructure for reasoning about hardware, e.g., data types for bit strings or machine words. This should make it much easier to re-produce this correctness result in a variety of verification systems (as long as these systems support higher-order predicates).

To give the reader an impression of how the generic specification techniques described in this paper can be applied to a more substantial example, this section of the paper presents the generic specification of the TAMARACK-3 programming level model.

The TAMARACK-3 microprocessor was designed as a verification example and is not seriously intended for practical applications.[3] It has just eight different programming level instructions and only one addressing mode. The only kind of hardware exception is a single level, non-vectored hardware interrupt. The microprocessor can be interfaced to external memory (or some other perpherial device) to operate in one of three possible modes: fully synchronous, fully asynchronous, and extended cycle mode. All I/O is memory-mapped. Figure 3 shows a functional diagram for the externally visible signals of TAMARACK-3.

The programming level model, or external architecture, of TAMARACK-3 is a description of its operation as seen by a programmer. This model hides all aspects of the internal architecture which the programmer does not need to know about when writing programs for this microprocessor. The programming level model can be viewed as an interpreter for manipulating a set of variables which corresponds to the externally visible state of the microprocessor. It consists of five main parts:

- Basic data types and primitive operations.

- Variables manipulated by the interpreter.

- Format of instructions.

- Instruction semantics.

- Instruction Cycle.

Basic Data Types and Primitive Operations

A total of seven different data types are used to specify the programming level model of TAMARACK-3. The data type :bool is used to represent voltage values or logical conditions. The data type :num is used when some lower level form of data is interpreted as the representation of a natural number. The remaining five data types are used to represent machine words (three different sizes), a particular field of bits within a machine word, and memory states.

---

[3] Although TAMARACK-3 is a very simple microprocessor, some aspects of its operation (support for interrupts and asynchronous interaction with external memory using handshaking signals) are more complex behaviours than found in the formal specification of the Viper microprocessor.

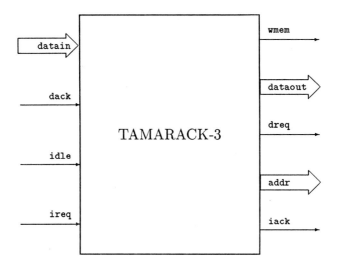

datain	- data from memory	wmem	- read/write select
dack	- data acknowledge	dataout	- data to memory
idle	- extended cycle mode	dreq	- data request
ireq	- interrupt request	addr	- address to memory
		iack	- interrupt acknowledge

Figure 3: Functional View of the TAMARACK-3 Microprocessor

:bool	- Boolean values {T,F}
:num	- natural numbers {0,1,2,...}
:*wordn	- full-size machine words
:*word3	- instruction opcodes
:*word4	- 4-bit words
:*address	- memory addresses
:*memory	- memory states

A conventional description of a microprocessor would typically be very specific about details such as the number of bits in a machine word and the size of memory. However, we avoid specifying these details by regarding :*wordn, :*word3, :*word4, :*address and :*memory as *uninterpreted types*. The actual representation of these basic data types may be thought of as implementation dependent details. The prefix * indicates our intention to use type variables for these data types.

Functional elements such as the ALU (*Arithmetic Logic Unit*) at the lowest level of architectural description perform various operations on data. These operations are regarded as *uninterpreted primitives*. The TAMARACK-3 programming level model is formally specified in terms of thirteen different primitives operations. Employing the generic specification technique outlined earlier in this paper, these thirteen different operations will be packaged into a single representation variable, rep. Each primitive will be selected (or extracted) from the representation variable by a unique selector function. These thirteen selector functions are listed below. Although the operations selected by these selectors are formally regarded as uninterpreted primitives, the following list also gives a suggested interpretation for each primitive operation.

(iszero rep)	- "test if zero"
(inc rep)	- "increment"
(add rep)	- "addition"
(sub rep)	- "subtraction"
(wordn rep)	- "full-size word representation of a number"
(valn rep)	- "value of a full-size word"
(opcode rep)	- "extract opcode field"
(val3 rep)	- "value of an opcode"
(address rep)	- "extract address field"
(fetch rep)	- "read memory"
(store rep)	- "write memory"
(word4 rep)	- "4-bit word representation of a number"
(val4 rep)	- "value of a 4-bit word"

Like every term in higher-order logic, the variable rep has a type. The type of rep is denoted by the following type abbreviation.[4]

---

[4]The built-in HOL system utility for creating type abbreviations does not allow this particular abbreviation since it contains type variables. However, there is an alternative way to introduce names to stand for fully expanded type expressions (using ML variables and ML antiquotation) - but these details are beyond the scope of this paper.

```
rep_ty =
  :(*wordn→bool)×                        % iszero %
   (*wordn→*wordn)×                      % inc %
   (*wordn×*wordn→*wordn)×               % add %
   (*wordn×*wordn→*wordn)×               % sub %
   (num→*wordn) ×                        % wordn %
   (*wordn→num) ×                        % valn %
   (*wordn→*word3)×                      % opcode %
   (*word3→num)×                         % val3 %
   (*wordn→*address)×                    % address %
   (*memory×*address→*wordn)×            % fetch %
   (*memory×*address×*wordn→*memory)×    % store %
   (num→*word4)×                         % word4 %
   (*word4→num)                          % val4 %
```

The selector functions are defined in the formal specification by composing various sequences of the two primitive selectors FST and SND. For instance, the first three selectors, iszero, inc, and add, have the following definitions.

```
⊢def iszero (rep:rep_ty) = FST rep

⊢def inc (rep:rep_ty) = FST(SND rep)

⊢def add (rep:rep_ty) = FST(SND(SND rep))
```

The rest of the selectors are defined in a similar manner such that the following theorem is true:

```
⊢thm rep =
        ((iszero rep),
         (inc rep),
         (add rep),
         (sub rep),
         (wordn rep),
         (valn rep),
         (opcode rep),
         (val3 rep),
         (address rep),
         (fetch rep),
         (store rep),
         (word4 rep),
         (val4 rep))
```

Externally Visible State

The set of variables manipulated by the programming level model corresponds to the externally visible state of the microprocessor. In TAMARACK-3, these variables are:

Instruction	Opcode Value	Effect
JZR	0	jump if zero
JMP	1	jump
ADD	2	add accumulator
SUB	3	subtract accumulator
LDA	4	load accumulator
STA	5	store accumulator
RFI	6	return from interrupt
NOP	7	no operation

Table 1: TAMARACK-3 Instruction Set

```
mem   - memory
pc    - program counter
acc   - accumulator
rtn   - return address register
iack  - interrupt acknowledge flag
```

The memory stores memory states, represented by the data type :*memory. Each of the registers stores full-size memory words, represented by the data type :*wordn. The interrupt acknowledge flag is stored internally by a flipflop whose value belongs to the data type :bool.

Instruction Word Format

Instructions are exactly one full-size machine word. Although specific details about word size and instruction word format are not given in this description, we can assume that the instruction word consists of a 3-bit opcode (since there are eight different instructions) with the remaining bits used as an operand address. The operand address is the absolute address of a memory word which may be used as the address of either data or an instruction.

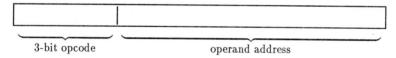

3-bit opcode   operand address

Opcodes and operand addresses are represented by the uninterpreted types :*word3 and :*address. They are extracted from an instruction word by the uninterpreted primitives opcode and address.

Instruction Set Semantics

The eight TAMARACK-3 programming level instructions are in Table 1. Their opcode values and a brief explanation of each instruction are also given in the table. The opcode is extracted from the current instruction word by opcode and its numerical value is then obtained by applying val3 to the extracted opcode.

Formally, the semantics of each instruction is given individually by the definition of a function which returns the next (externally visible) state of the microprocessor, i.e., the next values of the memory state mem, program counter pc, accumulator acc, return address register rtn and interrupt acknowledge flag iack. The following definitions specify how these values are computed from the current state of the microprocessor. In addition to a formal definition, the informal notation,

<destination> ← <expression>

is used to denote when a value computed from the current machine state is loaded into a register, flipflop or memory to form a component of the next machine state.

JZR - jump if zero

pc ← if (iszero rep) acc then inst else (inc pc)

```
⊢_def JZR_SEM (rep:rep_ty)
     (mem:*memory,pc:*wordn,acc:*wordn,rtn:*wordn,iack:bool) =
     let inst = (fetch rep) (mem,(address rep) pc) in
     let nextpc = ((iszero rep) acc) ⇒ inst | ((inc rep) pc) in
        (mem,nextpc,acc,rtn,iack)
```

If the result of applying iszero to the current contents of the accumulator acc is T, then the current instruction word is loaded into the program counter pc. Otherwise, the instruction is completed by incrementing the program counter pc.[5]

JMP - jump

pc ← inst

```
⊢_def JMP_SEM (rep:rep_ty)
     (mem:*memory,pc:*wordn,acc:*wordn,rtn:*wordn,iack:bool) =
     let inst = (fetch rep) (mem,(address rep) pc) in
        (mem,inst,acc,rtn,iack)
```

The current instruction word is unconditionally loaded into the program counter pc.

ADD - add accumulator

acc ← (add rep) (acc,operand)
pc ← (inc rep) pc

```
⊢_def ADD_SEM (rep:rep_ty)
     (mem:*memory,pc:*wordn,acc:*wordn,rtn:*wordn,iack:bool) =
     let inst = (fetch rep) (mem,(address rep) pc) in
     let operand = (fetch rep) (mem,(address rep) inst) in
        (mem,(inc rep) pc,(add rep) (acc,operand),rtn,iack)
```

---

[5]Here we have relaxed our presentation style by referring to an uninterpreted primitive, namely, inc, in terms of its suggested interpretation.

The **add** operation is applied to the current contents of the accumulator acc and the memory word addressed by the operand address field of the current instruction. The result is loaded into the accumulator acc. The instruction is completed by incrementing the program counter pc.

SUB - subtract accumulator

```
acc ← (sub rep) (acc,operand)
pc ← (inc rep) pc
```

```
⊢def SUB_SEM (rep:rep_ty)
     (mem:*memory,pc:*wordn,acc:*wordn,rtn:*wordn,iack:bool) =
     let inst = (fetch rep) (mem,(address rep) pc) in
     let operand = (fetch rep) (mem,(address rep) inst) in
       (mem,(inc rep) pc,(sub rep) (acc,operand),rtn,iack)
```

The **sub** operation is applied to the current contents of the accumulator acc and the memory word addressed by the operand address field of the current instruction. The result is loaded into the accumulator acc. The instruction is completed by incrementing the program counter pc.

LDA - load accumulator

```
acc ← operand
pc ← (inc rep) pc
```

```
⊢def LDA_SEM (rep:rep_ty)
     (mem:*memory,pc:*wordn,acc:*wordn,rtn:*wordn,iack:bool) =
     let inst = (fetch rep) (mem,(address rep) pc) in
     let operand = (fetch rep) (mem,(address rep) inst) in
       (mem,(inc rep) pc,operand,rtn,iack)
```

The memory word addressed by the operand address field of the current instruction is loaded into the accumulator acc. The instruction is completed by incrementing the program counter pc.

STA - store accumulator

```
mem ← (store rep) (mem,(address rep) inst,acc)
pc ← (inc rep) pc
```

```
⊢def STA_SEM (rep:rep_ty)
     (mem:*memory,pc:*wordn,acc:*wordn,rtn:*wordn,iack:bool) =
     let inst = (fetch rep) (mem,(address rep) pc) in
     let newmem = (store rep) (mem,(address rep) inst,acc) in
       (newmem,(inc rep) pc,acc,rtn,iack)
```

The current contents of the accumulator acc are stored in external memory at the location specified by the operand address field of the current instruction. The instruction is completed by incrementing the program counter pc.

RFI - return from interrupt

```
pc ← rtn
iack ← F
```

```
⊢_def RFI_SEM (rep:rep_ty)
        (mem:*memory,pc:*wordn,acc:*wordn,rtn:*wordn,iack:bool) =
        (mem,rtn,acc,rtn,F)
```

The current contents of the return address register rtn are loaded into the program counter pc and the interrupt acknowledge flag iack is reset to F. This instruction does not check whether the interrupt acknowledge flag iack is currently set.

NOP - no operation

```
pc ← (inc rep) pc
```

```
⊢_def NOP_SEM (rep:rep_ty)
        (mem:*memory,pc:*wordn,acc:*wordn,rtn:*wordn,iack:bool) =
        (mem,(inc rep) pc,acc,rtn,iack)
```

Hardware Interrupts

The processing of a hardware interrupt is described in a similar way by the definition of a function which computes the next state of the microprocessor from its current state.

```
pc ← (wordn rep) 0
rtn ← pc
iack ← T
```

```
⊢_def IRQ_SEM (rep:rep_ty)
        (mem:*memory,pc:*wordn,acc:*wordn,rtn:*wordn,iack:bool) =
        (mem,((wordn rep) 0),acc,pc,T)
```

An interrupt is processed by loading the hard-wired address of the interrupt routine (location 0) into the program counter, saving the current contents of the program counter in the return address register, and setting the interrupt acknowledge flag iack to T.

Instruction Cycle

The opcode of the current instruction word determines which instruction is executed during a particular instruction cycle. The following set of definitions specify the opcode value for each instruction.

86

```
⊢def  JZR_OPC = 0
⊢def  JMP_OPC = 1
⊢def  ADD_OPC = 2
⊢def  SUB_OPC = 3
⊢def  LDA_OPC = 4
⊢def  STA_OPC = 5
⊢def  RFI_OPC = 6
⊢def  NOP_OPC = 7
```

The opcode value of the current instruction is obtained by fetching the memory word addressed by the program counter, extracting the value of its opcode field and interpreting the opcode as a number between 0 and 7. This procedure is specified in the definition of OpcVal

```
⊢def  OpcVal (rep:rep_ty) (mem,pc) =
         (val3 rep) ((opcode rep) ((fetch rep) (mem,(address rep) pc)))
```

Every instruction cycle results in the execution of a programming level instruction unless a hardware interrupt is detected at the beginning of this cycle. The following definition of NextState specifies the overall control mechanism for determining what happens during a particular instruction cycle.

```
⊢def  NextState (rep:rep_ty) (ireq,mem,pc,acc,rtn,iack) =
         let opcval = OpcVal rep (mem,pc) in
           ((ireq ∧ ¬iack)     ⇒ IRQ_SEM rep (mem,pc,acc,rtn,iack) |
            (opcval = JZR_OPC) ⇒ JZR_SEM rep (mem,pc,acc,rtn,iack) |
            (opcval = JMP_OPC) ⇒ JMP_SEM rep (mem,pc,acc,rtn,iack) |
            (opcval = ADD_OPC) ⇒ ADD_SEM rep (mem,pc,acc,rtn,iack) |
            (opcval = SUB_OPC) ⇒ SUB_SEM rep (mem,pc,acc,rtn,iack) |
            (opcval = LDA_OPC) ⇒ LDA_SEM rep (mem,pc,acc,rtn,iack) |
            (opcval = STA_OPC) ⇒ STA_SEM rep (mem,pc,acc,rtn,iack) |
            (opcval = RFI_OPC) ⇒ RFI_SEM rep (mem,pc,acc,rtn,iack) |
                                 NOP_SEM rep (mem,pc,acc,rtn,iack))
```

Finally, we use the function NextState to define the predicate TamarackBeh which specifies the intended behaviour of the microprocessor as a relation on the time-dependent signals mem, pc, acc, rtn and iack.

```
⊢def  TamarackBeh (rep:rep_ty) (ireq,mem,pc,acc,rtn,iack) =
         ∀u:time.
           (mem (u+1),pc (u+1),acc (u+1),rtn (u+1),iack (u+1)) =
           NextState rep (ireq u,mem u,pc u,acc u,rtn u,iack u)
```

The programming level model not only hides structural details of the internal architecture but also timing details about the number of microinstructions executed for each instruction. To be more precise, the programming level model describes the operation of the microprocessor in terms of an abstract time scale where each instruction is uniformly executed in a single unit of time. This abstract time scale is different than the time scale used to specify the behaviour of register-transfer level components where a single unit of time corresponds to a single clock cycle. To emphasize this difference, we have used the explicit time variable u instead of t in the above definition of TamarackBeh (but there is no logical distinction between these two variable names). A major part of the task of formally verifying TAMARACK-3 is to establish a formal relationship between these two granularities of discrete time.

Minimal Assumptions about Uninterpreted Primitives

Formal verification of the register-transfer level implementation of TAMARACK-3 is not a trivial problem. For instance, this level of verification includes a rigorous analysis of how TAMARACK-3 interacts asynchronously with external memory using a handshaking protocol. However, these correctness results depend very little on computational aspects of the machine's operation.

In place of a full-scale computational model, the generic specification of TAMARACK-3 is supplemented by a minimal set of assumptions necessary to prove that the register-transfer level implementations is correct with respect to the programming level model. Just two assumptions are needed:

$\forall$w. ((val3 rep) w) < 8

$\forall$n. n < 16 $\implies$ (((val4 rep) ((word4 rep) n)) = n)

The first assumption states that the value of any 3-bit word, when interpreted as the representation of a natural number, is less than eight. The second assumption states that the functions selected by val4 and word4 from the representation variable are inverses for numbers less than sixteen. These two assumptions appear explicitly in the correctness results for the register-transfer level implementation of TAMARACK-3.

What is Proved ?

The formal verification of TAMARACK-3 at the register-transfer level is mostly concerned with three main issues:

- showing that the right actions occur at the right time, e.g, for an ADD instruction, that the ALU operation for addition is applied to the accumulator currents and the operand (fetched from memory) and that the result is stored in the accumulator.

- demonstrating that the microprocessor satisfies the handshaking protocol used for asynchronous interaction with external memory.

- establishing that a precisely defined timing relationship holds between the programming level model time scale and the register-transfer level time scale.

With the exception of the two assumptions mentioned above, these correctness results do not depend on any computational details about the functional units used in the register-transfer level implementation of TAMARACK-3. Functional units such as the ALU are specified generically with the same selector functions used to specify the TAMARACK-3 programming model. For instance, the four selectors inc, add, sub and wordn are used to generically specify the four primitive operations performed by the ALU.

```
⊢def ALU (rep:rep_ty) (f0,f1,inp1,inp2,out) =
        ∀t:time.
          out t =
            (((f0 t,f1 t) = (T,T)) → ((inc rep) (inp2 t)) |
             ((f0 t,f1 t) = (T,F)) → ((add rep) (inp1 t,inp2 t)) |
             ((f0 t,f1 t) = (F,T)) → ((sub rep) (inp1 t,inp2 t)) |
                                      ((wordn rep) 0))
```

Therefore, it should be clear that correctness results for TAMARACK-3 at the register-transfer level are not concerned with the implementation of functional units, for instance, whether the addition operation has been correctly implemented in the ALU. Using uninterpreted primitives instead of defined operations sharpens the distinction between what has and what has not been formally considered at this level of proof.

Creating Instances of a Generic Specification

The representation variable **rep** which appears as an extra parameter in definitions throughout the formal specification of TAMARACK-3 is effectively a parameterization of the formal theory. It provides a means of relating this theory to both lower and higher level models of computation.

For example, by assigning an appropriate value to the representation variable **rep**, the formal specification of the TAMARACK-3 programming level model can be made to stack upon a lower level theory about the implementation of register-transfer level devices. This lowel level theory might also, in turn, be a generic specification parameterized by its own representation variable and stacked upon an even lower level of representation at the transistor level.

To illustrate this idea with a simple example, the constant **REP16** is defined as a value for **rep** based on the built-in HOL data types described in [4, 5, 9]. In this case, we have created data types for a 16-bit version of TAMARACK-3.

```
⊢def ISZERO16 w = ((VAL16 w) = 0)

⊢def INC16 w = WORD16 ((VAL16 w) + 1)

⊢def ADD16 (w1,w2) = WORD16 ((VAL16 w1) + (VAL16 w2))

⊢def SUB16 (w1,w2) = WORD16 ((VAL16 w1) - (VAL16 w2))

⊢def OPCODE w = WORD3 (V (SEG (0,2) (BITS16 w)))

⊢def ADDRESS w = WORD13 (V (SEG (3,15) (BITS16 w)))
```

```
⊢_def  REP16 =
           ISZERO16,                         % iszero %
           INC16,                            % inc %
           ADD16,                            % add %
           SUB16,                            % sub %
           WORD16,                           % wordn %
           VAL16,                            % valn %
           OPCODE,                           % opcode %
           VAL3,                             % val3 %
           ADDRESS,                          % address %
           (λ(x,y). FETCH13 x y),            % fetch %
           (λ(x,y,z). STORE13 y z x),        % store %
           WORD4,                            % word4 %
           VAL4                              % val4 %
```

There are two main reasons for stacking correctness results upon lower level correctness results. One reason is to discharge assumptions introduced at one level by establishing them as theorems at lower levels. For instance, the two assumptions,

$\forall$w. ((val3 rep) w) < 8

$\forall$n. n < 16 $\Longrightarrow$ (((val4 rep) ((word4 rep) n)) = n)

needed to obtain correctness results at the register-transfer level could be established as theorems when the representation variable rep is instantiated to be REP16:[6]

$\forall$w. (VAL3 w) < 8

$\forall$n. n < 16 $\Longrightarrow$ ((VAL4 (WORD4 n)) = n)

The other main reason for stacking correctness results is to link correctness results at one level together with correctness results at lower levels to obtain a single correctness result spanning multiple levels of a hierarchical specification. This hierarchy can even extend upwards above the level of digital hardware. For instance, correctness results for a formally verified compiler [13] can be stacked upon correctness results for the TAMARACK-3 microprocessor to formally relate the semantics of a programming language to the execution of a compiled program by digital hardware. In this manner, a hierarchy of widely separated concerns can be treated in a truely hierarchical fashion - each level isolated from details only relevant to other levels.

Summary

This paper has argued that generic specification is a powerful concept in the context of formally verifying digital hardware. In addition to the well-known advantages of modularity, abstraction and reliable re-usability, the use of generic specification to eliminate non-essential detail from a formal specification sharpens the distinction between what has and what has not been formally considered. In a hierarchical proof effort, the elimination

---

[6]The current version of the built-in HOL data types (as given by the eval library in the HOL88 system) is not fully axiomatized or secure, but with a complete axiomatization it would be possible to derive these two assumptions as theorems.

of non-essential detail isolates each level from details only relevant to other levels. Finally, there is the practical benefit of reducing the need for special-purpose proof infrastructure, e.g., hardware-oriented data types.

As mentioned earlier in the introduction of this paper, most of the languages used for hardware specification do not provide explicit mechanisms for supporting and encouraging generic specifications. Some of the few exceptions include EHDM [17] and OBJ [8]. However, this paper shows that it is unnecessary to have explicit mechanisms for generic specification in the case of languages with (at least) the expressive power of higher-order logic. We have described a technique for expressing genericity based on the use of higher-order predicates parameterized by function variables and type variables. We believe that the use of higher-order predicates in this manner this is a very direct (if not the most direct) way to specify hardware generically. Therefore, we claim that the ability to express genericity is a very strong argument for why it is necessary, for all practical purposes, to use a formalism with (at least) the expressive power of higher-order logic.

Acknowledgments

The ideas presented in this paper are based on my Ph.D. research while a member of the Hardware Verification Group at Cambridge University. I am particularly indebted to my supervisor, Mike Gordon, who helped to refine and clarify many of these ideas. I am also grateful to a number of people who commented on drafts of my Ph.D. dissertation especially John Herbert and John Van Tassel. Pioneering work on microprocessor verification by Avra Cohn and Warren Hunt provided a very good starting point for this research. The idea of generic specification was prompted by discussions with John Rushby and his colleagues at SRI International. This research is currently supported by an NSERC (*Natural Sciences and Engineering Research Council*) Operating Grant.

References

[1] William R. Bevier, Warren A. Hunt, Jr., and William D. Young, in: Towards Verified Execution Environments, in: Proceedings of the 1987 IEEE Symposium on Security and Privacy, 27-29 April 1987, Oakland, California Computer Society Press, Washington, D.C., 1987 pp. 106-115. Also Report No. 5, Computational Logic, Inc., Austin, Texas, February 1987.

[2] W. Bevier, W. Hunt, J Moore, and W. Young, An Approach to Systems Verification, Journal of Automated Reasoning, Vol. 5, No. 4, November 1989. Also Report No. 41, Computational Logic, Inc., Austin, Texas, April 1989.

[3] Avra Cohn and Mike Gordon, A Mechanized Proof of Correctness of a Simple Counter, Report No. 94, Computer Laboratory, Cambridge University, July 1986.

[4] Avra Cohn, A Proof of Correctness of the Viper Microprocessor: The First Level, in: G. Birtwistle and P. Subrahmanyam, eds., VLSI Specification, Verification and Synthesis, Kluwer Academic Publishers, Boston, 1988, pp. 27-71. Also Report No. 104, Computer Laboratory, Cambridge University, January 1987.

[5] Avra Cohn, Correctness Properties of the Viper Block Model: The Second Level, in: G. Birtwistle and P. Subrahmanyam, eds., Current Trends in Hardware Verification

and Automated Theorem Proving, Springer-Verlag, 1989, pp. 1-91. Also Report No. 134, Computer Laboratory, Cambridge University, May 1988.

[6] Avra Cohn, The Notion of Proof in Hardware Verification, Journal of Automated Reasoning, Vol. 5, May 1989, pp. 127-139.

[7] H. Eveking, How to Design Correct Hardware and Know It. G. Milne, ed., The Fusion of Hardware Design and Verification, Proceedings of the IFIP WG 10.2 International Working Conference, Glasgow, Scotland, 3-6 July 1988, North-Holland, 1988, pp. 250-262.

[8] Joseph A. Goguen, OBJ as a Theorem Prover with Applications to Hardware Verification, in: G. Birtwistle and P. Subrahmanyam, eds., Current Trends in Hardware Verification and Automated Theorem Proving, Springer-Verlag, 1989, pp. 219-267. Also Report No. SRI-CSL-4R2, Computer Science Laboratory, SRI International, Menlo Park, August 1988.

[9] M. Gordon, LCF_LSM, Report No. 41, Computer Laboratory, Cambridge University, 1983.

[10] M. J. C. Gordon, Why Higher-Order Logic is a Good Formalism for Specifying and Verifying Hardware, in: G. Milne and P. Subrahmanyam, eds., Formal Aspects of VLSI Design, Proceedings of the 1985 Edinburgh Conference on VLSI, North-Holland, 1986, pp. 153-177.

[11] Michael J. C. Gordon et al., The HOL System Description, Cambridge Research Centre, SRI International, Suite 23, Miller's Yard, Cambridge CB2 1RQ, England.

[12] Jeffrey J. Joyce, Generic Structures in the Formal Specification and Verification of Digital Circuits, in: G. Milne, ed., Proceedings of the IFIP WG 10.2 Working Conference on The Fusion of Hardware Design and Verification, 4-6 July 1988, Glasgow, Scotland, pp. 51-75.

[13] Jeffrey J. Joyce, Totally Verified Systems: Linking Verified Software to Verified Hardware, in: M. Leeser and G. Brown, eds., Specification, Verification and Synthesis: Mathematical Aspects, Proceedings of a Workshop, 5-7 July 1989, Ithaca, N.Y., Springer-Verlag, 1989. Also Report No. 178, Computer Laboratory, Cambridge University, September 1989.

[14] Jeffrey J. Joyce, Multi-Level Verification of Microprocessor-Based Systems, Ph.D. Thesis, Computer Laboratory, Cambridge University, December 1989. Report No. 195, Computer Laboratory, Cambridge University, May 1990.

[15] J Strother Moore, Piton: A Verified Assembly Level Language, Report No. 22, Computational Logic Inc., Austin, Texas, September 1988.

[16] W. Luk and G. Jones, From Specifications to Parmeterised Architectures, in: G. Milne, ed., Proceedings of the IFIP WG 10.2 Working Conference on The Fusion of Hardware Design and Verification, 4-6 July 1988, Glasgow, Scotland, pp. 267-288.

[17] F. W. von Henke, J. S. Crow, R. Lee, J. M. Rushby and R. A. Whitehurst, The EHDM Verification Environment: An Overview, Proceedings of the 11th National Computer Security Conference, Baltimore, October 1988, pp. 147-155.

Sampling and Proof: A Half-Case Study

John Hughes*

Abstract

In this paper we give a brief introduction to the whiskies of Scotland and the way they are made, with emphasis on the factors affecting the flavour of the final product. Then we discuss the main regions of whisky production, with tasting notes on six exemplars. The paper is best accompanied by a practical session to verify our observations.

Introduction

Everyone has heard of Scotch whisky. Indeed, the words 'a Scotch' are so often heard one might think there was only one kind. In fact, Scotland has almost 120 whisky distilleries, which is probably more than the rest of the world put together. With so many producers, the variety of Scotch whisky is tremendous, and so although good whisky is made elsewhere, we feel justified in limiting our attention to Scotch whisky in this paper.

The well-known brands of Scotch, however, are not products of one distillery but blends of 30 to 40 different whiskies. About 65% of most blends is 'grain' whisky, which can be made from almost any kind of grain, but is usually made from maize. Grain whisky is made by a continuous process which is very cheap and efficient, but results in a rather tasteless product.

The remaining 35% of a blend is made up of 'malt' whiskies. These are the ingredients that give Scotch whisky its flavour. Malt whisky is made by a batch process, which is expensive and inefficient – but therein lies its secret. Just because the distillation process is poor at separating alcohol from other compounds, malt whisky retains a tremendous amount of taste.

Most malt whisky produced goes into blends, but it is also possible to buy 'single malt' whiskies – the unblended product of one malt distillery. Each malt is an individual, with its flavour subtly dependent on the distiller's every decision. Single malt whiskies are the pride of Scotland's whisky industry, and the topic of this paper.

The Making of Malt Whisky

Malt whisky is made from three simple ingredients: barley, water, and yeast. The production process, though, is long and complex, and each stage can affect the taste of the final product.

*Department of Computing Science, University of Glasgow, Glasgow, Scotland G12 8QQ. Email: rjmh@cs.glasgow.ac.uk

Malting the Barley

The alcohol in whisky is produced by the yeast, as it ferments sugars in the barley. The distiller's first problem is that barley does not contain sugar – it contains starch! To overcome this, the barley is soaked in water and allowed to germinate. During germination enzymes are produced that can break starch down into sugar, preparing the barley for fermentation. This process takes several days, and is known as 'malting' the barley. Once germination is complete, the wet barley is heated to kill it and stop it growing. The dried result, now known as malt, tastes like a kind of sweet muesli.

Traditionally, barley was malted on a large raised wooden floor. Tons of barley would be spread out over this 'malting floor', and distillery workers would turn the grain over regularly to prevent the heat generated by germination from cooking it. It would be dried by lighting a peat fire under the malting floor and allowing the smoke to rise up through the malt. The roof over the malting floor was of a traditional 'pagoda' style, designed to retain the smoke as long as possible. These pagoda roofs can still be seen on distilleries around Scotland.

Nowadays, few distillers find it economic to make their own malt, and most buy it from a commercial maltster. The malting floor and pagoda roof has been replaced by modern machinery, and peat has been replaced by coke or gas. However maltsters still burn some peat and pass the smoke through the malt according to the distiller's instructions because it imparts a smoky, peaty taste to the malt that survives through all the subsequent stages and is a distinctive component of the taste of Scotch whisky.

Making whisky from malt alone is almost unique to Scotland. Makers of Irish, American, or Canadian whisky prepare their grains for fermentation by a cooking process instead. Only in Japan is malt whisky made in the Scotch manner... and the Japanese distillers learned their trade in Scotland.

Preparing for Fermentation

When the malt arrives at the distillery it is ground up into a kind of coarse, sweet flour known as 'grist'. The grist is then fed into a large metal vessel with a filter in the base, called the 'mash tun' and resembling nothing so much as a giant washing machine. Hot water is added, and agitators in the mash tun mix the water and grist to dissolve the sugars in the water. Two or three batches of hot water, at increasing temperatures, are usually used to extract as much sugar as possible from the grist. The sugary liquid, known as the 'wort', is piped out of the mash tun for the next stage. The remainder of the grist is dried and sold as cattle cake.

Fermenting the Wort

From the mash tun the wort is piped into the fermentation vessels, the 'wash backs'. These are usually made of wood, and look like giant wooden buckets. At Glengoyne distillery, for example, the wash backs are made of Oregon pine and hold 16 *tons* of liquid each. Yeast is added, and the mixture allowed to ferment for two or three days. When the fermentation dies down the wort has become the 'wash', a kind of very strong beer of around 8% alcohol by volume.

Distillers may use just one yeast, or up to four different kinds, because the yeast used also affects the final flavour of the whisky. Yeast contributes a fruity flavour that is very pronounced in some whiskies.

Distillation in the Pot Still

The wash is now ready for distillation, and is fed into a pot still. The pot still is the secret of Scotch whisky. It is essentially a giant copper kettle with a long neck. It is heated from below using any convenient fuel, the wash boils, and the vapours pass up the neck and down into a condenser. The alcohol boils more readily than water, and so the liquid emerging from the condenser is stronger than that in the still.

Pot stills have a traditional lumpy shape, which distillers are careful to duplicate when they renew their stills, because *the shape matters*. The vapour driven off the wash contains many compounds other than alcohol and water, and the shape of the neck determines how much of each fraction of the distillate passes through into the condenser. For example, heavy fractions cannot ascend a long neck, and so tall stills produce a light whisky, while short stills produce an oily one.

The pot still is poor at separating alcohol and water, and expensive to operate because the wash must be distilled a batch at a time. Grain whisky, and most whisky made outside Scotland, is distilled in a 'Coffey' or 'patent' still, which passes a continuous flow of wash down through a cylinder, while a continuous flow of steam passes up. This kind of still is much cheaper to run, but loses more of the flavour components that the pot still retains.

The liquid flowing from the wash still is known as the 'low wines' and has an alcoholic strength of 20–25%, which is still much weaker than whisky. The low wines are therefore distilled again in a smaller (but otherwise similar) 'spirit still' to produce spirit with a strength something over 70% alcohol. However not all the spirit emerging from the still can be used to make whisky. The first to run through, called the 'foreshots', contains methyl alcohol and would be unsafe to drink. The 'middle cut' which follows is used for whisky making. Finally, the 'feints' have too low an alcoholic strength for maturation. The stillman must use his judgement to decide when the middle cut begins and ends – which is harder than it sounds since Customs and Excise insist that he has no physical contact with the spirit, on which duty has yet to be paid. The stillman makes his decision by measuring the density of the spirit inside a 'spirit safe', which is securely locked by Customs officers. The spirit coming from the still flows through the safe, and by turning handles outside it the stillman can divert the spirit into one tank or another, or into a vessel containing a hydrometer.

Although the foreshots and feints are not matured, neither are they thrown away. They contain alcohol, and so are returned to the low wines tank and mixed with the next batch of low wines ready for the next distillation. Eventually the proportion of methyl alcohol and other impurities builds up, and the middle cut becomes a smaller and smaller proportion of each distillation. Once each season the foreshots and feints are discarded and the process begins again.

Maturation

The spirit flowing from the still is a clear liquid, with a strength around 70% alcohol and a harsh and unpleasant taste. To convert it into whisky, it is diluted to around 60% alcohol and matured in oak barrels. Whisky must be matured for at least three years before it can legally be called whisky, but in practice single malts are matured for between eight and twenty-five years.

The barrels are not absolutely airtight, so during maturation the whisky can give up the harsh elements in its taste to the atmosphere and absorb flavour from the air. Distillers claim (credibly) that you can smell the sea in whisky matured by the coast for this reason. It also gives up 2–3% of its volume to the atmosphere each year, a proportion distillers resignedly call 'the angel's share'. Of course, if the angels take too much of this duty-free whisky, Customs and Excise become very interested!

During maturation the whisky also takes up flavours and colour from the wood. Distillers choose their barrels carefully to control the result. Traditionally many distillers used sherry barrels, and in some whiskies sherry is a pronounced element of the taste. The Macallan distillery even runs a sherry-maturing business in Spain to guarantee its supply! Other distillers may use Bourbon casks from the United States, or new wood, or a carefully chosen mixture of all three.

When the whisky is judged ready for drinking, it is diluted to around 40% alcohol and bottled. Once in an airtight bottle, whisky changes no more... so there is no point in buying a bottle of eight-year-old whisky and keeping it for four years in the hope that it will taste like a twelve-year-old – it will not. Sadly for those of us living in Scotland, there is no advantage in buying whisky 'fresh from the distillery' either!

The Whisky Regions of Scotland

Malts are available from over a hundred different distilleries in Scotland, each with its individual taste, but there are generally recognised regions with identifiable regional characteristics. These regions are:

- The Highlands

- The Lowlands

- Islay – an island off the west coast

- Campbeltown – a small town at the end of the Kintyre peninsula.

In its day Campbeltown had around thirty distilleries and was an important producer in its own right – so much so that Campbeltown loch was said to be full of whisky rather than water. Today, sadly, only two distilleries remain, so it is not included in our survey. We will discuss the other regions by describing six whiskies from around Scotland, ones that display the regional characteristics and the variety of Scotch whisky.

Glengoyne 10 year old

Glengoyne is our local malt, distilled 15 miles from Glasgow in a picturesque distillery at the foot of the Campsie Fells. It is (just) a part of the Highland region, which is by far the largest and most varied, with most of the distilleries in Scotland. Because there are so many, Highland whiskies have less in common than those of the other regions, but in general we may say they are smooth and smoky.

Glengoyne is unusual in that it is made from unpeated malt. It is a light whisky: smooth, with a slightly fruity nose and a long sweet finish. It is a very likeable whisky which displays none of its characteristics to excess, and is therefore both good for beginners who may find the more pungent malts offputting, and a useful standard against which to compare the other whiskies.

Glenfarclas 105 8 year old

The Glenfarclas distillery is in Speyside: the general vicinity of the river Spey which runs into the sea between Inverness and Aberdeen. Speyside is considered a part of the Highlands, and is Scotland's premium distilling region, with over 60 distilleries.

Why is Speyside so dominant? One reason is its naturally peaty water, which enables distillers to use lightly peated malt and allow the other flavours of their whisky to show through – Speyside malts are regarded as the most complex Scotland produces. Another reason lies in Scottish history... before the early nineteenth century, distilling was illegal in Scotland. Speyside is a mountainous region with many hidden glens where distilleries could be concealed, but is close to the major whisky markets of Perth and Dundee. Many of Speyside's distilleries can trace their origins to illicit activities in this period.

Glenfarclas, close to the Spey, is a classic of the region and one of Scotland's greatest malts. It is a big, sherry-ish whisky with the aroma of a rich fruit-cake covered in marzipan. The '105' in the name of this bottling is not the age, but the proof! Glenfarclas is one of the few whiskies bottled by the distiller at 'cask strength' – that is, without further dilution after maturation. It is 60% alcohol by volume, which at first sounds like madness. Is whisky not strong enough already?

Remember that dilution to 40% not only dilutes the alcohol, it dilutes the *taste*. Treated with care, a cask strength whisky like Glenfarclas 105 offers an explosion of flavour in the mouth. Treated carelessly, it offers an explosion of spluttering instead!

St. Magdalene 24 year old

The St. Magdalene distillery, now closed, is in the Lowlands of Scotland. The Lowlands lack the plentiful peat and babbling brooks of other parts of the country, and the regional style is correspondingly soft, sweet and fruity.

This bottling is the oldest in our selection, distilled in 1965, and displays a pronounced woodiness as a result. While the effect is very pleasant in St. Magdalene, it is quite strong enough. One can understand why whisky is usually said to deteriorate after around a quarter century in the cask.

St. Magdalene is no longer available from the distillers. This bottling comes from Gordon and MacPhail, based in Elgin, one of the two independent bottlers in Scotland. The independents offer whisky from distilleries that do not market their own single malt, or unusual ages or strengths from distilleries that do.

Highland Park 12 year old

The second half of our selection consists of three island whiskies. Traditionally, the islands produce peatier, more pungent whiskies than the mainland. Highland Park comes from Scotland's northernmost distillery, just outside Kirkwall, the capital of Orkney.

Highland Park still operates its own malting floor, using peat from island peat beds which are unusually shallow. The result is a higher proportion of heather in the peat than usual, which imparts a heathery-honey sweetness to the whisky and makes Highland Park one of Scotland's most distinctive malts. Highland Park is the only whisky ever to be awarded a rating of 100% by the *Scotsman*'s[1] tasting panel!

---

[1]The *Scotsman* is one of Scotland's two national papers, so should certainly know what it is talking about!

Talisker 10 year old

Talisker is the only distillery on the Isle of Skye, at the foot of the Cuillin Hills which are not hills at all, but the most challenging mountains in Britain for the mountaineer. It is a perfect example of an 'island whisky', with bags of peat on the nose and a sweet finish. I leave its description to Derek Cooper, writing in his *Century Companion to Whiskies*:

> The pungent, slightly oily, peaty ruggedness of the bouquet mounts into my nostrils. The corpus of the drink advances like the lava of the Cuillins down my throat. Then *VOOM!* Steam rises from my temples, a seismic shock rocks the building, my eyes water, cheeks aflame I steady myself against a chair...

Lagavulin 16 year old

Lagavulin hails from the island of Islay, which has a special place in the hearts of whisky-lovers. Just one small island, Islay is reckoned a whisky region in its own right. It produces the most pungent of Scotch whiskies, peaty and iodiney. First the island breezes with their lightly seaweed aroma, permeate the peat of the bogs. Then peaty island water is used in the distilleries, and the malt is heavily peated. Once the whisky is made it is matured in warehouses along the coast, some actually washed by the sea. Little wonder the whisky is so distinctive.

Lagavulin is one of the most pungent of Islay malts, and therefore of all malts. Perhaps it is not for all drinkers or all occasions, but at the right time it is absolutely wonderful. Imagine yourself striding across the moor in mist and pouring rain. You reach your croft and fling open the door, crying "Morag, I'm home!". You hang up your overcoat and sit down to toast your soaking toes by a roaring peat fire. *That's* the moment to enjoy Lagavulin!

Tasting Malt Whisky

Tasting malt whisky is very much like tasting wine. Admire the colour. Sniff the nose, which can be the most enjoyable aspect of a whisky. Then take a sip, chew it, and wait for the finish. The only difference between tasting whisky and wine is that, as far as I can tell, there is no advantage to making slurping noises when tasting whisky.

Personally I taste whisky as it comes from the bottle, but some like to add a little good quality water. This is not a sin, unless the whisky is diluted more than 50:50, which destroys the bouquet. On no account add ice – save that for drinks you do not really want to taste.

Conclusions and Future Work

The six whiskies surveyed here offer an introduction to the variety of Scotch malts, but no more than that. Between three and four *hundred* different bottlings are on the market at any one time, and await your pleasure.

A very enjoyable way to explore malt whisky is to visit the distilleries where it is made. All the distillers covered in this paper bar St. Magdalene, and many others, welcome visitors to their premises. Most make no charge, show you around explaining the production process as they go, and offer a taste of their single malt (but not enough to worry drivers). Since many distilleries are picturesque buildings in scenic locations this can be a very pleasant part of a Scottish holiday.

98

To those who wish to discover more about whisky, I recommend Jackson's excellent book *The World Guide to Whisky* [1]. Half taste-guide, half tour-guide, Jackson describes the whiskies themselves, their history, and the landscape in which they are made, with beautiful photographs throughout. His book is eminently readable, unlike many catalogues of malts with a few words about each. Although much of the book is devoted to Scotch, he covers the other major styles such as Bourbon, Rye, Irish and Canadian whiskey.

Slàinte mhath!

References

[1] Michael Jackson, *The World Guide to Whisky*, Dorling Kindersley, 1987.

High Level Test Generation via Process Composition

Venkatesh Akella*   Ganesh Gopalakrishnan [†]

Abstract

Specification driven design is gaining increasing popularity within the VLSI design community, mainly to contain the design complexity and capitalize on hierarchical and modular design techniques. Functional and behavioral abstraction and transformational approach to synthesis provide direct evidence to it. The notion of testing however, has not received sufficient attention in specification driven design environment. In this paper we shall introduce the notion of testing in the specification domain and investigate fault abstraction and high level test generation from abstract specifications. The approach taken by us consists of fault injection at the structural specification level, inferring the behavioral consequence of structural faults through process composition, and designing a tester process to distinguish the correct and faulty behaviors.

Keywords: Specification Driven Design, Design For Testability, Hardware Description Languages, High Level Test Generation, Process Composition, Fault Modeling

1   Introduction

Specification driven design efforts usually provide methods for formal verification of the design, but leave the issues of electrical testing to the VLSI testing community as a post-design activity. Unfortunately, a design has to be verified for correctness only once, but every single copy of the VLSI chip has to be tested for fabrication defects. By addressing testability issues in the specification driven environment itself, even when the design has only progressed through a few levels of refinement of a "functional specification", we can make the eventual testing of the chip easier and more efficient.

The focus of this paper will be a methodology for high level test generation in the framework of a hardware description language (HDL) and showing how design decisions can be taken during synthesis in a specification driven design environment so that testing of the final chip is easier.

Significance of High Level Test Generation

Although conventional scan-based design-for-testability (DFT) techniques have been widely researched, they have several drawbacks. They are intended for low gate-level models of circuits in which logic gates are primitive components. This is inconsistent with the modern views of VLSI design which include high level synthesis and hierarchical specification driven design. A design has to be flattened to gate level before the conventional testing strategies

---

*Dept. of Computer Science, University of Utah, Salt Lake City, Utah 84112 USA

[†]Dept. of Computer Science, University of Utah, Salt Lake City, Utah 84112 USA; Supported in part by NSF awards MIP-8710874 and MIP-8902558

can be applied. High level test generation circumvents this problem and also exhibits the potential for speeding up test generation because we abstract the low level details of the circuits and focus on *aggregate faults* like functional and sequencing errors. In addition, traditional testing strategies usually impose restrictions on the circuit design styles that are often unrealistic; for example, providing scan-paths in dynamic CMOS structures is not practically viable because it could potentially introduce charge sharing problems at storage nodes and offset the transistor savings promised by dynamic CMOS logic. High level test generation looks attractive in such scenarios.

Overview of our Approach

Generating tests at the level of functional specifications has been proposed before (see below)—however the problem has remained largely unsolved due to the following reasons:

1. Many of today's HDLs do not have a well specified and simple semantics; this makes many of the reasoning steps needed in functional testing hard, if not impossible.

2. In virtually all the HDLs, there is no algorithm to automatically infer *behavioral descriptions* from *structural descriptions*. The advantage of having such an algorithm would be that one can then automatically infer *the behavioral consequences of structural faults*. For example, if one connects an arbitrary wire in the circuit to ground ("stuck at zero"), what are *all* the functional consequences of this flaw? Does an *add* get changed to a *subtract*? Or does a certain control-flow branch change? Such information can be very useful when reasoning at a higher level of abstraction.

3. Given a correct behavioral description of a circuit and a faulty one (perhaps automatically inferred), how do we find a test that distinguishes them? In spite of past attempts, no efficient algorithms or heuristics exist for this problem.

To solve the first problem above we use the language HOP, which is a simple process model for synchronous hardware. The semantics of HOP has been specified in [8].

We solve the second problem (above) without any additional work because the design approach using HOP is centered around an algorithm called PARCOMP. Given a network of subcomponents as input, PARCOMP computes the behavior of this network for all possible inputs and states, and writes out (in HOP syntax) the behavior of the whole network, as if it were a single component. In this process, PARCOMP greatly simplifies the apparent complexity of the network, by detecting and throwing away those interactions between the subcomponents that are impossible. (It is a well-known fact that the behaviors possible for a sequential digital network are only a small fraction of the product of the behaviors possible for each of the subcomponents in the network.) A prototype of the HOP system consisting of PARCOMP and a symbolic simulator exist.

In our approach, the behavioral consequences of structural flaws resulting from only *single-stuck-at faults* [6], are deduced. Faults are introduced by modifying the structural description of a circuit (fault injection). The network is subsequently fed through PARCOMP to get a behavior that shows all the behavioral consequences of the structural flaw.

In order to construct tests, we classify the faulty behavioral descriptions into *event faults*—faults that affect some control/status information, and *data faults*—faults that affect data values, and possibly control flow that depends on data. The key step in our approach is the calculation of a *path predicate*. This is a conjunction of two predicates: a predicate that guides the chip into a state where the fault is internally triggered through a *sensitizing path*, and a predicate that makes the triggered fault observable, by forcing the chip to execute through an *observation path*.

Related Work

High level test generation has been addressed by several researchers but in different contexts. Earliest work in the area of *behavioral testing* could perhaps be traced to the *machine identification* problem and *fault-detection* experiments in automata theoretic models [11].

Functional testing has been be advocated as a promising alternative for testing micro-processors for many years now. A basis for language based testing has been proposed by Breuer and Friedman [1] where they introduce the notion of a set of *functional primitives* for test generation. This triggered research in extending the conventional test generation algorithms like the D-Algorithm to circuits described in a hardware description languages. Distante [5] has a fairly comprehensive survey of the various approaches to behavioral testing over the last couple of decades.

Recently, the notion of functional testing has been provided a completely new perspective by researchers like Devadas [2] who depict the symbiotic link between logic synthesis and test generation and advocate the coupling of synthesis and testability as the best alternative to design easily testable systems. Also recently, Singh [17] shows how certain high-level testing problems can be tackled in Ruby[16] by using non-standard interpretation.

We shall briefly summarize the approaches which influenced our work. Khorram [10] provides algorithms for generating test patterns for sequential circuits based on functional specifications in a ISPS like language. He uses a stimulus-response kind of model in the specification domain and generates the test patterns using a forward propagation and a backward propagation algorithm to control the execution of the system and propagate the results to known output ports. Levendal and Menon [12] describe an extension to the D-Algorithm to functions described in a computer hardware description language. Their approach is applicable to both procedural and non procedural languages and it contains a fairly sophisticated fault model encompassing variable stuck at 0 or 1, control faults and function faults with user-specified faulty behaviors. The CADOC work at IMAG laboratories [15] describes a compositional model for functional testing based on a strongly typed functional language.

O'Neill et al. [13] address test generation in the context of VHDL. They do not infer the behavioral consequences of structural faults, as we are doing; instead, they deliberately alter selected VHDL constructs (e.g. by removing one of the arms of a case statement) and finding ways to detect such alterations through tests. Our approach is much more accurate than their's because we actually insert structural faults in HOP's structural descriptions, and then infer the equivalent behavioral description.

Though our work is influenced by the above research we focus on a slightly different problem. Our specification domain is closer to the process calculi of Milner [14] and Hoare [9] than the imperative styles of many common HDLs. The major contribution of our work is the technique to derive behavioral consequences of structural faults (via PARCOMP). This implies that even though we are testing at functional level, we are testing for real faults rather than assumed functional faults, unlike most of the existing research in this area.

Organization of the Paper

In section 2, we explain HOP and PARCOMP, using the Huffman encoder as an example. In section 3, we define the testing problem to be solved, and chalk out our approach using HOP. In section 4, we apply our procedure on the Huffman encoder example for a few specific simulated faults. In section 5, we briefly touch upon some extensions to our basic method. Section 6 provides concluding thoughts and plans for future work—mainly how testability and synthesis ought to go hand-in-hand.

2   Language HOP, and Algorithm PARCOMP

In this section we specify the language HOP and the algorithm PARCOMP to a level of detail sufficient for understanding the rest of the paper. More details are provided in [8].

HOP is a simple language for specifying the *behavior* and *structure* of synchronous hardware systems. In synchronous hardware systems, modules share a set of central clocks. In response to every change in the state of the clock signals, each module computes new outputs and its next state based on its current inputs and state. New outputs and state are computed by a *combinational network* which reaches steady state before the clock changes state again. The combinational network may consist not only of boolean function blocks, but also bidirectional "pass" transistors. In specifying large VLSI synchronous systems, it is notationally more clear (and implementationally more efficient) to separate *control* aspects from *data* aspects, as best as possible. Of course, this separation is always not easy to identify.

A few notations are introduced. As in set theory, we shall treat a natural number as a set, with 0 denoting the empty set and $n > 0$ denoting $\{0 \ldots (n-1)\}$. $\{x_i \mid i \in N\}, N \geq 0$ denotes either the empty set (when $N = 0$) or the set $\{x_0 \ldots x_{N-1}\}$ (when $N > 0$). $[x_i \mid i \in N], N \geq 0$ denotes either the empty sequence (when $N = 0$) or the sequence $[x_0 \ldots x_{N-1}]$ (when $N > 0$). $(x_i \mid i \in N)$ denotes an N tuple. A one-tuple (x) is the same as x.

2.1   Behavioral Specification

A behavioral specification in HOP is a tuple (*ies, oes, me, ips, ops, S, s_0, ms*). *ies* is a set of *input events* that the module can respond to. *ies* are (truth-valued) conditions that are typically conveyed to a module by means of Boolean combinations of control inputs and clocks. Likewise, *oes* are a set of *output events* emitted by a module. These can be statuses or control points. *me* is a set of pairs of input events that are guaranteed (by the environment) to be not generated simultaneously (achieved by disjoint control encodings). *ips* are a set of *data input ports* and *ops* a set of *data output ports*. $S = C \times D$ is the set of states of the module, where C are *control states*, and D are *data states*. Data states range over the underlying types (such as sequences, arrays, etc.) s_0 is the start state and finally *ms* is the set of *moves* (also known as transitions) of the module. We define selector functions *ies*, etc., on a module M to mean the following: *ies*(M) is the component *ies* of M, and so on for the remaining fields of M.

ms contains *moves* which are triples $((c,d), ca_i, (c_i, d_i))$ that denote that a state (c,d) can evolve to a state (c_i, d_i) through the *compound action* ca_i. A compound action ca_i is a tuple of actions ($ies_i, dqs_i, g_i, oes_i, das_i$). ies_i is a possibly empty set of input events belonging to *ies*. dqs_i is a possibly empty set of *data queries* (see below). g_i is a guard—a boolean expression (if not mentioned, assumed to be *true*). oes_i is a possibly empty set of output events belonging to *oes*. das_i is a possibly empty set of *data assertions* (see below). The notation $a \in ca$ means that action a is present in any one of the constituents of ca.

A data query is a pair $(variable, port)$. In the HOP syntax, it is written as '*variable = input-port*'. This makes the intended meaning of the construct: obtaining a value from an input port and binding it to a variable, clear. *Input-port* must belong to *ips*. The variable belonging to a data query must not be part of any of the other data queries in the same ca_i nor must it be part of d, the data state. The scope of the variable is confined to the move in whose compound action the data query appears. Specifically, the variable defined in a data query may be used in the guard, in data assertions, and in the next data state expression.

A data assertion is a pair $(port, expression)$. It is usually written as '*output-port = expression*', and denotes the act of asserting a value on an output port. The *output-port* must belong to *ops*.

A move $((c, d), (ies1, dqs1, g1, oes1, das1), (c1, d1))$ means the following. If in state (c, d), at time t, if all the input events $ies1$ are asserted by the environment, if all the data queries $dqs1$ are performed at time t, and if the guard $g1$ is found true at time t, all the output events $oes1$ are asserted at time t, all the data assertions $das1$ are asserted at time t, and the module attains state $(c1, d1)$ at time $t + 1$. Further, the following conventions are followed: (i) all those output events that belong to the output event sort of the module, but are not present in $oes1$, are assumed to be *false*; (ii) all those ports that belong to the output port sort of the module, but are not used in any of the data assertions in $das1$, are assumed to have *unknown* values; (iv) it is also assumed that the functional expressions used in $das1$, as well as expression $d1$, are evaluable within one clock cycle; (v) it is assumed that port values and events asserted at time t are steady in the interval $[t-t+1)$; (vi) it is assumed that redundant data queries are removed; a data query dq belonging to a move m is redundant if the value of its variable is not used in any of the data assertions, the guard, or the next data state expression of m.

We sometimes abbreviate a state (c, d) by the letter s. The notation

$$M : s \xrightarrow{(ies1, dqs1, g1, oes1, das1)} s'$$

means that the move $(s, (ies1, dqs1, g1, oes1, das1), s')$ is in $ms(M)$. The notation

$$M : s \xrightarrow{[a_i | i \in K]} s'$$

for $K \geq 0$ means: (a) if $K = 0$ then $s = s'$; (b) if $K > 0$ then M evolves through the sequence of moves $[a_i \mid i \in K]$ to s'.

It is assumed that, of the moves possible from a state, at most one move will be eligible to occur at any time. This condition, called *determinacy*, will be guaranteed by the following conditions:

$$m = (ies1, dqs1, g1, oes1, das1) \in ms(M)$$
$$\wedge (ies2, dqs2, g2, oes2, das2) \in ms(M) \setminus \{m\} \Rightarrow$$
$$(\exists x \in ies1, y \in ies2 \, . \, (x, y) \in me) \vee \neg(g1 \wedge g2) \tag{1}$$

2.2 Structural Specifications

New modules can be obtained from existing ones using structural operations *hide*, *rename*, and *par*. HOP's structural operators were inspired by those in CCS[14] but are quite different in their semantics. Some of our ideas were inspired by studying the algebra of [4] (the use of bijections for renaming, and the decision to not hide input events or ports).

- If M is a module, $roe : oes(M) \mapsto oes(M)$ and $rop : ops(M) \mapsto ops(M)$ are bijections, and $rie : ies(M) \mapsto ies(M)$ and $rip : ips(M) \mapsto ips(M)$ are functions,

- $hoe \subseteq oes(M)$, $hop \subseteq ops(M)$,

- The following denote modules:

  $renameie(M, rie), renameoe(M, roe), renameip(M, rip), renameop(M, rop),$

  $hideoe(M, hoe), hideop(M, hop), par(M1, M2)$

renamee, renamep, hideoe, hideop, and *par* are called structural operations (or structural *combinators*). They are briefly explained in the next section.

Renaming functions *roe* and *rop* are restricted to be bijections to prevent renaming two distinct output events or ports to the same event/port name; doing so would be tantamount to electrically tying together two output wires. However, since it is permissible to tie together input wires, *rie* and *rip* are allowed to be unrestricted functions. Also, *par* is commutative and associative, and so $par(M_i \mid i \in N)$ is equivalent to $par(M_0, par(M_1, \ldots))$.

2.3 PARCOMP

In [8], an operational semantics for HOP has been specified by means of a labeled transition system. It is not presented here due to lack of space. The operational semantics describes the *module forming operators* introduced in the previous section. PARCOMP is an algorithm that essentially implements these operators; in other words, given a module described structurally, PARCOMP returns the equivalent behavioral presentation of the same module. Let us briefly examine how PARCOMP achieves this.

Operators of the *rename* variety are easy to implement: they simply change the names of the entities in question. Operators of the *hide* variety suppress the corresponding event or data assertion from being observed by the external world.

Operation *par* is the more interesting one. This operator simulates all possible executions of the pair of modules given as arguments, and discovers how they communicate with each other. Two facts make this task practically efficient: (i) the modules are driven by the same clock, and therefore only a subset of all possible pairs of states are reachable; (ii) from the states that are reachable, all pairs of moves possible for the modules are explored. Of these moves, only a small subset (usually one) of pairs of moves will actually *synchronize* with each other. For example, if move $m1$ awaits a set of input events while the other move $m2$ does not generate all these events even though the module whose move $m2$ is, is capable of doing so (i.e. these events are in the output sort of the second module), then move $m1$ will not happen. Only when a move $m1$ finds all its input events being generated either by one of the other submodules, or if the input events can be generated by the environment, will move $m1$ be retained.

As an illustration of the capabilities of the Huffman encoder (shown in figure 1) we present the moves of its submodules below. The moves of the whole Huffman encoder as inferred by PARCOMP, are shown below as process HENC-IABS.

```
                          ZERO GENERATOR

                  !out=T
(ZERO,[])  -----------> (ZERO,[])


                     HUFFMAN ENCODER TREE

             x=?datain, !dataout=(D x),
             !sentinel=(S x), !error=(E x)
(HTREE,[]) ---------------------------------> (HTREE,[])

where, functions D, E and S are defined as follows

(DEFUN
      (FUNCTION D ( x OF dintype) TO douttype
        d[3] =  x[1] \/ x[2] \/ x[3] \/ x[4] \/ x[5]
        d[2] =  x[4] \/ x[5]
        d[1] =  x[2] \/ x[3] \/ x[5]
        d[0] =  x[2] \/ x[3])
      (FUNCTION S (x OF dintype) TO douttype
        s[3] =  x[0] \/ x[1] \/ x[2] \/ x[3] \/ x[4] \/ x[5]
        s[2] =  x[1] \/ x[2] \/ x[3] \/ x[4] \/ x[5]
        s[1] =  s[2]
        s[0] =  x[2] \/ x[3])
      (FUNCTION E (x OF dintype) TO bit
       ~ ( x[0] \/ x[1] \/ x[2] \/ x[3] \/ x[4] \/ x[5])))


             PARALLEL-LOAD, SERIAL SHIFT REGISTER

               Iload, d=?din, !dout=dps
               !sout=(msb dps)
(SREG,[dps]) ---------------------------> (SR_NEG,[d])


               Ishift, s=?din, !dout=dps
               !sout = (msb dps)
(SREG,[dps]) ---------------------------> (SR_NEG,[(shift dps),s])


               OIdle, !dout=dps, !sout=(msb dps)
(SR_NEG,[dps]) ---------------------------> (SR,[dps])


where, functions msb and shift are defined as follows in lisp like notation,

(DEFUN
    (FUNCTION msb (d OF dtype) TO bit
      (index-vector dtype d 3)
    )
    (FUNCTION shift (d OF dtype sin OF bit) TO dtype
        (create-vector dtype
            (i (cond ( (> i 0) (index-vector dtype d (- i 1)))
                     (t sin)))))))
      ;for all i>0 result is d[i-1]; i=0 result is sin


                     HUFFMAN ENCODER CONTROLLER

              Iclock+, Inogo, Oconv-done, Oload
(HCTRL,[]) ---------------------------------> (HCTRL,[])
```

```
              Iclock+, Igo, Oconv-not-done, Oload
(HCTRL,[]) ----------------------------------> (SHIFT_LOOP,[])


                  Iclock+, (e=?error), (IF e),
                  Oconv-done, Oload
(SHIFT_LOOP,[]) ------------------------------>(HCTRL,[])


                  Iclock+, e=?error, sout=?sout,
                  (IF (and (not e) sout)), Ovalid-data, Oshift,
(SHIFT_LOOP,[]) -------------------------> (SHIFT_LOOP,[])


                  Iclock+, e=?error, sout=?sout,
                  (IF (and (not e) (not sout))), Oconv-done, Oload,
(SHIFT_LOOP,[]) -------------------------->(HCTRL,[])


                      CLOCK GENERATOR

                  Oclock+
(CLKGEN,[]) ----------------> (CLKGEN,[])


            INFERRED BEHAVIOR OF THE HUFFMAN ENCODER, HENC-IABS

                  Inogo, x=?datain, Oconv-done,
                  !dout=(msb dps2), !error=(E x)
(s0,[dps1,dps2]) ---------------------------> (s0,[(S x),(D x)])


                  Igo, x=?datain, Oconv-not-done,
                  !dout=(msb dps2), !error=(E x)
(s0,[dps1,dps2]) ---------------------------> (s1,[(S x),(D x)])


                  x=?datain, (IF (E x)), Oconv-done
                  !error=(E x),!dout=(msb (D x))
(s1,[dps1,dps2]) --------------------------->(s0,[(S x),(D x)])


                  x=?datain, (IF (and (not (E x)) (msb (S x)))),
                  Ovalid-data, !error=(E x), !dout=(msb (D x))
(s1,[dps1,dps2]) ---------------------------------------------->
                  (s1,[(shift dps1 f),(shift dps2 f)])


                  x=?datain, (IF (not (msb dps1))), Oconv-done,
                  !dout=(msb dps1),!error=(E x)
(s1,[dps1,dps2]) --------------------------->(s0,[(S x),(D x)])
```

3   The High Level Testing Problem

In this section we shall introduce high level test generation (HLTG) by providing the general definition of the problem and enumerating the basic requirements for a solution to such a problem.

3.1   HLTG Problem Specification

The HLTG problem addressed by us is defined using Fig 2. We assume that the HDL used has the ability to express *behavioral specifications* and *structural specifications*. Let S be the specification of a hardware module M in a suitable modeling domain D. Let I

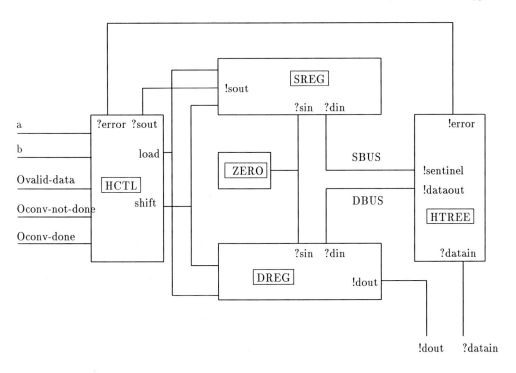

Figure 1: Schematic of the Huffman encoder chip

108

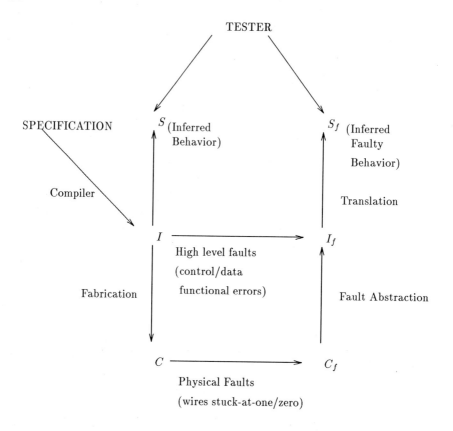

Figure 2: Characterizing High Level Test Generation

be a structural specification (interconnection of sub-modules) corresponding to S, obtained using some transformational approach. Let C be the circuit that realizes I. C consists of an interconnection of the circuits corresponding to each sub-module (called sub-circuits). Let C be susceptible to a fault f belonging to a class of faults F (typically fabrication faults) on its *interconnection wires*, resulting in a faulty circuit C_f. *We assume that the sub-circuits themselves are fault free and only the interconnections are faulty.* (Later we address how this can be relaxed by hierarchical reasoning.) Let h_F be the high-level equivalents of interconnection faults. For example, a stuck-at fault can result in a change in a control-point combination, thus triggering the wrong command. Reasonable definitions of h_F in the form of *event modification functions* and *data modification functions* will be presented later.

Let I_f be the structural specification corresponding to C_f. The first problem to be addressed is how I_f can be *reflected* into S_f, the faulty behavioral description. The second problem to be addressed is how a *tester process* may be constructed so as to distinguish S and S_f.

3.2   Essential Features of High Level Testing

The task of high level test generation can be decomposed into the following four subproblems independent of the HDL or the specification formalism used.

- *Translation:*

  This involves *transforming* the test generation problem from the implementation domain to the specification domain. *Translation* is also synonymous with the inference of behavioral consequences of structural faults, which was emphasized in the introduction of the paper.

- *Fault Modeling:*

  This involves developing *models* for physical faults like wires being *stuck-at-1* and *stuck-at-0* in the specification formalism and developing criteria to *detect* them. In the abstract specification domain one does not have handle on wires and gates to talk about conventional fault models like *stuck-at faults*, *bridging faults*, etc. So, we should invent the abstract counterparts of these faults which can be modeled in the specification domain of our interest.

- *Fault Detection:*

  A fault is detected by its manifestation at the *primary output* of the module. In the conventional *stuck-at* models, a fault is manifested by producing a zero instead of one or vice versa at a primary output pin. Since we have an abstract fault model like control faults and functional errors we would like to focus on a more abstract notion of detecting faults. A notion of an *observable* is needed to detect faults in the specification domain. Typically, an observable will produce unexpected data output and/or control flow, depending on the underlying specification calculus.

- *Tester Generation*

  Tester generation is the abstract counterpart of test vector generation in the conventional hardware testing setting. It involves synthesizing a tester process that is capable of providing the external stimulus to the module under question so that a given fault is manifested through an observable effect. In that sense it is similar to a distinguishing experiment to distinguish a faulty module from a good one.

3.3 Illustrating HLTG in HOP

In this section we shall describe our solution to the four major issues of HLTG i.e. *translation*, *fault modeling*, *fault detection* and *tester generation*.

3.3.1 Translation

The tool PARCOMP which was discussed in the previous section provides the *translation* mechanism. It takes a network of modules denoting the implementation of a given module and generates an equivalent module called the inferred behavior. PARCOMP has been applied to many large designs; the largest design (to date) is a pipelined cache memory system, and for this, it infers the behavioral description in a few minutes.

3.3.2 Fault Modeling

We shall model the following fault classes in HOP which provide complete coverage for pin and control faults and partial coverage for functional errors [12].

- *Event Fault* which can be informally defined as a fault on a control wire that is used to implement the event that results in a *different* event being received by the module.

- *Data Fault*, which is a fault on a data wire, changes the values sent/received by a module.

Let S be the specification of a module M in HOP. Let $E(M)$ denote the *event_sort* of M—the set of input events or output events that a module can participate in.

The abstract characterization of a *event fault* involves deriving a relationship between the sorts of the given module M and the faulty module M_f which have the corresponding HOP specifications S and S_f.

Mathematically, an *event fault* can be captured by an *event modification function* or *emf* for short which has the following type:

$$emf : event\_sort \mapsto event\_sort$$

This can be intuitively justified in the implementation domain, because a fault or a defect in a wire carrying information to a module will result in an unexpected or unknown control word being seen by the receiver.

Event faults may be further classified into *obvious event faults* and *non-obvious event faults*.

Definition 3.1 *If for some $a \in E(M)$, $emf(a) \notin E(M)$ then M is said to have an obvious event fault.*

Definition 3.2 *If for some $a \in E(M)$, $a \in ies$, and $emf(a) \in ies'$ for some ies and ies',* $emf(a) \in E(M)$, *and*

$$M : s \stackrel{(ies,dqs,g,oes,das)}{\longrightarrow} s' \Rightarrow M : s \stackrel{(ies',dqs,g,oes,das)}{\longrightarrow} s'$$

then M is said to have a non-obvious fault.

The latter class of faults can be harder to detect.

Data faults can cause errors in both data manipulations as well as control flows that depend on data. The distinction between event and data faults is natural in a language like HOP where control/data separation is encouraged. It is also very convenient because different (and more appropriate) procedures can be applied to detect faults in these categories. Data modification function dmf indicates ways in which data is corrupted.

$$dmf : port\_type, fault\_descriptor \mapsto port\_type$$

where $port\_type$ can be types such as a byte, and $fault\_descriptor$ is a way to model data faults. Currently, we take $fault\_descriptor$ as a specifier of which wire of the port (a bundle of wires) is stuck at what value (zero or one). Complete investigation of functional errors [12] is beyond the scope of this paper.

3.3.3 Fault Detection

Let us define a few basic concepts used:

Definition 3.3 *To detect a fault, it is necessary to identify an observable effect of a fault, or an* observable *for short. Observables used by us are*

- *a synchronization failure* inside *the module, that is manifest at the pins of the module through the raising of an error signal by the module;*

- *a different data assertion (than expected) or a different output event (than expected) at the output pins of the module.*

We now elaborate on these observables.

Synchronization Failure

A synchronization failure is said to occur within a module M when:

1. a sub-module M_1 awaits an input event e at time t while no other sub-module connected to M_1 generates a matching output event e;

2. a sub-module M_1 receives an input event e when it is not expecting it.

Since events are modeled as control wire combinations, the above can also be explained as (respectively) an expected control combination not arriving, and an unexpected control combination arriving. These errors must be detectable on *two* occasions: while doing PARCOMP and while operating the actual chip. Detecting synchronization failure during PARCOMP is already defined as a part of the PARCOMP procedure. For detecting synchronization failure in the real chip, it is the responsibility of the hardware synthesis procedure to explicitly introduce an *error* state inside every module that uses input events (i.e. every significant sequential block) and make the module enter the error state upon synchronization failure. In the error state, the module must assert an *error wire* that is then brought out as an *error pin* of the chip. *This is an example of addressing testability issues via synthesis in a specification calculus, which is one of our objectives.*

Thus, the observable of a synchronization failure can be used both during test vector generation at the HOP level and the actual testing of the chip.

A Different Data Assertion/Output Event

This observable needs no extra hardware to realize because test patterns include the *expected* output from the chip and a fault is detected when the expected output does not match the obtained output.

3.3.4 Tester Generation

In this section we shall describe a general procedure to generate a HOP process called a tester that helps detect data and event faults.

Assumptions

Only event and data faults as described thus far will be handled. Also, we assume that, there exists only *one* fault in the system at any given time which is similar to the *single stuck-at* fault assumption made in conventional testing.

Input

- A module which is expressed as the interconnection of k submodules $S_1 \ldots S_k$.

- Let $S = par(S_1, S_2 \ldots S_k)$, where, *par* is composition operator in HOP realized by PARCOMP. We assume that the inferred behavior denoted by S is reduced and non-redundant, i.e. it is a transition system where equivalent states are merged.

- Let $F_i = \{a_{i_1} \ldots a_{i_m}\}$ be the set of faults associated with the ports/events used by submodule S_i.
  Let $F = \bigcup F_i$ where $i \in \{1 \ldots k\}$.

- Let S_f be the behavior inferred from a fault-injected structural specification for $f \in F$.

Output

A tester process T which detects fault f in the module M. This tester can then be compiled into a sequence of physical test vectors.

Definition 3.4 *A physical test vector is a sequence of 0, 1, and x (don't care) that get loaded into typical VLSI testing equipment. Such a vector specifies both the system inputs and expected responses.*

Outline of the Tester Generation Algorithm

Let S denote the inferred behavior of the module M derived using PARCOMP. Let s_0 denote the initial (start) state of S. Let a denote an arbitrary action (a member of *ies,dqs,oes,das*). Let obs_a denote an action in M which is an *observable* for a (definition 3.3).

We shall define the following terms to facilitate the formulation of the tester generation procedure.

Definition 3.5 *A justification sequence J_a for action a is defined to be a sequence $[ca_i \mid i \in N], N \geq 0$ such that $M : s_0 \xrightarrow{[ca_i, i \in N]} s$ and $M : s \xrightarrow{a \in ca} s'$ for some ca, and s'. Further, an observation sequence O_a for action a is defined to be a sequence $[ca_i \mid i \in N], N > 0$ such that $M : s \xrightarrow{[ca_i \mid i \in N]} s''$ for some s'', $a \in ca_0$, and $obs_a \in ca_{N-1}$*

A tester is constructed by the following procedure (to be illustrated in the next section). For each $a \in F$ do the following steps:

1. Construct J_a as shown in definition 3.5

2. Construct O_a as shown in definition 3.5

3. Let $L_a = concatenate(J_a, O_a)$. Note that L_a will be one of the possible execution paths of S and *concatenate* is the standard concatenation function defined over sequences

4. Construct process T_a such that it interacts with S at every time step without synchronization failures, matches the data assertions and queries of S at every time step, and *guides* the execution of S along path L_a. T_a is known as the *tester* for the fault a

5. Let $M_{good} = par(T_a, S)$ and $M_{bad} = par(T_a, S_f)$, where S_f is the inferred behavior with a fault on action a

6. Let T_{good} and T_{bad} be sequences of actions performable by M_{good} and M_{bad} respectively

7. If $T_{good} = T_{bad}$ then a is an *undetectable* fault in M, otherwise the physical test vector corresponding to T_a *detects* a fault in the implementation of a. (Note that it is very easy to show that T_{good} and T_{bad} are strictly *sequential* processes and extracting the underlying *sequence* of actions described is routine.)

4 Illustration of Test Vector Generation

In this section we will illustrate the high level test generation algorithm on the Huffman encoder example. Figure 1 shows the schematic of the Huffman encoder, and the transition system of its inferred behavior is that of process `HENC-IABS` given above. Let us consider two different scenarios of faults and illustrate the test generation algorithm on each.

4.1 Testing Faults on Control Wires

Consider the problem of testing for faults on the control wire inputs a, b to the module shown in figure 1 These wires encode the *events* `Igo`, `Inogo` and `Ireset` in our specification S.
The following encoding was used to implement the control signals.

Event	Code (a,b)
Igo	01
Inogo	10
Ireset	11
Ixx (Not Used)	00

Example 1

Fault Abstraction: A fault in the implementation of event `Igo` can be abstracted by the event modification function in two ways.

- $emf(\texttt{Igo}) = \texttt{Ireset}$ (A *non-obvious* fault on `Igo`)

- $emf(\texttt{Igo}) = \texttt{Ixx}$ (An *obvious* fault on `Igo`)

A careful perusal of the above modification shows that the first abstraction corresponds to a stuck-at-1 fault on wire a and the second abstraction corresponds to a stuck-at-0 fault on wire b. So, we have modeled the stuck-at-1 fault on wire A and stuck-at-0 fault on wire B as an *event* fault on Igo.

Test Generation: The test generation involves two phases

1. We should discover a path in the specification S which will sensitize the event Igo and reveal the fault through an *observable* (output event or data action).

   The configuration or state in which action Igo will be performed is s_0 shown in the transition system of HENC-IABS. We choose event Oconvnotdone as an *observable* to reveal the fault. A path P in S which will justify the fault and reveal it to the external world is $s0 \rightarrow s1 \rightarrow s0$.

2. We should now compute the external stimulus which will guide the execution of S through P. We do this by back propagation. To guide the system along the arc $s1 \rightarrow s0$ we have to provide the following input: A data assertion to synchronize with p=?datain such that (E p) = TRUE. A data assertion !datain $= (0,0,0,0,0)$ will do it. (Here, bit vectors are shown as tuples.) The rest are data outputs which only have to be observed.

   To guide the system along the arc $s0 \rightarrow s1$ we have to provide the following inputs:

   - An event Ogo to synchronize with Igo
   - A data input which will synchronize with y=?datain. We obtain this from the previous step, because the intended operation of our huffman encoder system is such that data is fed into input port ?datain and is kept around till it is consumed by the system. So, the tester T_f which will lead the system from $s0 \rightarrow s1 \rightarrow s0$ is
   $$T_f[] \ \Leftarrow \ \text{Ogo}, !datain = (0,0,0,0,0) \ \rightarrow \ !datain = (0,0,0,0,0) \ \rightarrow \ T_f[]$$
   The physical test vectors for this testing sequence is:

A	B	?datain	Oconv-done	Oconvnotdone	Ovaliddata	!error	!dout
0	1	00000	X	1	X	X	X
X	X	00000	X	1	X	X	X

   Where an X denotes *don't care* for the present test case. As we remarked earlier this test sequence will detect a stuck-at-1 fault on wire a and stuck-at-0 on b wire.

Example 2

Let us repeat the same procedure to detect the stuck-at-0 fault on wire a and stuck-at-1 fault on wire b which corresponds to faults on event Inogo.

Fault Abstraction: A fault on event Inogo can also be abstracted in two ways:

- $emf(\text{Inogo}) = \text{Ireset}$ (A *non-obvious* fault on Inogo)

- $emf(\text{Inogo}) = \text{Ixx}$ (An *obvious* fault on Inogo)

This abstraction models wire b being *stuck-at-0* and wire a being *stuck-at-1*.

Test Generation: As usual this would involve computing the justification sequence and the observation sequence for the event Inogo in the inferred behavior S. We follow exactly the same procedure as in the previous example and choose event `Oconv-done` as the observable action and the execution sequence $s0 \rightarrow s0$ as the path P. The derivation of a tester process will again involve matching data actions and event actions to *guide* the execution of the module along the path P.

$$T_f[] \Leftarrow \texttt{Onogo}, !datain = (0,0,0,0,0) \rightarrow T_f[]$$

This notation is to be read as follows: tester T_f is a process that generates event `Onogo` at the first time step, asserts data `<00000>` on output port `!datain` also at the first time step, and, in the next time step (the $\rightarrow$ signifies moving to the next clock cycle), continues to behave as T_f. The [] signifies an empty list of data path state variables.

The physical test vector for this will be:

A	B	?datain	Oconv-done	Oconvnotdone	Ovaliddata	!error	!dout
1	0	00000	1	X	X	X	X

4.2 Testing Faults on Data Wires

So far we have focussed on faults in control wires which directly alter the control flow of the behavior and hence reveal faults through inconsistencies in the output events or data actions. This was always known to be the easier case. The more subtle case is the fault in data wires which does not alter the control flow behavior, so that good and faulty behavioral specifications follow the same execution sequence but probably produce a different output only when the faulty bit position is used. We shall illustrate how we can extend our algorithm to handle a typical data fault in the Huffman encoder example.

Consider a fault in the databus carrying the data signals from port `!sentinel` of the HTREE submodule to the port `?din` of the SREG submodule. Let us call it SBUS. Let us see how we can generate a tester process to reveal this fault. A databus typically consists of N wires (in our example N is 4) and each of them can be *stuck-at-0* or *stuck-at-1*.

From the specification of the Huffman encoder we find that the value being transmitted on SBUS is absorbed into the variable *dps1* in the module datapath state.

Fault Abstraction: We can model a fault on SBUS using a data modification function (dmf defined in section 3) which essentially corrupts the value on port `?din` of the SREG module. This manifests as the modification of the datapath variable *dps1* (refer to `HENC-IABS`.)

Test Generation: As in the case of control faults, the test generation involves two distinct phases:

1. Choosing a justification and an observation sequence for the datapath variable *dps1* (to be manifested later at the primary output `Oconv-done`). The execution sequence $s0 \rightarrow s1$ is an example of such a justification path. In this sequence, a data item `y` is input to the system, and then `(S y)` is bound to *dps1*.

   We discovered the *observable* by capitalizing on the fact that the boolean guard (path predicate) `(and (not ( E x)) (msb (S x)))` will be true as long as the most significant bit position in the `dps1` is 1 and will be false as soon as it becomes 0, which will result in the execution of the module to be pushed along the arc $s1 \rightarrow s0$ which will inturn produce `Oconv-done`.

   So, the execution path through which the system has to be guided is

   $$P = s0 \rightarrow s1 \rightarrow s1 \rightarrow s1 \rightarrow s1 \rightarrow s0$$

2. Using the same notion of backward propagation we can compute the external stimulus needed to keep the execution sequence of S along P.

To check for *stuck-at-0* fault on the SBUS we have to provide an input "y" to the module during the execution from $s0 \rightarrow s1$ such that $S(y) = (1,1,1,1)$. This has to be propagated through the HTREE sub module to arrive at the value to be supplied port datain. $y = (0,0,0,0,1)$ (which is encoding of character "r") serves as the appropriate input. If any bit position on SBUS is *stuck-at-0*, it will result in the premature exit of the loop $s1 \rightarrow s1$ and the production of the event Oconv-done. The tester process which achieves this effect is: $T_f[] \Leftarrow$ Ogo,$!datain = (0,0,0,0,1) \rightarrow$ OIdle $\rightarrow$ Oidle $\rightarrow$ OIdle $\rightarrow$ $T_f[]$

The physical test vectors for this fault are

A	B	?datain	Oconv-done	Oconvnotdone	Ovaliddata	!error	!dout
0	1	00001	0	1	0	X	X
X	X	00001	0	0	1	X	X
X	X	00001	0	0	1	X	X
X	X	00001	0	0	1	X	X
X	X	00001	1	0	0	X	X

Note that when the fault free system is in the loop $s1 \rightarrow s1$ you get a Ovaliddata and when the execution is in $s1 \rightarrow s0$ it produces Oconv-done A similar reasoning enables us to derive tester process and test vectors for the stuck-at-1 faults on SBUS.

5   Analysis of High Level Test Generation

In this section we shall conclude our discussion on HLTG by emphasizing on several important issues which are related to the notion of incorporating testability in a specification driven design environment.

Observability and Controllability

The construction of a *tester* to detect a fault on a given action, basically involves, determining a sequence of actions or a path in S which *guides* the execution in S to perform the action (justification path) and then bringing the result of the execution of that action to a primary (observation path) output. This is the general algorithm underlying many testing procedures [3] It is easy to see that the crux of the problem is in deriving the proper *justification* and *observation* paths for a given fault.

In general every action may not have a justification and observation path. Such an action could potentially result in a *undetectable fault* in the implementation. This brings us to the vital question of observability and controllability raised by Goldstein [7] among several other researchers.

Designing a piece of hardware such that all the actions are observable and controllable makes *testing* easy. We would like to add that the notions of observability and controllability can addressed in the specification domain itself and care should be taken that all the actions are made observable in one way or another.

Efficiency

The basic procedure described above could potentially be inefficient because a *tester* has to be generated for *each action* in the input specification S. The efficiency could be improved by incorporating the notion of *fault simulation* in the proposed algorithm to improve the efficiency. The idea is to take a given execution path L_j and the associated *tester* T_j (obtained by our algorithm) and analyze for the *Fault Coverage*. By *Fault Coverage* we mean, determining all the actions for which the tester T_j will be able to detect the faults.

For example, we have shown in our example that a tester for detecting fault on Igo event can detect both a *stuck-at-1* on wire A and *stuck-at-0* on wire B. This is a very simple example which illustrates the benefits of *fault simulation*.

Implementation Issues

The algorithm presented in section 3 has two apparently non mechanizable tasks, namely, discovering an *observable* for a given action and choosing an *observation sequence* to detect the fault. In practice, the first task is fairly easy in most cases. It involves finding a *unique* transition for the given action. It may result in exhaustive search of the underlying transition graph. However, the task gets fairly difficult for detecting *data faults*, which boils down to detecting the alteration of control flow due to data. Works needs to be done to completely automate this task.

Hierarchical Test Generation

In the presentation, we only considered the faults on the *interconnection* of the submodules alone. In general we would like to test the submodules themselves. Our technique can be extended to handle it in the following manner. In the first pass we detects faults in the internals of the submodules and make it available in the interconnect of the network of submodules and in the second pass *drive* these observables to a primary output so that it can be detected in essentially the same way as was outlined in our algorithm presented in section 3.

6   Conclusions and Future Work

The relation between test generation and behavioral modeling has been studied in the framework of a process oriented hardware description language. Specification driven design is a goal directed activity which involves successive refinement of the original specifications to physical hardware. Test generation is usually regarded as a *post fabrication* concern which many specification driven design approaches do not try to address.

Contemporary research has shown that *testability* and *synthesis* cannot be decoupled from each other and test generation is far too significant to dismiss it merely as a *post fabrication* activity.

Our investigation has shown that the specification formalism can address test generation issues from a fairly high level of abstraction and help in testing (or validating) the specifications at the behavioral itself capitalizing on the same tools and techniques used to contain the design complexity in behavioral modeling of hardware modules.

The significant contributions of this work are:

1. Developing a *high level fault model* for a process oriented hardware description language.

2. Developing methods for *fault abstraction* and *fault detection* in a hardware description language framework.

3. Devising an algorithm to construct test vectors to semi-automatically test a specification for the presence of a class of faults.

Our future work would involve developing a *unified methodology* to test synchronous and asynchronous circuits at the behavioral level and extend our approach to *hierarchical functional testing*.

Acknowledgements: Inspiring discussions with Rajiv Gupta of General Electric are gratefully acknowledged.

References

[1] M. A. Breuer and A. D. Friedman. Functional level Primitives in test generation. *IEEE Transactions on Computers*, 223–234, March 1980.

[2] Srinivas Devadas, H.K Tony Ma, A. Richard Newton, and A. Sangiovanni-Vincentelli. Optimal Logic Synthesis and Testability: Two Faces of the Same Coin. In *Proceedings of the International Test Conference*, pages 3–12, September 1988.

[3] Srinivas Devadas, H.K Tony Ma, A. Richard Newton, and A. Sangiovanni-Vincentelli. Synthesis and optimization procedures for fully and easily testable sequential machines. In *Proceedings of the International Test Conference*, pages 621–632, September 1988.

[4] David L. Dill. *Trace Theory for Automatic Hierarchical Verification of Speed-independent Circuits*. MIT Press, 1989. *An ACM Distinguished Dissertation*.

[5] F. Distante. Behavioral Testing of Programmable Systems. In F. Lombardi and M. Sami, editors, *Testing and Diagnosis of VLSI and ULSI*, Kluwer, 1988.

[6] Hideo Fujiwara. *Logic Testing and Design for Testability*. MIT Press, 1985.

[7] L. H. Goldstein. Controllability/Observability Analysis of Digital Circuits. *IEEE Transactions on Circuits and Systems*, CAS-26, September 1979.

[8] Ganesh C. Gopalakrishnan. *A Process Model for Synchronous Hardware*. Technical Report, Dept. of Computer Science, University of Utah, Salt Lake City, UT 84112, 1990. *In preparation. Draft available upon request.*

[9] C. A. R. Hoare. *Communicating Sequential Processes*. Prentice-Hall, Englewood Cliffs, New Jersey, 1985.

[10] R. Khorram. Functional Test Pattern Generation For Intergrated Circuits. In *Proceedings of the International Test Conference*, pages 246–249, 1984.

[11] Zvi Kohavi. *Switching and Finite Automata Theory*. McGraw-Hill, 1978.

[12] Y. H. Levendal and P. R. Menon. Test Generation Algorithms for Computer Hardware Description Languages. *IEEE Transactions on Computers*, 577–588, July 1982.

[13] M.D.O'Neill, D.D.Jani, C.H.Cho, and J.R.Armstrong. BTG: A Behavioral Test Generator. In *Proceedings of the Ninth International Symposium on Computer Hardware Description Languages and their Applications*, pages 347–361, August 1989.

[14] Robin Milner. *A Calculus of Communicating Systems.* Springer-Verlag, 1980. LNCS 92.

[15] G. Saucier and C. Bellon. CADOC: A System For Computer Aided Functional Test. In *Proceedings of the International Test Conference*, pages 680–686, 1984.

[16] Mary Sheeran. Retiming and Slowdown in Ruby. In *Proc. 1988 IFIP WG 10.2 International Working Conference on "The Fusion of Hardware Design and Verification", Univ. of Strathclyde, Glasgow, Scotland*, pages 285–304, July 1988.

[17] Satnam Singh. Application of Non-Standard Interpretation: Testability. In *Proceedings of the IMEC-IFIP Workshop on Applied Formal Methods for Correct VLSI Design, Leuven, Belgium*, pages 236–245, November 1989.

Towards Truly Delay-Insensitive Circuit Realizations of Process Algebras

Geoffrey M. Brown *

Abstract

Delay-insensitive circuits have the desirable property that their correct behavior is completely independent of propagation delays in either the set of primitive building blocks from which they are constructed or in the wires used to interconnect these blocks. While process algebras are widely recognized to provide a good specification language for delay-insensitive circuits, proposed compilation methods have required the use of delay-sensitive components such as "isochronic forks." The use of such delay-sensitive components can introduce subtle errors; we demonstrate that delay sensitive components are unnecessary, and hence pave the way for compilation of process algebras into truly delay insensitive circuits.

Introduction

We show how to compile programs written in a subset of occam [13] into delay insensitive circuits. The language we use does not have program variables; however, it is possible to compile programs written in a language with program variables into one without [12]. The subset of occam which we have chosen is sufficient to illustrate the implementation difficulties which other researchers have resolved by introducing delay-sensitive components. The use of such delay-sensitive components has proven to be error-prone [10].

Our compilation method builds upon results published by other researchers. In particular, there is a great similarity between our method and that used by Brunvand and Sproull [3]. Their work is related to that of Martin and Burns [9, 4]. However, our method does not use delay-sensitive components.

A compilation method for generating purely delay-insensitive circuits could be arrived at by applying known results. Ebergen has shown that circuits described using delay-insensitive traces can be compiled into purely delay-insensitive circuits [6]. Since the semantics of process algebras can be given in terms of traces [2], one would expect to be able to compile a suitably restricted process algebra into a delay-insensitive trace structure and then into a delay-insensitive circuit. However, this approach seems unnecessarily complex. Karjoth [7] has shown how to compile process algebra specifications into finite state machines and Keller has shown how to realize such finite state machines as purely delay-insensitive circuits [8]. This approach, while viable, is unattractive because of the loss of concurrency due to compiling the process algebra specification into a single finite state machine. The attraction of process algebras for circuit specification is that they allow the designer to benefit from the inherent concurrency available in VLSI realizations. Our compilation method provides

---

*School of Electrical Engineering, Cornell University, Ithaca, NY 14853; *gbrown@ee.cornell.edu*
This work supported by NSF Grant CCR-9058180

a direct and efficient path from process algebras to delay-insensitive circuits. Furthermore, it preserves concurrency.

The remainder of this paper is organized as follows. In the next section, we discuss delay-insensitive circuits and present a set of primitive circuit elements. We then present a subset of occam, show how some simple processes can be realized as delay-insensitive circuits and discuss the delay-insensitive implementation of processes which other researchers have realized with delay-sensitive components. We conclude with a discussion of related work.

Delay-Insensitive Circuits

In this section we discuss delay-insensitive circuits and present some primitive circuit elements which we later use to realize programs as circuits. A circuit consists of a set of primitive components connected by wires. Each of the primitive components has a number of input ports and output ports. A wire connects a single input port to a single output port. The unconnected ports of the constituent components of a circuit are the inputs and outputs of the circuit. The components of a circuit communicate by initiating events on their output ports or by absorbing events on their input ports. When two ports are connected by a wire, the initiation and absorption of an event are viewed as a single event identified by the name of the wire on which the event occurs.

There are numerous physical interpretations of events. For the purposes of this paper, we consider an event to be a transition in voltage level (e.g. $0V \to 5V$ or $5V \to 0V$). In physical devices, such voltage transitions take some time to propagate along a wire. Thus, there may be a delay between the initiation of a transition at an output port of a circuit and the arrival of that transition at a corresponding input port. Furthermore, the arrival of a transition at a circuit is assumed to cause some state change in the circuit. For example, in CMOS circuits this state change may consist of charging or discharging capacitors. Hence, even after a transition has arrived at the input of a circuit, it may be some time before it is absorbed, i.e. the effect of the transition on the state of the receiver is fully realized.

We can accurately describe the behavior of a circuit in terms of events, provided that we allow each voltage transition on a wire to be fully absorbed before initiating subsequent transitions on the wire. If we knew the delays in the wires and primitive components accurately, then we could satisfy this constraint by requiring a minimum delay between two transitions on a wire. Unfortunately, such detailed knowledge is implementation dependent and it is generally difficult to determine whether all the timing constraints are satisfied by a given circuit. Thus, we prefer to design circuits whose behavior is independent of the delays in either their constituent components or in the wires connecting these components. Such circuits are called *delay-insensitive*.

In the absence of detailed timing information, the only way in which we can "know" that a transition has been absorbed by a circuit is if the circuit subsequently produces a transition on one of its outputs. However, for an output transition to signal that an input transition has been absorbed, the two transitions must be causally related. Informal reasoning about the causal relationship of such events can lead to subtle design flaws. Thus, we need to be able to specify the input/output behaviors of a circuit which guarantee that all transitions on an input are absorbed before subsequent transitions occur on the input. These behaviors are delay-insensitive.

Udding has developed a formal definition of delay-insensitive behaviors described as sequences of the events of a circuit [16]. Each of these sequences is a *trace* while the set of traces of a circuit is a *trace structure*. While Udding's definition clearly distinguishes delay-insensitive traces from those which are not delay-insensitive, it does not provide a convenient way of establishing whether or not a circuit description is delay-insensitive. Furthermore, the definition of delay-insensitive trace structures does not provide a design methodology. In general we wish to specify circuits and verify that an implementation defined in terms of primitive circuit components satisfies this specification.

A usable design methodology based upon trace structures has been developed by Dill [5]. Dill's methodology provides procedures for checking whether a circuit satisfies its specification and whether a specification is delay-insensitive. Following Dill, we describe all of our primitive circuits and circuit specifications as finite state automata. Furthermore, the circuits presented in subsequent sections have been verified using Dill's tools.

We conclude this section with a description of the primitive circuit elements which are used in the remainder of this paper. We have not attempted to use a minimal set of components, but have chosen a set of components which are sufficient to implement the circuits presented later in this paper. All of the primitive components that we use have been described previously [8, 14, 3], and are physically realizable.

We present each primitive component as a symbol on the left and a specification on the right. Input ports are denoted by an inward arrow on the symbol while output ports are denoted by an outward arrow. The specification of a component consists of a finite-state machine. The initial state of the component is indicated by an arrow into the specification. All legal state transitions are indicated by labeled arcs in the specification. The label of each arc denotes the input or output event associated with the state transition.

The circuits we describe all have the property of *receptiveness*. In particular, all input events are possible in any state. Since some inputs may be incompatible with correct circuit operation, there is a distinguished failure state which results whenever an undesirable input event occurs. The failure state has all input and output events as self-looping transitions. Thus, after an undesired input event, all possible sequences of input and output events are possible. We do not show the transitions to the failure state explicitly because they can be inferred from the circuit descriptions which we give.

The simplest primitive component, besides a wire, is a FORK. For every input transition on its A port, a FORK produces a transition on its two output ports B and C. The FORK provides the only mechanism for duplicating a transition onto two wires.

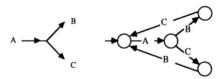

The dual of the FORK is the JOIN. A JOIN produces an output transition after every pair of transitions on its inputs. (JOIN is commonly realized as a *Muller C-element* with one or more inverters to satisfy initial constraints on the voltage levels of wires.)

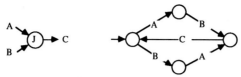

An alternative way to combine two input wires is with a MERGE which produces an output transition for each transition on either input. This component is commonly realized with an *XOR gate*.

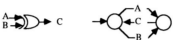

The primary state holding element is the SR. Its state is set by a transition on its S input, reset by a transition on its R input and tested by a transition on its T input. For correct operation, each input transition must by followed by an output transition.

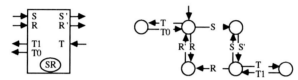

The interface to the SR module illustrates a signaling convention, two-phased handshaking, which is commonly used in implementing delay-insensitive circuits. In particular, each input "request" is matched by a corresponding "acknowledgement." For example, a request transition on the S input is acknowledged by a transition on the S' output. An SR can be used along with a MERGE to implement a CALL. The call module effectively merges two pair of input/output ports (A.req, A.ack and B.req, A.ack) into a single pair (C.req, C.ack).

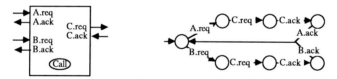

Like Brunvand and Sproull, we use the CALL module to share "procedures" among multiple processes. In addition, we use a variant of the CALL module, the BCALL, which provides the called procedure with the opportunity to return a boolean value with its acknowledgement by choosing among two acknowledgement signals.

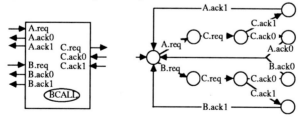

None of the preceding modules can choose between output ports based upon the order of concurrent input transitions. The traditional module for making such a choice is an arbiter (ARB).

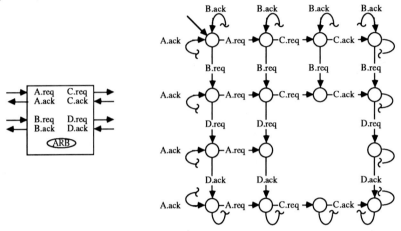

In this paper we make use of an alternative arbitration module, the "arbitrating test and set" (ATS). The "state" of an ATS module is initially 1 and is reset to 0 by a transition on its R input. The current state is tested and set to 1 by a transition on its T input. An ATS can be constructed from an ARB.

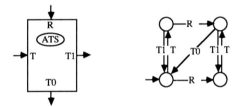

A Language of Communicating Processes

In this section we present a simple language of communicating processes and show how some primitive processes can be implemented as delay-insensitive circuits. The realization of processes which introduce implementation problems is postponed to the next section. The language description presented in this section closely follows that of Barrett [1], while the implementations of primitive processes (with the exception of the alternative and recursive constructs) were presented previously by Brunvand and Sproull [3].

Our language is a subset of occam [13] from which program variables and hence assignment, conditionals, and value-passing communication have been excluded. Furthermore, we do not consider process priorities. This subset is sufficient to illustrate the implementation difficulties which have led previous researchers to use delay-sensitive components.

The syntax of our language does not follow that of occam. In the following BNF-style syntax description, c is drawn from a set of channel identifiers CID and p is drawn from a set of process identifiers *PID*.

$$c \quad \in \quad CID$$
$$p \quad \in \quad PID$$

$$(\text{process}) \quad P \quad ::= \quad \texttt{stop} \mid \texttt{skip} \mid P_1; P_2 \mid P_1 \,\texttt{par}\, P_2$$
$$\mid \quad c! \to P \mid \texttt{alt}\, G \mid p \mid \mu p.P$$

$$(\text{guardP}) \quad G \quad ::= \quad c? \to P \mid G_1 [\!] G_2$$

Informally, the process terms stand for the following processes:

  stop   is the deadlocked process.

  skip   is a process which simply terminates.

  $P_1; P_2$ is the sequential composition of P_1 and P_2.

  $P_1 \,\texttt{par}\, P_2$ is the concurrent composition of P_1 and P_2.

  $c! \to P$ is a process which is ready to output along channel c and
            behaves like P after the output has been discharged.

  alt G is an arbitration. G can be either $c? \to P$ or $G_1 [\!] G_2$. In the
         first case the process is prepared to input along c and then
         behave like P. Otherwise a symmetric choice is made between
         some action on either side of the operator $[\!]$.

  $\mu p.P$ is the general recursive construction. A free p in the body P,
          behaves just like the whole process.

Legal occam programs must satisfy some further syntactic restrictions. In particular, the set of input channels used by two concurrently executed processes must be disjoint; similarly for output channels. Finally, since we intend that the processes will be realized with fixed hardware resources, we restrict recursion to ensure that any new processes which will be set in execution by the body of the recursion will have terminated when a further recursive call is reached. Barrett shows that this can be accomplished by not allowing "free" p's in parallel processes or in the first of a pair of sequential processes.

Before a program can be realized as hardware, it must first be compiled into a set of primitive processes. For example, the process (A! $\to$ A!) is compiled into two primitive processes which output to channel A. Similarly, programs which have more that one command to input from a channel are compiled into multiple processes which input from a common channel. Thus, most interesting programs are compiled into a set of processes which share channels.

In following, we present our primitive processes. Because most of the implementation difficulties arise from sharing communication channels among the primitive processes, we only discuss the implementation of private communication channels in this section. A private channel is accessed by at most one primitive process which inputs and at most one primitive process which outputs. In the next section we discuss the implementation of shared communication channels.

126

Following [3] we view the circuit realization of a process as a black box which begins execution when it absorbs a transition on its **start** port and indicates that it has terminated by initiating a transition on its **done** port.

The deadlock process **stop** is implemented with a broken wire.

start —— —— done

The process **skip** is implemented with a wire.

start ———— done

The sequential composition of two processes, $(P_1 \, ; P_2)$, is realized by connecting the **done** port of P_1 to the **start** port of P_2.

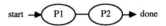

Notice that

$$(\text{skip}; \text{skip}) \approx \text{skip}$$

where $\approx$ is informally defined as "is behaviorally equivalent to." Similarly,

$$(\text{skip}; \text{stop}) \approx \text{stop}$$

The parallel composition of two processes $(P_1 \, \text{par} \, P_2)$ is implemented by tying the **start** ports of P_1 and P_2 together with a **FORK** element and combining the **done** ports P_1 and P_2 with a **JOIN** element.

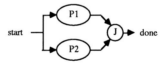

Notice that

$$(\text{skip} \, \text{par} \, \text{skip}) \approx \text{skip}$$

and

$$(\text{stop} \, \text{par} \, \text{skip}) \approx \text{stop}$$

Recursive processes are implemented by replacing each free p by a merge connection to the **start** port of the whole process. For example, $(\mu \, p. p_0 ; p)$ is implemented as

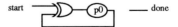

(Since this example is non-terminating, no connection is made to done.) Notice that

$$(\mu\, p.\texttt{skip}; p) \approx \texttt{stop}$$

A communication channel is realized as a pair of wires connecting an input process to an output process. For example, communication channel **A** is implemented by the wires **A.req** and **A.ack**. An output process indicates that it is ready to communicate over channel **A** by initiating a transition on **A.req**. The corresponding input process completes the communication event by initiating a transition on **A.ack**. For example, the primitive process (**A!**) is realized as

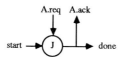

while (**alt A?** → **skip**) is implemented as

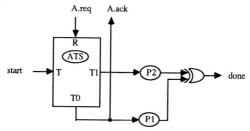

Notice that

$$(\texttt{A! par (alt A?} \rightarrow \texttt{skip)}) \approx \texttt{skip}$$

Implementing a general arbitration command is somewhat more complicated. The arbitration command must "test" its input channels until it detects that one is "ready." We implement this as a polling loop with a ring of "arbitrating test and set" components (**ATS**). For example, the process

$$(\texttt{alt A1?} \rightarrow P_1 \,[\!]\, \texttt{A2?} \rightarrow P_2)$$

is realized by the circuit illustrated in Figure 1. Recall that a transition on input port **R** of an **ATS** resets the state to 0 (initially the state is 1), while a transition on input port **T** tests the current state, produces an output transition on port **T0** (**T1**) if the state was 0 (1), and sets the state to 1. Thus, an input transition on port **start** will cause the circuit to repeatedly poll its inputs until a transition occurs on either **A1.req** or **A2.req**. After an input transition occurs on **A1.req** (**A2.req**) transitions will be initiated on **A1.ack** (**A2.ack**) and on the **start** port of process P_1 (P_2).

Our implementation of the general arbitration command can be understood in terms of recursion and a more primitive form of arbitration. Consider the following circuit constructed from an **ATS** module.

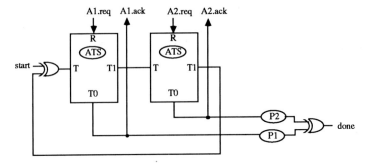

Figure 1: Implementation of an Arbitration Process

This circuit realizes the program

$$(\texttt{alt A?} \to \texttt{P}_1 \ [\!]\ \tau \to \texttt{P}_2)$$

where τ is the "silent" or internal command commonly included in process algebras. Thus, the circuit in Figure 1 implements

$$\mu\,\texttt{x.(alt A1?} \to \texttt{P}_1 \ [\!]\ \tau \to (\texttt{alt A2?} \to \texttt{P}_2 \ [\!]\ \tau \to \texttt{x}))$$

which is behaviorally equivalent to

$$(\texttt{alt A1?} \to \texttt{P}_1 \ [\!]\ \texttt{A2?} \to \texttt{P}_2)$$

The polling ring in Figure 1 is a "busy" implementation of the arbitration command. Although "static" implementations are possible, the "busy" implementation is more easily generalized to an arbitration command with n guards.

Shared Communication Channels

The circuit realizations of communicating processes presented in the preceding section are viable only when communication channels are not shared by primitive processes. In this section we show how to implement delay-insensitive circuits which allow processes to share communication channels. Although the problem has previously been solved for processes which share an output channel, the development of a delay-insensitive circuit which allows processes to share an input channel is novel. We begin by presenting a known implementation for shared output channels.

The basic approach to sharing an output channel among two processes is to introduce two new private channels, one for each process, and a CALL module which connects the new private channels with the original shared channel. The CALL module serves to manage access by the processes to the shared channel. For example, given two processes P:(C!) and Q:(C!), we implement the shared channel with a CALL.

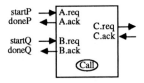

Multiple 2-way `call` modules can be combined to create an n-way `CALL` as illustrated by the following 3-way `CALL`.

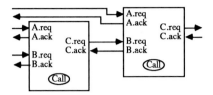

The situation for processes sharing an input channel is analogous. In the preceding section we developed a general arbitration command using the `ATS` module to test the state of a channel. This `ATS` interface can be shared among multiple processes using the `BCALL` module. For example, given two processes

$$P : (\text{alt}\, D? \rightarrow ...)$$

and

$$Q : (\text{alt}\, D? \rightarrow ...)$$

we implement the shared channel as follows.

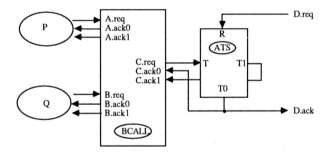

As with the `CALL` module, the 2-way `BCALL` can be used to implement an n-way `BCALL`

Our use of `CALL` and `BCALL` modules is only valid under the assumption that two processes which share an input or an output channel are never concurrently active. This assumption is guaranteed by the syntactic restrictions we have place on legal occam programs. Alternatively, the `CALL` and `BCALL` modules could be augmented with arbiters to allow concurrent access to an input or output channel.

Discussion

The implementation method presented in this paper builds largely upon by previous work by Sutherland, Sproull, Brunvand, and Martin [14, 9, 10, 3]. However, we were motivated by a single goal – to demonstrate that it is possible to build interesting and purely delay insensitive circuits using only a small set of basic building blocks. It is true, that our building blocks cannot be implemented without some knowledge of circuit delays; however, this delay-based reasoning can be strictly isolated. Thus, it is possible to use develop a compiler which uses a cell library and has no need to reason about circuit delays. Our predecessors have used similar sets of building blocks but have also compromised delay-insensitivity by using isochronic forks. As Martin has found, the use of such isochronic forks is dangerous [10]:

> The malfunctioning of the 1.6 μm chip for certain values of the instruction memory delay is caused by an implementation of an isochronic fork that does not always fulfill the delay requirement because of the unusually large capacitance of the fork node and because of the large discrepancies in the switching thresholds of the gates to which the fork is connected.

Is the implementation technique presented complete ? We have implemented a simple compiler in ML which translates occam programs into delay-insensitive circuits. The output of the compiler is a netlist of our basic building blocks.

Have we paid a price in terms of the complexity of the resulting circuits ? In order to address the question of feasibility, we have limited our attention to programs which do not pass values. Within this domain we believe our circuits are relatively efficient. One of the more expensive building blocks in delay-insensitive circuits is the arbiter. Our circuits do not use more arbiters than are strictly necessary (at most one per channel). Although it is possible to translate programs which pass values into ones which do not, this will lead to very inefficient circuits. Thus, our circuits need to be extended to include value passing. For boolean values this is relatively easy to accomplish; however, purely delay-insensitive circuits for arithmetic operations on integers are likely to be inefficient.

We believe that circuits to manipulate data will need to compromise delay-insensitivity. An interesting approach is the use of "micropipelines" as suggested by Sutherland and Sproull [14, 15] (similar work has been done by Meng et. al. [11]. By partitioning a circuit into a purely delay-insensitive controller and an asynchronous but delay-sensitive datapath a reasonable compromise between purity and efficiency may be achieved. In particular, the layout of a pipelined data path lends itself naturally to calculating worst case delays and thus can be implemented without introducing timing errors.

Acknowledgements

I gratefully acknowledge the helpful comments of Miriam Leeser, Bard Bloom, Jan Tijmen Udding, Mark Josephs, and the anonymous referees.

References

[1] Geoff Barrett. *The Semantics and Implementation of occam.* PhD thesis, Oxford University, 1988.

[2] S. D. Brookes, C. A. R. Hoare, and A. W. Roscoe. A theory of communicating sequential processes. *Journal of the Association for Computing Machinery*, 31(3):560–599, July 1984.

[3] E. Brunvand and R. F. Sproull. Translating concurrent communicating programs into delay-insensitive circuits. Technical Report CMU-CS-89-126, Carnegie-Mellon University, 1989.

[4] Steven M. Burns and Alain J. Martin. Syntax-directed translation of concurrent programs into self-timed circuits. In *Advanced Research in VLSI: Proceedings of the 5th MIT Conference*, pages 35–50, 1988.

[5] D. L. Dill. *Trace Theory for Automatic Hierarchical Verification of Speed-Independent Circuits.* MIT Press, 1989.

[6] Jo C. Ebergen. *Translating Programs into Delay-Insensitive Circuits.* PhD thesis, University of Eindhoven, 1987.

[7] Gunter Karjoth. Implementing process algebra specifications by state machines. In *Eighth International Symposium on Protocol Specification, Testing, and Verification*, 1988.

[8] Robert M. Keller. Towards a theory of universal speed-independent modules. *IEEE Transactions on Computers*, C-23(1):21–33, January 1974.

[9] Alain J. Martin. Compiling communicating processes into delay-insensitive VLSI circuits. *Distributed Computing*, 1:226–234, 1986.

[10] Alain J. Martin. The design of a delay-insensitive microprocessor: An example of circuit synthesis by program transformation. In *Hardware Specification, Verification and Synthesis: Mathematical Aspects*, volume 408 of *Lecture Notes in Computer Science*. Springer-Verlag, 1989.

[11] T. H.-Y. Meng, R. W. Brodersen, and D. G. Messerschmitt. Authomatic synthesis of asynchronous circuits from high-level specifications. 1988.

[12] R. Milner. *Communication and Concurrency.* Prentice Hall, 1989.

[13] D. Pountain and D. May. *A Tutorial Introduction to OCCAM Programming.* Inmos, 1987.

[14] Robert Sproull and Ivan E. Sutherland. *Asynchronous Systems.* Sutherland, Sproull & Associates, 1986.

[15] Ivan E. Sutherland. Micropiplines. *Communications of the ACM*, 32(6):720–738, June 1989.

[16] Jan Tijmen Udding. A formal model for defining and classifying delay-insensitive circuits and systems. *Distributed Computing*, 1:197–204, 1986.

The Design of a Delay-Insensitive Stack

Mark B. Josephs[*]   Jan Tijmen Udding[†]

Abstract

A novel process algebra is introduced and, as a case study, applied to the design of a delay-insensitive stack. In the algebra, expressions specify delay-insensitive circuits in terms of voltage-level transitions on wires. The approach appears to have several advantages over traditional state-graph and production-rule based methods. The wealth of algebraic laws makes it possible to specify circuits concisely and facilitates the actual designs. Individual components can be composed into circuits in which signals along internal wires are hidden from the environment.

Introduction

A circuit is connected to its environment by a number of wires. If the circuit functions correctly irrespective of the propagation delays in these wires, the circuit is called *delay-insensitive*. Delay-insensitive circuits are attractive because they can be designed in a modular way; indeed no timing constraints have to be satisfied in connecting such circuits together. As a result of the latest Turing Award Lecture [16], the design of delay-insensitive circuits has drawn renewed interest. Delay-insensitive circuit design, however, introduces a phenomenon absent in synchronous circuit design: one has to consider situations in which a signal (voltage-level transition) has been transmitted at one end of a wire but not yet received at the other end.

We have developed an algebraic notation in which we can concisely express delay-insensitive circuit specifications, including obligations to be met by the environment. Moreover, the above mentioned phenomenon of a signal being on its way is dealt with entirely within the algebra; the parallel composition of components remains straightforward. A state-machine implementation is often suggested by the form of our algebraic expressions. This is well-illustrated by the case study, the design of a stack, presented in this paper.

The algebra is based upon Hoare's CSP notation [7]. It adapts the theory of asynchronous processes [8, 9] to the special case of delay-insensitive circuits. The possibilities of *transmission interference* and *computation interference*, characterized by Udding [17, 18], are faithfully modeled in the algebra; the designer is able to reason about these errors, and so avoid them. Underpinning the algebra is a denotational semantics similar to those given in [2, 9]; the semantics is compatible with the failures-divergences model of CSP [1, 7].

Our approach complements that taken by Martin [12, 13] to the design of delay-insensitive circuits. Martin's approach, however, is more general in that he makes use of components

---

[*]Programming Research Group, Oxford University Computing Laboratory, 11 Keble Road, Oxford OX1 3QD, U.K., E-mail: mark%prg.oxford.ac.uk@nss.cs.ucl.ac.uk

[†]Department of Computer Science, Washington University, Campus Box 1045, St. Louis, MO 63130, U.S.A., E-mail: jtu@cs.wustl.edu

that are not delay-insensitive, namely his *isochronic forks*. We, on the other hand, do not make any assumptions on relative delays when connecting components.

The remainder of this paper provides an introduction to the constructs of the algebra. We give here only those laws necessary to understand the subsequent design of a delay-insensitive stack. For a comprehensive discussion of the algebra and all its laws the reader is referred to [10]. We verify the correctness of our design using the algebra. This is in contrast to verification at a semantics level, as advocated by Dill [3, 4]. Calculations in the delay-insensitive algebra are humanly feasible, though arduous. Tools for algebraic transformation might be useful, but our approach seems in any case to avoid a state explosion.

Basic Notions and Operators

A process is a mathematical model at a certain level of abstraction of the way in which a delay-insensitive circuit interacts with its environment. Typical names for processes are P and Q. A circuit receives signals from its environment on its input wires and sends signals to its environment on its output wires. Thus with each process are associated an alphabet of input wires and an alphabet of output wires. These alphabets are finite and disjoint. Typical names for input wires are a and b; typical names for output wires are c and d. The time taken by a signal to traverse a wire is indeterminate.

In the remainder of this section and the next, we consider processes with a particular alphabet I of input wires and a particular alphabet O of output wires.

The process P is considered to be "just as good" as the process Q ($P \sqsupseteq Q$) if no environment, which is simply another process, can when interacting with P determine that it is not interacting with Q. (This is the refinement ordering of CSP [1, 7], also known as the *must* ordering [6].) Two processes are considered to be equal when they are just as good as each other.

The refinement ordering is intimately connected with nondeterministic choice. The process $P \sqcap Q$ is allowed to behave either as P or as Q. It reflects the designer's freedom to implement such a process by either P or Q. (Thus $\sqcap$ is obviously commutative, associative and idempotent.) Now $P \sqcap Q = Q$ exactly when $P \sqsupseteq Q$.

A wire cannot accommodate two signals at the same time; they might interfere with one another in an undesirable way. This and any other error are modeled by the process $\bot$ (Bottom or Chaos). The environment must ensure that a process never gets into such a state. The process $\bot$ is considered to be so undesirable that any other process must be an improvement on it:

Law 0. $P \sqsupseteq \bot$

It follows that $\sqcap$ has $\bot$ as a null element.

We shall mostly be concerned with recursively-defined processes. The meaning of the recursion $\mu X.F(X)$ is the least fixpoint of F. Its successive approximations are $\bot$, $F(\bot)$, $F(F(\bot))$, *etc.* All the operators that we shall use to define processes are continuous (and therefore monotonic); all except for recursion are distributive (with respect to nondeterministic choice).

In earlier approaches to an algebra for delay-insensitive circuits, *cf.* [17, 2, 5], a particular input signal is allowed only when this is explicitly indicated, and otherwise is assumed to lead to interference. This is in contrast with the algebra presented here: an input need not result in interference even though the possibility of such an input has not been made explicit in the algebraic expression. This follows the approach taken in [9] and is more convenient in algebraic manipulation, even though at first it may appear less natural.

Thus we write $a?; P$ to denote a process that must wait for a signal to arrive on $a \in I$ before it can behave like P. It is quite permissible for the environment to send a signal along any other input wire b. Such a signal is ignored at least until a signal is sent along a (or a second signal is sent along b causing interference).

A process that waits for input on a and then for input on b before being able to do anything is actually just waiting for inputs on both a and b, their order being immaterial:

Law 1. $a?; b?; P = b?; a?; P$

Complementary to input-prefixing $a?; P$ is output-prefixing $c!; P$, where $c \in O$. This is a process that outputs on c and then behaves like P. The environment may send a signal on any input wire even before it receives the signal on c; whether or not it can do so safely depends on P.

Two outputs by a process on the same wire, one after the other, is unsafe because of the danger of the two signals interfering with one another before they reach the environment. Also, since any output of a process may arrive at the environment an arbitrary time later, the order in which outputs are sent is immaterial. Therefore, we have the following two laws:

Law 2. $c!; c!; P = \bot$

Law 3. $c!; d!; P = d!; c!; P$

Finally, as in CSP, prefixing is distributive (with respect to nondeterministic choice). For both input and output-prefixing we have the law

Law 4. $x; (P \sqcap Q) = (x; P) \sqcap (x; Q)$

Example 0   We are now in a position to specify a number of elementary delay-insensitive components, *viz.* the Wire, the Fork, and the C-element.

Consider a circuit with one input wire a and one output wire c. In response to each signal on a, the circuit should produce a signal on c. The precise behavior of this circuit is given by the following algebraic expression:

$$\mu X.\ a?; c!; X$$

which we shall refer to as the process W because it can be readily implemented by a wire. Now unfolding the recursion, we have that $W = a?; c!; W$. As in CSP, this equation itself uniquely defines W because its right hand side is guarded.

Next consider the process, with one input wire a and two output wires c and d, defined by the equation $F = a?; c!; d!; F$. This models the behavior of a fork.

Finally, the Muller C-element repeatedly waits for inputs on wires a and b before outputting on c. It is defined by $C = a?; b?; c!; C$.

When we introduce the *after* operator in the next section, it will become clear that the above expressions do indeed correctly specify the components.   ■

A more general form of input-prefixing is input-guarded choice. Such a choice allows a process to take different actions depending upon the input received. The choice is made between a number of alternatives of the form $a? \rightarrow P$. For S a finite set of alternatives, the guarded choice $[S]$ selects one of them. An alternative $a? \rightarrow P$ can be selected only if a signal has been received on a. The choice cannot be postponed indefinitely once one or more alternatives become selectable.

Choice with only one alternative is no real choice at all:

Law 5. $[a? \rightarrow P] = a?; P$

The environment cannot safely send a second signal along an input wire until the first signal has been acknowledged. Thus the result of sending two signals on a to the process $a?; a?; P$ is $\perp$ rather than P. The process is as useless as a choice with no alternative:

Law 6. $a?; a?; P = [\,]$

If two alternatives are guarded on a, then either may be chosen after input has been supplied on a. Indeed, the designer has the freedom to implement only one of the two. This is captured in the following law, where the symbol $\square$ separates the various alternatives:

Law 7. $\quad [a? \rightarrow P \;\square\; a? \rightarrow Q \;\square\; S]$
$= [a? \rightarrow (P \sqcap Q) \;\square\; S]$
$= [a? \rightarrow P \;\square\; S] \sqcap [a? \rightarrow Q \;\square\; S]$

Until a process acknowledges receipt of an input signal, a second signal on the same wire can result in interference. So, for S_0 and S_1 sets of alternatives, we have

Law 8. $[a? \rightarrow [S_0] \;\square\; S_1] = [a? \rightarrow [a? \rightarrow \perp \;\square\; S_0] \;\square\; S_1]$

Indeed, if it is unsafe for the environment to send a signal along a particular input wire, it remains unsafe at least until an output has been received. Therefore, we also have the following absorption law.

Law 9. $[a? \rightarrow \perp \;\square\; b? \rightarrow [a? \rightarrow P \;\square\; S_0] \;\square\; S_1] = [a? \rightarrow \perp \;\square\; b? \rightarrow [S_0] \;\square\; S_1]$

Example 1   With the input-guarded choice we can model somewhat more interesting delay-insensitive components, such as the Merge and the Decision-Wait element.
The Merge is a circuit with two input wires a and b and one output wire c. In response to a signal on either a or b, it will output on c:

$M = [a? \rightarrow c!; M \;\square\; b? \rightarrow c!; M]$

We shall discover, in the next section, that this definition implies that it is unsafe for the environment to supply input on both a and b before receiving an output on c.
Finally, we can define the Decision-Wait element (2×1 in this case). It expects one input change in its row and one input change in its column. It produces as output the single entry which is indicated by the two changing inputs – there are two entries in this case:

$DW = [\; r0? \rightarrow [r1? \rightarrow \perp \;\square\; c? \rightarrow e0!; DW]$
$\square\; r1? \rightarrow [r0? \rightarrow \perp \;\square\; c? \rightarrow e1!; DW]\,]$

(A C-element can be viewed as a 1×1 Decision-Wait element.) $\qquad\blacksquare$

It quite often happens that several alternatives in a guarded choice differ only in their guards. (Usually, these alternatives are of the form $a? \rightarrow \perp$.) We introduce the notation $[S \text{ else } P]$ as a shorthand for the guarded choice consisting of the alternatives of S, together with an alternative $a? \rightarrow P$ for each $a \in I$ which does not occur as one of S's guards.

More Advanced Constructs

In the last section we provided enough operators to allow us to specify many interesting delay-insensitive components from which larger circuits might be constructed. To better understand these specifications we need to be able to determine how a circuit will behave after some signals have been exchanged with its environment. Before we can do this, it turns out that we need a more general form of guarded choice which allows for *skip* guards as well as input guards.

Recall that a guarded choice $[S]$ consists of a set S of alternatives of the form $a? \rightarrow P$. We shall now allow S to include also alternatives of the form $skip \rightarrow P$. Such an alternative can be selected whether or not any input is supplied. (As in CSP, if no input is supplied, it must eventually be selected.)

The laws of the last section remain valid, but in addition we have several laws involving *skip* guards. (These are also laws in occam [15].) As before, a choice with one alternative is no real choice at all:

Law 10. $[skip \rightarrow P] = P$

Nondeterministic choice can be regarded as a special case of guarded choice:

Law 11. $[skip \rightarrow P \ \Box \ skip \rightarrow Q] = P \sqcap Q$

The selection of a *skip*-guarded alternative is an internal (unobservable) action of a process. This gives rise to the following three laws. In the first, a nondeterministic choice arises after input has been supplied on a because the signal may arrive before the selection of a *skip*-guarded alternative:

Law 12. $\quad [a? \rightarrow P \ \Box \ skip \rightarrow [a? \rightarrow Q \ \Box \ S_0] \ \Box \ S_1]$
$\quad = \ [skip \rightarrow [a? \rightarrow (P \sqcap Q) \ \Box \ S_0] \ \Box \ S_1]$

The second law states that a nested *skip*-guarded alternative can be selected in preference to any other alternative:

Law 13. $[skip \rightarrow [skip \rightarrow P \ \Box \ S_0] \ \Box \ S_1] = [skip \rightarrow P \ \Box \ S_0 \ \Box \ S_1]$

The third law is a convexity property of guarded choice:

Law 14. $[skip \rightarrow [S_0] \ \Box \ skip \rightarrow [S_0 \ \Box \ S_1] \ \Box \ S_2] = [skip \rightarrow [S_0] \ \Box \ S_1 \ \Box \ S_2]$

Example 2 Two *skip*-guarded alternatives can be combined together:

$\quad [skip \rightarrow P \ \Box \ skip \rightarrow Q \ \Box \ S]$
$= \quad \{$ nesting the *skip* guards using Law 13. $\}$
$\quad [skip \rightarrow [skip \rightarrow P \ \Box \ skip \rightarrow Q] \ \Box \ S]$
$= \quad \{ \sqcap$ as guarded choice, Law 11. $\}$
$\quad [skip \rightarrow (P \sqcap Q) \ \Box \ S]$

■

Example 3 A *skip*-guarded alternative can always be chosen, and so no other alternative need be offered, *i.e.*, $P \sqsupseteq [skip \rightarrow P \ \Box \ S]$.

$P \sqcap [skip \rightarrow P \,\square\, S]$

= $\{\, \sqcap$ as guarded choice, Law 11. $\}$

$[skip \rightarrow P \,\square\, skip \rightarrow [skip \rightarrow P \,\square\, S]\,]$

= $\{\,$ unnesting the $skip$ guards, Law 13. $\}$

$[skip \rightarrow P \,\square\, S]$

In particular, $[skip \rightarrow \perp \,\square\, S] = \perp$ by Law 0.   ∎

Example 4   As another example of interference between two consecutive outputs on a wire, we have

$c!; [skip \rightarrow c!; P \,\square\, S]$

$\sqsubseteq$ $\{\,$ Example 3 and monotonicity of prefixing $\}$

$c!; c!; P$

= $\{\,$ interference between outputs, Law 2. $\}$

$\perp$

which means that $c!; [skip \rightarrow c!; P \,\square\, S] = \perp$, by Law 0.   ∎

We are now able to define how a process behaves after the environment has sent input to it or received output from it. In this paper we consider only the after-input case.

The process $P/a?$ behaves like P after its environment has sent it a signal on $a \in I$. Notice that this does not mean that P has received this input yet; the signal may still be on its way. Indeed it is impossible to tell whether P has received the signal until some acknowledging signal has been received from P.

The first two laws for after-input are concerned with undesirable behavior. A process which has entered an unsafe state remains unsafe. Also, sending two signals in a row on an input wire may cause interference and is therefore unsafe.

Law 15. $\perp/a? = \perp$

Law 16. $P/a?/a? = \perp$

The order in which signals are sent does not determine the order in which they are received, and so

Law 17. $P/a?/b? = P/b?/a?$

An output-prefixed process can do nothing but output, even when sent input:

Law 18. $(c!; P)/a? = c!; (P/a?)$

After-input (on a) distributes through the alternatives in a guarded choice, except for those alternatives guarded on a. Those become $skip$-guarded. Furthermore, an extra alternative is required to indicate that interference can result after a second input on a.

Law 19. $[S]/a? = [a? \rightarrow \perp \,\square\, S']$,
       where S' is formed by substituting for each alternative $A \in S$ the new alternative $A/a?$, defined by

138

$$(skip \to P)/a? = skip \to (P/a?)$$
$$(a? \to P)/a? = skip \to P$$
$$(b? \to P)/a? = b? \to (P/a?), \text{ for } b \neq a.$$

As a consequence of Laws 5. and 19., we have that

$$(a?; P)/a? = [a? \to \perp \square \ skip \to P]$$

and

$$(b?; P)/a? = [a? \to \perp \square \ b? \to (P/a?)].$$

Example 5   When $\perp$ is guarded on a, the environment must not supply input on a.

$[a? \to \perp \square \ S]/a?$
= { after through guarded choice, Law 19.,
$\quad\quad\quad S'$ being some set of alternatives derived from S }
$[a? \to \perp \square \ skip \to \perp \square \ S']$
= { unguarded $\perp$, Example 3 }
$\perp$

∎

The following law allows us to expand the set of alternatives in a guarded choice to make the behavior after a particular input explicit:

Law 20. $[S] = [a? \to [S]/a? \square \ S]$

Example 6   Here is a case in which $skip$ can be eliminated:

$[a? \to \perp \square \ skip \to [S]]$
= { adding an a-guarded alternative with Law 20. }
$[a? \to \perp \square \ skip \to [a? \to ([S]/a?) \square \ S]]$
= { postponing alternative until after $skip$, Law 12. }
$[skip \to [a? \to (([S]/a?) \sqcap \perp) \square \ S]]$
= { one choice is no choice and $\perp$ is null element of $\sqcap$ }
$[a? \to \perp \square \ S]$

∎

Example 7   Now we can determine how components such as the C-element and the Merge behave after they have interacted with their environment. For the C-element we derive

$(a?; b?; c!; C)/a?$
= { after through input-prefixing, corollary to Law 19. }
$[a? \to \perp \square \ skip \to b?; c!; C]$
= { one choice is no choice and eliminating $skip$ as in Example 6 }
$[a? \to \perp \square \ b? \to c!; C]$

Hence, a C-element that has been sent one input on a must not be sent another (until a signal on c has been received). Before it will output on c, however, it has to input on b. This is exactly how we want a C-element to behave after being sent a signal on a. We can now also compute $C/a?/b?$. A little calculation shows that the result is $[a? \rightarrow \bot \ \Box \ b? \rightarrow \bot \ \Box \ skip \rightarrow c!; C]$, as desired. Had we defined after-output as well, we could have shown that $C = C/a?/b?/c!$.

A more interesting example of the possibility of interference is seen in the specification of Merge. Once a signal has been sent on either input wire, both input wires become unsafe to use. In this case we compute

$$M/a?$$

$$= \quad \{ \text{ definition of } M \ \}$$

$$[a? \rightarrow c!; M \ \Box \ b? \rightarrow c!; M]/a?$$

$$= \quad \{ \text{ after through choice and prefixing, Laws 18. and 19. } \}$$

$$[a? \rightarrow \bot \ \Box \ skip \rightarrow c!; M \ \Box \ b? \rightarrow c!; (M/a?)]$$

$$= \quad \{ \ M/a? \text{ is of the form } [skip \rightarrow c!; P \ \Box \ S], \text{ Example 4 } \}$$

$$[a? \rightarrow \bot \ \Box \ b? \rightarrow \bot \ \Box \ skip \rightarrow c!; M]$$

This shows that signals on both a and b should be withheld until the Merge outputs on c.

■

Composition

In this section we define a parallel composition operator. With it we can determine the overall behavior of a circuit from the individual behavior of its components. It is understood that if the output wire of one component has the same name as the input wire of another, then these wires are supposed to be joined together; any signals transmitted along such a connection are hidden from the environment. The parallel composition operator is fundamental to a hierarchical approach to circuit design. It permits an initial specification to be decomposed into a number of components operating in parallel, and each of these components can be designed independently of the rest.

The simplicity of the laws enjoyed by parallel composition is one of the main attractions of our algebra. Indeed, in [17] certain restrictions had to be placed on processes before their composition could even be considered; and in [2] the fixed-point definition of parallel composition was rather unwieldy.

Parallel composition is denoted by the infix binary operator $\|$. All the operators we have met so far do not affect the input and output alphabets of their operands; so, for example, in the nondeterministic choice $P \sqcap Q$, we insist that the input alphabet of P is the same as that of Q, and declare that it is the same as that of $P \sqcap Q$. In the parallel composition $P \| Q$, however, the input alphabet of P should be disjoint from that of Q; likewise, the output alphabet of P should be disjoint from that of Q. (These rules prohibit fan-in and fan-out of wires; the explicit use of Merges and Forks is required.) The input alphabet of $P \| Q$ then consists of those input wires of each process P and Q which are not output wires of the other. Similarly, the output alphabet of $P \| Q$ consists of those output wires of each process which are not input wires of the other.

Parallel composition is commutative. It is also associative, provided we ensure that a wire named in the alphabets of any two processes being composed is not in the alphabets of a third process. If one process in a parallel composition is in an undesirable state, then the overall state is undesirable:

Law 21. $P \parallel \perp = \perp$

When an output-prefixed process $c!; P$ is composed with another process Q, the output is transmitted along c. Depending on whether or not c is in the input alphabet of Q, the signal on c is sent to Q or to the environment:

Law 22. $(c!; P) \parallel Q = \begin{cases} P \parallel (Q/c?) & \text{if } c \text{ is in the input alphabet of } Q \\ c!; (P \parallel Q) & \text{otherwise} \end{cases}$

It remains only to consider parallel composition of guarded choices. The following law specifies the alternatives in the resulting guarded choice.

Law 23. $[S_0] \parallel [S_1] = [S]$,

where S is formed from the alternatives in S_0 and S_1 in the following way. For each alternative in S_0 of the form $skip \rightarrow P$, we have $skip \rightarrow (P \parallel [S_1])$ in S. For each alternative in S_0 of the form $a? \rightarrow P$ with a not in the output alphabet of $[S_1]$, we have $a? \rightarrow (P \parallel [S_1])$ in S. The alternatives in S_1 contribute to the alternatives in S in a similar way.

Example 8   If one component is able to send a signal that it is unsafe for the other to receive, then their parallel composition is $\perp$.

$(a!; P) \parallel [a? \rightarrow \perp \square S]$

$=$ { internal communication on a, Law 22. }

$P \parallel [a? \rightarrow \perp \square S]/a?$

$=$ { Example 5 and $\perp$ null element of parallel composition, Law 21. }

$\perp$

∎

Example 9   We compute a simple composition in this example. Although the result of the composition is well-known, it has never previously been possible to give a straightforward algebraic derivation.

We compose a "one-hot" C-element and a Fork in the following way. The C-element is specified by $C = a?; b?; c!; C$ and the Fork by $F = c?; a!; d!; F$. This is a circuit involving feedback.

$C/a? \parallel F$

$=$ { Example 7 and definition of F }

$[a? \rightarrow \perp \square b? \rightarrow c!; C] \parallel (c?; a!; d!; F)$

$=$ { one choice is no choice and parallel composition through guarded choice, using that a and c are internal }

$b?; ((c!; C) \parallel (c?; a!; d!; F))$

$=$ { internal communication on c }

$b?; (C \parallel (c?; a!; d!; F)/c?)$

= { definition of C and after through prefixing }

$b?; ((a?; b?; c!; C) \parallel [c? \rightarrow \perp \; \square \; skip \rightarrow a!; d!; F])$

= { one choice is no choice, parallel composition through guarded choice, using that a and c are internal, and definition of C }

$b?; [skip \rightarrow (C \parallel (a!; d!; F))]$

= { one choice is no choice, internal communication on a and external communication on d }

$b?; d!; (C/a? \parallel F)$

By uniqueness of guarded recursion, this combination of C-element and Fork behaves just like a wire. Although the Fork signals on a and d "in parallel", this did not lead to a doubling of the number of states which we had to analyze. We could deal with a entirely before d was pulled out of the parallel composition. This technique can be more generally applied and that is why these algebraic manipulations do not lead to a state explosion. ∎

A Case Study: the Stack

We shall now put the constructs and algebraic laws of the previous sections to use in a case study, in which we investigate delay-insensitive stacks of finite capacity. We first show how such stacks can be specified and then go on to suggest a decomposition into a number of identical stack elements. We verify formally that the composition of a stack element with a stack of capacity N yields a stack of capacity $N + 2$. We also argue that these stacks have constant response time: the time required for a stack to respond to a push or a pop does not depend upon the current size of the stack or its capacity. Finally, from the algebraic expression for the stack element we derive its delay-insensitive implementation as a state-machine, using a 2×3 Decision-Wait element and several Forks and Merges.

To keep this presentation simple, we have not modeled the actual storage of values in the stack. Indeed it is common practice in asynchronous circuit design to separate the control path from the data path. Actually, we can easily extend the algebra so as to incorporate data. The method is briefly sketched at the end of this section. A stack element designed to meet a full specification, incorporating the storage and transfer of data, is to be found in [11].

The Specification of a Stack of Finite Capacity

A stack has two inputs, *push* and *pop*. If the environment wants to push an item on to the stack it sends a *push* signal; if it wants to pop an item from the stack it sends a *pop* signal. The stack acknowledges a successful push with *ack-push* and a successful pop with *ack-pop*. A push is unsuccessful when the stack is already full; a pop is unsuccessful when the stack is already empty. In these cases, the stack responds with *full* or *empty*, respectively. One push can follow another once a response to the first has been received. The same is true for pops. Pushing and popping are independent activities, perhaps performed by two different users of the stack. These considerations lead us to specify the stack as follows.

Definition 0   A delay-insensitive stack S_n^N, where N is its capacity and n its current size:

$$S_0^0 \;=\; [push? \rightarrow full!; S_0^0 \;\square\; pop? \rightarrow empty!; S_0^0]$$

For $N > 0$,

$$S_0^N \;=\; [push? \rightarrow ack\text{-}push!; S_1^N \;\square\; pop? \rightarrow empty!; S_0^N]$$
$$S_N^N \;=\; [push? \rightarrow full!; S_N^N \;\square\; pop? \rightarrow ack\text{-}pop!; S_{N-1}^N]$$

For $0 < n < N$,

$$S_n^N \;=\; [push? \rightarrow ack\text{-}push!; S_{n+1}^N \;\square\; pop? \rightarrow ack\text{-}pop!; S_{n-1}^N]$$

∎

Notice the symmetry between the push and pop operations. Our design will exhibit the same symmetry.

It is obvious how to implement a stack S_0^0 of zero capacity: connect *push* to *full* and *pop* to *empty*. This requires just two wires. This seemingly useless component will be used in every stack that we design!

The Stack Element

We intend to implement a stack of capacity $N + 2$ by putting a stack element on top of a stack of capacity N. This is to be done in such a way that only the stack element communicates with the environment. Hence, the stack element has twice the number of input and output wires as the stack itself: it engages in "upward" communications with the environment above and "downward" communications with the stack below. We shall use the label "d" to indicate a downward communication. By using stack elements of capacity 2 we are able to achieve constant response time, as we shall soon see.

A stack element can be in one of three states, E(mpty), P(artially full) or F(ull). In the empty state a push is immediately acknowledged and the state changes to P. (Only if the next transaction is a push does it make sense to push this item further down the stack. That is why we need a stack element of capacity 2.) In the partially full state a push is immediately acknowledged and the previous item is pushed downwards at the same time. The state remains P if the push downwards is successful, *i.e.*, acknowledged with a *d.ack-push*, but becomes F if the response to the push downwards is *d.full*. In state F a push results in the output *full*. The actions for a pop are similar because of symmetry. In particular, only in the partially full state is a pop propagated downwards. It should be apparent that a stack constructed in this way can always respond in constant time to pushes and pops from its environment. Formally, an (empty) stack element is specified by E, defined in the following way.

Definition 1

$$E \;=\; [push? \rightarrow ack\text{-}push!; P \;\square\; pop? \rightarrow empty!; E \;\textbf{else}\; \bot]$$

$$P \;=\; [push? \rightarrow ack\text{-}push!; d.push!; W\,push$$
$$\square\; pop? \rightarrow ack\text{-}pop!; d.pop!; W\,pop$$
$$\textbf{else}\; \bot]$$

$$F = [push? \rightarrow full!; F \,\square\, pop? \rightarrow ack\text{-}pop!; P \text{ else } \bot]$$

$$Wpush = [d.ack\text{-}push? \rightarrow P \,\square\, d.full? \rightarrow F$$
$$\square\, d.ack\text{-}pop? \rightarrow \bot \,\square\, d.empty? \rightarrow \bot]$$

$$Wpop = [d.ack\text{-}pop? \rightarrow P \,\square\, d.empty? \rightarrow E$$
$$\square\, d.ack\text{-}push? \rightarrow \bot \,\square\, d.full? \rightarrow \bot]$$

∎

The auxiliary processes $Wpush$ and $Wpop$ correspond to the quiescent states in which the stack element is waiting for the stack below to acknowledge a downward push or pop respectively. The strategy of giving all quiescent states a name turns out to be extremely valuable in the decomposition of specifications into separate components. This is demonstrated when we decompose the stack element into a Decision-Wait element and several Forks and Merges.

In order to show that we can implement a stack of capacity $N + 2$ by placing stack element E on top of a stack of capacity N, we prove that

$$(E \parallel d : S_0^N) = S_0^{N+2} \tag{0}$$

(As in CSP, $d : P$ is the process P with all communications labeled with d.) It then follows that N stack elements on top of S_0^0 implement a stack of capacity $2 \times N$. Thus stacks of arbitrarily large capacity can be built from stack elements.

The definition of S_0^{N+2} involves $N + 3$ mutually recursive equations, one for each S_n^{N+2}, $0 \le n \le N + 2$. All equations are guarded which implies that the solution for each S_n^{N+2}, $0 \le n \le N + 2$, is unique. We show that $E \parallel d : S_0^N$ is governed by exactly the same $N + 3$ equations, which proves (0). More specifically, we show the following correspondences for $N \ge 0$.

$$
\begin{aligned}
S_0^{N+2} &= E \parallel d : S_0^N, \\
S_{n+1}^{N+2} &= P \parallel d : S_n^N \quad \text{for } 0 \le n \le N, \text{ and,} \\
S_{N+2}^{N+2} &= F \parallel d : S_N^N.
\end{aligned}
\tag{1}
$$

We do so by unfolding the parallel compositions on the right hand sides in (1) once, and then assuming (1) itself to be valid. In this way we obtain the following derivation for $E \parallel d : S_0^N$.

$E \parallel d : S_0^N$

= { parallel composition through guarded choice, using that all d-labeled communications are internal }

$[push? \rightarrow ((ack\text{-}push!; P) \parallel d : S_0^N) \,\square\, pop? \rightarrow ((empty!; E) \parallel d : S_0^N)]$

= { external communication of $ack\text{-}push$ and $empty$ and folding according to (1) }

$[push? \rightarrow ack\text{-}push!; S_1^{N+2} \,\square\, pop? \rightarrow empty!; S_0^{N+2}]$

= { definition of S_0^{N+2} }

S_0^{N+2}

For $P \parallel d : S_n^N$, $0 \le n \le N$, we derive

$$P \parallel d : S_n^N$$

$=$ { parallel composition through guarded choice, using that all d-labeled communications are internal }

$[push? \rightarrow ((ack\text{-}push!; d.push!; W push) \parallel d : S_n^N)$
$\square\ pop? \rightarrow ((ack\text{-}pop!; d.pop!; W pop) \parallel d : S_n^N)]$

$=$ { external communication on $ack\text{-}push$ and $ack\text{-}pop$, internal communication on $d.push$ and $d.pop$ }

$[push? \rightarrow ack\text{-}push!; (W push \parallel d : (S_n^N/push?))$
$\square\ pop? \rightarrow ack\text{-}pop!; (W pop \parallel d : (S_n^N/pop?))]$

To complete the proof that $S_{n+1}^{N+2} = P \parallel d : S_n^N$ for $0 \leq n \leq N$, all that remains is to show using (1) that $W push \parallel d : (S_n^N/push?) = S_{n+2}^{N+2}$ and that $W pop \parallel d : (S_n^N/pop?) = S_n^{N+2}$. We confine ourselves to the former. The latter then follows by symmetry. A short calculation, using the law of after through guarded choice, reveals that

$$S_n^N/push? = \begin{cases} \begin{aligned} &[push? \rightarrow \perp \square\ skip \rightarrow full!; S_0^0 \\ &\square\ pop? \rightarrow empty!; (S_0^0/push?)] \end{aligned} & \text{in case } 0 = n = N, \\[2ex] \begin{aligned} &[push? \rightarrow \perp \square\ skip \rightarrow ack\text{-}push!; S_1^N \\ &\square\ pop? \rightarrow empty!; (S_0^N/push?)] \end{aligned} & \text{in case } 0 = n < N, \\[2ex] \begin{aligned} &[push? \rightarrow \perp \square\ skip \rightarrow full!; S_N^N \\ &\square\ pop? \rightarrow ack\text{-}pop!; (S_{N-1}^N/push?)] \end{aligned} & \text{in case } 0 < n = N, \text{ and} \\[2ex] \begin{aligned} &[push? \rightarrow \perp \square\ skip \rightarrow ack\text{-}push!; S_{n+1}^N \\ &\square\ pop? \rightarrow ack\text{-}pop!; (S_{n-1}^N/push?)] \end{aligned} & \text{in case } 0 < n < N. \end{cases}$$

Using the definition of $W push$, we find

$$W push \parallel d : (S_n^N/push?) = \begin{cases} F \parallel d : S_N^N & \text{in case } 0 \leq n = N \\ P \parallel d : S_{n+1}^N & \text{in case } 0 \leq n < N \end{cases}$$

By symmetry, we also have

$$W pop \parallel d : (S_n^N/pop?) = \begin{cases} E \parallel d : S_0^N & \text{in case } 0 = n \leq N \\ P \parallel d : S_{n-1}^N & \text{in case } 0 < n \leq N \end{cases}$$

Using (1), we conclude that $P \parallel d : S_n^N = S_{n+1}^{N+2}$ for $0 \leq n \leq N$.

Finally, we have to show that $S_{N+2}^{N+2} = F \parallel d : S_N^N$. This follows by symmetry from $E \parallel d : S_0^N = S_0^{N+2}$.

Removing Arbitration

The specifications of the stack and the stack element E (and P and F for that matter) allow inputs $push$ and pop to occur concurrently. It is left to each element to decide in which order to push or to pop whenever both signals arrive. If we construct a stack of E's, however, then the non-top elements will never have to make this decision: by the definition of $W push$ and $W pop$, the element above requires a response to each push and pop downwards before it will push or pop downwards again. This leads us to redefine the stack element under the assumption that pushes and pops are mutually exclusive since otherwise we would need one arbiter per stack element. A single arbiter can be inserted between the environment and the resulting stack in any environment that does not guarantee mutual exclusion.

The reason that we did not insist on mutual exclusion from the outset was that capturing this property tends to clutter up our specifications with ⊥'s. Of course, the more ⊥'s there are in a specification, the easier it is to implement.

Below we give the specification of a stack element, E, in which we have removed the arbitration between *push* and *pop*. Making similar changes to the definition of a stack, the reader should be able to redo the verification of the previous section, although the expressions will become more complicated. We respecify the stack element as follows.

Definition 2

$$E = [push? \to [skip \to ack\text{-}push!; P \text{ else } \bot]$$
$$\square\ pop? \to [skip \to empty!; E \text{ else } \bot]$$
$$\text{else } \bot]$$

$$P = [push? \to [skip \to ack\text{-}push!; d.push!; W push \text{ else } \bot]$$
$$\square\ pop? \to [skip \to ack\text{-}pop!; d.pop!; W pop \text{ else } \bot]$$
$$\text{else } \bot]$$

$$F = [push? \to [skip \to full!; F \text{ else } \bot]$$
$$\square\ pop? \to [skip \to ack\text{-}pop!; P \text{ else } \bot]$$
$$\text{else } \bot]$$

$$W push = [d.ack\text{-}push? \to P \ \square\ d.full? \to F$$
$$\square\ push? \to\ [d.ack\text{-}push? \to P/push?$$
$$\square\ d.full? \to F/push?$$
$$\text{else } \bot]$$
$$\square\ pop? \to\ [d.ack\text{-}push? \to P/pop?$$
$$\square\ d.full? \to F/pop?$$
$$\text{else } \bot]$$
$$\text{else } \bot]$$

$$W pop = [d.ack\text{-}pop? \to P \ \square\ d.empty? \to E$$
$$\square\ push? \to\ [d.ack\text{-}pop? \to P/push?$$
$$\square\ d.empty? \to E/push?$$
$$\text{else } \bot]$$
$$\square\ pop? \to\ [d.ack\text{-}pop? \to P/pop?$$
$$\square\ d.empty? \to F/pop?$$
$$\text{else } \bot]$$
$$\text{else } \bot]$$

■

Performance Analysis

We have claimed earlier that a stack consisting of elements E has constant response time. A proof that a stack constructed out of stack elements has constant response time relies upon the fact that certain communications will take place concurrently. In particular, the top

146

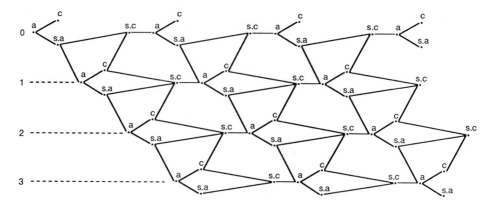

Figure 0: Dependency-graph induced by $Q = a?; c!; s.a!; s.c?; Q$.

stack element is ready to deal with the next push or pop as soon as it has acknowledged the last one, even though elements lower down the stack have not yet entered their quiescent states. The point is that those elements will have entered such a state by the time the next push or pop has propagated down to them. To argue this formally it is convenient to re-specify the behavior of the stack in which concurrent activity can be shown explicitly. In essence we draw a dependency-graph, in which a communication is preceded by all the communications that must have occurred first. (In general, something a little more sophisticated is required to handle nondeterministic behavior, e.g. POM-sets [14].)

Of interest to our performance analysis of the stack are the longest paths (from the start) leading to the occurrence of an input (push or pop) or an output (ack-push or ack-pop). The events on such a path must take place one after the other, which puts a lower bound on the occurrence of the last event. We say that a process has constant response time if the maximum length of any path leading to the occurrence of one of those events grows linearly with the occurrence number of that event. This means that production of an acknowledgement can start a bounded number of steps after the corresponding request has been processed, and also that a next request can be processed a bounded number of steps after the previous acknowledgement has been received.

Notice that a constant response time does not necessarily mean that the number of actions to be performed between a push and its acknowledgement is bounded by a constant. But if that number increases then the amount of parallelism must increase accordingly in order to have paths in the dependency-graph of bounded length.

By way of example we study the specification defined by

$$Q = a?; c!; s.a!; s.c?; Q,$$

where s is a process defined by the same equation. We show that it has constant response time. Pictorially the dependency graph is represented in Figure 0. Each row represents the communication actions of a process and the arrows denote the order between a node and its immediate successors and predecessors. The top process, Q, has been given number 0, its subprocess 1, etc. The $s.a$ and $s.c$ symbols of process i correspond to the a and c symbols of process $i + 1$. As we can see from the specification, input a must have been processed before c and $s.a$ can be produced, which has to precede the processing of input $s.c$, which precedes the processing of input a again. Outputs c and $s.a$ are considered to be unordered, although that is immaterial for the core of the analysis. For the sake of a simpler figure we have ordered the events a and $s.c$, although that is immaterial too. Of course, the ordering between the inputs and the outputs is crucial. The following theorem shows that the maximum length of any path ending in a for process 0 grows linearly with the number of occurrences of a. Since c always immediately follows a, this suffices to show that we have constant response time.

Theorem 0   For all k, $k \geq 1$, and for all processes m, $0 \leq m < k$, the maximum length of any path ending in the $(k - m)$th a of process m is $5k - 3m - 4$.

Proof   We use induction on k.

Base: $k = 1$. We have to show for process 0 that the maximum length of any path ending in the first a of process 0 is 1. This is obvious, since it is the first element in the dependency-graph on account of the specification for Q.

Step: Assume that the theorem holds for some k, $k \geq 1$. We have to show that for all processes m, $0 \leq m < k + 1$, the maximum length of any path ending in the $(k + 1 - m)$th a of process m is $5k - 3m + 1$. We prove this by induction on m.

Base: $m = k$. We have to show that the maximum length of any path ending in the first a of process k is $2k + 1$. The one and only predecessor of the first a of process k is the first $s.a$ of process $k - 1$, since $k \geq 1$ and since the first a of a process does not have any predecessors in that process itself. The first $s.a$ of process $k - 1$ has 1 immediate predecessor, viz. the first a of process $k - 1$, upon which we can apply the induction hypothesis. Hence, the longest path ending in the first a of process k is $2k - 1 + 2 = 2k + 1$.

Step: Assume, in addition to the first hypothesis, that for some m, $0 < m < k + 1$, the maximum length of any path ending in the $(k + 1 - m)$th a of process m is $5k - 3m + 1$. We have to show that the maximum length of any path ending in the $(k + 2 - m)$th a of process $m - 1$ is $5k - 3m + 4$.

The $(k + 2 - m)$th a of process $m - 1$ has possibly two immediate predecessors. If $m \geq 2$ then the $(k + 2 - m)$th a is immediately preceded by the $(k + 2 - m)$th $s.a$ of process $m - 2$ and by the $(k + 1 - m)$th $s.c$ of process $m - 1$. In case $m = 1$ it has only the latter as an immediate predecessor. First we consider the paths through an $s.a$-predecessor of a, which is only possible if $m \geq 2$.

Assuming in this paragraph that $m \geq 2$ we show that the maximum length of any path to the $(k + 2 - m)$th $s.a$ of process $m - 2$ is $5k - 3m + 3$. This $s.a$ has only one immediate predecessor, viz. the $(k+2-m)$th a of process $m-2$. Applying the first induction hypothesis we infer that the longest path to this a is $5k - 3(m - 2) - 4$, which is $5k - 3m + 2$, as desired.

Looking at the other immediate predecessor of the $(k + 2 - m)$th a of process $m - 1$, being the $(k + 1 - m)$th $s.c$ of process $m - 1$, it suffices to prove that the maximum length of any path to this $s.c$ is $5k - 3m + 3$. This $s.c$ has three immediate predecessors, viz. the $(k + 1 - m)$th $s.a$ and c of process $m - 1$ and the $(k + 1 - m)$th c of process m. The first two predecessors give rise to paths of length up to $5k - 3m + 1$ ending in $s.c$ on account of the first induction hypothesis. The other predecessor gives rise to a path of length $5k - 3m + 3$ on account of the second induction hypothesis, as desired.   ∎

We have deliberately chosen to analyze the performance of this process Q. It turns out that E satisfies a similar equation. We can transform the equation for E into that of Q by

148

no longer distinguishing the various inputs and the various outputs. The generic input is a and the generic output is c and no input leads to $\bot$. Any execution of the original processes can be mapped onto an execution of the new process. Therefore, if we can show that the new process has constant response time with respect to a and c, then so does the original process. (The converse does not necessarily hold.) The equations become

$$
\begin{aligned}
E &= [a? \to c!; P \;\square\; a? \to c!; E] \\
P &= [a? \to c!; s.a!; Wpush \;\square\; a? \to c!; s.a!; Wpop] \\
F &= [a? \to c!; F \;\square\; a? \to c!; P] \\
Wpush &= [s.c? \to P \;\square\; s.c? \to F] \\
Wpop &= [s.c? \to P \;\square\; s.c? \to E]
\end{aligned}
$$

From this we conclude that E and F do no longer differ and neither do $Wpush$ and $Wpop$. Hence, this set of equations reduces to

$$
\begin{aligned}
E &= a?; c!; (P \sqcap E) \\
P &= a?; c!; s.a!; s.c?; (E \sqcap P)
\end{aligned}
$$

It is clear that we add more ordering between events if we add to the equation of E the sequence $s.a!; s.c?$, right after $c!$. The resulting equation is then exactly the one that we analyzed earlier to have constant response time.

Decomposition of a Stack Element

For the actual design it is easier to look at the original specification, keeping in mind that *push* and *pop* are mutually exclusive. Apparently, a stack element can be in one of five quiescent states, E, P, F, $Wpush$ or $Wpop$. In the first three cases, the next state is determined by the current state and one of the inputs *push* or *pop*. This can be implemented with a 2×3 Decision-Wait element (*cf.* Example 1). The row inputs are *push* and *pop* and the column inputs are e, p and f. To begin with there is a signal on e because the element is empty. In states $Wpush$ and $Wpop$, an input from below moves the element into one of the first three states, and so these inputs can be fed into e, p and f as appropriate. If more than one signal is to be produced in a certain state, we use Forks. If more than one signal can lead to the same state, or to the same output, they are combined by means of Merges. This completes the informal design, which immediately suggests itself to us from the formal specification. Thus E can be decomposed into the following components.

$$
\begin{aligned}
DW/e? \text{ where } DW &= [push? \to R_0 \;\square\; pop? \to R_1 \\
&\quad \square\; e? \to C_0 \;\square\; p? \to C_1 \;\square\; f? \to C_2] \\
R_j &= [e? \to O_{j0} \;\square\; p? \to O_{j1} \;\square\; f? \to O_{j2} \textbf{ else } \bot] \\
C_j &= [push? \to O_{0j} \;\square\; pop? \to O_{1j} \textbf{ else } \bot] \\
O_{ij} &= [skip \to m_{ij}!; DW \textbf{ else } \bot]
\end{aligned}
$$

$$F00 \quad = \quad m00?; y0!; x00!; F00$$

$$F01 \quad = \quad m01?; d.push!; x01!; F01$$

$$F02 \quad = \quad m02?; full!; x02!; F02$$

$$F10 \quad = \quad m10?; empty!; x10!; F10$$

$$F11 \quad = \quad m11?; d.pop!; x11!; F11$$

$$F12 \quad = \quad m12?; y1!; x12!; F12$$

$$M0 \quad = \quad [x00? \to ack\text{-}push!; M0 \;\square\; x01? \to ack\text{-}push!; M0]$$

$$M1 \quad = \quad [x11? \to ack\text{-}pop!; M1 \;\square\; x12? \to ack\text{-}pop!; M1]$$

$$M2 \quad = \quad [x10? \to e!; M2 \;\square\; d.empty? \to e!; M2]$$

$$M3 \quad = \quad [y0? \to p!; M3 \;\square\; y1? \to p!; M3$$
$$\square\; d.ack\text{-}push? \to p!; M3 \;\square\; d.ack\text{-}pop? \to p!; M3]$$

$$M4 \quad = \quad [x02? \to f!; M4 \;\square\; d.full? \to f!; M4]$$

This decomposition is represented in Figure 1. The formal verification of this design can be found in [11].

Incorporating Data

As stated earlier, we have not modeled the storage and movement of data. Our original specification could therefore serve equally well as a description of a buffer or, for that matter, a simple counter. On the other hand, it should be clear that our design is more suited to the control of a stack than the control of a buffer.

Our algebraic notation, as presented above, describes only the transmission of signals. It can, however, be extended in a straightforward way to describe the transmission of data. For example, we could modify the stack specification so that S is subscripted with a sequence of values (recording the contents of the stack), rather than simply their number; the values being communicated could be input with $push?x$ and output with $ack\text{-}pop!x$. We shall not investigate this here, but refer the reader to [11] for a comprehensive discussion.

Conclusion

An algebraic approach has been taken to the specification and verification of delay-insensitive circuits. It has not been necessary to express explicitly all the states that such a circuit can enter; instead the possibility of them arising can be deduced using algebraic laws. This has lead to concise specifications and short proofs. Another simplifying factor has been

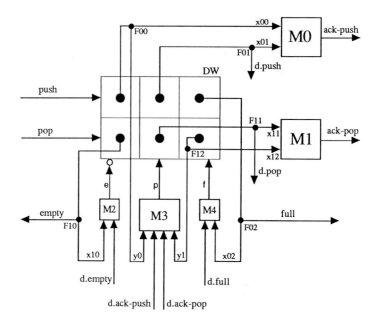

Figure 1: The decomposition of a stack element

that, following [17], we do not distinguish between high and low-going transitions; this exposes many symmetries that would not otherwise be apparent. The main advantage of our approach is the ease with which we can compute the parallel composition of components.

We have demonstrated that the algebra facilitates design. It was proved that a delay-insensitive stack of arbitrarily large capacity can be validly implemented by connecting a sufficient number of identical elements together. This can be done in such a way that the response time of the stack does not depend upon its capacity or current size. Another interesting aspect of our design was in the implementation of a stack element as a state-machine controlled by transition signaling. It may very well be the case that this is a widely-applicable implementation strategy in delay-insensitive circuit design; further study is necessary.

Acknowledgements

We are grateful for the comments that 3 referees made upon an earlier version of this paper. It prompted us to include the section on the performance analysis of the stack. Discussions with Paul Lucassen, Rudolf Mak, and Tom Verhoeff helped clarify some of the issues in this analysis. This research was partially funded by the ESPRIT Basic Research Action CONCUR.

References

[1] S. D. Brookes and A. W. Roscoe. An improved failures model for communicating sequential processes. In G. Winskel, editor, *Proceedings of the NSF-SERC Seminar on Concurrency*, number 197 in Lecture Notes in Computer Science, pages 281–305. Springer-Verlag, 1985.

[2] W. Chen, J. T. Udding, and T. Verhoeff. Networks of communicating processes and their (de)-composition. In J. L. A. van de Snepscheut, editor, *The Mathematics of Program Construction*, number 375 in Lecture Notes in Computer Science, pages 174–196. Springer-Verlag, 1989.

[3] D. L. Dill. *Trace Theory for Automatic Hierarchical Verification of Speed-Independent Circuits*. PhD thesis, C.S. Dept., Carnegie Mellon Univ., Pittsburgh, PA, Feb. 1988.

[4] D. L. Dill and E. M. Clarke. Automatic verification of asynchronous circuits using temporal logic. In H. Fuchs, editor, *1985 Chapel Hill Conference on Very Large Scale Integration*, pages 127–143. Computer Science Press, 1985.

[5] J. C. Ebergen. *Translating Programs into Delay-Insensitive Circuits*. PhD thesis, Dept. of Math. and C.S., Eindhoven Univ. of Technology, 1987.

[6] M. Hennessy. *Algebraic Theory of Processes*. Series in Foundations of Computing. The MIT Press, Cambridge, Mass., 1988.

[7] C. A. R. Hoare. *Communicating Sequential Processes*. Prentice-Hall, 1985.

[8] H. Jifeng, M. B. Josephs, and C. A. R. Hoare. A theory of synchrony and asynchrony. In *Proceedings IFIP Working Conference on Programming Concepts and Methods*, volume (to appear), 1990.

[9] M. B. Josephs, C. A. R. Hoare, and He Jifeng. A theory of asynchronous processes. *J. ACM*, (submitted), 1989.

[10] M. B. Josephs and J. T. Udding. An algebra for delay-insensitive circuits. Technical Report WUCS-89-54, Dept. of C.S., Washington Univ., St. Louis, MO, 1989.

[11] M. B. Josephs and J. T. Udding. Designing a delay-insensitive stack. Technical Report CS9004, Groningen University, Dept. of Comp. Sci., 1990.

[12] A. J. Martin. Compiling communicating processes into delay-insensitive VLSI circuits. *Distributed Computing*, 1(4):226–234, 1986.

[13] A. J. Martin. Programming in VLSI: From communicating processes to delay-insensitive circuits. Technical Report Caltech-CS-TR-89-1, Caltech Computer Science, 1989.

[14] V. Pratt. Modelling concurrency with partial orders. *International Journal of Parallel Programming*, 15(1), 1986.

[15] A. W. Roscoe and C. A. R. Hoare. The laws of occam programming. *Theoretical Computer Science*, 60(2):177–229, 1988.

[16] I. E. Sutherland. Micropipelines. *Comm. ACM*, 32(6):720–738, 1989. Turing Award Lecture.

[17] J. T. Udding. *Classification and Composition of Delay-Insensitive Circuits.* PhD thesis, Dept. of Math. and C.S., Eindhoven Univ. of Technology, 1984.

[18] J. T. Udding. A formal model for defining and classifying delay-insensitive circuits. *Distributed Computing*, 1(4):197–204, 1986.

Specifying the Micro-program Parallelism for

Microprocessors of the Von Neumann style

Hélène COLLAVIZZA[*]   Dominique BORRIONE[+]

Abstract

In order to verify significant micro-processors, we believe that the proof process must be decomposed into successive verifications between adjacent description levels. Furthermore, we recommend the use of a functional formalism. In this paper, we first recall the functional semantics defined at the "micro-program" level, level which takes into account the memory/processor information exchanges. Then we characterize some validity conditions required by the "implicit" or "explicit" parallel execution of two micro-programs. We emphasize that our functional formalism and proof methodology are suitable to express the parallelism encountered during instruction execution, in particular for pipelined micro-processors.

1.Introduction

As digital circuits became increasingly complex, and simulation could no longer be considered a secure validation tool, considerable awareness of the necessity to formally verify hardware designs has developed over the past decade. However, as discussed in [28], post-design verification of big circuits is likely to lead to very large and complex proofs. The task can be handled with reasonable effort only if formal verification is performed step by step [9], and integrated in the design process. A modelling framework, uniform among the types and levels of abstraction [25], is needed. Yet we believe that, for efficiency reasons, a "Design for Verifiability" methodology [28] calls for the development of specialized modelling features and proof tools, for well identified levels of abstraction and classes of digital circuits, together with recommendations and guidance given to the hardware designer.

Along these lines, we have proposed a proof methodology for micro-processor verification, which can be applied to a large class of processors of the "Von Neumann" type [2]. We consider several specification and description levels and associate a functional semantics to each level. The three most abstract levels, under consideration in this paper, can be listed as:

- level_1, the "Machine Instruction" level, which describes the processor behaviour as seen by the programmer,
- level_2, the "Micro-program" level, which takes into account the memory/processor information exchanges and the internal operations executed in parallel,
- level_3, the "Micro-instruction" level, which reflects the data transfers between data path ressources.

[*]Université de Provence, Case S, 3 Place Victor Hugo, 13331 Marseille cedex, FRANCE
[+]Université Joseph Fourier, Laboratoire IMAG/ARTEMIS, BP 53X, 38041 Grenoble cedex, FRANCE

If some specification efforts are required for each of these levels, the advantage of a stepwise decomposition is double: the proof is reduced to simple verifications between successive adjacent levels and, furthermore, more properties about each level can be specified and then verified.

At each level, the semantics that we define for a processor is inspired from the functional semantics of programming languages [33]. Functional formalisms [20] have gained acceptance for the specification of digital devices. They provide a uniform framework for the various abstraction levels, allow the expression of sequentiality by function composition and of parallelism by tuple composition, and are suitable for mathematical manipulations. However, the above mentioned two composition methods appear to be insufficient to portray specifications that state the successive actions performed by pipelined stages of hardware, in a way that imposes verification of validity conditions on the data flow; these composition methods are also inadequate to express that two functions can be executed either sequentially or in parallel, the decision being deferred to a later design step.

In this paper, we focus on the specification of micro-program parallelism. In particular, for pipelined micro-processors, we define the "explicit parallelism" of two microprogram fragments executed into two independent pipeline stages, and the "partial parallelism" of two contiguous pipeline stages. Furthermore, we show how to specify the "Implicit parallelism" of several internal operations, which modify different state variables, and can possibly be executed during the same micro-instruction. Principles of specification at levels 1 and 2 are described at length in [29] and [11].

Related works

Much research in hardware verification is based upon functional formalisms. Some formal systems have specially been built, such as LCF-LSM [15], muFP [31] (an extension of FP [1]), or the CIRCAL system [27]. Common functional languages have been also used, such as LISP, associated with the automatic Boyer & Moore theorem prover, for the description and verification of a microprocessor [23] or the verification of pipelines, at the Register Transfer level [7]. Higher-order functions have been recommended as a better formalism for specifying and verifying hardware [16], [17], [HD85], and simple micro-processors have been proven in HOL [9], [24]; but the price paid for the increased generality of higher-order functions is the necessity of an expert user to guide the proof process. A unifying approach is the concept of "System Semantics", an extension to Denotational Semantics which allows for the definition of several interpretations in various modelling domains for a given circuit description [4]. Functional formalisms are also helpful in the scope of synthesis, a cooperative approach to hardware verification [Ev, 87]. For example, the Digital Design Derivation system [3] works by transformation of programs written in a dialect of lambda-calculus. A more complete survey of formal hardware verification can be found in [12].

Few authors have addressed the specific problem of specifying and verifying the abstract levels of pipe-lined hardware. The usual view point in attacking this task is inspired by CCS [26], CSP [21], and all the derived formalisms used in specifying communication networks and protocols [32]; for instance, in [18], the interface behaviour of two processes is checked for identity, where one process is constructed as the composition of a pipelined implementation with some "tester" circuitry, and the other process is the composition of a non-pipelined specification with another "tester". To our knowledge, the verification of a subset of the Cayuga processor in Clio [6] is the only piece of work which resembles ours: the authors use a functional approach for modelling the instruction level and the structural decomposition of the processor, they express the processor state and formulate the correspondence between the representations of the state at two levels in the same way as we do; the main difference is that they do not consider a micro-program level, and must prove their instruction set against an implementation decomposed at the clock cycle grain of timing, which we believe to be too big a jump.

The remainder of this paper is organized as follows. Section 2 recalls some general principles for the specification at level_2. Section 3 defines properties of state transition functions, to be used in stating the parallelism validity conditions. Section 4 shows how to specify the parallelism for pipelined micro-processors. Section 5 deals of the "implicit parallelism" between micro-program fragments. We conclude on the present development of a specialized editor to help the designer build such functional specifications.

2. Principles of specification at level_2

2.1. Processor state

The state includes the set of level_1 state variables plus the set of instruction registers and the set of internal registers used to buffer the results of the several pipeline stages. The level_1 state variables are the set of memorizing components available to the programmer (i.e main memory, register banks, program counter... In addition, we introduce a state variable which represents the current value read in the main memory, in order to model the read/write memory operations. Furthermore, if the memory is managed by a cache system, we introduce as many state variables as caches.

Registers are represented by 0-ary functions with value in Numi (Numk represents the set of bit vectors of length k); memories (resp. register banks) are represented by functions of type Numi $\rightarrow$ Numj where "j" is the memory word length (resp. register length) and "i" is the smallest integer large enough to address the memory (resp. the register bank).

The state can be represented by the list of functions:

$$STATE2=(MEM,REG1,REG2,...,PC,SR,...,I1,I2,...,DI1,DI2,...$$
$$P1,P2,...,DATA\_IN1,DATA\_IN2,...)$$

where MEM is the main memory, the REG#i represent some internal register banks, PC is the Program Counter, SR the status register, I#i are the instruction words, DI#i are used to buffer the instruction code at the several instruction decoding stages, P#i are used to buffer the results of the different pipeline stages and DATA_INi represents the current value read by means of the cache i.

2.2. Semantics of the machine instructions at level_2: the "implμpgm" function

At the two highest description levels, each instruction is represented by a list of parameters, called "abstract syntax" of the instruction [29]. This list symbolizes the set of actual instruction fields and includes some parameters used to specify the instruction mnemonic, the addressing mode and the operands. If the number and meaning of parameters change from one instruction to another, the instruction set is decomposed into instruction classes in a such way that all the instructions in the class have the same abstract syntax. The meaning of the operands is defined by operand functions which express the operand value in terms of the state and instruction syntax parameters.

The *"implµpgm"* function expresses the decomposition of an instruction into a set of successive micro-sequences. It associates to each instruction, represented in abstract syntax, its implementation by one or more micro-sequences. Each micro-sequence is defined as a transition function on the state at level_2. It corresponds either to a read/write memory operation, either to an internal operation (which can be a micro-program or a micro-program fragment) delimited by two successive memory accesses, or by another internal operation which can be executed in parallel.

The *"implµpgm"* function is split up into several subfunctions according to the different instruction formats and operative kinds. Since the memory accesses depend on the addressing mode, each subfunction is defined by cases from the different modes.

Because, at level_2, we model all the memory accesses required to realize an instruction, we must also define the memory accesses involved in reading and loading the instruction words. So the first sequence of *"implµpgm"* is the function *"seq_fetch"* which specifies these accesses according to the instruction abstract syntax. The actual instruction registers are only considered at level_3, in order to prove the correctness of the *"seq_fetch"* function.

3. Arguments and modified variables of a state transition function

3.1. Definitions

Here we set-up some concepts to express the parallelism validity conditions of two state transition functions of type:

$$X_1 \times X_2 \times \ldots \times X_n \rightarrow X_1 \times X_2 \times \ldots \times X_n$$

where $X_1, X_2, \ldots$ and X_n are the sets of values taken by the state variables.
Generally, the functions under consideration modify only a subset of the state variables, and depend only on another subset of state variables. In particular, it is the case for the micro-sequences, which modify only a part of the processor state.

Intuitively, two state transition functions f1 and f2 can be executed in parallel if the state variables modified by f1 (resp. f2) are not real arguments of f2 (resp. f1), and furthermore if f1 and f2 do not modify the same state variables.
We thus need to give a precise definition of the set of state variables modified by a state transition function, and of the set of variables actually used as arguments by a function.
We consider in fact the sets of indices included in $\{1,2,\ldots,n\}$, denoted modif(f) and arg(f), such that:

- if $i \in$ modif(f), then state variable x_i is modified by the function f

- if $i \in$ arg(f) then state variable x_i is actually used as argument by f.

Notations:

- $X_1 \times X_2 \times \ldots \times X_n$ is denoted X
- x_i denotes a state variable with value in X_i
- X_i denotes the set of tuples of length n-1 defined by:

$$X\_i = X_1 \times \ldots \times X_{i-1} \times X_{i+1} \ldots \times X_n$$

- The set of the state transition functions from X to X is denoted $\mathcal{T}(X)$.
- The functional composition is denoted o
- The selection function from X to X_i is denoted sel_i. To simplify the expressions, we denote sel_i_f the function sel_i o f.

Definition 1

*Let $f \in \mathcal{T}(X)$. Then **modif** (f) = {i $\in$ {1,2,...,n} / sel_i_f $\neq$ sel_i }*

Definition 2

*Let $f \in \mathcal{T}(X)$. Then sel_k_f is a selection function of f **constant with respect to** X_i if:*

$$\forall \ (x_1, x_2, \ldots, x_{i-1}, x_{i+1}, \ldots, x_n) \in X_{-i}$$
$$\exists ! \ c \in X_k \ such \ that \ \forall \ x_i \in X_i, \ sel\_k\_f(\ x_1, \ldots, x_i, \ldots, x_n) = c$$

Definition 3

*Let $f \in \mathcal{T}(X)$. f is **almost-constant with respect to** X_i if:*

(i) If i $\in$ modif(f) then:

$\forall k \in \{1,2,\ldots,n\}$ *sel_k_f is a selection function of f constant with respect to X_i*

(ii) If i $\notin$ modif(f) then:

$\forall k \neq i$, *sel_k_f is a selection function constant with respect to X_i*

In fact, a function f is almost-constant with respect to the set Xi, if the values of the variables xj for j≠i, which are computed by this function, do not depend on xi, and furthermore, if xi is either unchanged, or modified with a value which does not depend on itself.

Definition 4

Let $f \in \mathcal{T}(X)$.

$$arg \ (f) = \{ \ i \in \{1,2,\ldots,n\} \ / \ f \ is \ not \ almost\text{-}constant \ with \ respect \ to \ X_i\}$$

The arguments of a function f correspond to the variables actually used to compute the values modified by f. In other words, if sel_i_f = sel_i (i.e $\forall$ x $\in$ X, sel_i_f (x) = xi) then i is not considered as an argument of f.

3.2. Application to the micro-sequences

We now give a practical means to determine the sets modif(m) and arg(m) when m is a micro-sequence.

Each micro-sequence at level_2 is a transition function of $\mathcal{T}$(State2) defined in our formalism by means of the "subst" function:

m: State2 → State2

state2 → subst(state2,list_nval)

where "list_nval" is a list of couples (vari,vali). "subst(state2,list_nval)" substitutes in the tuple "state2" the current value of each var#i which belongs to "list_nval", with the corresponding val#i. For example, subst(state2, ((PC, sel_PC(state2)+1))) substitutes in state2 the current value of PC with its value incremented by one.

Notations

To make the expressions clearer, State2 is denoted Var1 x Var2 x ... x Varn where var#i are the indentifiers of the state variables. So, we denote "sel_VAR" the selection function of the variable "VAR", such as sel_PC, sel_MEM... The index of a state variable is then defined by its place in the tuple which represents the state.

So, an easy way to determine the set modif(m) is to enumerate the indices which correspond to the state variables in the list "list_nval".

On the other hand, the expressions given by val#i depend only on a part of the state. If the value "vali" depends on the state variable "vark" then it contains an occurence of the selection function "sel_vark". So, to determine if index "k" is in arg(m), we make a syntactic analysis of the expressions "var#i" for all "vari" in "list_nval", and answer positively if "sel_vark" occurs in these expressions.

4. Specifying the explicit parallelism. Application to pipelined micro-processors

4.1. Definitions

Definition 5

*Let $m_1 \in \mathcal{T}(State2)$ and $m_2 \in \mathcal{T}(State2)$. m_1 and m_2 can be **explicitely executed in parallel** if they verify the three conditions:*

(i) $modif(m_1) \cap arg(m_2) = \emptyset$

(ii) $modif(m_2) \cap arg(m_1) = \emptyset$

(iii) $modif(m_1) \cap modif(m_2) = \emptyset$

(i) expresses that the variables used as arguments by m_2 are not modified by m_1.
(ii) expresses that the variables used as arguments by m_1 are not modified by m_2.
(iii) expresses that m_1 and m_2 do not modify the same variables.

This expresses that m_1 and m_2 define the operations performed into two independent processor units which work in parallel. We call this "explicit" parallelism since this parallelism is explicitly specified by the designers, in particular for pipelined microprocessors.

This parallelism corresponds to a control graph for the sequencer, which has a structure illustrated on figure 1:

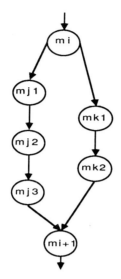

Fig1: μ-instruction sequencing.
Case of explicit parallelism

Property

   The composition of two micro-sequences m_1 and m_2 which verify the conditions of definition 5 is commutative and associative. Moreover, $m_1 o m_2$ is defined by:

   $\forall S \in State2,$

   if $i \notin modif (m_1)$ and $i \notin modif (m_2)$ then $sel\_i (m_1 o m_2) (S) = sel\_i (S)$

   if $i \in modif (m_1)$ then $sel\_i (m_1 o m_2) (S) = sel\_i\_m_1 (S)$

   if $i \in modif (m_2)$ then $sel\_i (m_1 o m_2) (S) = sel\_i\_m_2 (S)$

A demonstration can be found in [10].

4.2. Specifying pipelined micro-processors

   For these processors, several instructions are partly executed in parallel in different pipeline stages. At each point in time, each stage executes a micro-sequence for one of these instructions; a particular instruction is completely executed when it has passed through all the stages.

   In order to specify the several pipeline stages, we introduce in the processor state all the registers used to store the pipeline stage results. Then we decompose each instruction into the micro-sequence composition which corresponds to the instruction pass through the successive pipeline stages.

   The parallelism of the operations consists of:

   - the explicit parallelism of the micro-sequences which correspond to not

successive pipeline stages: these micro-sequences are independent.
- a partial parallelism of each couple of consecutive stages: two consecutive stages execute in parallel two computation steps for two distinct instructions. This involves for the sequencer control graph, the same structure as shown in figure 1. However, if m_1 and m_2 correspond to two successive pipeline stages, the arguments used by m_2 are some variables modified by m_1. So, they are not independent and do not verify the conditions of definition 5.

Nevertheless, some pipeline validity conditions can be set:

Definition 6

We say that two micro-sequences m_1 and m_2 can define two successive pipeline stages if:

(i) modif(m_1) $\cap$ modif(m_2) = $\emptyset$

(ii) modif(m_2) $\cap$ arg(m_1) = $\emptyset$

(we denote m_2 o_p m_1 the composition of two such micro-sequences)

Definition 6 expresses that:
- the sets of output buffers of the pipeline stages defined by m_1 and m_2 are distinct.
- the input buffers of the pipeline stage defined by m_1 are distinct from the output buffers of the pipeline stage defined by m_2.

So, at level_2, each instruction of a pipelined micro-processor is described by a micro-sequence composition of the type: m_n o_p m_{n-1} o_p ... o_p m_1 where "m_i" defines the state modifications involved by the pipeline stage i.
During the proof between levels 1 and 2, "o_p" is considered as a classical composition; however, the specification of the pipeline validity conditions enforces additional verifications at levels 2 and 3.

We have to verify:

- between levels 1 and 2: for each instruction, its correct implementation by the micro-sequence composition defined by the *"implμpgm"* function
- at level_2: the independence conditions and pipeline validity conditions
- between level 2 and 3: the implementation of each micro-sequence by a set of successive micro-instructions
- at level_3: the actual parallelism of the micro-instruction sequences which implement two explicit parallel micro-sequences or two micro-sequences which correspond to successive pipeline stages.

Remark

If we consider the pipeline stages as several communicating units, we can see a micro-processor as a very restricted case of a communicating system: the several units communicate by means of the pipeline input and output buffers, but there is no complex communication protocol between them. However, we can make some remark about the similarity between our formalism and some operators used in the specification of communicating systems. As stated in [26], one may compare a function argument to an input port of a process. This lead to the following remark in [5], where a lambda-calculus for communicating systems is proposed: "λ x. p" of the λ_calculus and "α x. p" of CCS behave quite similarly. In our formalism, the input ports of a pipeline unit are the arguments of the corresponding micro-sequence, where "argument" has the meaning given in part 2.1.

4.3. Example: the CLIPPER microprocessor

The CLIPPER microprocessor, developped by Intergraph Corporation [22], presents the main features of a RISC architecture: limited and simple instruction set, maximum use of registers and minimal references to the memory, optimizing the instruction execution pipeline. This processor is divided into three parts: the central processing unit and two caches and memory management units, one for the data (called D_CAMMU) and the other for the instructions (I_CAMMU).

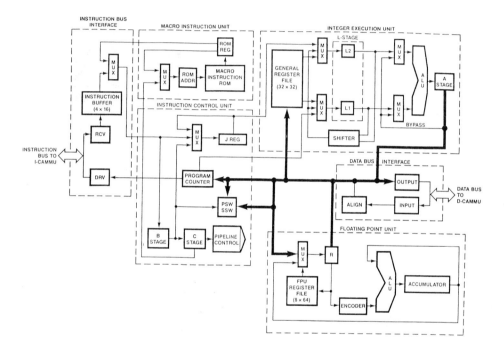

Fig2: CLIPPER architecture [22]

The central processing unit includes six main blocks:
-   an instruction bus interface
-   a data bus interface
-   a macro-instruction unit (complex instructions are directly implemented in a ROM)
-   an instruction control unit "ICU" which is responsible for decoding instructions and controlling instruction execution.
-   an integer execution unit "IEU"
-   a floating point execution unit "FPU"
(each one of these last two units includes an ALU)

For this processor, the several pipeline stages are:
- two stages of instruction decoding (two instructions partly decoded are in the CPU)
- three stages in the IEU: operand fetch (L stage), arithmetic stage (A stage) and operand write stage (O stage).

The explicit parallelism consists of the parallel processing of the FPU and the IEU. This implies the explicit parallelism of each IEU micro-sequence with respect to the FPU micro-sequence.

We give below two micro-sequence compositions which realize an integer computation instruction and a floating point computation instruction. Since we lack a complete documentation about CLIPPER, we only illustrate our specification principles without detailing the values assigned to the several state variables.

The state of the CLIPPER processor can be represented by the tuple of functions:

state2_CLIPPER = < MEM, PC, PSW, SSW, IB, B, C,
IGPR, L1, L2, AIEU, FGPR, AFPU,
DATA_IN_INS, DATA_IN_DAT>

where MEM is the main memory, PC is the Program Counter (contains the address of the instruction to be issued), PSW is the Program Status Word, SSW the System Status Word, IB the "Instruction Buffer" is a bank of four registers which contains the address of the last four instructions, B contains the instruction code after the first decoding step, C contains the instruction code after the second decoding step, IGPR is a register bank of "General Purpose Registers" in the IEU, FGPR is a register bank of "General Purpose Registers" in the FPU, AIEU and AFPU are the accumulators of the IEU and FPU, L1 and L2 are the buffers which contain the operands in the IEU, DATA_IN_INS represents the memory word read in the I_CAMMU, DATA_IN_DAT represents the memory word read in the D_CAMMU.

Like most of RISC machines, CLIPPER has a load/store architecture in which memory accesses are most of the time realized by load and store instructions. The memory operands are computed according to nine addressing modes and the internal operands according to six addressing modes.

Since the operand instruction fields differ according to addressing modes, the operand parameters are defined by lists whose first element is the instruction mode and the rest of the list gives the operand fields for this mode [29]. We already used such a formalization for the Motorola 68000 [10]: on the basis of the detailed description of the instruction set (in the programmer's manual), we decomposed the instruction set into instruction classes and specified precisely two operand parameters, one for the source and the other for the destination.

Unfortunately, we are lacking precise information about the addressing modes actually allowed for each instruction class, in the documentation we have about CLIPPER. So we only illustrate our modelling principles and define the instruction syntax of CLIPPER by the couple: <MNEM, OPERANDS>
where
    MNEM takes its value in a set of 85 instruction mnemonics
    OPERANDS takes its value in a set of 15 lists of operand specification

For example, we give below the lists used to specify the operands for internal addressing

modes (see [22], page 203):
- register to register mode: (REG R1 R2)
- quick mode: (QUICK Q R2)
- 16-bit immediate mode: (IM16 R2 S WIM)
- 32-bit immediate mode: (IM32 R2 S WIML WIMH)
- control mode: (CONT B)
- macro mode: (MACRO CODE R1 R2)

where
R1, R2, Q are in Num4, S represents the sign of type Num1, WIMH and WIM are in Num15, WIML is in Num16, B in Num8 and CODE in Num6.

The CLIPPER implementation function has the form:

$$\text{impl}\mu\text{pgm\_CLIPPER} = \lambda \text{ inst state2.}$$
$$\underline{\text{case}} \text{ inst } \underline{\text{in}}$$
$$\text{Int\_calc: impl\_int\_calc(inst, state2)}$$
$$\text{Fp\_calc: impl\_fp\_calc (inst, state2)}$$
$$\text{Branch: impl\_branch (inst, state2)}$$
......
where "inst" stands for an instruction represented in an abstract syntax, "Int_calc" is the set of integer arithmetic instructions, "Fp_calc" the set of floating point arithmetic instructions, "Branch" the set of branch instructions.

λ inst. is the notation of functional programming [20] from lambda calculus [8].
Each subfunction associates to an instruction of the considered class, a composition of micro-sequences.

For example we have:

$\text{impl\_int\_calc} = \lambda$ inst state2.
$\quad$ write_data_int o_p comp_ALU_int(inst) o_p fetch_op(inst) o_p decod_C o_p
$\quad$ decod_B o_p seq_fetch(inst) (state2)

and:

$\text{impl\_fp\_calc} = \lambda$ inst state2.
$\quad$ assign_ALU_fp(inst) o_p decod_C o_p decod_B o_p seq_ fetch (inst) (state2)

where
- seq_fetch(inst): defines the memory accesses required to read the instruction words and to store them into the instruction buffer IB. These accesses depend on the "OPERANDS" parameter of "inst" (for example, if OPERAND is (REG R1 R2) then one read access is required; if it is (IM32 R2 S WIML WIMH), then three memory accesses are required).
- decod_B and decod_C: partly decode the instruction at the top of the IB stack and store the results in the local registers B, C and J_REG
- fetch_op(inst): fetches the operands in the IGPR at the address given by the registers B, C and J_REG and loads the registers L1 and L2 with the read values
- comp_ALU_int(inst): computes the operation defined by the instruction in the ALU of IEU, from the values of L1 and L2 and stores the result in the AIEU register.
- write_data_int: assigns a data memory word or an internal register with the result

contained in the AIEU register.

- assign_ALU_fp(inst): computes the operation defined by the instruction in the ALU of FPU and stores the result in the AFPU register. The operands are read in the FGPR register file according to the instruction fields.

The difference between the two above micro-sequence compositions, is that there is only one micro-sequence for the instruction pass through the FPU, while there are three micro-sequences for the IEU, one for operand fetch, one for arithmetic and logic computation and the other for result writing.

We detail below some micro-sequences:

comp_ALU_int(inst) = λ state2.
   subst (state2, ((AIEU,
         res_calc_int(mnem(inst), sel_L1(state2), sel_L2(state2))),

where "res_calc_int" is a function which determines the IEU ALU result according to the instruction mnemonic.

 fetch_op(inst) = λ state2.
   subst (state2, ((L1, sel_IGPR(ad_op1(inst))
        (L2, sel_IGPR(ad_op2(inst)))

where "ad_op1" and "ad_op2" determine the operand address of an instruction according to its abstract syntax.

 assign_ALU_fp(inst) = λ state2.
   subst (state2, ((AFPU, res_calc_fp (mnem(inst),
           sel_FGPR(ad_op1(inst)),
           sel_FGPR(ad_op2(inst))))))

where "res_calc_fp" is a function which determines the FPU ALU result according to the instruction mnemonic.

We have:
  modif(comp_ALU_int) = {11}   arg(comp_ALU_int) = {9,10}
  modif(fetch_op) = {9,10}   arg(fetch_op) = {8}
  modif(assign_ALU_fp) = {13}   arg(assign_ALU_fp) = {12}

The index 8 corresponds to state variable "IGPR", index 9 to "L1", index 10 to "L2", index 11 to "AIEU", index 12 to "FGPR" and index 13 to "AFPU".

So we see that the independence conditions of "comp_ALU_int" and "fetch_op" with respect to "assign_ALU_fp" as well as the pipeline validity conditions of "comp_ALU_int" and "fetch_op" are verified.

Remark

   We give here only a chronological (timing order) specification and not a chronometric (timing measure) one. We do not specify the pass time in the FPU with respect to the pass time in the IEU but we only specify that these passes must be executed in parallel. We take into account the chronometric properties only at level_3 for which an elementary function (i.e a micro-instruction) corresponds to a machine cycle (for more details on the chronology vs chronometry modelling, see [13]).

5. Specifying the implicit parallelism

5.1.Definition

The explicit parallelism, depends on the processor architecture, decomposed into sub-units which work in parallel. On the other hand, the implicit parallelism does not require a specific processor architecture and does not imply a particular sequencer structure (no parallel branches). It only expresses that an operation can execute at the same time as another. In fact, this parallelism is inherent in our formalism. Defining a micro-sequence as a global state transition function, implicitly specifies the parallel modification of several state variables.

However, it seems to be essential for the verification between levels 2 and 3 to clearly express this parallelism in two cases:
- when two operations can possibly be executed during a same micro-instruction
- when an internal operation can take place at any time during a micro-sequence series. This case means that no early decision should be made that could prevent the designers from optimizing the micro-code.

We express below some implicit parallelism validity condition:

Definition 7

Let $m_1 \in \mathcal{T}(State2)$ *and* $m_2 \in \mathcal{T}(State2)$*.We say that* m_1 *and* m_2 *can be* **implicitly executed in parallel** *if they verify the condition:*

$$modif(m_1) \cap modif(m_2) = \emptyset$$

(we denote m_1 */o/* m_2 *the composition of two such micro-sequences)*

So, in the specification at level_2, we denote "m_1 o m_2" each time that the state changes defined by m_2 <u>must</u> be executed before the ones defined by m_1; we denote "m_1 /o/ m_2" if the state changes defined by m_1 and m_2 can possibly be executed at the same time during the same micro-instruction.

Furthermore, we denote "m /o/ (m_1 o m_2 o...o m_n)" if the micro-sequence "m" defines an internal operation which can be executed at any time during the sequence (m_1 o m_2 o...o m_n) (in fact, this means during any micro-instruction of the sequence which implements one of the m#i). In this case, all the m#i can be implicitly executed in parallel with m.

For the proof between levels 1 and 2, we consider "/o/" as the classical functional composition. On the other hand, between levels 2 and 3, the operator "/o/" gives some indications on the verication process:
- m_1 /o/ m_2 can possibly be identified with respect to a single micro-instruction
- for the sequence "m /o/ (m_1 o m_2 o...o m_n)" we do not identify m with a particular micro-instruction sequence but have only to verify that the global state obtained after the sequence (m_1 o m_2 o...o m_n), includes the state changes defined by m.

Remark

The implicit parallelism is also taken into account in hardware synthesis, but with an opposite view point. In fact, if at level_i, two operations are performed in parallel, some implementation constraints may induce that these operations be executed in sequence at level_i+1 [3]. In this case, we do not specify that two operations are possibly executed in parallel at a lower level but on the contrary, express that two parallel operations must not be parallel at a lower level.

5.2. Example: the MTI processor

We consider the MTI processor, a 16 bit microprocessor with a single instruction format, developed at CNET in France [30]. This processor works according to the based address principle; its instruction set includes 22 arithmetic, logic, branch, and stack handling instructions.

The MTI state can be defined by the list of functions [11]:

state2_MTI= <MEM, REG, DEP, BASE, PC, SR, IR,W,DATA_IN>

where MEM is the main memory, REG is a general purpose register bank, DEP a special purpose register bank used for internal interrupts, BASE is a special purpose register bank used to compute the based addresses, PC is the Program Counter and SR the Status Register, IR the instruction register, W the second instruction word, DATA_IN represents the current word read in the memory.

We first illustrate our formalism with a simple example: the implicit parallelism during the execution of a computation (i.e arithmetic or logic) instruction.
In general, for these instructions, two kinds of variables are set up:
- the variable which receives the computed result
- the program status registers such as the carry or the overflow bit.
We give below the MTI implementation function and then the implementation sub-function for the computation instructions.

IMPLμP_MTI = λ inst state2.
    <u>case</u> mnem(inst) <u>is</u>
        <u>in</u> Calc: IMPL_CALC(inst,state2)
        <u>in</u> {LOAD,STORE}:   IMPL_TRANSF(inst,state2) ....

where IMPL_CALC is defined by:

IMPL_CALC = λ inst state2.
    <u>case</u> mode(inst) <u>is</u>
        IM: (assign_res_im(inst) /o/ assign_code_im(inst))
        <u>in</u> {SD,XD}: (assign_res(inst) /o/ assign_code(inst)) o read(ad_inst(inst))
        <u>in</u> {SI,XI}: (assign_res(inst) /o/ assign_code(inst)) o read_data o
                  read(ad_inst(inst))
        o fetch) (state2)
where

* IM is the immediate addressing mode, SD and XD are two direct addressing modes and SI and XI two indirect addressing modes.
* assign_res_im (resp. assign_res): assigns the REG register defined by the instruction with the value computed by the ALU from the source operand register and the immediate operand (resp. from the value read in the memory).
* assign_code_im (resp. assign_code): assigns the condition codes in the SR with the

indicators value computed by the ALU from the source operand register and the immediate operand (resp. from the value read in the memory).

* read(ad_inst(inst)): reads the memory word at the address defined by the instruction
* read_data: used for indirect addressing; reads the memory word at the address defined by the previous word read in the memory (i.e defined by DATA_IN(state2)).
* fetch: realizes the instruction fetch
* mnem and mode: are some selection functions which determine respectively the instruction mnemonic and the mode from the abstract syntax of the instruction [11].

We have modif(assign_res) = {2} and modif(assign_code) = {6} (where index 2 corresponds to the state variable "REG" and index 6 to "SR"), so these two micro-sequences verify the implicit parallelism validity condition.

A more complex example is the fetch sequence of the MTI. An informal specification of this sequence is given by:

- the memory word at the address defined by the current value of PC is stored into the IR register
- the memory word at the address defined by the current value of PC + 1 is stored into the W register
- at the end of the sequence, the PC has been incremented by two.

Two specifications of this sequence can be given, depending on the implementation chosen at level_3.

A first solution is:

fetch = λ state2.
    inc_PC o assign_W o read_PC o inc_PC o assign_IR o read_PC(state2)

where "inc_PC" increments the PC by 1, "read_PC" reads the word at the address defined by PC, "assign_IR" and "assign_W" respectively assign the IR register and the W register with the value read in the memory.

Another solution is:

fetch = λ state2.
    inc_PC_2 /o/ (assign_W o read_PC+1) o assign_IR o read_PC (state2)

where "read_PC+1" reads the word at the address defined by PC+1, inc_PC_2 increments PC by 2.

The first solution is an easy way to specify the fetch sequence but implies that the PC is modified twice. This is not required by the informal specification and furthermore, induces an implementation choice for level_3 which might turn to be an unnecessary constraint, which would lead to the flagging of "false errors" during the verification between levels 2 and 3. On the other hand, the second solution leaves it free to increment PC at any time during the sequence "assign_IR o read_PC+1".

In fact, the detailed study of the MTI micro-instruction sequences shows that the second solution is needed to provide a proper specification for what has actually been implemented. The PC incrementation is done by a micro-instruction which modifies the memory address pins, during the micro-sequence "read_PC+1"; as a matter of fact, the value PC+1 is never stored in PC, but the value PC+2 is.

Some specification principles can be stated, in order to avoid "over specification":

- use "/o/" whenever the condition for implicit parallelism is satisfied, and the successive execution of two micro-sequences is not required;

- specify a state change only when it is needed and observable at the end of the micro-sequence execution, and avoid referring in the specification to intermediate state values.

Conclusion

We have shown that the specification at level_2, and more specifically the use of several forms of functional composition, are adequate to express some parallelism properties on the processor behaviour at level_3. In particular, our decomposition principle and functional formalism are suitable to model the behaviour of pipelined micro-processors.

A LISP implementation of level_1 and level_2 specifications has been made for the MTI micro-processor. Owing to the decomposition principle, the expressions to be proven between these two levels are quite close. Furthermore, some level_3 micro-instruction sequences have been proven correct with respect to level_2 micro-sequences.

We are now building an interactive, menu driven, specification editor, in order to help the designer specify their processors at levels 1, 2 and 3 (the other levels are covered by classical hardware description languages for which specialized compiler back-ends are being developped by other members of the group). This tool will get the descriptions in a user-friendly way and automatically translate the descriptions into our functional formalism.

Acknowledgements

This work was partly supported by CNET (MEYLAN), under contract #883 B09 100 790 9245 CNS, and by "CHARME" Basic Research Action ESPRIT #3216

References

[1] J.BACKUS: "*Can Programming be liberated from the von Neumann style? A functional style and its Algebra of Programs*", CACM, Vol. 21 N°8, August 1978.

[2] D. BORRIONE, P. CAMURATI, J.L. PAILLET, P. PRINETTO. "*A functional approach to formal hardware verification: The MTI experience*", Proc. IEEE International Conference on Computer Design ICCD'88, Port Chester, New York. October 1988.

[3] C.D. BOYER, S.D JOHNSON. "*A derived Garbage Collector*", Proc. 9th IFIP Int. Conf. CHDL, Washington D.C., USA, June 89 (North Holland)

[4] R.T. BOUTE: "*System Semantics and Formal Circuit Description*", IEEE Trans. on Circuits and Systems, Vol 33, N°12, Dec. 1986.

[5] G. BOUDOL: *"Towards a Lambda-Calculus for Concurrent and Communicating Systems"*, INRIA Research Report n°885, Rocquencourt, France, 1988

[6] M. BICKFORD, M. SRIVAS: *"Verification of a Pipelined Microprocessor Using Clio"*, Proc. of the Workshop on "Hardware Specification, Verification and Synthesis: Mathematical Aspects", Cornell University, Ithaca, USA, July 1989 (Springer Verlag, Lecture Notes in Computer Science N° 408).

[7] A. BRONSTEIN, C.TALCOTT: *"Formal Verification of Pipelines based on String-Functional Semantics"*, Proc. of the IMEC_IFIP workshop on "Applied Formal Methods For Correct VLSI Design". Leuven, Belgium, Nov. 1989

[8] A.CHURCH: *"The calculi of lambda conversion"*, Annals of Mathematics studies. N°6. Princeton University Press 1941

[9] A. COHN: *"A Proof of Correctness of the Viper Microprocessor: The First Level "*, in "VLSI Specification, Verification and Synthesis", ed. by G. Birtwistle and P.A. Subrahmanyam, Proc. Workshop Calgary, Canada, Jan. 1987 (Kluwer Academic Publishers, 1988)

[10] H. COLLAVIZZA:*"Sémantique fonctionnelle des micro-processeurs: le niveau Micro-programme"*, Technical Report N°89-08. Université de Provence, Marseille, France, 1989. (in French)

[11] H. COLLAVIZZA : *"Functional Semantics of Microprocessors at the Micro-program level and Correspondence with the Machine Instruction level"*, Proc of the EDAC Conf. Glasgow, Scotland, 12-15 March, 1990.

[12] P. CAMURATI, P. PRINETTO: *"Formal verification of hardware correctness: an introduction "*, Proc. IFIP 8th Int. Conf. CHDL, Amsterdam, April 1987 (North Holland)

[13] E. DECAMP: *"Methodology for the specification of temporal behaviours applied to the formal verification of circuits"*, R.R. N°580, IMAG-ARTEMIS, Grenoble, France, January 1986.

[14] H. EVEKING: *"Verification, synthesis and correctness-preserving transformations - cooperative approaches to correct hardware design"*, In "From HDL Description to Guarantees Correct Circuits Designs" ed. by D. Borrione. Proc. IFIP WG 10.2 Working Conf., Grenoble, France, Sept. 86 (North-Holland 1987).

[15] M.GORDON: *"LCF-LSM"*, Tech. Report 41, Computer Laboratory, University of Cambridge, England, 1983.

[16] M.GORDON: *"A Machine Oriented Formulation of Higher-Order Logic "*, Tech. Report 68, Computer Laboratory, University of Cambridge, England, 1985.

[17] M.GORDON: *"Why Higher-Order Logic is a good formalism for specifying and verifying hardware"*, in "Formal aspects of VLSI design", ed. G.J. Milne and P.A. Subrahmanyam (North Holland, 1986)

[18] G.C. GOPALAKRISHNAN: *"Specification and verification of pipelined hardware in HOP"*, Proc. 9th IFIP Int. Conf. CHDL, Washington D.C., USA, June 89 (North Holland)

[19] F.K. HANNA, N. DAECHE: "*Specification and Verification using Higher-Order Logic* ", Proc. IFIP 7th Int. Conf. CHDL'85, Tokyo, August 29-31 1985, (North Holland).

[20] P. HENDERSON: "*Functional Programming: Application and Implementation* ", Prentice Hall. 1980.

[21] C.A.R. HOARE: "*Communicating Sequential Processes*", Prentice Hall, Englewood Cliffs,New Jersey, 1985.

[22] W. HOLLINGSWORTH. H. SACHS. A.J. SMITH: "*The CLIPPER processor: instruction set architecture and implementation* ", Communications of the ACM. Vol 32 N°2. Feb. 89.

[23] W. A. HUNT: "*FM8501 : A Verified Microprocessor* ", Technical Report 47, Institute for Computing Science. University of Texas at Austin, Feb. 1986.

[24] J.J. JOYCE: "*Formal Verification and Implementation of a Microprocessor* " in "VLSI Specification, Verification and Synthesis", ed. by G. Birtwistle and P.A. Subrahmanyam, Proc. Workshop Calgary, Canada, Jan. 1987 (Kluwer Academic Publishers, 1988)

[25] T.F. MELHAM: "*Abstraction Mechanisms for Hardware Verification* ", in "VLSI Specification, Verification and Synthesis", ed. by G. Birtwistle and P.A. Subrahmanyam, Proc. Workshop Calgary, Canada, Jan. 1987 (Kluwer Academic Publishers, 1988)

[26] R. MILNER: "*A Calculus of Communicating Systems* ", Lecture Notes in Computer Science, Springer Verlag, 1980.

[27] G.MILNE: "*CIRCAL and the Representation of Communication, Concurrency and Time* ", ACM Trans. on Prog. Lang. and Systems, v.7 n°2, April 1985.

[28] G.J. MILNE: "*Design for Verifiability*", Proc. of the Workshop on "Hardware Specification, Verification and Synthesis: Mathematical Aspects", Cornell University, Ithaca, USA, July 1989 (Springer Verlag, Lecture Notes in Computer Science N° 408)

[29] J.L. PAILLET: "*Functional Semantics of Microprocessors at the Machine Instruction Level*", Proc. 9th IFIP Int. Conf. CHDL, Washington D.C., USA, June 89 (North Holland)

[30] J. PULOU, J.L RAINARD, P. THOREL: "*Microprocesseur à Test Intégré (MTI). Description fonctionnelle et architecture*", Technical report NT/CNS/CCI/59. CNET Grenoble. France. January 1987 .

[31] M.SHEERAN: "*muFP, a language for VLSI design* ", ACM Symposium on LISP and Functional Programming, Austin, Texas, 1984.

[32] J. SIFAKIS, editor: "*Automatic Verification Methods for Finite State Systems*" Proc. Workshop, Grenoble, France, June 12-14, 1989 (Springer Verlag, Lecture Notes in Computer Science N° 407)

[33] J.E.STOY: "*Denotational Semantics: The Scott-Strachey Approach to Programming Language Theory* ", MIT Press, 1977.

The Implementation and Proof of a Boolean Simplification System

Mark Aagaard and Miriam Leeser *

Abstract

We have implemented and proved a Boolean simplification system. Our algorithm is based on the weak division algorithm used in MIS; our implementation is in the programming language ML. We began with a proof of the algorithm presented previously and extended it to a level of detail sufficient for proving the implementation of the system. In the process of developing the proof we clarified many definitions presented in previous accounts of the algorithm, and discovered several errors in our implementation. The result is that the designs generated by our implementation can be claimed to be *correct by construction*, since we have proved the correctness of our system.

Introduction

It is both desirable and feasible to integrate formal synthesis tools into the hardware design process. As of yet, no realistic formal synthesis system has been produced. Boolean simplification provides an excellent candidate for a preliminary formal tool because this task is commonly automated and the results can be rigorously proved based upon the theories of Boolean algebra. In addition, a *post hoc* proof technique is not sufficiently powerful; proving that the input and outputs to a Boolean simplification system are functionally equivalent is NP complete. Rather than prove the result every time we use the system, we prove the correctness of the system once and for all. We have implemented and proved PBS: Proven Boolean Simplification. We are in the process of mechanizing our proof using Nuprl [8], a proof development system developed at Cornell.

There are many different products available which do some form of Boolean simplification. One of the most widely used is Espresso [3]. It has been recently superseded by MIS (Multilevel Logic Interactive Synthesis System) [5], which contains both Espresso and some newer algorithms for treating an entire system of Boolean equations. We implemented a subset of MIS, namely the *weak division* algorithm. We chose this algorithm because it can be concisely described in formal mathematical terms; this has greatly enhanced the development and proof of a correct implementation of our system.

Weak division seeks common subexpressions among the divisors of a set of Boolean equations and then substitutes in new variables for the subexpressions appearing in multiple equations. This is equivalent to replacing several identical sections of combinational logic, each feeding a single input, with a single section of logic feeding several inputs.

A drawback to current Boolean simplification programs is that they rely on the iterative procedure of debugging and testing the output to arrive at a final (and hopefully error free) system. While it is impossible to guarantee the total correctness of any final product, a

---

*School of Electrical Engineering, Cornell University, Ithaca NY 14853

proved Boolean simplification tool can greatly enhance the designer's confidence that a circuit has been correctly implemented.

Many researchers are considering proving hardware design tools correct, and synthesis by proved correct transformation. For example, Martin [12] uses proved correct transformations to synthesize delay insensitive circuits, Chin [7] uses verified design procedures to synthesize array multipliers, Sheeran [14] uses category theory to reason about behavior preserving transformations, and Hanna [11] uses constructive type theory to produce a proved correct implementation of a digital circuit. None of this work, however, is aimed at the task of Boolean simplification.

The rest of the paper is organized as follows: we discuss the origination of the weak division algorithm and provide some general information on Boolean simplification in the Background. We then describe the algorithm in detail, which leads into a presentation of our proof. We conclude with a discussion of our proof and implementation and some remarks about future work. Our presentation depends on many definitions, these are presented in the first appendix.

Background

In general, Boolean simplification algorithms can be classified either as local or global. Weak division [4] is a global approach to Boolean simplification; the algorithm works with an entire system of Boolean equations at once. Local optimization techniques (such as Espresso [3], SOCRATES [10], LSS [9]) examine and optimize each equation independently.

Local techniques attempt to rewrite an individual Boolean function so that the implementation uses the minimum amount of hardware. To do this, a mapping (such as a Karnaugh map) of the inputs and outputs is constructed. This mapping is examined, manipulated and rewritten in some minimal form that takes advantage of knowledge such as *don't cares*.

Global techniques are based upon the premise that a system containing a large number of functions which use the same set of input variables will contain sections of duplicated hardware. That is, there will be multiple groups of logic gates which perform the same Boolean function on the same input variables. These multiple sub-circuits can be implemented once, and their outputs fed into the different parts of the circuit which originally had their own sub-circuit. By implementing each unique sub-circuit exactly once, redundant hardware is eliminated, and there is a great potential for savings in circuit area.

MIS [5] is part of the Berkeley Synthesis System. It supersedes the earlier program Espresso IIC [3] which performed two-level local optimizations on a system of Boolean equations. MIS is interactive in that it allows the user to choose from a variety of algorithms, and to specify the order in which the algorithms are to be applied. This also allows the user to explore the design space by experimenting with different speed/area tradeoffs. MIS uses primarily a global approach, the weak division algorithm. But it also has the ability to perform two level local optimizations and make use of the *don't care* set. This is done by using Espresso as a subroutine to manipulate the equations.

Brayton and McMullen [4] present descriptions of some of the algorithms which are used in the weak division process and outlines of the proofs of correctness for the overall algorithm. While their presentation may be suitable for convincing the reader that the algorithms work as promised, the proofs are sketchy and the definitions are somewhat vague. In a later article [5], more details about the algorithms and expanded definitions of the terminology are included. We have based our work upon the definitions, algorithms, and proof outlines presented in these articles. In some cases we have clarified previous definitions and algorithms, and in many instances we have developed formal proofs from the informal outlines presented earlier. The aim of our work is to prove an *implementation* of the weak division algorithm. Because of this, we reason about the algorithms at a much more specific and lower level than that of the earlier work.

Our proof of the algorithm consists of a formal description, its various properties, and a fairly detailed paper proof. We have begun the process of mechanizing the proof using the Nuprl proof development system. Nuprl is based on constructive type theory and a *proofs as programs* paradigm. In Nuprl everything, including functions, has a specific type. An algorithm is proved correct by describing its type and then producing a proof that the algorithm's type is inhabited by a function. This can be done by either explicitly entering the function or by developing a proof using Nuprl's proof refinement tools. If this second approach is used, an executable implementation of the function can be automatically synthesized. In our case, we will be using a mixture of the two approaches to prove that there exists an algorithm which, for any valid system of Boolean equations, will produce an equivalent system with the additional property that this new system is minimal in some sense.

In our descriptions of the algorithm and proof we further formalize these statements of valid systems, equivalence of systems, and minimality of systems. Before considering the proof, we describe the weak division algorithm in more detail.

Algorithm

In this section we begin with an overview of the weak division algorithm, and then proceed with a more detailed description of the division operation itself. We then present a portion of the algorithm known as *distill*. Distill is the first phase of a two phase process, and is used as an example of the types of operations which we use.

Overview

The *weak division* algorithm seeks to decrease circuit area by removing redundant combinational logic. A sub-circuit contains redundant logic if it implements precisely the same function as another. Consider Figures 1 and 2 and the Boolean equations for outputs p and q. Initially, both equations are in disjunctive normal form and both are minimal in the sense that neither equation can be rewritten in a simpler form. Figure 1 shows a simple implementation of the system of two equations. Notice that in both equations, the term $(b \wedge c)$ appears. In Figure 2 the common subexpression $(b \wedge c)$ has been factored out of each equation. This process can be described as common subexpression elimination, because the redundant logic is identified by examining the Boolean expressions implemented by the circuit. The new variable x now acts as an input to both of the two output variables. This has decreased the area of the circuit, because the factor $(b \wedge c)$ has only been implemented once. The tradeoff is that the delay through the circuit has increased from two gate delays to three.

174

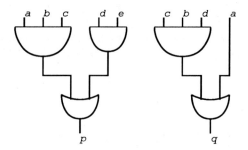

Figure 1: Original Circuit

$$p = (a \wedge b \wedge c) \vee (d \wedge e)$$
$$q = (d \wedge b \wedge c) \vee a$$

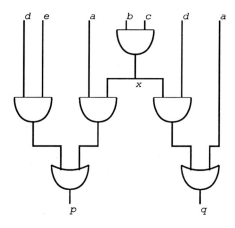

Figure 2: Simplified Equations and Circuit

$$x = b \wedge c$$
$$p = (a \wedge x) \vee (d \wedge e)$$
$$q = (d \wedge x) \vee a$$

Weak division finds the obvious common subexpressions among different Boolean functions, but it gains real power by being able to identify common subexpressions among the *divisors* of different functions. For example, consider the the system of functions:

$$p = (a \wedge b \wedge c) \vee (a \wedge b \wedge d)$$
$$q = (g \wedge c) \vee (g \wedge d) \vee h$$

Each of these functions can be rewritten in factored form as:

$$p = (a \wedge b) \wedge (c \vee d)$$
$$q = g \wedge (c \vee d) \vee h$$

From this it can be seen that the sets of divisors of p and q are:

$$p : \{(a \wedge b), (c \vee d \vee e)\}$$
$$q : \{g, (c \vee d), h\}$$

There is one common subexpression, $(c \vee d)$, among the divisors of p and q. A new variable z can be substituted in for $(c \vee d)$ and the system becomes:

$$p = (a \wedge b) \wedge z$$
$$q = (g \wedge z) \vee h$$
$$z = c \vee d$$

Furthermore, if the system contained another function which had a divisor containing $a \wedge b$, that too could be substituted for. So the system

$$p = (a \wedge b) \wedge z$$
$$q = g \wedge z \vee h$$
$$r = (a \wedge b \wedge c) \vee (g \wedge d)$$
$$z = c \vee d$$

would become:

$$p = y \wedge z$$
$$q = g \wedge z \vee h$$
$$r = (y \wedge c) \vee (g \wedge d)$$
$$y = a \wedge b$$
$$z = c \vee d$$

This example illustrated substitution of two different types of divisors: cube-free divisors, such as $c \vee d$ (these are defined as kernels); and cubic divisors, such as $a \wedge b$.

The description of PBS makes use of a great deal of terminology; the symbols and definitions of all *italicized* terms are presented in the first appendix. PBS is a two phase process [4]. In the first phase, called *distill* by Brayton and McMullen, all *common cube-free divisors* are removed from the system, and in the second phase, called *condense*, *common cubes* are removed from the system. The final result of this substitution of new variables for common divisors is a system of Boolean equations with a minimum amount of duplicated combinational logic. A more formal way to state this is that the largest divisors shared by any pair of equations in the system consist solely of single literals [4].

The two phases of PBS are similar, except that distill works with *kernels* and condense works with *cubes*. There are several reasons for the two phase approach, rather than trying to eliminate all *common divisors* in a single step. First, it is much faster to generate just the kernels than to produce all of the divisors of a function. Second, the substitution of

```
exprDIVcube a_expr d_cube =
    quot = ∅;
    for each cube cₐ ∈ a_expr
        if d_cube ⊆ cₐ
        then quot = quot ∪ (cₐ − d_cube);
    return quot;
```

Figure 3: Pseudo Code for Dividing an Expression by a Cube

new variables for the kernels may create common cubes which did not exist before. So, to remove these new cubes would require a second phase.

In PBS we use an algorithm which generates the complete set of kernels. This allows us to guarantee that the resulting system is minimal. If a fast algorithm is important, it is possible to use just a subset of the kernels; the tradeoff is that the resulting system may not be minimal. In practice, the difference in quality may be quite small, especially compared to the enormous gains in speed. Unfortunately, these results are strictly empirical averages which cannot be easily reasoned about in a formal manner. For this reason, we produce the complete set of kernels.

Weak Division

The entire process of minimization is commonly referred to as *weak division*, when in fact division refers only to the method by which an expression can be divided by another expression. The name is fitting though, because this division operation makes the entire process possible.

To describe the algorithm for performing the division of two expressions, we begin with the example of dividing an expression by a cube, which produces an expression. The algorithm for dividing an expression (a_expr) by a cube (d_cube) is presented in pseudo code in Figure 3, and discussed in the following paragraphs.

The expression to be divided (a_expr) is broken up into the individual cubes making up the expression, and the following operation is performed on each of the cubes.

If d_cube (the divisor cube) is a subset of c_a (the cube from a_expr), then a new cube is added to the quotient expression ($quot$). This new cube consists of all literals of c_a, except for those literals which appear in d_cube, (i.e. $c_a - d\_cube$). If d_cube is not a subset of c_a, then nothing is done. The process is then repeated for the next cube in the expression.

To divide an expression by another expression, the above operation is performed with each of the cubes in the divisor. This produces a set of expressions, one for each of the cubes in the divisor. The quotient is defined as the intersection of these expressions. The following example illustrates this:

To divide $((a \wedge b) \vee (a \wedge c) \vee (a \wedge p) \vee (d \wedge b) \vee (d \wedge c) \vee (d \wedge q))$
　　　by $(a \vee d)$
We first divide by each of the cubes
　　　$((a \wedge b) \vee (a \wedge c) \vee (a \wedge p) \vee (d \wedge b) \vee (d \wedge c) \vee (d \wedge q))/(a) = (b \vee c \vee p)$
and
　　　$((a \wedge b) \vee (a \wedge c) \vee (a \wedge p) \vee (d \wedge b) \vee (d \wedge c) \vee (d \wedge q))/(d) = (b \vee c \vee q)$

These divisions are done by calling **exprDIVcube** first with the expression as a_expr and a as d_cube and then with the expression as a_expr but d now as d_cube. These expressions resulting from dividing the cubes into the expression are intersected to produce the quotient.

$$(b \lor c \lor q) \cap (b \lor c \lor q) = (b \lor c)$$

The resulting quotient is : $(b \lor c)$

Distill

The rest of this discussion will concentrate on the distill phase. The condense phase is just a simplified version of the distill phase, because the algorithms involved in finding and substituting cubes are degenerate cases of finding and substituting kernels.

Distill substitutes new variables for cube-free divisors which appear in multiple functions of a system. The process consists of four steps.

1 Generate the kernels of each function.

2 Find common subexpressions among the kernels.

3 Substitute in new variables for common subexpressions.

4 Back-substitute subexpressions for those new variables which were only used once in the substitution.

The first step is to calculate the set containing the kernels of each of the functions in the system. There are several different algorithms for doing this. These algorithms each provide a different tradeoff between time and quality. In general the faster algorithms return a smaller subset of the kernels. PBS implements an algorithm that returns the complete set of kernels. This is done because we can formally guarantee that our results are minimal only by using the full set of kernels.

The distill algorithm divides an expression by each of the literals appearing in the expression. Each of these division operations produces a divisor which can be divided by the literals appearing in it, thereby producing more divisors of the original expression. This process can continue until the entire set of divisors has been produced. Since we are interested in only finding cube free divisors, we make each divisor cube free before it is factored.

This algorithm is shown in Figure 4 in ML-like pseudo code. In order to compute the list of kernels of an expression, the function **Kernels** is called with the expression being passed as the argument. The expression is made cube free in the function **Mk_cube_free**, and then passed to the function **Kernels2**. Because the expression is now cube free, it is a kernel, so it is added to the list of kernels. This kernel may itself contain other kernels, so **Kernels** is called again, this time passing the expression divided by the first literal. The kernels resulting from dividing the expression by the remaining literals are produced by calling **Kernels2** again, this time without the literal that was previously divided into the expression. The *support* of the expression is calculated in **Get_support**; this is done in order to provide the list of literals which **Kernels2** will recurse over. The *support* of an expression is the set of all variables which appear in the expression.

Now that we have computed the set of kernels of the system, we could search for matching kernels from different expressions, and then substitute new variables back into the system

```
Kernels( expression ) =
    Kernels2( Mk_cube_free( expression), Get_support( expression));

Kernels2( expression, s :: support ) =
    expression ∪ Kernels( expression divided by s) ∪ Kernels2(expression, support);

Mk_cube_free( expression ) =
    if expression is cube free then
        expression;
    else
        let
            c = largest cube dividing expression evenly
        in
            expression divided by c
        end

Get_support( expression ) = list of all literals appearing in expression;
```

Figure 4: Pseudo code for Computing Kernels of an Expression

for these common kernels. This won't yield very good results because it is quite rare that two kernels from two different functions are identical. We are trying to eliminate logical subexpressions which appear in multiple expressions. To do this, we find all sets of two or more cubes appearing in multiple kernels. It is these common subexpressions of the kernels that we substitute into the system. Brayton and McMullen present an informal proof that this is equivalent to eliminating all common cube free divisors among expressions. In the next section we give a formal and complete version of the proof.

Even though each of the cube-free divisors is a divisor of at least two different functions, it is not guaranteed that all of them can be simultaneously substituted into the system. It is possible that the substitution of one divisor into a function will prevent some other divisor from later being substituted in. This could mean that the second divisor is only substituted into one of the functions, in which case we would not be saving any hardware by performing this substitution. This potential problem is dealt with in three steps. First, the cube free divisors are sorted by the total number of literals in the expression. This heuristic will usually result in the substitutions which will save the most area being done first. Second, after having performed all possible substitutions, those divisors which were only used once are back-substituted out of the system. Third, the entire process is iterative. We continue calculating kernels, finding common sub-expressions, and substitution until no more common sub-expressions are found. The iterations are guaranteed to terminate because in each iteration we reduce the number of literals in at least two functions.

Having previously discussed the algorithm for the production of kernels, we now turn our attention to the other major part of the distillation process. After finding common subexpressions among the kernels of the functions in the system, we must substitute the new variables into the functions in place of the common subexpressions. We begin with two systems of functions, one is the original system, and the other is the sorted set of all common subexpressions. We iterate through the subexpressions, attempting to substitute each one into all of the functions of the system. After having attempted to substitute all of the common subexpressions into the system, we find those which were substituted only once and back-substitute them out of the system. The method used to substitute a common subexpression into a function is discussed in the following paragraphs.

The substitution operation is based on the division operation; it requires a definition for *Remainder*:

Remainder The remainder of dividing an expression f by g is those cubes which are members of f, but not of $(f/g) * g$.

The basic property which division operations must obey is:

$$f = Quot(f, g) * g + Rem(f, g)$$

Where $Quot(f, g)$ is the quotient of f and g, $Rem(f, g)$ is the remainder of f and g, and $+$ and $*$ are a sum and a product operation respectively [1]. This property is the basis for the substitution operation used in PBS. Let $a = F$ be a function, (i.e. a is a variable and F is the expression associated with a) and let K be a divisor of F. If we create the new function $x = K$ then we can substitute x into F in place of K. The property shown above can be rewritten to reflect the algorithm as follows:

$$F = Quot(F, K) * x + Rem(F, K)$$

In the substitution operation $f = F$ would be the function from the system and $x = K$ would be a common subexpression. To test if the common subexpression K is a divisor of the expression F we must compute the quotient of F and K. This may seem to be an expensive operation to perform for each function and common subexpression, but it is actually the most efficient way known to test if an expression is a divisor of another expression. For a small improvement in efficiency, if the quotient is empty, we simply return the original expression F and do not calculate the remainder.

In this section we examined some of the more important operations used in the weak division algorithm. After presenting an overview of PBS, we demonstrated the division operation and outlined the different components of the distillation process, which is the first of two phases which make up PBS. The next section relates the algorithms to our work on a formal proof of the implementation.

Proof

We have completed a paper proof of the weak division algorithm and are in the process of producing a proved implementation. We are simultaneously mechanizing our proof and developing an implementation using the Nuprl proof development system. Nuprl [8] is very well suited for this type of task, because of its *proofs as programs* paradigm. Another advantage of Nuprl is that we are able to reason about logical functions using a mixture of logic and set theory. This is of great benefit to us, because set notation is sometimes more expressive for the manipulations that are involved in weak division.

We use the *constructive type theory* of Nuprl to describe a type for each of the algorithms in the component sections of PBS. We then write a theorem claiming that there exists a function which inhabits the type. The theorem can be proved either by explicitly providing the function and then proving that the function inhabits the correct type, or by completing the proof without regard to an implementation, and then using Nuprl to automatically synthesize a function. The advantages to providing a function is that the implementation will usually be more efficient, the code will be more readable, and the structure of the algorithm can be used to guide the development of the proof. In general, though, it is not necessarily easier to verify the type of a function than it is to prove that there exists a function of the specified type. In particular, proofs done in the synthesis mode will not be cluttered with explicit representations of the functions and may allow for proof styles closer to the mathematical proof of the existence of an algorithm.

As an example, consider proving that a function correctly calculates the kernels of an expression. To do this, we would define a *parameterized type*, $Kern\_type(e)$, whose single element would be the set of kernels of the expression e. By doing this we are including the definition of what a kernel is in the type of functions which compute kernels. We would then seek to prove that there exists a function of the type $(e : expr\_t \rightarrow Kern\_type(e))$, where $expr\_t$ is expression type. We could now either verify that some pre-existing function correctly computes the kernels of an expression, or prove that there exists a function matching the type specification and then use Nuprl to extract the function from the proof of existence. With either method we produce a proof of the algorithm and a proved function simultaneously.

In our case, we are proving the existence of a function which can produce a system which is minimal in some sense and which is equivalent to the system used as input to the function. We will be using both styles of proof available to us with Nuprl, choosing between the two for individual theorems as appropriate.

Our proofs are based on some sketchy proofs of some parts of the weak division algorithm. These proofs are quite abstract and not at all formal. For example, to prove that the condense algorithm is correct Brayton and McMullen present the following algorithm [4]:

1 Select cubes $c \in f_i, c' \in f_j, i \neq j$, such that $|c \cap c'| \geq 2$. If no such pair exists, stop.

2 Record $(v, c \cap c')$ for some new variable v.

3 Set $f_i = s(v, c \cap c', f_i)$ for each i.

4 Go to 1.

Their complete proof is:

The f_i coming into the condense algorithm are relatively kernel free, having passed through distillation; and it is not hard to verify that the outgoing f_i must therefore be relatively kernel free. Hence their common divisors are cubes. But it is clear that any cube dividing two of the f_i must consist of a single literal; otherwise we would not have terminated at step 1.

This level of discussion may be suitable for informal arguments, but it is not a formal proof of correctness of either the algorithm or an implementation of the algorithm. We began with several proofs similar to this which have been previously presented, and formalized them at a level more appropriate for describing implementations of the algorithm in Nuprl.

In the rest of this section we discuss an overview of our proof technique and then present two examples of our proofs. These examples have been referred to in a previous section, where we presented the algorithms for the operations which we now prove.

Overview

We now present an outline of the proof, which uses a divide and conquer technique and a mixture of set theory and predicate calculus. In general we prove two claims about each part of the algorithm: that the manipulation performed has some desired properties, and that it preserves the equivalence of the system being manipulated. The equivalence claim is proved by isolating the specific operations which change the system. By proving that these operations preserve equivalence and that no other operations affect the system, we can claim that the entire algorithm preserves equivalence.

Before beginning our outline of the proof, we must define the notion of a *valid system* and *equivalence of systems*. A *valid* system is a set of Boolean functions such that no variable appears on the left and right hand sides of the same equation, and which contains no circularity of definitions. This is consistent with the common practice of describing a system of Boolean equations as a directed acyclic graph, with each variable in the system representing a node in the graph.

More formally, there is a partial ordering of the variables of a system such that no variable x which is in the transitive closure of the *support* of a variable v contains v in the transitive closure of its support. The support of a variable v is the set of all variables which appear in the expression defining v. In a circuit this means that if v can affect the value of x, then x must not be able to affect the value of v.

We define two systems to be *equivalent* if they can be reduced to the same standard form, where the standard form of a system is defined as a rewritten version the system with all of the substitution variables removed and the functions restored to their unfactored form. It is important to note that this standard form is a theoretical concept which is only used for the sake of the proof. The algorithm never performs this reduction.

Our definition is a behavioral definition, because the steady state behavior of the two equivalent systems will be identical. This allows for some transient difference in the behavior of two equivalent systems; the factoring process introduces more layers of logic in the functions, thereby varying the propagation time for the signals.

Figure 5 gives the notation we use in our proof and Figure 6 shows the hierarchy of algorithms which comprise PBS. It also represents a rough outline of the proof tree for PBS. At the top of the tree we have some overall theorem describing the algorithm for PBS and at the leaves (not shown) we have elementary operations on sets. Each node of the tree contains a function which makes calls to the functions in the nodes below it. The node also has several theorems which describe the properties of the inputs and outputs of the function.

∧	logical and
∨	logical or
∈	element of
∩	intersection
∪	union
⇒	implies
⇔	logical equivalence
∀	for all
∃	there exists
$sup(f)$	the support of function f
$\delta(f)$	the set of divisors of function f.
$\mathcal{D}(f)$	the set of primary divisors of function f
$\mathcal{K}(f)$	the set of kernels of function f
$=_s$	equivalence of systems
$x : x\_t$	x is of type x_t

The type symbols are:

$syst\_t$	system
$fnct\_t$	function
$expr\_t$	expression
$cube\_t$	cube
var_t	variable
$FUNS$	function

Figure 5: Proof Notation

At each node of the tree we define three relations:

$\mathcal{I}_i(a)$ a meets the input condition for node i

$\mathcal{O}_i(b)$ b meets the output condition for node i

$\mathcal{F}_i(fun)$ fun is a function which satisfies the functional relation of node i

The input and output conditions define the properties that we wish the input and output of the node to have. The functional relations of the nodes are usually similar to:

$$\mathcal{F}(fun) = \forall a, b. \ (\mathcal{I}(a) \ \wedge \ b = fun(a)) \Rightarrow \mathcal{O}(b)$$

The implementation and the proof are tied together by showing that the functions used in the implementation satisfy the functional relations of the nodes in the proof tree.

Proving the Root Node

We now describe the relations we use and the method by which we build the proof in more detail. We will use the root node (PBS) of the tree as our example. The only input relation is that the input is a valid system. The output relation describes the property of minimality which we claim that the output system has. The claim is an output system s'' is minimal in the sense that the functions in s'' contain common divisors consisting only of single literals.

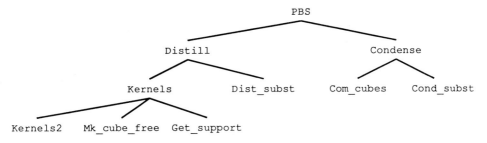

Figure 6: Hierarchy of PBS

This property of minimalism is stated formally by claiming that the size of the support of the intersection of any two divisors of any two functions in s'' is at most one. We write this in mathematical terms as:

$$\mathcal{O}_{\text{PBS}}(s'' : syst\_t) =$$
$$\forall f_1, f_2 : fnct\_t. \ f_1, f_2 \in s'' \ \wedge \ f_1 \neq f_2$$
$$\forall d_1, d_2 : expr\_t.d_1 \in \delta(f_1) \ \wedge \ d_2 \in \delta(f_2).$$
$$|sup(d_1 \cap d_1)| \leq 1$$

The functional relation for PBS is that for any valid system s which is an input to the function, the output of the function satisfies the output relation, and the output system is equivalent to the input system:

$$\mathcal{F}_{\text{PBS}}(fn : FUNS) =$$
$$\forall s, s'' : syst\_t.$$
$$s'' = fn(s) \ \Rightarrow \ \mathcal{O}_{\text{PBS}}(s'') \wedge s'' =_s s$$

PBS is a two phase process, distill followed by condense, so we can break the proof down into two subproofs, one for distill and one for condense and then tie the two subproofs together to prove the overall proof. This is illustrated in Figure 7.

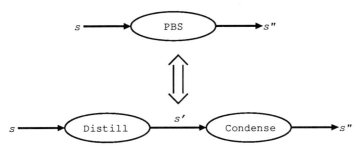

Figure 7: Distill and Condense

In general, when we build a proof for node in the tree from the children, we must show that the relations of the children are somehow equivalent to the parent's relations. In this case, it is quite simple, because we build the function for PBS by concatenating the functions for distill and condense. The proof consists of proving that the input relations of PBS and distill are equivalent, that the output relation of distill is equivalent to the input relation of condense and that the output relation of condense is equivalent to the output condition of PBS. We begin this proof by defining the relations for condense and distill and then show how the various connections are proved.

As with PBS the input relation for distill is just that the input is a valid system. The output relation for distill is that the intersection of any two kernels of any two functions in s' consists of at most a single cube.

$$\mathcal{O}_{\text{distill}}(s' : syst\_t) =$$
$$\forall f_1, f_2 : fnct\_t.f_1, f_2 \in s' \wedge f_1 \neq f_2$$
$$\forall k_1, k_2 : expr\_t.k_1 \in \mathcal{K}(f_1) \wedge k_2 \in \mathcal{K}(f_2).$$
$$|k_1 \cap k_2| \leq 1$$

The functional relation for distill is similar to that of PBS. We need to prove that for any valid input system, the output relation is satisfied by the output system and the output system is equivalent to the input system.

$$\mathcal{F}_{\text{distill}}(fn : FUNS) =$$
$$\forall s, s' : syst\_t.$$
$$\mathcal{I}_{\text{distill}}(s) \wedge (s' = fn(s)) \Rightarrow \mathcal{O}_{\text{distill}}(s) \wedge (s' =_s s)$$

The claim for condense uses the relation that the input system s' is a valid system and has had all common cube-free divisors removed. In other words, the intersection of any two divisors of any two functions consists of at most a single cube. Notice that this is similar, but not identical to, the output relation for distill.

$$\mathcal{I}_{\text{condense}}(s' : syst\_t) =$$
$$\forall f_1, f_2 : fnct\_t.f_1, f_2 \in s' \wedge f_1 \neq f_2$$
$$\forall d_1, d_2 : expr\_t.d_1 \in \delta(f_1) \wedge d_2 \in \delta(f_2).$$
$$|d_1 \cap d_2| \leq 1$$

The output relation is identical to that for PBS: the size of the support of the intersection of any two divisors of any two functions in s'' is at most one.

$$\mathcal{O}_{\text{condense}}(s'' : syst\_t) =$$
$$\forall f_1, f_2 : fnct\_t.f_1, f_2 \in s'' \wedge f_1 \neq f_2$$
$$\forall d_1, d_2 : expr\_t.d_1 \in \delta(f_1) \wedge d_2 \in \delta(f_2).$$
$$|sup(d_1 \cap d_2)| \leq 1$$

The functional relation for condense is that if the input system satisfies the input relation then the output of the function satisfies the output relation, and the output system is equivalent to the input system:

$$\mathcal{F}_{\text{condense}}(fn : FUNS) =$$
$$\forall s', s'' : syst\_t.$$
$$\mathcal{I}_{\text{condense}}(s') \wedge (s'' = fn(s')) \Rightarrow \mathcal{O}_{\text{condense}}(s'') \wedge (s'' =_s s')$$

In order to link together the proofs for distill and condense, we must show three things: (1) the input relation for PBS is equivalent to the input relation for distill, (2) the output relation for distill is equivalent to the input relation for condense, and (3) the output relation for condense is equivalent to the output relation for PBS.

$$
\begin{aligned}
(1) &\quad \mathcal{I}_{\text{PBS}} &&\Leftrightarrow \mathcal{I}_{\text{distill}} \\
(2) &\quad \mathcal{O}_{\text{distill}} &&\Leftrightarrow \mathcal{I}_{\text{condense}} \\
(3) &\quad \mathcal{O}_{\text{condense}} &&\Leftrightarrow \mathcal{O}_{\text{PBS}}
\end{aligned}
$$

The first and last equivalences are trivial, because the input relation for PBS is identical to the input relation of distill and the output relation for PBS is identical to the output relation for condense. The middle relation, which connects distill and condense, is more difficult, and is presented in the next subsection. The difference between the two relations is that the relation for distill reasons about kernels, and the relation for condense reasons about divisors. For now we will continue with the procedure of linking together the functions from distill and condense to create a proved function for PBS.

Assuming that we have proved that the output relation of distill is equivalent to the input relation of condense, we construct a function which is the concatenation of condense and distill. The output of the function will satisfy the output relation of condense for all inputs which meet the input relation of distill. We have shown that the input relation for distill is identical to the input relation for PBS and that the output relation for condense is identical to the output relation for PBS for. So we have proved that the function for PBS is simply the concatenation of the functions for distill and condense:

$$
\forall fn_1, fn_2 : FUNS.
$$
$$
\mathcal{F}_{\text{distill}}(fn_1) \wedge \mathcal{F}_{\text{condense}}(fn_2) \Rightarrow \mathcal{F}_{\text{PBS}}(fn_2 \circ fn_1)
$$

We use this same technique of building up the nodes of the proof tree by connecting the relations of the children of a node with the relations of the parent node. The example used here was not too difficult because the parent node's function was the concatenation of the two children's functions. In nodes with more children and complicated connections the proofs will be considerably more difficult.

Connection of Distill and Condense

In the previous subsection we deferred the proof that the output relation for distill is equivalent to the input relation for condense. We now present our proof as well as an earlier proof of this same statement. This provides a comparison between an informal proof style and a formalized reasoning suitable for proving implementations of algorithms.

In order to connect the two phases of PBS and complete the proof, we need to show that the output relation of distill is equivalent to the input relation of condense:

$$
\mathcal{O}_{\text{distill}} \Leftrightarrow \mathcal{I}_{\text{condense}}
$$

Repeating the definitions of the relations:

$\mathcal{O}_{\text{distill}}(s' : syst\_t) =$
$\quad \forall f_1, f_2 : fnct\_t. \ f_1, f_2 \in s' \ \wedge \ f_1 \neq f_2$
$\quad \forall k_1, k_2 : expr\_t. \ k_1 \in \mathcal{K}(f_1) \ \wedge \ k_2 \in \mathcal{K}(f_2).$
$\quad |k_1 \cap k_2| \leq 1$

$\mathcal{I}_{\text{condense}}(s' : syst\_t) =$
$\quad \forall f_1, f_2 : fnct\_t. \ f_1, f_2 \in s' \ \wedge \ f_1 \neq f_2$
$\quad \forall d_1, d_2 : expr\_t. \ d_1 \in \delta(f_1) \ \wedge \ d_2 \in \delta(f_2).$
$\quad |d_1 \cap d_2| \leq 1$

The difference between the two relations is that $\mathcal{O}_{\text{distill}}$ makes a claim about the kernels of two functions and $\mathcal{I}_{\text{condense}}$ makes a claim about the divisors of two functions. The statement that we need to prove in order to show that these two relations are equivalent is:

$\forall f_1, f_2 : fnct\_t.$
$\quad \forall k_1, k_2 : expr\_t. \ k_1 \in \mathcal{K}(f_1) \ \wedge \ d_2 \in \mathcal{K}(f_2).$
$\quad |k_1 \cap k_2| \leq 1$
$\Leftrightarrow$
$\quad \forall d_1, d_2 : expr\_t. \ d_1 \in \delta(f_1) \ \wedge \ d_2 \in \delta(f_2).$
$\quad |d_1 \cap d_2)| \leq 1$

That is, claiming that the intersection of any two <u>kernels</u> of some two functions consists of at most a single cube is equivalent to claiming that the intersection of any two <u>divisors</u> of those same functions consists of at most a single cube. A proof of this statement appears in [4], we show this proof below to give a flavor for the distinction between previous work in this area and our proofs.

Two new symbols are used in this proof:

$g|f$ g *divides* f: $g|f \Leftrightarrow f/g \neq \emptyset$.
$\mathcal{D}(f)$ The primary divisors of function f. Recall that we use $\delta(f)$ for the divisors of f; and that the primary divisors are those divisors which can be produced by dividing an expression by a cube.

The proof requires the use of a proposition proved earlier in their paper.

[†]**Proposition**: If $g|f$, then $g \subseteq d \in \mathcal{D}(f)$ for some d.
Theorem: f and g have a common divisor d with $|d| \geq 2 \Leftrightarrow |K \cap K'| \geq 2$ for some $K \in \mathcal{K}(f), K' \in \mathcal{K}(g)$.
Proof: $\Leftarrow$ is clear since $|K \cap K'|$ is a common divisor. Therefore, suppose $d|f, d|g, |d| \geq 2$. Then there is a cube-free e such that $e|d$. Now $e|f$ so by the preceding proposition[†], $e \subseteq K \in \mathcal{D}(f)$ similarly $e \subseteq K' \in \mathcal{D}(g)$ for some K and K'. But e is cube-free, so K and K' are as well; hence $K \in \mathcal{D}(f), K \in \mathcal{D}(f)$ and $e \subseteq K \cap K'$ therefore $|K \cap K'| \geq 2$.

We have formalized this proof; and now outline our version. We begin by rewriting our equivalence relation between the output relation of distill and the input relation of condense: there exists two kernels whose intersection contains two or more cubes if and only if there exists a common divisor of two or more cubes:

$\forall f_1, f_2 : fnct\_t.$
$\quad \exists k_1, k_2 : expr\_t. \ k_1 \in \mathcal{K}(f_1) \ \wedge \ k_2 \in \mathcal{K}(f_2).$
$\quad |k_1 \cap k_2| \geq 2$

$\Leftrightarrow$

$\quad \exists d_1, d_2 : expr\_t. \ d_1 \in \delta(f_1) \ \wedge \ d_2 \in \delta(f_2).$
$\quad |d_1 \cap d_2| \geq 2$

First we prove the forward direction of the equivalence: if there are two kernels from different expressions whose intersection consists of two or more cubes then the two expressions have a common divisor containing at least two cubes. We next prove the reverse direction: if two expressions have a common divisor with at least two cubes then there must also be two kernels from these expressions whose intersection contains at least two cubes.

As Brayton and McMullen say, proving the first direction is quite simple. A kernel must be a divisor of an expression; and it straightforward to show that any subset of cubes from a divisor of an expression is also a divisor the expression:

$\forall e_1 : expr\_t :$
$\quad \forall k_1, d : expr\_t. \ k_1 \in \delta(e_1) \ \wedge \ (d \subseteq k_1) \ \Rightarrow$
$\quad\quad d \in \delta(e_1)$
Similarly: $d \in \delta(e_2)$

The subset of any kernel of an expression is also a divisor of the expression. Therefore the expression comprised of the cubes in the intersection of the two kernels is a divisor of both of the two expressions. We assume that there are at least two cubes in the intersection of the kernels, thus, there are also at least two cubes in the common divisor of the two expressions.

$\forall e_1, e_2 : expr\_t.$
$\forall k_1, k_2 : expr\_t. \ k_1 \in \mathcal{K}(e_1) \ \wedge \ k_2 \in \mathcal{K}(e_2)$
$\quad \forall d : expr\_t. \ d = (k_1 \cap k_2) \ \wedge \ |d| \geq 2 \Rightarrow$
$\quad\quad d \in \delta(e_1) \ \wedge \ d \in \delta(e_2)$

This completes our proof of the first direction of the equivalence: If d is the intersection of two kernels of two expressions and d has at least two cubes, then d is also a common divisor of the two expressions.

It is more involved to show that if two expressions have a common divisor then there must be two kernels from the expressions whose intersection contains at least two cubes. The proof is based upon the theorem that if a is a divisor of e then there must exist a primary divisor of e (say b), such that $a \subseteq b$:

$$\forall a, e : expr\_t. \ a \in \delta(e) \ \Rightarrow \ \exists b : expr\_t. \ b \in \mathcal{D}(e) \ \wedge \ a \subseteq b \tag{1}$$

The outline of our approach is as follows: Let d be the common divisor of two expressions e_1 and e_2; construct a cube free expression q which is a divisor of d; then use the just mentioned theorem to show that there must exist two expressions k_1 and k_2 such that k_1 is a primary divisor of e_1 and k_2 is a primary divisor of e_2 and q is a subset of both k_1 and k_2.

$\forall d : expr\_t. \ (|d| \geq 2) \ \wedge \ (d \in \delta(e_1)) \ \wedge \ (d \in \delta(e_2)) \ \Rightarrow$
$\quad \exists k_1, k_2 : expr\_t. \ (k_1 \in \mathcal{K}(e_1)) \ \wedge \ (k_2 \in \mathcal{K}(e_2)) \ \wedge \ (|k_1 \cap k_2| \geq 2)$

By proving that if any two cubes of an expression are cube free then the entire expression must be cube free, we can arrive at our claim that k_1 is a kernel (cube free primary divisor) of e_1 and k_2 is a kernel of e_2. The details of this proof are shown in the second appendix.

We have proved that if two expressions have a common divisor of at least two cubes then there must exist two kernels of the expressions whose intersection also contains at least two cubes. We have already proved the opposite direction of the equivalence; therefore, this completes our proof that the output relation of distill is equivalent to the input relation of condense. This allows us to concatenate any function which satisfies the functional relation of distill with any function which satisfies the functional relation of condense to produce a function which will satisfy the functional relation of PBS. This last step results in a proved implementation of the weak division algorithm.

Proof of Equivalence

The previous discussion has given a flavor of the general methods used in proving that the operations involved in the weak division algorithm are correct. We must also prove that equivalence is preserved between the input and output systems. This is done by proving that a single operation preserves equivalence, and then showing that this operation is the only operation which could alter the system. The operation in question is the method by which a new variable is substituted into a function in place of some existing divisor. Each of the two phases has its own substitution method, but as before, the version in condense is just a simple case of the more general method used in distill.

It is very easy to prove that the substitution operations are the only parts of the algorithm which modify the system. This is because the processes of generating common subexpressions and common cubes just extract information from the system, they never output to the system.

There are actually two operations which change the system, substitution and back-substitution. For substitution we must prove that the operation preserves the equivalence of systems. The substitution operation takes two functions as inputs, and returns a single function. The output function is the result of substituting the variable from the second function into the first function. For back-substitution, we prove that it is the inverse function of substitution. This is because the purpose of back-substitution is to remove those new variables which were only used once in the substitution operation. When we remove a substitution variable from a function, we would like to have the function restored to its original form.

Following our earlier methodology, we define input, output, and functional relations for the substitution operation. The input relation says that two functions, f_a and f_x, are both members of the same system (f_a is the original function and f_x is the subexpression to be substituted into f_a) and the variable from f_x must not be in the support of f_a, that is, it must be a new variable. The substitution operation will alter the function f_a by introducing a new variable into its expression. This new variable only has meaning within a system in which it is defined by a function. So substituting a new variable into f_a, but not including the function for the variable in the system with f_a would be a meaningless operation. The second condition preserves the validity of the system by preventing circular definitions of variables or redefining variables.

$$\mathcal{I}_{subst}(f_a, f_x : func\_t) =$$
$$\forall s : syst\_t.\ (f_a \in s \Rightarrow f_x \in s) \wedge Var(f_x) \notin sup(Expr(f_a))$$

We use $Var(f)$ to denote the variable on the lhs of function f, and $Expr(f)$ to denote the expression on the rhs function f.

There is no output relation for substitution. The operation only produces a single function; the relationship between this new function and the two functions used as input to the operation is defined in the functional relation:

$$\mathcal{F}_{subst}(fun : FUNS) =$$
$$\forall f_a, f'_a, f_x : func\_t$$
$$\mathcal{I}_{subst}(f_a, f_x : func\_t) \wedge (f'_a = fun(f_a, f_x)) \Rightarrow$$
$$f'_a = (f_a / f_x) * x + Rem(f_a, f_x)$$

The first part of the relation says that the original function f_a and the substitution function f_x satisfy the input relation for the substitution operation. We next define a new function, f'_a, which is the result of performing the substitution operation. The definition of division is used to define the relationship between the two functions f_a and f_x and the resultant function f'_a. The formal statement defining a division operation is:

$$g = G \wedge (f = Quot(f, g) * g + Rem(f, g)) \Rightarrow$$
$$f = Quot(f, g) * G + Rem(f, g)$$

A division operation is defined only in terms of other operations. In algebraic structures we cannot say that the quotient of two items really has any specific properties by itself. It is only by combining the quotient and remainder operations that we can make any logical claims. It is exactly this equivalence preserving relationship of the quotient and remainder operating together that we use in proving that the substitution operation preserves the equivalence of a system.

An interesting remark to make about the substitution operation is that its correctness does not require that the function (f_x) which substituted in possess any particular properties with regard to the function (f_a) which it is substituted into, although this is crucial for the correctness of the overall algorithm.

For back-substitution we do not define either an input or an output relation, because the functional relation is that the operation is the inverse of the substitution operation, which is the only claim we need to make about the operation:

$$\mathcal{F}_{Back\_sub}(fun : FUNS) =$$
$$\forall fun_{sub} : FUNS.$$
$$\forall f_a, f_x : func\_t$$
$$\mathcal{F}_{subst}(fun_{sub}) \Rightarrow f_a = fun\,(fun_{sub}\,(f_a, f_x)\,, f_x)$$

We prove the above relations for substitution and back-substitution using our methodology of defining relations and proving theorems for the various component functions which make up the quotient and remainder operations. Proving these relations and inserting them into the appropriate nodes of the proof tree will allow us to prove that our quotient and remainder functions perform properly and thereby support our claim that PBS preserves the equivalence of the input system.

Discussion

In this section we describe our experiences in implementing PBS, some errors we discovered in our work as we were formalizing the proof, and some relevant areas we would like to explore in the future.

We first implemented PBS in the programming language ML [15] in order to gain a better understanding of how the *weak division* algorithm worked and to experiment with various modifications. We chose to use ML because it is a functional language, which means that it came quite close to capturing the ideas we wanted to reason about in the proof. By isolating individual operations into separate functions we were able to quite easily describe the desired properties of the functions, and are now translating these into propositions in the proof as it is being developed in Nuprl.

By examining the code and algorithm in great detail as we formalized our work, we discovered several obscure errors in our implementation and formal description of the algorithm. The nature of the errors is such that they would most probably manifest themselves only in rare occurrences in large systems of equations, exactly the times when they would be least likely to be detected. The two most important errors that we found are discussed below.

There is a subtle difference between a <u>divisor</u> and a <u>primary divisor</u>. In confusing these definitions we produced an implementation which makes use of a very small subset of the kernels (the *level zero kernels*). With this incorrect algorithm, the speed up was tremendous, and the results appeared to be correct. In the process of working on the proof we discovered that this implementation does not generate a minimal result in all cases.

An earlier error that was made involved the back-substitution of variables into the system. We originally thought that by using only the *level zero kernels* we could ensure that all intersections of two or more kernels would be substituted into at least two functions. This means that we would not have to perform the back-substitution algorithm at the end of each iteration of the distill and condense phases. Again this produces a great speed up of the algorithm and yields results identical to a correct algorithm in most cases.

In Nuprl we have been working at both the very top of the proof tree and at the leaves of the tree. At the root node of the tree we have written specifications for PBS, distill and condense. We have proved that the input specifications of PBS and distill are equivalent and that the output specifications of PBS and condense are also equivalent. In addition, we have proved that under the assumption that the output specification for distill is equivalent to the input specification for condense, we can concatenate the functions for distill and condense to create a function which satisfies the specification for PBS. At the lower levels of the proof we began by defining Nuprl analogs of our ML datatypes: var_t, lit_t, $cube\_t$, $expr\_t$, $fnct\_t$ and $syst\_t$. For each of these datatypes we have written and proved constructor and destructor functions. We have also written and proved functions in Nuprl for determining if an element is a member of a list, to decide if one list is contained in another, and if two lists contain identical sets of elements. From these functions we have created and proved equality functions for variables, literals and cubes.

Our most substantial function written in Nuprl so far is one which calculates the conjunction of a literal and a cube. We have completed the specification for this function and are in the process of proving that the implementation meets the specification. Overall we have created approximately 145 theorems, 45 definitions, and 4 tactics in Nuprl.

Although we are still in the process of completing the Nuprl proof, there are several areas that we would like to extend our work into. Among these is considering the use of *don't cares* in multilevel logic, a performance comparison with conventional systems, and area/delay tradeoffs in the design space. In addition, the BOLD system [2] uses a different division algorithm which they claim produces better results than MIS. In the future, we will investigate proving their algorithms.

The manipulation of the *don't care* set of an equation is best handled by Boolean minimization. This is because the goal is to exploit the *don't care* set in order to minimize the disjunctive normal form of an equation. Weak division works by simplifying two level disjunctive normal form equations into multi-level equations, and does not have any knowledge of the *don't care* set of an equation. We realize though, that *don't cares* are an important topic of current research [6, 13], and we plan to investigate several methods of extending the weak division algorithm to allow the use of *don't cares* within PBS.

We do not expect our implementation to run as fast as the conventional systems. These other programs have been optimized with the goal of extracting as much speed from the computer as possible. It is fairly obvious that a data structure based on arrays of bits mapped to a computer's internal architecture will run much faster than a data structure based on lists of text. But there is a tradeoff: if a proved system runs reasonably fast, then an engineer may decide that the extra time invested in the design cycle is worth the added assurance that a final product has been correctly implemented. A lot of time would be lost in redesign if the conventional tool does have a bug in it, and the error is not found until the product has reached the market.

We intend to compare PBS with the MIS system both in terms of speed of execution and quality of results. We do not implement the complete set of algorithms used by MIS, but by using the interactive control of MIS we should be able to restrict MIS to only use those algorithms which we have implemented. This will provide a meaningful comparison between a proved synthesis tool and its conventional counterpart.

In the future we hope to be able to allow the designer to explore the design space by providing methods of evaluating different tradeoffs between propagation delay and circuit area.

Conclusions

There is a great deal of work being done with mechanized formal reasoning and hardware design, but most of the results are quite theoretical and are not yet suitable for an industrial environment. At the same time, synthesis tools (albeit non-formal ones) are becoming increasingly accepted by the industrial community. We believe that although much of the current work in formal design tools is not yet suitable for industry, it is still possible to bridge the gap between theory and the real world. Our system is neither an extremely sophisticated formal tool, nor an extremely impressive industrial tool. Instead, it is preliminary attempt to provide a formal tool which can be realistically used in the industrial design community.

Acknowledgements

We would like to thank the following people for their helpful discussions in the development of this paper and of our system: Geoffrey Brown, Robert Constable, Paul Jackson, and the rest of the Nuprl group. We would also like to thank Geoffrey Brown and Robert Cooper for carefully reading earlier drafts of this paper. We are especially grateful to Paul Jackson for his help in describing our proof in Nuprl.

References

[1] Mario Benedicty and Frank R. Sledge. *Discrete Mathematical Structures*. Harcourt Brace Jovanovich, 1987.

[2] D. Bostick, G. D. Hachtel, R. Jacoby, M. R. Lightner, et al. The Boulder optimal logic design system. In *International Conference on Computer-Aided Design*, pages 62–65, 1987.

[3] R. K. Brayton, G. D. Hachtel, C. T. McMullen, and A. L. Sangiovanni-Vincentelli. *Logic Minimization Algorithms for VLSI Synthesis*. Kluwer Academic Publishers, 1984.

[4] R. K. Brayton and C. McMullen. Decomposition and factorization of boolean expressions. In *International Symposium on Circuits and Systems*, 1982.

[5] R. K. Brayton, R. Rudell, et al. MIS: A multiple-level logic optimization system. *IEEE Transactions on Computer-Aided Design*, CAD-6(6), 1987.

[6] R. K. Brayton, R. Rudell, et al. Multi-level logic optimization and the rectangular covering problem. In *International Conference on Computer-Aided Design*, pages 66–69, November 1987.

[7] Shiu-Kai Chin. Combining engineering vigor with mathematical rigor. In Miriam Leeser and Geoffrey Brown, editors, *Proceedings of the MSI Workshop on Hardware Specification, Verification, and Synthesis: Mathematical Aspects*. Springer Verlag, 1990. LNCS 408.

[8] R. L. Constable et al. *Implementing Mathematics with the Nuprl Proof Development System*. Prentice Hall, 1986.

[9] J. A. Darringer et al. LSS: A system for production logic synthesis. *IBM Journal of Research and Development*, 28(5):537–545, September 1984.

[10] A. de Geus and W. Cohen. A rule-based system for optimizing combinational logic. *IEEE Design and Test of Computers*, 2(4):22–32, 1985.

[11] F. K. Hanna, M. Longley, and N. Daeche. Formal synthesis of digital systems. In L. J. M. Claesen, editor, *Applied Formal Methods for Correct VLSI Design*. IMEC-IFIP, North-Holland, 1990.

[12] A. J. Martin. The design of a delay-insensitive microprocessor: An example of circuit synthesis by program transformation. In Miriam Leeser and Geoffrey Brown, editors, *Proceedings of the MSI Workshop on Hardware Specification, Verification, and Synthesis: Mathematical Aspects*. Springer Verlag, 1990. LNCS 408.

[13] Alexander Saldanha, Albert R. Wang, and Robert K Brayton. Multi-level logic simplification using don't cares and filters. In 26th *Design Automation Conference*, pages 277–282. ACM/IEEE, June 1989.

[14] Mary Sheeran. Categories for the working hardware designer. In Miriam Leeser and Geoffrey Brown, editors, *Proceedings of the MSI Workshop on Hardware Specification, Verification, and Synthesis: Mathematical Aspects*. Springer Verlag, 1990. LNCS 408.

[15] Ake Wikstrom. *Functional Programming Using Standard ML*. Prentice Hall, 1987.

Definitions

	Variable	A simple string of characters (e.g. a, $write$, $carry\_out$).
	Literal	A variable or its complement (e.g. a, $\neg b$).
	Cube	A conjunction of literals (e.g. $a \wedge b \wedge c$, $write \wedge \neg carry\_out$).
	Expression	A disjunction of cubes (e.g. $a \wedge b \wedge c \vee d \wedge \neg e$).
	Function	A variable associated with an expression (e.g. $a = b \wedge c \vee e \wedge d$).
	System	A set of functions.
$sup(f)$	*Support*	The set of all variables appearing in expression f.
$f * g$	*Product*	The pairwise union of all cubes from two expressions f and g.
	Orthogonal	Two expressions are orthogonal if they do not have any common variables.
f/g	*Divide*	The expression f divided by the expression g is the largest set of cubes h such that:
		$\quad h$ is orthogonal to g
		$\quad$ the product of h and g is a subset of f.
	Divide evenly	g divides f evenly if $(f/g) * g = f$.
	Cube free	An expression is cube free if no cube divides it evenly.
$\delta(f)$	*Divisors*	The divisors of an expression f are any cubes or expressions which can be produced by dividing an expression by a cube or expression.
$\mathcal{D}(f)$	*Primary Divisors*	Those divisors of f which can be produced by dividing the expression by a cube.
$\mathcal{K}(f)$	*Kernels*	The set of all cube free primary divisors of expression f.
	Remainder	The remainder of dividing an expression f by g is those cubes which are members of f, but not of f/g.

Proof of Equivalence

In this appendix we prove the reverse direction of the equivalence of the distill output condition and the condense input condition. The proof of the forward direction appears in the section Connection of Distill and Condense. Specifically, the statement we are proving is: there exists two kernels whose intersection contains two or more cubes only if there exists a common divisor of two or more cubes.

$\forall f_1, f_2 : fnct\_t.$
$\quad \exists k_1, k_2 : expr\_t. \ k_1 \in \mathcal{K}(f_1) \ \wedge \ k_2 \in \mathcal{K}(f_2).$
$\quad |k_1 \cap k_2| \geq 2$
$\Leftarrow$
$\quad \exists d_1, d_2 : expr\_t. \ d_1 \in \delta(f_1) \ \wedge \ d_2 \in \delta(f_2).$
$\quad |d_1 \cap d_2| \geq 2$

Let d be the common divisor of e_1 and e_2; we assume that d contains at least two cubes. Any expression with two or more cubes has a cube free divisor. (Recall that an expression is defined as cube free if there is no cube which divides the expression evenly). We can produce this cube free divisor (q) of d using the algorithm Mk_cube_free, which was presented in Figure 4. We use the predicate *cubefree(e)* to denote that the expression e is cube free:

194

$$\forall d : expr\_t. \ |d| \geq 2$$
$$\exists q : expr\_t. \ q \in \delta(d) \ \wedge \ cubefree(q)$$

We have constructed q so that it is a divisor of d, and d is a divisor of e_1 and of e_2; therefore, q is also a divisor of e_1 and e_2.

$$q \in \delta(d) \ \wedge \ d \in \delta(e_1) \ \Rightarrow \ q \in \delta(e_1)$$
Similarly: $q \in \delta(e_2)$

We now make use of Theorem 1:

$$\forall a, e : expr\_t. \ a \in \delta(e) \ \Rightarrow \ \exists b : expr\_t. \ b \in \mathcal{D}(e) \ \wedge \ a \subseteq b$$

We know that q is a divisor of e_1. The theorem tells us that there must then exist a primary divisor of e_1 (say k_1) such that q is a subset of k_1. An identical argument can be used to show that there must exist an expression k_2 such that k_2 is primary divisor of e_2 and q is a subset of k_2.

$$\forall q, e_1 : expr\_t.$$
$$q \in \delta(e_1) \Rightarrow$$
$$\exists k_1 : expr\_t. \ k_1 \in \mathcal{D}(e_1) \ \wedge \ q \subseteq k_1$$

Because it is a subset of both primary divisors k_1 and k_2, q is a subset of the intersection of k_1 and k_2:

$$(q \subseteq k_1 \ \wedge q \subseteq k_2) \Rightarrow (q \subseteq (k_1 \cap k_2))$$

Linking together the previous steps, we can show that if two expressions (e_1 and e_2) have a common divisor (d) consisting of at least two cubes then there must exist two primary divisors (k_1 and k_2) of the expressions whose intersection (q) contains at least two cubes:

$$\forall e_1, e_2 : expr\_t.$$
$$\forall d : expr\_t. \ |d| \geq 2 \ \wedge \ d \in \delta(e_1) \ \wedge \ d \in \delta(e_2) \ \Rightarrow$$
$$\exists k_1, k_2 : expr\_t. \ k_1 \in \mathcal{D}(e_1) \ \wedge \ k_2 \in \mathcal{D}(e_2) \ \wedge \ |k_1 \cap k_2| \geq 2$$

Thus we need only show that k_1 and k_2 are cube free to complete the proof. In other words, we need to show that k_1 and k_2 are kernels as well as primary divisors.

If an expression is not cube free, then by definition, there must exist some cube which divides the expression evenly. In order to *divide the expression evenly*, the cube must be a subset of each of the cubes of the expression; this results from the definition of to divide evenly and from the algorithm exprDIVcube for dividing an expression by a cube. A cube c divides an expression e evenly if and only if $(e/c) * c = e$. This means that the remainder must be the empty set. In order to not have any cubes in the remainder each cube in e must contain c. If this condition does not hold then, according to the algorithm, there will be some cubes from e which will not be represented in the quotient. In order to preserve the definition of division, these cubes must be part of the remainder. But the remainder must be empty; therefore, c must be a subset of each of the cubes in e. More formally, c must be a subset of every cube in e in order to divide e evenly:

$$\forall e : expr\_t; c : cube\_t. \ c \ divides \ e \ evenly \Rightarrow$$
$$\forall c_e : cube\_t. \ c_e \in e \Rightarrow c \subseteq c_e$$

The contrapositive of this theorem is: if any two cubes (c_1, c_2) of an expression have an empty intersection, there does not exist any cube c which evenly divides the expression. Thus, the expression is cube free:

$\forall e : expr\_t.$
$\forall c_1, c_2 : cube\_t.\ c_1, c_2 \in e\ \wedge\ (c_1 \cap c_2 = \emptyset) \Rightarrow$
$\quad \neg \exists c : cube\_t.\ c\ divides\ e\ evenly \Rightarrow$
$\quad\quad cubefree(e)$

We are trying to show that k_1 and k_2 are cube-free, based upon our knowledge that q is a cube free expression which is a subset of both k_1 and k_2. Since q is a subset of both k_1 and k_2; there are at least two cubes in each of k_1 and k_2; whose intersections are empty. Therefore k_1 and k_2 are cube free:

$\forall q, k_1 : expr\_t.\ q \subseteq k_1\ \wedge\ cubefree(q)$
$\forall c_1, c_2 : cube\_t.\ (c_1, c_2 \in q)\ \wedge\ (c_1, c_2 \in e) \Rightarrow$
$\quad (c_1 \cap c_2 = \emptyset) \Rightarrow cubefree(k_1)$

We began by defining d to be the common divisor of two expressions e_1 and e_2. We then constructed the expression q: a cube free divisor of d. From these properties we showed that there must exist a primary divisor (k_1) of e_1 and a primary divisor (k_2) of e_2 such that q is a subset of the intersection of k_1 and k_2. Having now proved that k_1 and k_2 are cube free proves that k_1 is a kernel of e_1 and k_2 is a kernel of e_2. Thus, if there exists a common divisor (d) of two expressions $(e_1$ and $e_2)$, then there must exist a cube free expression of at least two cubes which is a subset of the intersection of two kernels $(k_1$ and $k_2)$ of the expressions e_1 and e_2:

$\forall e_1, e_2 : expr\_t.$
$\exists d : expr\_t.\ (|d| \geq 2)\ \wedge\ (d \in \delta(e_1))\ \wedge\ (d \in \delta(e_2)) \Rightarrow$
$\quad \exists q : expr\_t.\ cubefree(q)\ \wedge\ (q \in \delta(d)) \Rightarrow$
$\quad\quad \exists k_1, k_2 : expr\_t.\ (q \subseteq (k_1 \cap k_2))\ \wedge\ (k_1 \in \mathcal{D}(e_1))\ \wedge\ (k_2 \in \mathcal{D}(e_2)) \Rightarrow$
$\quad\quad\quad (k_1 \in \mathcal{K}(e_1))\ \wedge\ (k_2 \in \mathcal{K}(e_2))\ \wedge\ (|k_1 \cap k_2| \geq 2)\quad \square$

A Model for Synchronous Switching Circuits and its Theory of Correctness

Zhou Chaochen[*]   C. A. R. Hoare[†]

Abstract

Following Bryant [2], an algorithm is given for translating a switching circuit design into a program which simulates its dynamic behaviour. A theory of assertions based on Dijkstra [4] and UNITY [3] is then developed to formalise specifications of hardware circuit designs, and to establish their correctness. Both combinational and sequential circuits are taken into account, and both in N-mos and C-mos; the latter turns out to be much simpler.

Introduction

This paper is an attempt to build a bridge between formal methods for the design of software and of hardware. It tackles the lowest level of discrete reasoning in hardware design, just above the interface between digital electronics and analogue circuit theory. The behaviour of a hardware design at the switching level can with reasonable accuracy be simulated by a program; and this allows a circuit to be specified, and proved correct by standard assertional techniques. More specialised techniques are developed to take advantage of the particular structure and properties of the simulation program.

There are three goals in constructing a formal theory of design of hardware: they are similar to those for software. The first is to provide a final check for the design before committing to the expense and delays of fabrication. The efficacy of the check is increased if it can be made at the lowest possible level of detail and at the latest possible stage before production. A potential advantage of a check at the switching level is that the details of the design and interconnection can be read back almost directly from the final instructions for laying out the fabrication masks.

A second goal of a formal theory is to provide the basis for a rigorous design method. Such a method starts with a mathematical specification, which is perhaps in its turn the outcome of an earlier design phase, conducted at a higher level of abstraction. The method then permits a number of alternative or successive design steps, whose validity may be separately checked, perhaps even by computer. Some of the steps can be wholly automated, but in other cases the need for ultimate efficiency may require the judgement or invention of the human engineer. But in all cases, the rigour of the design method may reduce the expense of checks on the final design, in the reasonable confidence that it is correct by construction.

---

[*]Programming Research Group, 11 Keble Road, Oxford OX1 3QD, England (on leave from the Software Institute, Academia Sinica); *zcc@uk.ac.oxford.prg*

[†]Programming Research Group, 11 Keble Road, Oxford OX1 3QD, England; *carh@uk.ac.oxford.prg*

A third goal of a formal theory at a low level of abstraction is to establish exact conditions for the validity of design methods and paradigms used at a higher level of abstraction. For example, switch level design is used mainly to provide a fixed library of small assemblies (gates and latches), each of them with a fixed set of input and output wires. Gate level design proceeds by connecting output wires of one gate only to the input wires of another gate, with strict rules preventing the introduction of cycles. A theory of switch level circuit behaviour can give a precise formulation and justification for these rules. Formalisation also makes precise the interface between switch level design and lower level design tasks. For example, it sets the objectives that must be achieved by ascribing appropriate sizes to the transistors and geometries to the wires. The problems of sizing are far more difficult than those tackled by the theory expounded in this paper.

In the case of hardware design, there is an additional advantage of a formal theory, if it can predict the results of arbitrary random faults arising from production errors, for example, a switch that will not go on or will not go off. An analysis of these faults can help to define a battery of tests which are applied during production to reject faulty chips. One goal would be to ensure that any chip with just a single fault will be rejected; but it is also important to minimise the total time spent on testing.

Finally a successful formal theory may be the basis for the design of silicon compiler that translates specifications automatically into sufficiently economic designs. Some preliminary work on this is reported in [1].

Of course, it is far too early to predict whether the theory of this paper (or some improvement of it) will ever achieve any of the goals described above. That will depend on a determined effort to integrate the theory into existing design method and tools, and to use it in the actual production of circuits on a commercial scale. Neither of the authors has the skill or the competence to engage in such experimental validation of theory, which is at least as difficult as an experimental test of a theory put forward by a theoretical physicist.

Simulation

We follow the usual convention of giving alphanumeric names $(w, g, s, d, \ldots)$ to the wires of a circuit. For each wire w, we introduce two boolean variables Hw and Lw: truth of Hw at the end of a typical cycle of operation means that the wire w is connected to $High$ voltage; and Lw similarly indicates connection to Low voltage. We also let Hw^- and Lw^- stand for the values of Hw and Lw at the end of the previous cycle of operation.

It will be convenient to abbreviate the pair (Lw, Hw) as just w; and to use the propositional connectives componentwise, so

$$s \vee d = (Ls \vee Ld, Hs \vee Hd).$$

Now there are four possible values for a wire (Lw, Hw)

$(false, true)$	abbrev.	1,
$(true, false)$	abbrev.	0,
$(false, false)$	abbrev.	$\perp$, and
$(true, true)$	abbrev.	$\top$.

When the wire w takes 1 as its value, the wire is connected to power. When w takes value 0, the wire is connected to ground. When the wire w takes value $\perp$, i.e. Hw and Lw are both $false$, the wire is connected neither to power nor to ground; such a wire is said to be

198

floating. When the wire w takes value $\top$, i.e. Hw and Lw are both *true*, the wire w is equally connected both to power and ground. This is considered to be an error in the design of the circuit (often due to a *race* condition); it results in excessive flow of current, and prevents proper determination of the results output by the circuit. Our simulation program will detect such an error, and so need not give an accurate description of its effects.

At the beginning of each cycle of the simulation, all the wires are set to $\bot$. Then, for each input wire w, the value 1 or 0 is assigned, depending whether the input voltage is high or low. This is the *initialisation* phase of the simulation, abbreviated by *INIT*. This phase of the simulation is the least realistic, since in practice each non-input wire retains the value it had at the end of the previous cycle of operation. As a result, there are certain errors in real circuits (e.g., sneak paths) which cannot be detected by our simulation.

The voltage on each input wire remains unchanged throughout the current cycle, but the value of the other wires change as a result of the switching action of the transistors of the circuit (described below). Enough time is allowed for all switching to complete; the value of the output wires can then be read out, and the next cycle can start. In practice, a circuit may fail to stabilise, because one of its wires alternately takes values 1 and 0. In our simulation this wire will take the value $\top$, signalling an error. Our theory will not deal with circuits which are intended to oscillate.

A *transistor* is an electronic switch connected to its environment by three wires, its gate (g), its source (s) and its drain (d). The voltage at the gate determines whether the switch is on or off. When a transistor is on it establishes an electrical connection between its source and its drain. As a result, if the source is already connected to a given voltage, the drain acquires the same connection; and similarly, the source acquires any previous connection which the drain has. Of course, each wire also retains its own previous connection.

The effect of joining the two wires s and d is simulated by the multiple assignment

$$s, d := s \vee d, d \vee s$$

hereafter abbreviated as $join(s,d)$. For connection to power (or ground), the effect is simulated by the assignment

$$s := s \vee 1 \text{ (or } s := s \vee 0)$$

abbreviated as $join(s,1)$ (or $join(s,0)$). Note that these assignments can change the values of the relevant variables only from *false* to *true*, never the other way round; they are therefore *increasing* operations in the ordering which places *true* above *false*.

In a C-mos circuit design there are two kinds of transistors, the N-transistor and the P-transistor. The N-transistor is switched on when the gate is connected to high voltage; whereas for a P-transistor, it is a low voltage at the gate that switches it on. So the propagation action of an N-transistor is simulated by the conditional statement

if Hg **then** $join(s,d)$

and for a P-transistor it is

if Lg **then** $join(s,d)$

Note that both these operations are *monotonic*, in the sense that if any variable is increased *before* the operation, the result of the operation is at least as high as if the increase had not taken place. In N-mos circuits, P-transistors are not available, and more complicated techniques must be used; their treatment is postponed to the end of this section.

Unfortunately, even in C-mos, this is an oversimple model of the switching behaviour of transistors. The problem is that a P-transistor, even when switched on, offers resistance to low voltages, and the N-transistor conversely offers resistance to high voltages. A signal that passes through such resistances may be weakened to such an extent that it no longer reliably operates a gate. A neat solution, described in [5], is to introduce for each wire an additional boolean variable δw which means that the voltage on the wire is strongly driven, either to high voltage through a series of P-transistors or to low voltage through a series of N-transistors. A similar solution can be introduced into the model of this paper; but in the interests of simplicity of exposition we refrain from doing so.

When a collection of transistors is assembled into a circuit, we adopt the usual convention that all wires with the same name are connected together, so that they are forced to take the same value (in fact, each wire takes the *disjunction*, i.e. the least upper bound, of the values they would have taken separately). This is exactly the same effect as when two fragments of a simulation program are put together: naturally, variables with the same name in the two fragments denote the same variable in the combined program. Of course in a real circuit a change in the voltage on a wire takes a time dependent on the length, thickness and shape of the wire. Also in a real circuit the voltage on a wire varies continuously, and it may even oscillate, causing temporary short circuits, before settling down to a final value. Such transient phenomena are ignored by our theory.

To assemble a complete simulation program for a circuit from the single statements which simulate its individual transistors, we use the union operator [] of UNITY [3]. The propagation phase ($PROP$) of the simulation, which follows the initialisation, is defined for a circuit with n transistors

$$PROP \stackrel{\text{def}}{=} T_0 \;[]\; T_1 \;[]\; \ldots \;[]\; T_{n-1},$$

where each T_i is a conditional statement that simulates a single transistor. The meaning of this construction is as follows: all the statements T_i are executed repeatedly at random, until any further execution of any of them makes no difference. The propagation phase then terminates. This is bound to happen, because each individual statement is an increasing operation (in the order that places *true* above *false*), and there are only a finite number of states.

In a real circuit, of course, all the propagations occur simultaneously. The sequential simulation gives the same result as the real parallel execution, in other words the simulation is *deterministic*, because each of the operations T_i is increasing and monotonic [6]. This greatly simplifies our model and its analysis.

Example 1. The simulation for C-mos circuit *NOR*

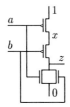

A *NOR*-circuit (as in the figure) has a and b as its input wires, z as the output wire, and x as the internal wire. The initialisation is to decay z and x to the floating state, denoted by *INIT-NOR(a, b, z, x)*

$$z, x := \bot, \bot.$$

The propagation phase, denoted by *PROP-NOR(a, b, z, x)*, is the union combination of the statements which simulate its four transistors:

$$\textbf{if } La \textbf{ then } join(1, x) \tag{1}$$
$$[] \quad \textbf{if } Lb \textbf{ then } join(x, z) \tag{2}$$
$$[] \quad \textbf{if } Ha \textbf{ then } join(z, 0) \tag{3}$$
$$[] \quad \textbf{if } Hb \textbf{ then } join(z, 0) \tag{4}$$

The simulation program for the combinational behaviour of $NOR(a, b, z, x)$ is the sequential composition of the two phases described above

$$INIT\text{-}NOR(a, b, z, x); \ PROP\text{-}NOR(a, b, z, x).$$

Consider the case where the input wires a and b are both set to 0. *INIT-NOR* initialises the other wires z and x with $\bot$, and transfers to the next phase *PROP-NOR*. *PROP-NOR* starts with $(a, b, z, x) = (0, 0, \bot, \bot)$ and only the conditions of statements (1) and (2) are true. The program will terminate directly after the execution of (1) followed by (2), and reaches the final state $(0, 0, 1, 1)$.

The following table lists the simulation result for all combinations of the values (except $\top$) of the input wires.

input		final state			
a	b	a	b	z	x
1	1	1	1	0	$\bot$
1	0	1	0	0	0
0	1	0	1	0	1
0	0	0	0	1	1
1	$\bot$	1	$\bot$	0	$\bot$
$\bot$	1	$\bot$	1	0	$\bot$
0	$\bot$	0	$\bot$	$\bot$	1
$\bot$	0	$\bot$	0	$\bot$	$\bot$
$\bot$	$\bot$	$\bot$	$\bot$	$\bot$	$\bot$

Rows 5 and 6 show that *NOR* is a symmetric non-strict operator. It can give a determinate answer on the output wire z, even when one of its input wires is undetermined.

Of course, the wire x is not intended to be used for input or output. It could be declared as a local variable of the simulation, invisible from the outside. Techniques for removing such internal wires from the specification of the circuit will be given later. □

The program described above simulates the behaviour of a *combinational* circuit, in which each successive cycle of operation is wholly independent of the previous cycle, and there is no storage of information from one cycle to the next. If such storage is desired, the circuit is called *sequential*. The designer of a sequential circuit must specify some subset C containing just those wires c which are to be capable of retaining (as charge) the same voltage which they had at the end of the previous cycle of operation. But this retention is overridden for a wire c on any cycle on which the wire is found to be connected to high or low voltage at the end of the preceding phase *PROP* of combinational propagation. Such prior connections are of course necessary to initialise the wire and to change the stored value when so desired.

The retention of charge and its effects are simulated in a second propagation phase called *CPROP*. We first define the new symbol $\sim$ which is employed in the phase

$$\sim w \stackrel{\text{def}}{=} (\neg H w, \neg L w),$$

and obtain

$$
\begin{aligned}
\sim 1 &= 1, \\
\sim 0 &= 0, \\
\sim \perp &= \top, \\
\sim \top &= \perp.
\end{aligned}
$$

The fact, that a wire c in C will retain its charge from the previous cycle when c is not connected to high nor low voltage at the end of *PROP*, is then simulated by

$$c := c \vee (\sim c_0 \wedge c^-)$$

where c_0 is a *snapshot* of the value c that has at the end of *PROP* and does not change during *CPROP*. The table below shows the simulation result of the retention of c, where c starts with the value from the previous phase, i.e. the value of c_0.

c_0	c
$\perp$	c^-
1	1
0	0
$\top$	$\top$

It shows that c is set back to the value it had at the end of the previous cycle only in the case that the combinational propagation leaves it floating; of course in the real hardware, the wire retains its previous value all along. The simulation program of the retention of all the wires in C is the union composition of the statements which simulate the individual wires in C: it is denoted by *RET*.

The retained charges may switch on or off transistors, and may be propagated between the source and drain of an open transistor. That is exactly what the preceding phase *PROP* simulates. The whole simulation could then have two phases: a sequential composition of *RET* and *PROP*; however the union composition gives the same result, since each of them is monotonic. We therefore simplify them to a single phase:

$$RET \,[\!]\, PROP,$$

and abbreviate this whole second phase to *CPROP*.

In summary, the whole simulation program for a single cycle of operation of a C-mos circuit is the sequential composition of the three phases described above

$$INIT;\ PROP;\ CPROP$$

Of course in a real circuit, the propagation does not divide neatly into phases; consequently a real circuit is subject to errors such as transient charge sharing which are not detected by our simulation (though in some cases charge sharing is signalled by a short circuit $\top$). Some of these risks can be avoided by introducing δw [5]. Others will have to be avoided (or at least detected) at the next lower level of design, by careful choice of the sizes of transistors and the length of wires and the exact timing of the input signals.

Example 2. The simulation program of an RS flip-flop

A C-mos RS flip-flop circuit is made of two NOR circuits, $NOR(r,q,p,x)$ and $NOR(s,p,q,y)$, where p and q are storage wires and x and y are the internal wires. The simulation program for its sequential behaviour consists of three phases

$$INIT\text{-}RS;\ PROP\text{-}RS;\ CPROP\text{-}RS,$$

where the first two phases are the union combination of the corresponding phases of its subcircuits NORs

$$INIT\text{-}RS \overset{\text{def}}{=} INIT\text{-}NOR(r,q,p,x) \ [\!]\ INIT\text{-}NOR(s,p,q,y),$$
$$PROP\text{-}RS \overset{\text{def}}{=} PROP\text{-}NOR(r,q,p,x) \ [\!]\ PROP\text{-}NOR(s,p,q,y).$$

Unioning $PROP\text{-}RS$ with the statements which simulate the retention of storages p and q, we obtain $CPROP\text{-}RS$

$PROP\text{-}RS$
$[\!]\quad p := p \lor (\sim p_0 \land p^-)$
$[\!]\quad q := q \lor (\sim q_0 \land q^-.$

Let $r = s = q^- = 0$ and $p^- = 1$, and start the simulation program. $INIT\text{-}RS$ simply sets p, q, x and y to $\bot$, and transfers to the next phase $PROP\text{-}RS$. This terminates in the state $x = y = 1$ and $p = q = \bot$. The latter become the snapshots of p and q at the beginning of the phase $CPROP\text{-}RS$, and the retention part RET in $CPROP\text{-}RS$ assigns to p and q their previous charges 1 and 0. The whole program at last terminates with the final state

$$r = s = q = 0,\quad p = x = y = 1.$$

The main part of the simulation result is shown in the following table, where we do not list the possible stored charges in the case that they are irrelevant or equal to $\top$.

input		store		final state					
r	s	p^-	q^-	r	s	p	q	x	y
1	1			1	1	0	0	0	0
1	0			1	0	0	1	$\bot$	1
0	1			0	1	1	0	1	$\bot$
0	0	$\bot$	$\bot$	0	0	$\bot$	$\bot$	1	1
0	0	1	0	0	0	1	0	1	1
0	0	0	1	0	0	0	1	1	1
0	0	0	0	0	0	$\top$	$\top$	$\top$	$\top$

Some of the rows of this table are worthy of comment. The first line states that if r and s are held at $(1,1)$, then the values of p and q will go to $(0,0)$, so on the following cycle

p^- and q^- will both be 0. The last line states that if in this state both r and s go to zero simultaneously the result will be a short circuit. This is a warning that RS may oscillate; our theory states that it should be used only in an environment which will not cause it to do so. Rows 2 and 3 show that p and q can be successfully initialised by setting r and s to different voltages. This takes advantage of the non-strict property of NOR. In practice, a suitably designed RS flip-flop can be used as an *arbiter*, to decide between two signals r and s which both go from 1 to 0 almost simultaneously. The decision is made by random fluctuations in the wires p and q, which are then amplified by the transistors. We do not model such physical effects; but the theory is "fail-safe" in the sense that it signals its own failure by giving $\top$. □

We now proceed to describe the more complicated measures needed in N-mos circuit design, where P-transistors are not available. Instead, transistors are classified either as *strong* or *weak*. In the physical layout, the strong transistors will usually have a wider channel between source and drain, and the weak transistors a narrower one. The classification of transistors according to strength is not wholly realistic, but it does seem to follow quite closely the features of the Bryant model [2]. The strong transistors behave exactly like the C-mos transistors described above. The weak transistors, even when switched on, act like resistors, and therefore make only a *weak* connection between their source and their drain. Thus a resistor is modelled as a weak transistor which is always switched on. The weak connection has the usual effect on any wire that is otherwise unconnected. However, if a wire is already *strongly* connected to either high or low voltage, a subsequent weak connection has no effect at all. Thus a connection between the source s and drain r of a weak transistor is simulated by

$$weakjoin(s,d) \stackrel{\text{def}}{=} s, d := s \vee (\sim s_0 \wedge d), d \vee (\sim d_0 \wedge s),$$

where the zero-subscripted variables refer to their values at the beginning of the phase, and therefore stand for any previously established strong connection.

The simulation of the combinational behaviour of an N-mos circuit consists of two phases. The first is the strong propagation phase $SPROP$, which uses the same program $PROP$ as for C-mos, except that only the *strong* transistors take part in it. The next phase is that of weak propagation ($WPROP$). All transistors play a part, strong as well as weak, but they only accomplish weak joins instead of strong ones:

if Hg **then** $weakjoin(s,d)$.

Let us suppose that there is only a single strength for charge retention, and that it is weaker than the strength of signals propagated by transistors. Then the last phase of N-mos design of sequential circuits is the same as that for C-mos design, except that again the propagation is only by weak join. In summary, the overall simulation program is the sequential composition of the four phases

$$INIT; \ SPROP; \ WPROP; \ CPROP.$$

In Bryant's model [2] of N-mos switching circuits, there may be more than two different strengths for transistors. This can be simulated by additional phases of weak propagation, with the weaker transistors joining only in the later phases. Similarly, in Bryant's model the wires which retain charge may be classified as doing so either strongly or weakly. The weakly charged wires are simulated in the last phase, as described above. We can simulate the strong charges by introducing a strong retention program $SRET$, which is the same as RET but only the strong wires take part in it.

In principle, there may be more than two different capacities for charge retention; these may be simulated by more than two retention phases, with more weakly charged wires participating only in the later phases. The strengths of transistors may be classified and modelled in different ways. Our general method can therefore be applied to a variety of models of hardware and a variety of design styles. A designer should select the simplest one which is adequately realistic and supports the relevant design skills. Fortunately for C-mos design the simplest model is adequate for many purposes.

Assertions

In the previous section, we split the simulation of a switching circuit into a number of phases, to be executed in sequence. In this section we explore the assertions which are true at the end of each phase.

We consider first just the first and simplest case, namely a combinational C-mos circuit, whose simulation consists of initialisation followed by a single propagation phase $PROP$. The definition of the $[]$ operator guarantees that at the end of this phase, further execution of the code T_i corresponding to each transistor will have no effect. The logic of UNITY therefore states that all the assignments can be translated into equations, and all of the resulting assertions will be true at the end of the phase. This is known as the fixed point of a UNITY program. The assignment $join(s, d)$ translates to the equation

$$(s, d) = (s \vee d, d \vee s),$$

which simplifies just to

$$s = d,$$

and the assignment $join(s, 1)$ (or $join(s, 0)$) translates to

$$s = s \vee 1 \text{ (or } s = s \vee 0)$$

which simplifies to

$$Hs \text{ (or } Ls).$$

Thus each N-transistor contributes an assertion

$$Hg \Rightarrow s = d$$
or
$$Hg \Rightarrow Hs$$
or
$$Hg \Rightarrow Ls,$$

and each P-transistor contributes

$$Lg \Rightarrow s = d$$
or
$$Lg \Rightarrow Hs$$
or
$$Lg \Rightarrow Ls.$$

Thus at the end of $PROP$ we may make the assertion

$$B \stackrel{\text{def}}{=} \bigwedge_{0 \leq i < n} B_i$$

where each B_i is the assertion contributed by one of the transistors of the circuit.

This assertion describes the all possible final states of all variables on termination of *PROP*, and is called the *fixed point* assertion. The variables Hw and Lw in B are called input variables, when w is an input wire; and the other variables of B are called non-input variables. However B itself is rather uninformative; for example, given any values to the input variables, it holds when *all* the non-input variables take the value *true*. In fact, the set of combinations of values which satisfy B is a complete lattice in the sense of Tarski [7]. This is because the simulation terminates at the fixed point of a monotonic operation.

Example 3.   The assertions for *NOR*
The fixed point assertion of $NOR(a, b, z, x)$ is

$$B\text{-}NOR(a, b, z, x)$$
$$= \qquad La \Rightarrow Hx$$
$$\wedge \quad Lb \Rightarrow (z = x)$$
$$\wedge \quad Ha \Rightarrow Lz$$
$$\wedge \quad Hb \Rightarrow Lz$$
$$= \qquad La \Rightarrow Hx$$
$$\wedge \quad Lb \Rightarrow (z = x)$$
$$\wedge \quad (Ha \vee Hb) \Rightarrow Lz.$$

As expected, we see that $a = b = 0$ makes $Hz = true$, i.e. z is connected to power; and $a = 1 \vee b = 1$ makes $Lz = true$, i.e. z is connected to ground. It is easy to check that all the final states of the simulation program of *NOR* circuit (which are shown in Example 1) satisfy this assertion. However it does not exactly characterise the simulation results. For example, when $a = b = 1$ (i.e. $Ha = Hb = true$ and $La = Lb = false$), both $z = 0$ and $z = \top$ satisfy the assertion; it is not as deterministic as the simulation result. That is why we need the minimalisation described below. □

To give a more informative assertion, we must express it as a relation between the final state of the iteration of *PROP* and the values of the input wires. Because the loop *PROP* is monotonic, it is easy to show [6] that the final state of a UNITY iteration of monotonic operations is the *least* state above the initial state which satisfies the fixed point property B.

More formally, let B' be the result of replacing every occurrence of non-input variables $v, w, \ldots$ by $v', w', \ldots$ The statement that the non-input variables take the minimum value consistent with B can be formalised

$$minB \quad \overset{\text{def}}{=} \quad B \wedge (\forall v', w' \ldots B' \Rightarrow (v \Rightarrow v') \wedge (w \Rightarrow w') \wedge \ldots).$$

We will call this the *exact* specification of the circuit, because it uniquely defines the final values of the wires of the circuit with respect to given initial values of the input wires. For example, the non-input variable Lw takes the final value *true* only if there is no way in which it could take the value *false*, i.e. there is no combination of the final values for the non-input wires of the circuit which will allow Lw to be *false*. More formally,

$$Lw \quad = \quad \neg\exists v, w, \ldots (\neg Lw \wedge B) \tag{5}$$

where $v, w, \ldots$ are the non-input wires of B. A similar equation holds for Hw

$$Hw \quad = \quad \neg\exists v, w, \ldots (\neg Hw \wedge B) \tag{6}$$

206

These facts are established by the theorem

$$minB \quad \Rightarrow \quad (1) \wedge (2).$$

Actually, $minB$ is equivalent to the conjunction of equations like (1) and (2) for all non-input wires of the circuit. The proof is simple, and uses the complete lattice property that the conjunction of the values which satisfy B also satisfies B.

Although $minB$ is the strongest assertion which can be made about the program $PROP$, for many purposes it is convenient to use the simpler and weaker assertion B. For example these simpler assertions are compositional in the following sense: if $B0$ is the assertion for one circuit and $B1$ is the assertion for another circuit, and if these two circuits are connected by their like-named wires, then the assertion for the resulting composite circuit is just the conjunction

$$B0 \wedge B1.$$

In other words, the fixed point assertions are compositional. The same is not true for $minB0$ and $minB1$ (except in the useful but trivial case when these assertions share no non-input variables).

A circuit is usually connected into its environment only by a subset of its wires, namely those which are used on each cycle for input of data or output of results. The majority of wires of a large circuit are never connected to the environment; they are used only to convey intermediate results from one part of the circuit to another. They are like the local variables of a computer program, and their names (and even their existence) are entirely at the discretion of the designer of the circuit: they are certainly of no interest to its user. Consequently, they should not appear anywhere in the assertions which specify the externally visible behaviour of the circuit.

Consider $minB$ rewritten in the form of equations (1) and (2). The equations define the final values of each non-input wire in terms of the values of the input wires. Now the final values of the local variables can be removed from the specification simply by omitting the equations which define their values from the rewritten form of $minB$. This can be taken as the exact specification of the circuit when implemented in such a way that these wires are unconnected to its environment.

But there is a much easier way to formalise the concealment operator, with the advantage that it also gives a compositional fixed point specification of concealment. Consider an equation for a *non*-local and *non*-input wire x and a local wire w

$$Lx \quad = \quad \neg \exists v, w, x, \ldots (\neg Lx \wedge B).$$

By predicate calculus this equals

$$\neg \exists v, x, \ldots (\neg Lx \wedge \exists w B)$$

But this is exactly the equation that would have been obtained if the *fixed point* specification had been $\exists w B$. We can therefore define the concealment operator of w for fixed point assertion B simply as $\exists w B$. This is short for $\exists Lw, Hw.B$, and can be simplified as the disjunction of four versions of B, each with a different combination of values for Lw and Hw.

The validity of the definition of the concealment operator be checked by exploring its relationship with minimalisation. The exact characterisation of the behaviour of $PROP$ is not B but $minB$. What we are interested in is the exact characterisation of the program in which w is treated as a local variable, initialised to $\perp$

begin new w; $w := \bot$; *PROP* **end.**

Since *PROP* starts with $\bot$ as the initial value for w also, the only difference between *PROP* and the above program is that the value of the variable w at the end of the block is irrelevant. We get the exact specification of the program:

$$\exists w.minB \tag{7}$$

But if we take $\exists w B$ as the fixed point specification of the circuit we will be led to suppose that the exact characterisation of the circuit will be

$$min(\exists w B) \tag{8}$$

Fortunately, it is easy to prove that (3) and (4) are equivalent.

There is one danger in the above account of hiding, that the hidden wire in the real circuit will take the value $\top$, indicating that it connects power with ground. This can cause loss of power, overheating etc, leading perhaps to failure of the whole circuit. In order to allow the circuit designer to avoid the problem, it is essential that our model should not conceal it.

We therefore introduce a global variable sh, which is set to *false* initially, and then is set to *true* in the simulation if for any wire w it is found that Lw and Hw are both *true*

if $Lw \wedge Hw$ **then** $sh := true$.

This is fortunately a monotonic and increasing operation. Then every fixed point assertion should have the additional clause

$$\bigwedge_w (Lw \wedge Hw \Rightarrow sh).$$

Now if a short-circuited wire is concealed, the fact that it has made sh *true* is still visible. Like the other non-input variables sh will be *true* only if it has to be; so it should be included in the minimalisation. But we will omit further mention of sh.

Example 4. The assertions for *NOR* (continued from Example 3)
Hide the local wire x in $B\text{-}NOR(a, b, z, x)$

$$\exists x.B\text{-}NOR(a, b, z, x)$$
$$= \exists x.(La \Rightarrow Hx) \wedge (Lb \Rightarrow (z = x)) \wedge (Ha \vee Hb \Rightarrow Lz).$$

By substituting for x all possible values from $\{\bot, 0, 1, \top\}$, we can replace the quantified formula by the disjunction

$$
\begin{array}{llll}
(& La \Rightarrow false & \wedge & Lb \Rightarrow (z = \bot) \\
\vee & La \Rightarrow true & \wedge & Lb \Rightarrow (z = 1) \\
\vee & La \Rightarrow false & \wedge & Lb \Rightarrow (z = 0) \\
\vee & La \Rightarrow true & \wedge & Lb \Rightarrow (z = \top) \quad) \wedge (Ha \vee Hb \Rightarrow Lz)
\end{array}
$$

This simplifies to

$$(La \wedge Lb \Rightarrow Hz) \wedge (Ha \vee Hb \Rightarrow Lz).$$

Obviously, the Hz and Lz take their minimal values when the implications are replaced by equations. So these two formulae

$$Lz \;=\; (Ha \vee Hb),$$
$$Hz \;=\; (La \wedge Lb)$$

constitute an assertion which exactly specifies the simulation result of the NOR circuit in the table of Example 1, provided the inputs are restricted to $\{0,1\}$, and only the non-local wires are mentioned. □   □

Example 5.   The assertions for RS

Due to compositionality the fixed point assertion of RS is a conjunction of the assertions for its two subcircuit NORs:

$$B\text{-}RS \;=\; B\text{-}NOR(r,q,p,x) \wedge B\text{-}NOR(s,p,q,y).$$

Concealment maintains compositionality also. Concealing x and y of $B\text{-}RS$ are simply done by concealing them from the individual subformula $B\text{-}NOR$s.

$$\begin{aligned}
\exists x,y.B\text{-}RS \;&=\; (\exists x.B\text{-}NOR(r,q,p,x)) \wedge \exists y.B\text{-}NOR(s,p,q,y) \\
&=\; (Lr \wedge Lq \Rightarrow Hp) \wedge ((Hr \vee Hq \Rightarrow Lp) \\
&\quad \wedge (Ls \wedge Lp \Rightarrow Hq) \wedge (Hs \vee Hp \Rightarrow Lq).
\end{aligned}$$

However minimalisation can be done only after the whole circuit is assembled. We have to derive $min(\exists x,y.B\text{-}RS)$ directly from the definition

$$\begin{aligned}
Lp \;&=\; \neg \exists p,q.\neg Lp \wedge \exists x,y.B\text{-}RS, \\
Hp \;&=\; \neg \exists p,q.\neg Hp \wedge \exists x,y.B\text{-}RS.
\end{aligned}$$

and similar equations for Lq and Hq. They simplify to

$$\begin{aligned}
Lp \;&=\; Hr, \\
Hp \;&=\; Lr \wedge Hs, \\
Lq \;&=\; Hs, \\
Hq \;&=\; Ls \wedge Hr.
\end{aligned}$$

This specifies the simulation result of RS, when the charge retention is not considered (see the first four rows of the table of the simulation result in Example 2). □

We now turn to the last phase in the simulation of a C-mos circuit, namely $CPROP$. This is also an iteration of increasing and monotonic operations which can be treated in the same way as $PROP$. The assignment

$$c := c \vee (\sim c_0 \wedge c^-)$$

is translated into an implication

$$(\sim c_0 \wedge c^-) \Rightarrow c$$

, and the snapshots Lc_0 and Hc_0 are defined by the final values of Lc and Hc after the $PROP$ phase. Their negations are the formulae X and Y:

$$X \;\overset{\text{def}}{=}\; \exists v,w,c,\ldots \neg Lc \wedge B,$$
$$Y \;\overset{\text{def}}{=}\; \exists v,w,c,\ldots \neg Hc \wedge B.$$

The simulation of the charge retention of c is translated to assertion R_c.

$$((Y,X) \wedge c^-) \Rightarrow c.$$

So we define

$$R \stackrel{\text{def}}{=} \bigwedge_{c \in C} R_c,$$

where C contains all the storage wires of the circuit. R is then the assertion for the charge retention of the circuit.

The assertion for propagation in the $CPROP$ phase is the same as in the phase $PROP$, namely B. The conjunction of R and B describes the possible final states of the all variables on termination of the whole cycle of $(INIT; PROP; CPROP)$, abbreviated to RB. RB is called the *fixed point* assertion of the whole simulation program. However it does not uniquely prescribe the results of the simulation. To give an exact specification, we need to minimalise as before.

$$minRB \stackrel{\text{def}}{=} RB \wedge \forall v', w', \ldots RB' \Rightarrow ((v \Rightarrow v') \wedge (w \Rightarrow w') \wedge \ldots),$$

where RB' be the result of replacing every occurrence of non-input variables $v, w, \ldots$ with $v', w', \ldots$ in RB.

The assertion $minRB$ uniquely defines the minimum final state of the circuit with respect to given input values and stored charges from the previous cycle. $minRB$ can also be rewritten as a set of equations which define the minimum final values of individual non-input variables:

$$Lw = \neg \exists v, w, \ldots \neg Lw \wedge RB$$
$$Hw = \neg \exists v, w, \ldots \neg Hw \wedge RB.$$

$minRB$ is the strongest assertion about the whole simulation program of a C-mos circuit, and it is considered the *exact* specification of the sequential behaviour of the simulated circuit.

The concealment operator for local wires is still valid for the whole simulation program. It can be checked by the fact, when h is a local wire,

$$\exists h.minRB = min(\exists h.RB).$$

It is also valid to use this formula to hide the value of any wire c in C. However the value of c^- which records its previous charge is not allowed to be hidden in this way.

Example 6. The assertions for RS (continued from Example 5)
The retention assertion of RS is

$$R = R_p \wedge R_q,$$

where

$$R_p = (((Y,X) \wedge p^-) \Rightarrow p),$$

and (from Example 5)

$$X = \neg H r,$$
$$Y = \neg(Lr \wedge Hs).$$

R_p can be rewritten as

$$(\neg(Lr \wedge Hs) \wedge Lp^-) \Rightarrow Lp$$
$$\wedge \quad (\neg Hr \wedge Hp^-) \Rightarrow Hp.$$

Similarly we can write R_q as

$$(\neg(Ls \wedge Hr) \wedge Lq^-) \Rightarrow Lq$$
$$\wedge \quad (\neg Hs \wedge Hq^-) \Rightarrow Hq.$$

The fixed point assertion RB of RS is

$$RB = B\text{-}RS \wedge R.$$

The concealment of x, y in RB, $\exists x, y.RB$, is equivalent to

$$(\exists x, y.B\text{-}RS) \wedge R,$$

as x and y do not occur in R. $\exists x, y.B\text{-}RS$ has been given in Example 5 and we are not copying it here. The minimalisation of $\exists x, y.RB$ will produce long formulae also. However we are probably only interested in the practically meaningful inputs, which are the values from $\{0, 1\}$. More formally, we will assume the following assertions always true:

$$Lw = \neg Hw, \qquad\qquad \text{for } w \in \{r, s\}.$$

With these assumption, we can at last simplify $min(\exists x, y.RB)$ to the equations

$$\begin{aligned}
Lp &= Hr \vee (Ls \wedge (Lp^- \vee Hq^-)), \\
Hp &= Lr \wedge (Hs \vee Hp^- \vee Lq^-), \\
Lq &= Hs \vee (Lr \wedge (Lq^- \vee Hp^-)), \\
Hq &= Ls \wedge (Hr \vee Hq^- \vee Lp^-),
\end{aligned}$$

which exactly specifies the simulation result of the sequential behaviour of RS partially shown in the table of Example 2. □

The assertional technique described above for the two-stage C-mos sequential circuit can be generalised to the larger number (n) of stages of the Bryant model [2]. In this generalisation, each circuit is modelled as a list of n fixed-point assertions (one for each strength level). Each assertion describes the fixed points of the corresponding loop in the simulation program. A transistor of strength k has its fixed point assertion in all the last k positions of the list. A wire c with capacitive strength k has the retention assertion

$$(\sim c_0 \wedge c^-) \Rightarrow c$$

in the kth position from the end. When transistors and circuits are put together, the resulting assertion is just the component-wise conjunction of the list of assertions for its components.

The list of assertions gives an abstract compositional semantics for the behaviour of switching circuits. The exact specification is a single assertion about the behaviour of a circuit as a whole. It is obtained by a complex sequence of minimalisations, starting at the left hand end of the list. The concealment of local wires can be done, with existential quantifier, just before the last minimalisation of the sequence, since we must keep recording their values and passing them as snapshots to the later stages. Clearly it is not practical to carry out this minimalisation over a circuit with many thousands of transistors. That is why such circuits are in practice constructed from small subassemblies (gates and latches).

The first compositional semantics for switch-level circuit designs was given by Winskel [8]; the research reported in this paper has been an attempt to simplify Winskel's pioneering achievement, and to demonstrate the relationship between a more abstract assertional semantics and an underlying model of physical circuit behaviour, as described by a simulation program. It is hoped that the methods which have been applied to this example may also be useful in building bridges between theories of computation at differing levels of abstraction, either in hardware or in software, or in the interface between them.

References

[1] D. A. Basin, G. M. Brown and M. E. Leeser, Formally verified synthesis of combinational CMOS circuits. in *Formal VLSI specification and synthesis, VLSI design methods I*, L. J. M. Claesen (ed), North Holland, 1990, pp 197-206.

[2] R. E. Bryant, A switch-level model and simulation for the MOS digital systems. IEEE Trans. Comput., c-33 (Feb. 1984) pp 160-177.

[3] K. M. Chandy and J. Misra, *Parallel program design: a foundation*. Addison-Wesley, 1988.

[4] E. W. Dijkstra, Guarded commands, non-determinacy, and the formal derivation of programs. Comm. ACM 18 (August 1975) pp 435-457.

[5] C. A. R. Hoare, A theory for the derivation of C-mos circuit designs. in *Beauty is our business*, W. H. J. Feijen et al (ed), Springer-Verlag, 1990.

[6] C. A. R. Hoare, Fixed points of increasing functions. Information Processing Letters 34 (April 1990) pp 111-112.

[7] A. Tarski, A lattice-theoretical fixpoint theorem and its application. Pacific J. of Math. 5 (1955) p 285.

[8] G. Winskel, Models and logic of MOS circuits. Proc. of Intl. Summer School on Logic of Programming and Calculi of Discrete Design (July 1986).

Efficient Circuits as Implementations of Non-Strict Functions

Carlos Delgado Kloos *   Walter Dosch **

Abstract

In this paper we derive two adders, viz. the ripple-carry adder and the completion recognition adder, from a common specification. For this development, we describe the adder algorithms by functional programs processing streams of binary digits. We explain the design decisions leading to the implementations and relate the efficiency gain to concepts known from the theory of programming language semantics. In particular, we relate the synchronism of digital circuits to the strictness of functions.

Introduction

The study of the denotational semantics of programming languages has given rise to the family of functional languages. They were designed putting main emphasis on the semantic concepts to be included. Contrary to this approach, imperative languages evolved as abstractions of the behaviour of von Neumann machines. Thus functional languages support the design of algorithms on a high level, whereas procedural programs support their efficient execution on conventional machines.

In the area of hardware, the design of digital circuits has been driven by experience and analogy. New and more efficient versions of a circuit were developed by local optimizations from other existing circuits. The overall design proceeded bottom-up: new and more complex circuits were designed by composing simpler circuits.

In several places ([3, 12]) it has been proposed to understand a digital circuit as an algorithm constructed in terms of primitives that constitute physical devices. If a digital circuit is described by a program, then programming techniques may support its top-down development from a specification. Having this analogy in mind, we examine efficient hardware designs from the view point of functional languages; in particular we relate the efficiency gain to concepts known from the theory of programming language semantics.

When describing circuits formally, synchronism is often assumed, and some assumptions are made concerning the length of the clock cycle and the correct building of loops. However, it is a major design decision, whether a specified function is implemented as a synchronous or an asynchronous circuit. Therefore, we start the design process with a purely functional specification which is free from such implementation concerns, and systematically derive both implementations from it.

In the present paper, we study the design of circuits for digital adders, compare [6, 10, 11]. We specify them in a stream-based functional language and discuss two major implementation lines, viz. the synchronous ripple-carry adder and the more efficient, asynchronous completion recognition adder. In the same way as non-strict functions may speed

---

*Depto. Ingeniería de Sistemas Telemáticos, Universidad Politécnica de Madrid, ETSI Telecomunicación, Ciudad Universitaria, E–28040 Madrid, Spain; *cdelgado@dit.upm.es*

**Institut für Mathematik, Universität Augsburg, Universitätsstr. 2, D–8900 Augsburg, Germany

up the computation of algorithms, they allow an efficiency increase in the performance of circuits.

The Specification

For the development and the description of the adder algorithms we will use a notation that resembles modern functional languages, like [1, 13, 14]. Since adders work on the representation of natural numbers as sequences of binary digits, we first introduce appropriate data structures.

Streams

We use streams to model the linear succession of values. The domain of streams over a set $\mathcal{A}$ of atoms

$$\mathcal{S} = \mathcal{A}^* \cup \mathcal{A}^\infty$$

comprises finite and infinite streams. The approximation order on streams

$$\forall s, t \in \mathcal{S}: \ s \sqsubseteq t \ \Leftrightarrow \ \exists r \in \mathcal{S}: s \hat{\ } r = t$$

expresses that a progress in computation leads to a prolongation of the stream; here, the operator $\hat{\ }$ denotes the concatenation of two streams. Infinite streams are completely determined by the set of their finite approximations.

Note that streams can be used to model the linear succession of atoms both in time and in space, see fig. 1.

Figure 1: Spatial and temporal interpretation of streams

In the syntax, the type constructor **stream**, used in postfix notation, denotes the type of streams over a given base type. For example, **bit stream** is the type of streams of binary digits. In the sequel, the identifiers starting with an apostrophe denote type variables.

On streams, the infix operator

    :: : 'a × 'a stream → 'a stream

prefixes an element of a base type 'a to a corresponding stream.

Moreover, for every arity $n \in \mathcal{N}$ the map operator ∞ used in postfix notation maps a total n-ary function

    f: 'a₁ × 'a₂ × ··· × 'aₙ → 'aₙ₊₁

on base types a_i to the corresponding function

$$f^\infty\colon \text{'}a_1 \text{ stream} \times \text{'}a_2 \text{ stream} \times \cdots \times \text{'}a_n \text{ stream} \to \text{'}a_{n+1} \text{ stream}$$

over streams that applies f componentwise:

```
f∞(x₁::s₁, ..., xn::sn) = f(x₁, ..., xn) :: f∞(s₁, ..., sn)
```

If some argument stream is empty, then the result stream of f^∞ is empty as well.
    For representing binary digits we use

```
type bit = 0 | 1  .
```

In the sequel, we will identify truth values and binary digits, with the correspondence

```
true  ↔ 1
false ↔ 0
```

in order to simplify the expressions.
    For representing natural numbers as infinite streams of binary digits, we use the coding function

```
code: nat → bit stream
```

given by

```
code(n) = (n mod 2) :: code(n div 2)  .
```

In the representation, the least significant bit is at the head of the stream; for example

```
code(13) = 1::0::1::1::0∞  .
```

    In the sequel, we assume all algorithms to process infinite streams. Of course, in every concrete instance one is only interested in a finite approximation.

Definition of the Adder Function

The addition of two streams of binary digits is described by the following algorithm (compare [4, 5])

```
add: bit stream × bit stream → bit stream
add(x::r, y::s)
    = ((x+y) mod 2) :: if x+y>1 then succ(add(r,s)) else add(r,s)
```

where the successor algorithm

```
succ: bit stream → bit stream
```

on bit streams is given by

```
succ(x::r) = if x then 0::succ(r) else 1::r  .
```

Correctness

An adder function on bit streams correctly implements the addition if the representations of two natural numbers are mapped to the representation of their sum, compare the commuting diagram in fig. 2.

```
add o (code, code) = code o (+)
```

Here "o" denotes the function composition operator and "," the pair building constructor.

$$\begin{array}{ccccc} \texttt{nat} & \times \ \texttt{nat} & \xrightarrow{\ +\ } & \texttt{nat} \\ \downarrow\texttt{code} & \downarrow\texttt{code} & & \downarrow\texttt{code} \\ \texttt{bit stream} \times \texttt{bit stream} & \xrightarrow{\ \text{add}\ } & \texttt{bit stream} \end{array}$$

Figure 2: Addition as an induced operation

Developing Adder Algorithms

When analysing the operational behaviour of the algorithm add, we see that bit positions in the stream might be treated twice: once for calculating the sum, and once for performing the successor operation.

Introducing the Carry Bit

To fuse these two subtasks, we introduce the generalization

```
sum: bit stream × bit stream × bit → bit stream
sum(a, b, z) = if z then succ(add(a, b)) else add(a, b)
```

where the additional parameter z denotes the carry bit. The original adder function can be retrieved with the embedding

```
add(a, b) = sum(a, b, 0)  .
```

With a program development employing fold and unfold transformations combined with algebraic simplificactions, we can derive the following direct recursion for the routine sum:

```
sum(x::r, y::s, z) = ((x+y+z) mod 2) :: sum(r, s, (x+y+z) div 2)  .
```

As an abbreviation we introduce the antivalence and majority functions for three arguments

```
A: bit × bit × bit → bit
M: bit × bit × bit → bit
```

defined as

```
A(x,y,z) = (x+y+z) mod 2
M(x,y,z) = (x+y+z) div 2  .
```

216

Their tables read:

A	0	1
00	0	1
01	1	0
10	1	0
11	0	1

M	0	1
00	0	0
01	0	1
10	0	1
11	1	1

When switching from arithmetic to boolean expressions, we obtain for example

```
A(x,y,z) = x ≢ y ≢ z
M(x,y,z) = (x ∧ y) ∨ (y ∧ z) ∨ (z ∧ x)   .
```

Using the conditional, equivalent characterizations read:

```
A(x,y,z) = if x≡y then z else ¬z
M(x,y,z) = if x≡y then x else z   .
```

In summary, the adder algorithm reads:

```
sum(x::r, y::s, z) = A(x, y, z) :: sum(r, s, M(x, y, z))   .
```

Introducing a Stream of Carries

Next we aim at expressing the adder algorithm in a more iterative style using the map operator. To this end, we consider the sequence of carries $c = c_1::c_2::c_3::...$ occurring in the computation of sum(a, b, z):

```
c₁    = z
cᵢ₊₁ = M(aᵢ, bᵢ, cᵢ)     (i>0)
```

Hence the stream c of carries can be computed independently from the antivalence function with the recursion equation

```
c: bit stream
c = z :: M∞(a, b, c)   .
```

This suggests the following generalization of the adder function

```
plus: bit stream × bit stream × bit stream → bit stream
plus(a, b, z::t) = sum(a, b, z)   ,
```

where the third parameter denotes the stream of carries occurring in the computation of sum(a, b, z):

```
z::t = z::M∞(a, b, z::t)   .
```

To derive a direct recursion for plus, we use unfold and fold transformations

```
plus(x::r, y::s, z::t)                          {unfold plus}
   = sum(x::r, y::s, z)                         {unfold sum}
   = A(x, y, z) :: sum(r, s, M(x, y, z))        {fold plus}
   = A(x, y, z) :: plus(r, s, t)   ,
```

and obtain

    plus(x::r, y::s, z::t) = A(x, y, z) :: plus(r, s, t) .

The solution of this recursion equation for `plus` can be expressed with the map operation:

    plus(a, b, c) = A^∞(a, b, c)

Together with the initialization

    add(a, b) = sum(a, b, 0) ,

we obtain the following adder algorithm:

    add(a,b) = A^∞(a, b, c)
        where c = 0 :: M^∞(a, b, c)

Parallel Adder

When we interpret the recursion of the map operator in space, we get the regular repetition of the elementary circuitry implementing A and M, compare fig. 3.

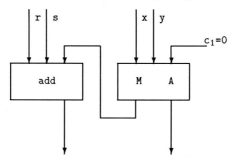

Figure 3: Parallel Adder

In the parallel adder, addend and augend are added bitwise starting with the least significant position. Unwinding the recursion n times in the gives gives a finite approximation for the potentially infinite network, viz. an n-bit parallel adder, compare fig. 4.

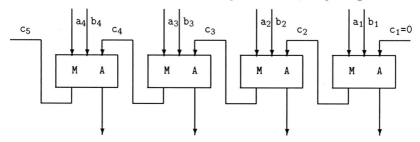

Figure 4: 4-bit Parallel Adder

The operational behaviour of the parallel adder will be analysed in more detail in the next section.

Serial Adder

When we interpret the linear order on streams as temporal succession, the same algorithm add describes the serial adder, compare fig. 5.

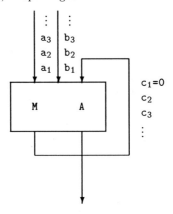

Figure 5: Serial Adder

Here, the bits of augend and addend arrive serially one after the other. In every recursion step one pair of bits is added and both carry and result are transferred. The feedback is done by a 1-bit carry register, which is initially set to 0. Although the adder algorithm is recursive, the network can be kept static since the full adder device (M, A) is reused in every incarnation. Of course, in practice, we only deal with a finite approximation of this infinite computation.

Modelling the Availability of Data

We started from a specification with streams of binary digits, which model the linear succession in time or in space. To discuss the operational behaviour of adder circuits in more detail, we now provide a richer structure as an implementation for it.

Ternary Digits

We consider streams of trits [1]

```
type trit = ? | 0 | 1
```

where the additional element ? is intended to model the non-availability of a binary digit in a computation. Using this additional value, computations resulting from different implementations can be compared w.r.t. their efficiency.

On type trit, we assume a flat ordering

$$a \preceq b \quad \Leftrightarrow \quad a=? \ \lor \ a=b$$

---

[1] Already Knuth gives the name of trits to the ternary digits in [9], but there they have the values -1, 0, and 1

reflecting the availability of binary digits. Here ? is the least element indicating that a binary digit is not (yet) available; the bits 0 and 1 are incomparable.

This approach is motivated by the denotational semantics, where the symbol $\bot$ is used as an additional value to denote an erroneous or divergent computation. In our approach, the symbol ? models a binary digit that is not yet available.

Monotonic Extensions

For formulating the adder algorithm on ternary digits, we have to extend the antivalence and the majority function from binary to ternary digits. These extensions have to respect the original function, that is, their restriction to binary digits should coincide with the original one. Additionally, we require the extensions to produce better output, if better input is available. For the description of this constraint, we call a function

$$f: \underbrace{\text{trit} \times \cdots \times \text{trit}}_{n} \rightarrow \text{trit}$$

monotonic, if for all trits a_i, b_i

$$\bigwedge_{i=1}^{n} \quad a_i \preceq b_i \Rightarrow f(a_1, \ldots, a_n) \preceq f(b_1, \ldots, b_n) \quad .$$

It is called *strict* in the j-th argument, if for all trits a_i

$$f(a_1, \ldots, a_{j-1}, ?, a_{j+1}, \ldots, a_n) = ? \quad .$$

Hence a strict function actually needs its j-th argument: if this argument is not available, the result is not available.

Extension of the Addition

The addition algorithm over trit streams reads:

```
addt : trit stream × trit stream → trit stream
addt(a,b) = At∞(a, b, c)
    where c = 0 :: Mt∞(a, b, c)   .
```

Here

```
At : trit × trit × trit → trit
Mt : trit × trit × trit → trit
```

are some monotonic extensions of the antivalence function and of the majority function to ternary digits:

```
At |bit×bit×bit = A
Mt |bit×bit×bit = M   .
```

These two properties ensure the correctness of this implementation step:

```
addt |bit stream×bit stream = add   .
```

Extension of the Antivalence

For the antivalence there is exactly one monotonic extension, which is strict in all three arguments:

A_t	?	0	1
??	?	?	?
?0	?	?	?
?1	?	?	?
0?	?	?	?
00	?	0	1
01	?	1	0
1?	?	?	?
10	?	1	0
11	?	0	1

Operationally, the antivalence function always has to wait until binary digits are available for all three arguments. The value table does not allow a more efficient implementation where the result is already available although some inputs are still missing.

Extensions of the Majority

For the majority function there are, however, more possibilities. The following table indicates all possible choices that can be taken for monotonic extensions of the majority function:

M_t	?	0	1
??	?	?	?
?0	?	0/?	?
?1	?	?	1/?
0?	?	0/?	?
00	0/?	0	0
01	?	0	1
1?	?	?	1/?
10	?	0	1
11	1/?	1	1

Operationally, for six bit combinations the majority function can deliver a result bit without having to wait for the input bit of some argument. This non-strictness is the reason for speeding up the adder algorithm.

In the next two chapters we will elaborate two major design lines showing how different choices lead to different hardware implementations. We denote strictly extended functions with a hat (^) and non-strictly extended functions with a tilde (~).

Strict Majority

As a first design line, we study the majority function, which is strict in all three arguments.

Value Table

In the value table for the strictly extended majority function $\hat{M}_t$ we choose ? whenever one of the arguments is ?. Operationally, the majority device always waits for all three argument bits in order to compute the result bit.

$\hat{M}_t$	?	0	1
??	?	?	?
?0	?	?	?
?1	?	?	?
0?	?	?	?
00	?	0	0
01	?	0	1
1?	?	?	?
10	?	0	1
11	?	1	1

We can express this function with the following expression

$$\hat{M}_t(x,y,z) = (x \; \hat{\wedge}_t \; y) \; \hat{\vee}_t \; (y \; \hat{\wedge}_t \; z) \; \hat{\vee}_t \; (z \; \hat{\wedge}_t \; x) \quad ,$$

where $\hat{\wedge}_t$ and $\hat{\vee}_t$ denote the strictly extended conjunction and disjunction.

Implementing Ternary Digits

As we aim at a binary technology, we implement the type `trit` with pairs of bits:

    type bb = bit × bit .

We choose the following abstraction function (for this notion compare [7])

    abst: bb → trit
    abst = fun (0,0) -> ?
             | (1,0) -> ?
             | (0,1) -> 0
             | (1,1) -> 1

converting bit pairs into trits. The second component of a bit pair characterizes the availability of a binary digit, whereas the first one indicates which bit it is, provided one is available. In this representation, we have the freedom to code the not yet available bit ? by the pair (0,0) or (1,0).

Implementing Dyadic Functions

First we uniformly define how to transfer a strictly extended dyadic function

$$\hat{f}_t: \quad \text{trit} \times \text{trit} \rightarrow \text{trit}$$

to the implementation type

$$\hat{f}_{bb}: \quad bb \times bb \rightarrow bb \quad .$$

It is specified using the abstraction function (compare this equation with the concept of simulation, as defined in [8]):

$$\text{abst} \circ \hat{f}_{bb} = \hat{f}_t \circ (\text{abst}, \text{abst})$$

The specification deliberately leaves freedom how to represent the result ?. Nevertheless, it uniquely determines the function $\hat{f}_{bb}$:

$$\hat{f}_{bb}((x_1, x_2), (y_1, y_2)) = (f(x_1, y_1), x_2 \wedge y_2) \quad .$$

Hence, the single result components only depend on the respective input components. In particular, for conjunction and disjunction we obtain:

$$(x_1,x_2) \; \hat{\wedge}_{bb} \; (y_1,y_2) = (x_1 \wedge y_1, \; x_2 \wedge y_2)$$
$$(x_1,x_2) \; \hat{\vee}_{bb} \; (y_1,y_2) = (x_1 \vee y_1, \; x_2 \wedge y_2) \quad .$$

Implementing the Majority Function

For the strictly extended majority function on bit pairs

$$\hat{M}_{bb}: \; bb \times bb \times bb \rightarrow bb$$

we calculate:

$$\hat{M}_{bb}((x_1,x_2), (y_1,y_2), (z_1,z_2))$$
$$= ((x_1,x_2) \hat{\wedge}_{bb}(y_1,y_2)) \; \hat{\vee}_{bb} \; ((y_1,y_2) \hat{\wedge}_{bb}(z_1,z_2)) \; \hat{\vee}_{bb} \; ((z_1,z_2) \hat{\wedge}_{bb}(x_1,x_2))$$
$$= ((x_1 \wedge y_1) \vee (y_1 \wedge z_1) \vee (z_1 \wedge x_1), \; (x_2 \wedge y_2) \wedge (y_2 \wedge z_2) \wedge (z_2 \wedge x_2))$$
$$= (M(x_1,y_1,z_1), \; x_2 \wedge y_2 \wedge z_2)$$

The interpretation of this result is simple: if all three input bits are available, that is, their second components are equal to 1, we compute the majority of the first components and signal the result as available, that is, we put the second bit to 1; otherwise the result is not yet available, as indicated by the second bit 0.

Implementing the Antivalence Function

The dyadic antivalence function

$$\hat{\neq}_{bb}: \; bb \times bb \rightarrow bb$$

on the implementation type can again be computed componentwise:

$$(x_1,x_2) \; \hat{\neq}_{bb} \; (y_1,y_2) = (x_1 \neq y_1, \; x_2 \wedge y_2)$$

For the strictly extended ternary antivalence function

$$\hat{A}_{bb}: \; bb \times bb \times bb \rightarrow bb$$

we obtain with a simple calculation:

$$\hat{A}_{bb}((x_1,x_2), (y_1,y_2), (z_1,z_2))$$
$$= (x_1,x_2) \; \hat{\neq}_{bb} \; (y_1,y_2) \; \hat{\neq}_{bb} \; (z_1,z_2)$$
$$= (x_1 \neq y_1 \neq z_1, \; x_2 \wedge y_2 \wedge z_2)$$

Thus, the strict antivalence shows the same operational behaviour as the strict majority function. If all three argument bits are available, then the antivalence of the first components is computed. If one or more argument bits are missing, however, the antivalence does not produce an output.

Detailed Behaviour of the Ripple-Carry Adder

The complete definition of the ripple-carry adder reads:

```
rc-add: bb stream × bb stream → bb stream
rc-add(a,b) = Âbb∞(a,b,c)
   where c = (0,1) :: M̂bb∞(a,b,c)
```

To analyse the time efficiency of this adder, we take a closer look at the streams. For this purpose, we first turn every atom x into an infinite constant stream x^∞. This stream models a finer behaviour, since the single value considered up to now is spread into a sequence of values at subsequent time instants. Similarly, a stream (when interpreted in space) can be refined componentwise into a stream of constant streams. This leads to two-dimensional space-time diagrams, compare fig. 6.

Figure 6: Space-Time Diagram

In this detailed view, we furthermore assume that each of the basic functions has a certain delay. We model this delay by prefixing the symbol ? to the output stream of the function. For example, the output of the negation function with input 1^∞ will be $?::0^\infty$.

For addend and augend

$$a = a_1^\infty :: a_2^\infty :: a_3^\infty :: \ldots$$
$$b = b_1^\infty :: b_2^\infty :: b_3^\infty :: \ldots$$

the following carries are generated:

$$c_1 = 0^\infty$$
$$c_{i+1} = ? :: M̂_t^\infty(a_i^\infty, b_i^\infty, c_i) \qquad (i>0)$$

Thus the stream of streams of carries satisfies the following recursion equation

$$c = 0^\infty :: (?::)^\infty(M̂_t^{\infty\infty}(a, b, c)) \quad,$$

where $(?::)^\infty$ is the componentwise extension of the monadic function $(?::)$ on streams to streams of streams.

The two-dimensional space-time diagram for the stream of streams of carries reads:

							↑ time
	m_{44}	m_{34}	m_{24}	m_{14}	0	5	
...	?	m_{33}	m_{23}	m_{13}	0	4	
...	?	?	m_{22}	m_{12}	0	3	
...	?	?	?	m_{11}	0	2	
...	?	?	?	?	0	1	
space ←	c_5	c_4	c_3	c_2	c_1		

where $m_{ij} = \hat{M}_t(a_{ij}, b_{ij}, c_{ij})$. Since we have implemented a strict majority, all the ?'s propagate. This yields the above diagram — independently of the value of addend and augend.

The carries of successive stages are computed later, because they depend on the carries of the stage before. This gave the name to the "ripple-carry" adder. Switching from trits to bit pairs, we see that the availability bit is set to 1 at successively later instants for the successive stages. Instead of interpreting the second bit as an availability signal, we may also look at it as a clock line.

Suppose we know beforehand an upper bound for the (real-time) delays of the components. Then we may replace all the availability bit lines by a single bit line that signalises the instants of these upper bounds. In general, we get then a worse performance, because we may receive some results later. But as an advantage, we need not compute the availability signal for each component. We indicate with this separate line the instants at which the results at the other lines are to be taken seriously. This additional line then corresponds to a clock line.

The detailed algorithm for the ripple-carry adder reads:

```
fine-rc-add: bb stream stream × bb stream stream → bb stream stream
fine-rc-add(a,b) = ((0,0)::)∞ (Âbb°°°(a,b,c))
     where c = (0,1)∞ ::  ((0,0)::)∞ (M̂bb°°°(a,b,c))
```

Non-Strict Majority

As discussed before, there are several non-strict but monotonic extensions of the majority function. The choice of the particular extension used in this section is uniquely determined by the following two design decisions:

- We aim at developing an adder circuit where recursion is put into space. Thus, we may assume that all input bits of augend and addend are simultaneously available. Hence we can choose the majority function to be strict in the first and in the second argument.

- We aim at disentangling the computations for the single positions of addend and augend as much as possible. Since the carry is the only dependence between adjacent positions, we choose the majority function non-strict in the third argument whenever possible.

Value table

The subsequent development is therefore based on the following non-strict extension:

$\widetilde{M}_t$	?	0	1
??	?	?	?
?0	?	?	?
?1	?	?	?
0?	?	?	?
00	**0**	**0**	**0**
01	?	0	1
1?	?	?	?
10	?	0	1
11	**1**	**1**	**1**

Vertically, the two first arguments represent the input bits of augend and addend, and horizontally the third one corresponds to the carry from the next lower position. The result of the majority can be computed independently of the (not yet available) carry bit, iff the bits of addend and augend are equal (compare the bold-faced entries in the value table).

We may define this non-strict majority function with an expression similar to that for the majority function defined over bits:

$$\widetilde{M}_t(x,y,z) = \widetilde{if}_t \ x\,\widehat{\widetilde{=}}_t\,y \text{ then } x \text{ else } z$$

Here we take the strict extension of the equivalence and the following extension of the conditional:

$$\widetilde{if}_t \ u \text{ then } v \text{ else } w = \begin{cases} ? & \text{if } u=? \\ v & \text{if } u=1 \\ w & \text{if } u=0 \end{cases}$$

which is non-strict in the first argument.

Implementing Ternary Digits

Again we implement ternary digits with pairs of binary digits. The representation function

```
repr': trit → bb
repr' = fun 0 -> (1,0)
          | 1 -> (0,1)
          | ? -> (0,0)
```

defines a two-rail coding: the bit 1 as the first component indicates the value 0, and the bit 1 as the second component represents the value 1.

Conversely, an abstraction function is given by

```
abst': bb → trit
abst' = fun (0,0) -> ?
          | (1,1) -> ?
          | (1,0) -> 0
          | (0,1) -> 1   .
```

Hereby, the contradictory bit combination $(1,1)$ is interpreted as if no proper binary digit were available.

Implementing the Majority Function

First, we express the strict equivalence on bit pairs

$$\hat{\equiv}_{bb}: \quad bb \times bb \rightarrow bb$$

in terms of boolean functions. As an abbreviation, we introduce the predicate

$$P: bb \rightarrow bit$$
$$P(x_1,x_2) = x_1 \neq x_2$$

which yields 1 iff the pair represents an available binary digit. From the specification

$$abst' \circ \hat{\equiv}_{bb} = \hat{\equiv}_t \circ (abst', abst')$$

and the requirement to represent the missing result bit always by $(0,0)$, we get

$$(x_1,x_2) \hat{\equiv}_{bb} (y_1,y_2)$$
$$= \text{if } P(x_1,x_2) \wedge P(y_1,y_2) \text{ then } (x_1 \neq y_1, x_2 \equiv y_2) \text{ else } (0,0) \quad .$$

In a similar way, the conditional function on bit pairs can be split into a pair of conditionals:

$$\widetilde{if}_{bb} (u_1, u_2) \text{ then } (v_1, v_2) \text{ else } (w_1, w_2)$$
$$= \text{if } P(u_1, u_2) \text{ then } (\text{if } \neg u_1 \text{ then } v_1 \text{ else } w_1,$$
$$\qquad\qquad\qquad \text{if } u_2 \text{ then } v_2 \text{ else } w_2) \text{ else } (0,0)$$

For the majority function

$$\widetilde{M}_{bb}: \quad bb \times bb \times bb \rightarrow bb$$

induced on pairs of bits, we calculate:

$$\widetilde{M}_{bb}((x_1,x_2), (y_1,y_2), (z_1,z_2))$$
$$= \widetilde{if}_{bb} (x_1,x_2) \hat{\equiv}_{bb} (y_1,y_2) \text{ then } (x_1,x_2) \text{ else } (z_1,z_2)$$
$$= \text{if } P(x_1,x_2) \wedge P(y_1,y_2) \text{ then } (\text{if } \neg x_1 \neq y_1 \text{ then } x_1 \text{ else } z_1,$$
$$\qquad\qquad\qquad\qquad\qquad \text{if } x_2 \equiv y_2 \text{ then } x_2 \text{ else } z_2)$$
$$\qquad\qquad\qquad\qquad \text{else } (0,0)$$
$$= \text{if } P(x_1,x_2) \wedge P(y_1,y_2) \text{ then } (M(x_1,y_1,z_1), M(x_2,y_2,z_2)) \text{ else } (0,0)$$

Altogether this leads to a duplication of the circuit: There is one majority function for the first or 0 component and one for the second or 1 component.

Implementing the Antivalence Function

As a preparation, we first implement the dyadic antivalence function on pairs of bits:

$$\hat{\neq}_{bb}: \quad bb \times bb \rightarrow bb$$
$$(x_1, x_2) \hat{\neq}_{bb} (y_1, y_2)$$
$$= \text{if } P(x_1,x_2) \wedge P(y_1,y_2) \text{ then } (x_1 \equiv y_1, x_2 \neq y_2) \text{ else } (0,0)$$

For the implementation of the strictly extended ternary antivalence function

$\hat{A}_{bb}$: bb $\times$ bb $\times$ bb $\rightarrow$ bb

we calculate

```
Âbb((x₁,x₂), (y₁,y₂), (z₁,z₂))
   = (x₁,x₂) ≇bb (y₁,y₂) ≇bb (z₁,z₂)
   = if P(x₁,x₂)∧P(y₁,y₂)∧P(z₁,z₂)
        then (x₁≡y₁≡z₁, x₂≠y₂≠z₂) else (0,0)
   = if P(x₁,x₂)∧P(y₁,y₂)∧P(z₁,z₂)
        then (A(x₁,y₁,z₁), A(x₂,y₂,z₂)) else (0,0)
```

If all argument bits are available, we can again split the ternary antivalence function on bit pairs into a pair of antivalence functions on single bits. In the circuit, this leads to a duplication of all lines, one signalling the arrival of a 0 (a 1 on the first line) and the other signalling the arrival of a 1 (a 1 on the second line).

Detailed Behaviour of the Completion Recognition Adder

The completion recognition adder is described by the following algorithm:

```
cr-add: bb stream × bb stream → bb stream
cr-add(a,b) = Âbb∞(a,b,c)
    where c = (1,0) :: M̃bb∞(a,b,c)
```

Performing the same refinement as for the ripple-carry adder, we obtain as a detailed algorithm:

```
fine-cr-add: bb stream stream × bb stream stream → bb stream stream
fine-cr-add(a,b) = ((0,0)::)∞(Âbb∞∞∞(a,b,c))
    where c = (1,0)∞ ::  ((0,0)::)∞(M̂bb∞∞∞(a,b,c))
```

However, in this implementation we may get proper bits earlier. As an example consider addend and augend

```
a = 1∞::0∞::1∞::1∞:: ...
b = 0∞::1∞::1∞::1∞:: ... .
```

For a comparison, we compute the stream of ternary carries for the ripple-carry adder

						$\uparrow$ time
$\ddots$	:	:	:	:	:	
...	1	1	0	0	0	5
...	?	1	0	0	0	4
...	?	?	0	0	0	3
...	?	?	?	0	0	2
...	?	?	?	?	0	1
space $\leftarrow$	c_5^{rc}	c_4^{rc}	c_3^{rc}	c_2^{rc}	c_1^{rc}	

and for the completion recognition adder:

						↑ time
⋱	⋮	⋮	⋮	⋮	⋮	
...	1	1	0	0	0	5
...	1	1	0	0	0	4
...	1	1	0	0	0	3
...	1	1	?	0	0	2
...	?	?	?	?	0	1
space ←	c_5^{cr}	c_4^{cr}	c_3^{cr}	c_2^{cr}	c_1^{cr}	

For the ripple-carry adder, each subsequent carry stream has an additional delay (?) compared with its predecessor. Due to the non-strictness of the majority function, this does not apply to the completion recognition adder, if in some positions the bits of addend and augend streams coincide. Hence, corresponding entries in the space-time diagram are related by the availability order:

$$\forall \; i,j \in \mathcal{N}: \quad c_{ij}^{rc} \preceq c_{ij}^{cr} \quad .$$

Thus, the extension $\preceq^{\infty\infty}$ of the availability ordering on trits to streams of streams allows to compare circuits w.r.t. their time efficiency.

Conclusion

We don't want to draw the conclusion that a semantic analysis supersedes the traditional engineering and design techniques. However, we conclude that the knowledge of semantic issues like the ones presented here may complement the usual engineering techniques: they provide a formal framework that guides the design and supports the reasoning. Informal and intuitive ideas are still needed to produce good and efficient designs. However, the design activity should be supported by the use of formal methods based on sound theories. In the present paper, we have used the framework of functional programming with infinite streams for the design and description of adder algorithms.

To shorten the exposition, we have not mentioned all the single transformation steps and rules; rather, the above derivation provides a skeleton for a transformational development.

This case study also shows that hardware description using streams is not a priori restricted to the modelling of synchronous or asynchronous systems. Streams model sequences of values without relation to time or space. Only a further refinement or interpretation leads to the different timing techniques. This approach is also related to the work in [2], where an applicative language for real time programming, called **ART**, is presented. Note, however, that we don't model real time by assuming a priori that the elements of the streams correspond to given time instants: there are no time tags associated with them.

For discussing the operational behaviour of adder algorithms in more detail, we have introduced an absence value into the domain, compare the notion of "hiatons" in data flow programming. Of course, there are a number of different possibilities how to define the operations on the extended domain. As a guideline, we used an ordering which reflects the availability of binary digits.

In the adder networks presented, we have assumed that the addition is only performed once. Hence in the detailed view, all streams stay constant once a proper value has become available. This does not capture the reuse of components, which will be the subject of further investigations.

Acknowledgement

This work has been partially carried out in the project "Modelado funcional de sistemas distribuidos/Funktionale Modellierung verteilter Systeme" within the programme "Acciones integradas hispano-alemanas", supported by the Spanish CICYT (Comisión Interministerial de Ciencia y Tecnología) and the German DAAD (Deutscher Akademischer Austauschdienst). We gratefully acknowledge interesting discussions with M. Broy, and various improvements suggested by B. Möller and the anonymous referees.

References

[1] F.L. Bauer, R. Berghammer, M. Broy, W. Dosch, F. Geiselbrechtinger, R. Gnatz, E. Hangel, W. Hesse, B. Krieg-Brückner, A. Laut, T. Matzner, B. Möller, F. Nickl, H. Partsch, P. Pepper, K. Samelson (†), M. Wirsing, and H. Wössner. *The Munich Project CIP. Volume I: The Wide Spectrum Language CIP-L*, volume 183 of *Lecture Notes in Computer Science*. Springer, Berlin, 1985.

[2] Manfred Broy. Applicative real-time programming. In R.E.A. Mason, editor, *IFIP 1983*, pages 259–264. North-Holland, 1983.

[3] Carlos Delgado Kloos. *Semantics of Digital Circuits*, volume 285 of *Lecture Notes in Computer Science*. Springer, Berlin, 1987.

[4] Carlos Delgado Kloos and Walter Dosch. Transformational development of digital circuit descriptions: A case study. In W.E. Proebster and H. Reiner, editors, *CompEuro87*, pages 319–322. IEEE Computer Society Press, 1987.

[5] Carlos Delgado Kloos and Walter Dosch. Transformational development of circuit descriptions for binary adders. In M. Broy and M. Wirsing, editors, *Methodik des Programmierens — Eine Festschrift zu Ehren von F.L. Bauer*, pages 99–117, Universität Passau, Germany, 1989.

[6] I. Flores. *The Logic of Computer Arithmetic*. Prentice-Hall, Englewood Cliffs, 1963.

[7] C.A.R. Hoare. Proof of correctness of data representations. *Acta Informatica*, 1:271–281, 1972.

[8] C.A.R. Hoare. Refinement Algebra and Compilation. Lectures at the International Summer School on Programming and Mathematical Method, Marktoberdorf, Germany, 24 July–5 August 1990.

[9] Donald E. Knuth. *The Art of Computer Programming*, volume 2. Addison-Wesley, Reading, Mass., 1969.

[10] M.M. Mano. *Digital Design*. Prentice-Hall, Englewood Cliffs, 1984.

[11] R.K. Richards. *Digital Design*. Wiley, New York, 1971.

[12] M. Sheeran. μFP, a language for VLSI design. In *ACM Symposium on LISP and Functional Programming*, pages 104–112, August 1984. Austin, Tx.

[13] D.A. Turner. Miranda — a non-strict functional language with polymorphic types. In *Proc. Conference on Functional Programming Languages and Computer Architecture*, volume 201 of *Lecture Notes in Computer Science*, pages 1–16, Berlin, 1985. Springer.

[14] Åke Wikström. *Functional Programming Using Standard ML*. Prentice-Hall, Englewood Cliffs, 1987.

Verification of Synchronous Concurrent Algorithms Using OBJ3: A Case Study of the Pixel-Planes Architecture[*]

S. M. Eker[†]   V. Stavridou[†]   J. V. Tucker[‡]

Abstract

This paper is concerned with the mechanical verification of synchronous concurrent algorithms using OBJ3. Our case study is a graphics engine, the Pixel Planes architecture which has been previously specified as a synchronous concurrent algorithm and has been manually verified. Our aim is to show that OBJ3 is a viable theorem proving tool for complex synchronous concurrent algorithms.

1 Introduction

A synchronous concurrent algorithm (SCA) consists of a network of modules and channels which are synchronised by a global clock and compute and communicate data in parallel. Many algorithms and architectures occurring in science and engineering, are in fact instances of SCAs. Such examples include clocked hardware, systolic algorithms, neural networks, cellular automata, deterministic data flow systems and coupled map lattice dynamical systems. The mathematical theory of SCAs is based on several computationally equivalent models of deterministic parallel computing devised for the theory of computable functions on many sorted algebras. This theory unifies the study of the above disparate systems and provides general methods for their design, analysis and verification. The theory of SCAs is studied thoroughly in [31, 25, 18, 24, 32, 20, 17, 26, 3, 19].

These parallel algorithms are complex and require extensive simulation to understand their behaviour. They are also increasingly employed in many safety critical applications and therefore their thorough analysis and verification is desirable. Although some work has been reported on the mechanical verification of SCAs using the Boyer-Moore [29, 28] and Nuprl [1] theorem provers, both analysis and proof are by and large done manually. In this paper, we investigate and report on a first attempt to use OBJ3 as theorem proving tool for the verification of SCAs. We will present a systematic method applicable to a wide variety of SCAs which formulates algorithms and specifications algebraically, maps them in a routine way to OBJ3 programs and permits their verification.

For this purpose we have chosen the example of a VLSI–intensive graphics system, Pixel Planes [7, 8], which has been studied as an SCA and manually verified in [4]. Pixel Planes is a high speed rendering system composed of custom logic enhanced memory chips that can be programmed to perform most of the time consuming pixel oriented tasks in

[*]Work partially supported under SERC/IED grant No. GR/F 38839/4/1/1324.

[†]Department of Computer Science, Royal Holloway and Bedford New College, Egham, Surrey TW20 0EX, England.

[‡]Department of Mathematics and Computer Science, University College of Swansea, Singleton Park, Swansea SA2 8PP, Wales.

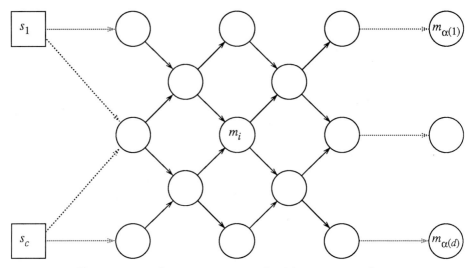

Figure 1: A synchronous concurrent algorithm as a network.

parallel at each pixel. The architecture supports an efficient tree structured computation unit called the *Linear Expression Evaluator* or LEE which calculates values for every pixel in parallel. The implementation reported in [5] contains 512 × 512 pixels × 72 bits per pixel implemented with 2,048 custom 3 micron nMOS chips (63,000 transistors in each, operating at 10 million micro-instructions per second). This two dimensional LEE is composed of one dimensional LEEs with trees of depth 9. Here we will deal with an abstract model of a one dimensional LEE with a small computation tree, which will be sufficiently complex to demonstrate clearly the applicability and viability of OBJ3 as an SCA verification tool. Note that here we are concerned with the verification rather than the specification of Pixel Planes.

The next three sections contain informal introductions to synchronous concurrent algorithms, OBJ3 and Pixel Planes Linear Expression Evaluator. We then present the specification of the Linear Expression Evaluator (LEE). The main results of our verification work are shown in section 6.

We thank B. C. Thompson and K. Meinke for useful discussions on matters arising in this paper.

2   Synchronous concurrent algorithms

We consider a synchronous concurrent algorithm (SCA) as a network of *sources*, *modules* and *channels* computing and communicating data, as depicted in Figure 1. For simplicity we will assume that all the data is drawn from a single set A. The network has a global discrete clock $\mathbf{T} = \{0, 1, \ldots\}$ to synchronise computations and the flow of data between modules. There are c *sources* labelled $s_1, \ldots, s_c$, and k *modules* labelled $m_1, \ldots, m_k$. The sources perform no computation; they are simply input ports where fresh data arrives at each clock cycle. Each module m_i has $p(i)$ inputs and a single output as depicted in Figure 2. The action of a module m_i is specified by a function

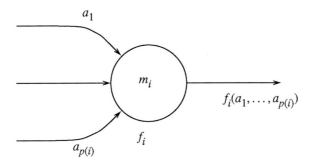

Figure 2: Module m_i.

$$f_i : A^{p(i)} \rightarrow A.$$

If the diagram in Figure 1 is to be a *graph* then edges may not branch. Thus where the output of a module is required as an input to several other modules, extra output channels that copy the value must be added to the module (a number of conventions handling this point are discused in §2.2). Results are read out from a subset of the modules $m_{\alpha(1)}, \ldots, m_{\alpha(d)}$ which may be termed output modules or *sinks*.

The interconnections between the sources and modules are represented by a pair of partial functions

$$\gamma : \mathbf{N}_k \times \mathbf{N} \rightarrow \{S, M\}$$

and

$$\beta : \mathbf{N}_k \times \mathbf{N} \rightarrow \mathbf{N}$$

where $\mathbf{N}_k = \{1, 2, \ldots, k\}$. Intuitively $\gamma(i, j) = S$ indicates that the jth input to module m_i comes from a source whereas $\gamma(i, j) = M$ indicates it comes from another module. The index of the source or module in question is given by $\beta(i, j)$.

To ensure that our networks are well defined we impose the following conditions on γ and β:

$$\forall i, j.[(i \in \{1, \ldots, k\}) \wedge (j \in \{1, \ldots, p(i)\}) \Rightarrow \beta(i, j) \downarrow] \tag{1}$$

$$\forall i, j.[(i \in \{1, \ldots, k\}) \wedge (j \in \{1, \ldots, p(i)\}) \Rightarrow \gamma(i, j) \downarrow] \tag{2}$$

$$\forall i, j.[(\gamma(i, j) = S) \Rightarrow (\beta(i, j) \in \{1, \ldots, c\})] \tag{3}$$

$$\forall i, j.[(\gamma(i, j) = M) \Rightarrow (\beta(i, j) \in \{1, \ldots, k\})] \tag{4}$$

Here the notation $\beta(i, j) \downarrow$ means that $\beta(i, j)$ is defined on the specified arguments i, j given in the expression. The first two conditions ensure that β and γ are defined for every input of every module. The latter two conditions ensure that the sources or modules named by β and γ actually exist.

We will assume that each module is initialised with a well defined output assigned to its output channel. Thus the initial state of the network is an element $b \in A^k$ and we will use the notation b_i to denote the initial value of the output of module m_i for $i = 1, \ldots, k$.

In terms of our intuitive picture, new data are available at each source, and new results at each sink, at every tick of the global clock $\mathbf{T}$. Thus the algorithm processes infinite sequences or streams of data. A stream $\underline{a}(0), \underline{a}(1), \ldots$ of data from A is represented by a map $\underline{a} : \mathbf{T} \rightarrow A$ and the set of streams of data is represented by the set $[\mathbf{T} \rightarrow A]$ of all such maps. Thus we will specify the input-output behaviour of an architecture, initialised by b, by a mapping V_b from source streams into sink streams:

$$V_b : [\mathbf{T} \to A]^c \to [\mathbf{T} \to A]^d$$

We call V_b a *stream transformer* and the *i/o specification* of the algorithm.

2.1 Representing stream algorithms

We represent each module m_i by a *value function* $v_i : \mathbf{T} \times [\mathbf{T} \to A^c] \times A^k \to A$. Intuitively $v_i(t, \underline{a}, b)$ represents the output of module m_i at time t, when the network is initialised with values b and is computing on the input stream $\underline{a}$. The function v_i is specified as follows

$$v_i(0, \underline{a}, b) = b_i$$

$$v_i(t + 1, \underline{a}, b) = f_i(A_1, \ldots, A_{p(i)})$$

where for $j = 1, \ldots, p(i)$:

$$A_j = \begin{cases} \underline{a}_{\beta(i,j)}(t) & \text{if } \gamma(i,j) = S \\ v_{\beta(i,j)}(t, \underline{a}, b) & \text{if } \gamma(i,j) = M \end{cases}$$

We can now write down the i/o specification of the algorithm V_b when initialised with values b and executed on input stream $\underline{a}$ as

$$V_b(\underline{a})(t) = (v_{\alpha(1)}(t, \underline{a}, b), \ldots, v_{\alpha(d)}(t, \underline{a}, b)).$$

where $\alpha(1), \ldots, \alpha(d)$ are the labels of the sinks. We often work with V_b in the following form:

$$V_b : [\mathbf{T} \to A]^c \times \mathbf{T} \to A^d$$

2.2 Conventions on the network model

Looking at the synchronous network depicted in Figure 1 a number of conventions are involved in this informal notation that are motivated by the formalisation by means of the value functions above. In particular channels do not branch and modules only have a single distinct output value. Where the output of a module is required in several places we need separate channels which carry duplicate outputs of the module in question. In the Pixel Planes example later on, we will find it convenient to draw networks with more than one distinct output value and branching channels (such networks are no longer graphs). When we formalise these networks as shown above we deal with this pictorial convention in the following way. Modules with more than one distinct output are split into separate single output modules, one for each output and each module takes all the inputs of the original; see the translation in Figure 3. Branching channels are replaced by a set of non-branching channels, one for each of the branches of the original; see the translation in Figure 4.

2.3 User specifications

In order to be able to prove a given algorithm correct we need a formal specification of the task which the algorithm is supposed to perform i.e. a *user specification* or *behavioural specification* which defines the task in terms of outputs required at particular times. Formally a user specification is a stream transformer of the form

$$S : [\mathbf{T} \to A]^c \to [\mathbf{T} \to A \cup \{u\}]^d$$

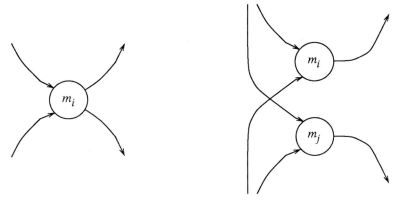

Figure 3: Splitting modules with more than one output.

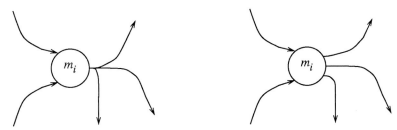

Figure 4: Replacing branching channels.

where u is a special undefined element. An i/o specification $I : [\mathbf{T} \to A]^c \to [\mathbf{T} \to A]^d$ of an algorithm is said to *directly satisfy* or *directly meet* a user specification $S : [\mathbf{T} \to A]^c \to [\mathbf{T} \to A \cup \{u\}]^d$, if and only if, for all input streams $\underline{x} \in [\mathbf{T} \to A]^c$, for each $i \in \{1, \ldots, d\}$ and $t \in \mathbf{T}$, either

$$S_i(\underline{x})(t) = u \text{ or } I_i(\underline{x})(t) = S_i(\underline{x})(t)$$

where S has coordinate functions S_i and I has coordinate functions I_i. There are occasions when the definition of correctness of an algorithm with respect to a specification is more complicated. For example, correctness can involve the scheduling or translation of input-output streams: see [20, 25].

With these notions we may formulate mathematically two problems in hardware design. The SCA verification problem is as follows: Given a user specification and a SCA which is claimed to satisfy the user specification, we have to provide a formal proof that it indeed does so. A related but harder problem is the SCA synthesis problem: Given a user specification and a data type containing the constants and basic operation from which module functions may be constructed, we have to design a SCA which meets the user specification.

2.4 Component, program and task algebras

We note that in formulating a SCA, the functions f_i that specify the actions of the modules together with the constant 0 and operations $t + 1$ and *eval* form a stream algebra with carriers $\mathbf{T}$, A and $\mathbf{T} \to A$. We call this the *component algebra*. The value functions v_i that defined the SCA similarly give rise to a stream algebra which we call the *program algebra*. Finally if we just consider the value functions $v_{\alpha(i)}$ of the output modules we get a third stream algebra which we call the *task algebra*.

The sort A and its operations in the component algbebra may be defined abstractly by a set of equations in which case we have a class of component algebras which are *standard algebras* in that time $\mathbf{T}$ has its standard interpretation. In this case the algorithm determines classes of program and task algebras which are also standard algebras.

3   OBJ3

3.1   Overview

OBJ3 [16] is the latest in a series of incremental implementations of OBJ which was designed by J. A. Goguen in the mid seventies [12]. Although that original language was intended as an attempt to extend algebraic data type theory to handle errors and partial functions, in the years hence, OBJ has come to be viewed and used, first as an (executable) algebraic specification language [15, 9], then as a programming language [14] and finally as a theorem proving tool [13]—it can of course be used in all three ways. It is this latest guise of OBJ that we are interested in this paper. In what follows we will use the term **OBJ** to refer to the family of languages and **OBJ3** to refer to the latest implementation.

There are two major syntactic entities in OBJ, *objects* which contain executable code and *theories* which contain non-executable assertions. We are fortunate in dealing with a language with well defined formal semantics. OBJ has denotational semantics given by order sorted algebra and operational semantics given by ordered sorted term rewriting. The denotation of an OBJ3 text P is a *standard (initial) model* of P if P is an object and the *variety of all models* of P if P is a theory. The operational semantics of objects is defined by equations which are interpreted as *left→right* rewrite rules. The latest version of OBJ3 supports (limited) rewriting on theories which corresponds to reasoning about the variety.

Objects and theories support two fundamental features of OBJ, namely *subsorting* and *parameterisation*. We do not go into a detailed description of OBJ3 here; we will instead comment on relevant features as we come across them in the text of this paper. For a full exposition of OBJ3 see [16].

3.2   Theorem proving

The fact that OBJ has formal semantics is not just opportune for our work; it is in fact essential. As J. A. Goguen points out [13], it is only because the semantics of OBJ *is* the semantics of equational logic that allows us to use it as a theorem prover for equational logic. Our theorem proving approach is motivated on the following principles:

- *Use the simplest logic possible for a given application*, because reasoning overheads are proportional to the expressive power of the logic.

- *A usable theorem prover should help the user discover a proof* rather than simply check a fully constructed proof or generate a fully automatic proof, because the former is tedious and the latter often not viable.

Equational logic is very simple but is powerful enough to allow the encoding and verification of many correctness problems for synchronous concurrent algorithms. This is because any recursive equations can be mapped into an algebraic specification; see [32]. Thus the essence of our method for the mechanical verification of hardware is as follows:

- Formulate the hardware in terms of SCAs.

- Formalise the data and component modules of each SCA as a class of stream algebras and find an appropriate axiomatisation of this class.

- Formalise each SCA by means of value functions over the class of its component algebras.

- Translate the axiomatisation of the component algebras and the primitive recursive equations that define the value functions into appropriate OBJ3 theories.

Stream transformers which are perceived as second order functions can be encoded directly in first order logic by using unconstrained function symbols (that is function symbols for which there exists no equation that define their properties) as shown later in this paper. This is really the standard trick in logic of replacing universally quantified variables by new constants but here we also do the same thing with universally quantified function (stream) variables. This effectively allows reasoning with equations that are universally quantified over variables and function symbols without ever leaving the domain of many sorted first order logic. This is discussed in more detail in §6.

Furthermore, SCAs' simultaneous primitive recursive definitions are expressed in OBJ3 in a very natural way which eliminates the need for counter intuitive encodings required by other theorem provers [29, 28].

The operational semantics of OBJ3 provides us with an essentially gratis theorem prover implementation. The available proof techniques include associative-commutative (AC) order sorted reduction (of ground terms), deduction (with terms containing variables interpreted as constants), induction (via the encoding of inductive schemata), reasoning with conditional equations and reasoning about parameterised modules (and hence parameterised proofs)[1]. We feel that this is an impressive array of proof methods for OBJ3 which after all was designed as language, not a theorem prover.

There is a large body of work on the use of term rewriting in theorem proving (for a survey see [2]. The main direction in this respect is Knuth-Bendix completion [23] and proof by consistancy (so called 'inductionless induction') [21, 22]. We have chosen not to go this way in spite of the term rewriting operational semantics of OBJ3. Experience shows that inductionless induction is a weak proof method compared with structual induction [10, 30]. Moreover to our knowledge, there exists no satisfactory order sorted completion procedure for conditional equations which is what we would need in the case of OBJ3. Term rewriting theorem proving systems such as LP [11] at present only implement unsorted unconditional rewriting. It is furthermore the case that the uncontrollable search space of completion algorithms results in an explosion of less and less relevant rules (particularly in the case of AC completion) which can be very counter-intuitive when a proof fails. OBJ3 proofs, however, are much easier to control, do not require termination proofs for new rule sets and failed proofs often provide intuition into the cause of the failure. Such failures normally produce a rule similar to a critical pair which offers hints about required lemmas for a successful proof.

---

[1] J. A. Goguen develops the theoretical foundations of these methods in [13].

238

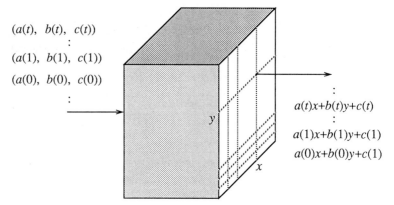

$(a(t), \quad b(t), \quad c(t))$
$\vdots$
$(a(1), \quad b(1), \quad c(1))$
$(a(0), \quad b(0), \quad c(0))$

$\vdots$

$a(t)x+b(t)y+c(t)$
$\vdots$
$a(1)x+b(1)y+c(1)$
$a(0)x+b(0)y+c(1)$

Figure 5: The LEE section of Pixel Planes.

4   Informal description of Pixel Planes' LEE

In this section we discuss an example of a synchronous concurrent algorithm which we will verify later using OBJ3. This algorithm is the *Linear Expression Evaluator* (LEE) section of the Pixel Planes architecture [7, 8]. Further extensions are described in [6] and implementation details are given in [27]. A review of current experimental and commercial VLSI graphics systems, including Pixel Planes, is given by Fuchs [5]. We shall examine the algorithm in its 'pure' form without the modifications (such as super trees) required to implement it in current VLSI technology.

The Pixel Planes LEE has the task of taking an input stream

$$(a(0), b(0), c(0)), (a(1), b(1), c(1)), \ldots$$

of triples of numbers, and generating in parallel for each point (x, y) on a discrete $n \times m$ grid, the stream

$$a(0)x + b(0)y + c(0), a(1)x + b(1)y + c(1), \ldots$$

of values of the linear expression $ax + by + c$. This is shown diagramatically in Figure 5. At this top level of description it suffices to assume that input and output data are numbers (such as integers or reals); in more specific accounts, including the original paper, the input and output data are bit representations.

The architecture that implements this specification consists of 1-dimensional LEE modules which evaluate $w+vz$ on an input (v, w) for each value of z. Note that the 2-dimensional expression $ax + by + c$ is evaluated as $(c + ax) + by$. The way the 1-dimensional LEE modules are connected together to perform this is shown in Figure 6 with the 1-dimensional LEE modules represented by triangles. Each output of the first 1-dimensional LEE module, which computes the $ax + c$ terms in parallel for each value of x, is connected to a 1-dimensional LEE module, which adds the by term in parallel for each value of y. It is these 1-dimensional LEE's that we will specify and mechanically verify in the following sections.

The internal structure of the 1-dimensional LEE module is shown in Figure 7. It is composed of a tree of smaller modules. The structure of the tree nodes is shown in Figure 8. The left output is simply the top input delayed by one clock cycle. The right output is

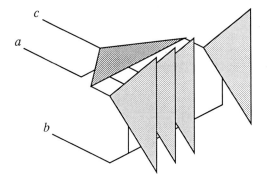

Figure 6: Inside the LEE section.

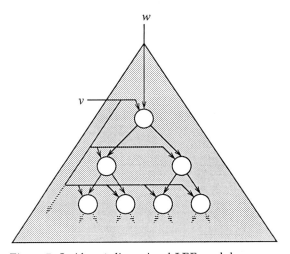

Figure 7: Inside a 1-dimensional LEE module.

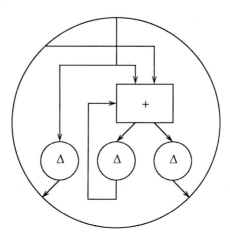

Figure 8: Inside a tree module.

formed by adding the two inputs, together with the carry bit saved from the previous addition.

5   Specification of the 1-dimensional LEE

Rather than specify and verify the Pixel Planes 1D LEE at the bit level where numbers are represented by a finite sequence of bits and are processed bit serially we choose a higher level model where each number is considered to be an element of an abstract data type, whose equational axioms are chosen to be just strong enough so that the design can be verified. This approach considerably simplifies the verification process but there is a price to be paid.

In the real bit level Pixel Planes 1D LEE numbers are represented by sequences of bits, the least significant bit first (earliest). Thus multiplication by two can be done cheaply by a one cycle delay. Similarly division by two can be done by letting the bit sequence representing the number to be divided 'get ahead' by one cycle of the bit sequences representing the other numbers being pumped around the architecture. In the real Pixel Planes 1D LEE each number fed in to the v input is multiplied by 2^{n-1} by proceeding it with $n-1$ zeros and is effectively divided by two at each level in the tree as it gets progressively 'out of step' with the numbers generated by each tree processor.

In our abstract model of the Pixel Planes 1D LEE each clock cycle represents a whole new element being fed into each input, not just the current bit of a number and therefore streams of elements cannot be allowed to 'get out step'. Thus we have to add explicit one cycle delays and multipliers to keep the elements 'in step' and to handle the implicit computations on the elements sent to the v input.

5.1   Abstract data types

The data type we choose to specify Pixel Planes 1D LEE is built from three smaller data types. Time is represented by a copy $\mathbf{T} = \langle \mathbf{T} \mid 0, t+1 \rangle$ of the natural numbers without the addition and multiplication operations. The natural numbers $\mathbf{N} = \langle \mathbf{N} \mid 0, n+1, +, \times \rangle$

are used to generate particular abstract numbers via a mapping which we define below. In order to generate abstract numbers to play the role of powers of two in the multiplier modules, it is convenient to add the operation 2^n to the natural numbers. We also need the abstract numbers on which we actually do the computations. We need two operations to represent addition and multiplication and a constant to represent the zero element. We thus have an algebra $\langle R \mid 0, +, \times \rangle$. It was shown in [4] that this algebra needs to satisfy just four equational axioms.

$$(a + b) + c = a + (b + c) \tag{5}$$
$$a + 0 = a \tag{6}$$
$$0 \times a = 0 \tag{7}$$
$$(a + b) \times c = (a \times c) + (b \times c) \tag{8}$$

We can thus consider the abstract data type R to be the class of all algebras which satisfy these axioms.

In order to generate abstract numbers to represent particular natural numbers we define the following function. Let α be any element of R. Then we define the function $r_\alpha : \mathbf{N} \to R$ inductively.

$$r_\alpha(0) = 0$$

$$r_\alpha(n + 1) = r_\alpha(n) + \alpha$$

Thus $r_\alpha(0) = 0$, $r_\alpha(1) = 0 + \alpha$, $r_\alpha(2) = 0 + \alpha + \alpha$ and so on.

Lemma 1 *The mapping r_α is a homomorphism w.r.t. the the '+' operations in $\mathbf{N}$ and R; i.e. $r_\alpha(a + b) = r_\alpha(a) + r_\alpha(b)$.*

This fact is easily proved by induction and we shall prove it in the section 6 as an illustration of how to do inductive proofs with OBJ3. We note that every ring satisfies these axioms. Particularly important is the case where $R = \mathbf{Z}$ and $\alpha = 1$.

5.2   Implementation specification

The specification is taken from [4] with some of the modules and their functions renamed for clarity.

This specification is for a generic 1D LEE of height n with 2^n outputs. Since the number of modules (and hence functions and equations defining them) is dependent on n we cannot write a fixed list of equations. Instead, we subscript the module and function names with natural numbers and write *equation templates*. In writing these equation templates we need definition by cases, odd and even tests and various arithmetic operations that are only partial functions on the natural numbers such as subtraction and division by two. This extra copy of the natural numbers together with its extra operations take no part in the actual computations performed by the architecture and can be eliminated whenever n is instantiated to a particular natural number as we shall see in §6. They are simply part of the mechanism for writing down the equation templates.

The abstract version of the Pixel Planes 1D LEE which we specify is shown in Figure 9 (compare it with Figure 7).

The process of writing down the implementation specification is straight-forward—for each module shown in Figure 9 we assign a value function. (Note that under our convention, modules have more than one distinct output are split and each output gives rise to a value

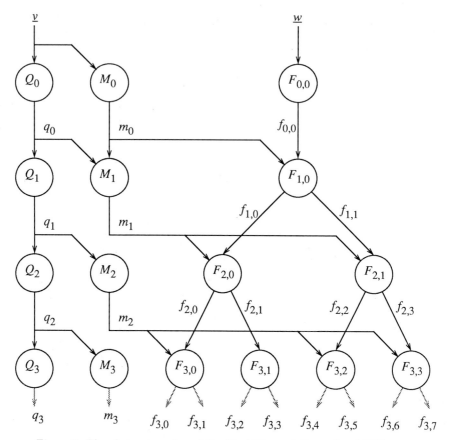

Figure 9: The abstract version of the Pixel Planes 1-dimensional LEE.

function.) The value functions are defined using the scheme in §2.1. Here all modules are initialised to $0 \in R$ at time 0.

We start with the one cycle delays, $Q_0, \dots, Q_{n-2}$. Module Q_0 takes its input from the $\underline{v}$ input stream; the others each take their input from their immediate predecessor. The value functions for the delay modules are q_i for $i \in \{0, \dots, n-2\}$:

$$q_i : \mathbf{T} \times [\mathbf{T} \rightarrow R]^2 \rightarrow R$$

$$q_i(0, \underline{v}, \underline{w}) = 0$$

When $i = 0$:

$$q_0(t + 1, \underline{v}, \underline{w}) = \underline{v}(t)$$

Otherwise:

$$q_i(t + 1, \underline{v}, \underline{w}) = q_{i-1}(t, \underline{v}, \underline{w})$$

Next we have the multiplication processors $M_0, \dots, M_{n-1}$. Module M_0 takes its input directly from the $\underline{v}$ input stream; the others take their inputs from the preceeding delay module. Each multiplication processor M_i multiplies its input by the element $r_\alpha(2^{n-1-i})$. The value functions for the multiplication processors are m_i for $i \in \{0,\ldots,n-1\}$:

$$m_i : \mathbf{T} \times [\mathbf{T} \to R]^2 \to R$$

$$m_i(0, \underline{v}, \underline{w}) = 0$$

When $i = 0$:

$$m_0(t+1, \underline{v}, \underline{w}) = r_\alpha(2^{n-1}) \times \underline{v}(t)$$

Otherwise:

$$m_i(t+1, \underline{v}, \underline{w}) = r_\alpha(2^{n-1-i}) \times q_{i-1}(t, \underline{v}, \underline{w})$$

Finally we have the tree processors $P_{i,j}$. Module $P_{0,0}$ has a single output and a single value function $f_{0,0}$. All the other tree processors $P_{i,j}$ have two outputs; a left one with value function $f_{i,2j}$ and a right one with value function $f_{i,2j+1}$. We define these value functions as follows, for $i \in \{0,\ldots,n\}$, $j \in \{0,\ldots,2^i-1\}$:

$$f_{i,j} : \mathbf{T} \times [\mathbf{T} \to R]^2 \to R$$

$$f_{i,j}(0, \underline{v}, \underline{w}) = 0$$

When $i = j = 0$:

$$f_{0,0}(t+1, \underline{v}, \underline{w}) = \underline{w}(t)$$

Otherwise:

$$f_{i,j}(t+1, \underline{v}, \underline{w}) = \begin{cases} f_{i-1,j/2}(t, \underline{v}, \underline{w}) & \text{if } j \text{ is even} \\ f_{i-1,(j-1)/2}(t, \underline{v}, \underline{w}) + m_i(t, \underline{v}.\underline{w}) & \text{if } j \text{ is odd} \end{cases}$$

The stream transformer defined by this implementation specification is

$$LEE^n : [\mathbf{T} \to R]^2 \to [\mathbf{T} \to R]^{2^n}$$

$$LEE^n(\underline{v}, \underline{w})(t) = (f_{n,0}(t, \underline{v}, \underline{w}), \ldots, f_{n,2^n-1}(t, \underline{v}, \underline{w}))$$

5.3   User specification

Let R be any structure satisfying equations (5)-(8). Our user specification is

$$U^n : [\mathbf{T} \to R]^2 \to [\mathbf{T} \to R \cup \{u\}]^{2^n}$$

defined by its coordinate functions; for $j \in \{1,\ldots,2^{n-1}\}$:

$$U^n_j(\underline{v}, \underline{w})(t) = \begin{cases} u & \text{if } t < n+1 \\ \underline{w}(t-(n+1)) + r_\alpha(j) \times \underline{v}(t-(n+1)) & \text{otherwise} \end{cases}$$

Here $(n+1)$ is the time delay between the data arriving at the sources and valid results being available at the sinks.

Now for verification we want the i/o specification to satisfy the user specification. We derive the following equivalent condition on value functions; for $j \in \{0,\ldots,2^n-1\}$:

$$\forall t \in \mathbf{T}.[t \geq n+1 \Rightarrow f_{n,j}(t, \underline{v}, \underline{w}) = \underline{w}(t-(n+1)) + r_\alpha(j) \times \underline{v}(t-(n+1))]$$

For automatic verification it is convenient to eliminate the subtraction operations and the implication. An equivalent condition is given in the following theorem.

Theorem 1 *If R satisfies equations (5)-(8) then for $j \in \{0, \dots, 2^n - 1\}$:*

$$\forall t \in \mathbf{T}.[f_{n,j}(t + n + 1, \underline{v}, \underline{w}) = \underline{w}(t) + r_\alpha(j) \times \underline{v}(t)]$$

It is this condition which expresses the correctness of the algorithm for any structure R that satisfies our abstract arithmetic axioms.

6 Verification using OBJ3

Following the general plan for verification in §3.2 the plan for the verification is as follows. First we specify the data type in OBJ3. Then we prove Lemma 1 by induction on $\mathbf{N}$. Next we treat the informal recursive equations that define the value functions of the pixel planes SCA as formal equations and write them as OBJ3 code. Finally we prove the equations that are the user specification by rewriting.

Two important principles are used in these proofs. The first is the 'Constants Lemma' which allows us to replace universally quantified variables with unconstrained variables. We state this theorem informally—its formal statement and proof is given in [13].

Lemma 2 *Let Σ, X be disjoint signatures, let E be a set of Σ-equations and let A be a ground $(\Sigma \cup X)$-equation. We can consider A as a Σ-equation, $\forall X.A(X)$ by universally quantifying all constant and function symbols drawn from X. Then $\forall X.A(X)$ is true in every $\langle \Sigma, E \rangle$ model if and only if A is true in every $\langle \Sigma \cup X, E \rangle$ model.*

The second principle is proof by induction. The general structural induction scheme for initial models is stated and proved in [13]. We however require induction for a class of models, called *standard models* in which certain sorts (including time and natural numbers) have their usual interpretations but other sorts may not.

6.1 Data types in OBJ3

Recall from §5.1 that our data type is constructed from three smaller data types. We will now write an OBJ3 module to describe each of these.

First we have time $\mathbf{T}$. Recall that this has just one constant , '0' (which must be written in OBJ3 as an operation of zero arity) and one operation '$t + 1$' (which we will write as 's'). There are no properties to be defined by equations and we want initial semantics in order to exclude non-standard models of time. We therefore declare time with following OBJ3 object.

```
obj TIME is sort Time .
        op 0 : -> Time .
        op s_ : Time -> Time .
endo
```

Next we have the natural numbers, $\mathbf{N}$ augmented by the '2^n' operation. Here we have a single constant '0' and four operations, '$n + 1$', '$+$', '$\times$' and '2^n'. The '$+$' and '$\times$' operations are associative and commutative and we specify this in OBJ3 by means of the 'assoc' and 'comm' attributes. Putting commutativity in as an equation (with the operational semantics being *left→right* rewrite rules) would lead to non-termination. Similarly including the associativity law both ways around would also lead to non-termination. The 'prec' attribute is used to specify the precedences of the operations for the OBJ3 mix-fix parser. We also need to add equations to define the other properties of the operations. These are just standard primitive recursive definitions of the '+', '*' and '2^n' operations. Again we want initial semantics to exclude non-standard models of arithmetic so we use an OBJ3 object.

```
obj NAT is sort Nat .
        op 0 : -> Nat .
        op s_ : Nat -> Nat [prec 1] .
        op _+_ : Nat Nat -> Nat [assoc comm prec 3] .
        op _*_ : Nat Nat -> Nat [assoc comm prec 2] .
        op 2^_ : Nat -> Nat [prec 1] .

vars A B C : Nat .
        eq A + 0 = A .
        eq A + s B = s(A + B) .
        eq A * 0 = 0 .
        eq A * s B = A + A * B .
        eq 2^ 0 = s 0 .
        eq 2^ s A = s s 0 * 2^ A .
endo
```

Finally we need the abstract arithmetic data type R. Recall that this has one constant, '0' and two operations, '+' and '×' and satisfies four equational axioms. Since operationally these are considered as rewrite rules which way around they are declared is important. For instance if the associtivity axiom is written as $(A + B) + C = A + (B + C)$ some of our proofs would fail. In the case of associativity the effect of having both versions without the problem of non-termination can be avoided by using the 'assoc' attribute. The initial model of this signature and set of equations is in fact the unit algebra. Our intention is to verify the LEE over all the class of all algebras which satisfy these equations and thus we want variety semantics and so we use an OBJ3 theory.

```
th ABS is sort Abs .
        op 0 : -> Abs .
        op _+_ : Abs Abs -> Abs [prec 3] .
        op _*_ : Abs Abs -> Abs [prec 2] .

vars A B C : Abs .
        eq A + (B + C) = (A + B) + C .
        eq A + 0 = A .
        eq 0 * A = 0 .
        eq (A + B) * C = (A * C) + (B * C) .
endth
```

We now need the r_α operation to map natural numbers into our abstract numbers. We introduce this as another module defined in terms of the NAT and ABS modules above.

```
th RMAP is protecting NAT + ABS .
        op alpha : -> Abs .
        op r_ : Nat -> Abs [prec 1] .

var N : Nat .
```

```
          eq r(0) = 0 .
          eq r(s N) = r(N) + alpha .
endth
```

Here 'protecting' is one of OBJ3's several module importation modes and the expression 'NAT+ABS' forms the module containing all the sorts, operations and equations of both NAT and ABS (module union). The idea of the protecting mode is that the semantics of the imported modules is protected—no new elements are created and no previously unequal elements are equated.

6.2 Proving the homomorphism property of r_α

Recall from §5.1 that we stated that Lemma 1 could be easily proved by induction. We now do this proof as an example of how to do inductive proofs with OBJ3. We do induction on the second argument of r_α.

We start with the basis case: $r_\alpha(a,0) = r_\alpha(a) + r_\alpha(0)$. To prove this in OBJ3 we first create a new module that includes an 'unconstrained' constant to represent the variable a (recall that OBJ3 can only rewrite ground terms).

```
th BASIS is protecting RMAP .
          op a : -> Nat .
endth
```

We then ask OBJ3 to do the proof by rewriting the terms on either side of the equality symbol to a normal form and then checking for syntactic equivalence.

```
reduce in BASIS : r(a + 0) == r(a) + r(0) .
```

We then do the induction step; assume that $r_\alpha(a+b) = r_\alpha(a) + r_\alpha(b)$ and prove $r_\alpha(a + b + 1) = r_\alpha(a) + r_\alpha(b + 1)$. We write the induction hypothesis as another OBJ3 module:

```
th INDUCT is protecting BASIS .
          op b : -> Nat .
          eq r(a + b) = r(a) + r(b) .
endth
```

And do the proof by rewriting as before:

```
reduce in INDUCT : r(a + s b) == r(a) + r(s b) .
```

Now that the lemma is proven we create a new module LEMMA1 containing it so we can use it later.

```
th LEMMA1 is protecting RMAP .
vars A B : Nat .
          eq r(A + B) = r(A) + r(B) .
endth
```

6.3 Converting the implementation specification to OBJ3

In order to verify the design using OBJ3 we need to make a number of simplifications. First we choose a particular value for n—we choose $n = 3$. This gives us a finite set of functions and equations defining them. For the one cycle delays:

$$q_0(0, \underline{v}, \underline{w}) = 0 \qquad q_0(t+1, \underline{v}, \underline{w}) = \underline{v}(t)$$
$$q_1(0, \underline{v}, \underline{w}) = 0 \qquad q_1(t+1, \underline{v}, \underline{w}) = q_0(t, \underline{v}, \underline{w})$$

For the multipliers

$$m_0(0, \underline{v}, \underline{w}) = 0 \qquad m_0(t+1, \underline{v}, \underline{w}) = r_\alpha(2^2) \times \underline{v}(t)$$
$$m_1(0, \underline{v}, \underline{w}) = 0 \qquad m_1(t+1, \underline{v}, \underline{w}) = r_\alpha(2^1) \times q_0(t, \underline{v}, \underline{w})$$
$$m_2(0, \underline{v}, \underline{w}) = 0 \qquad m_2(t+1, \underline{v}, \underline{w}) = r_\alpha(2^0) \times q_1(t, \underline{v}, \underline{w})$$

The tree processors

$$f_{0,0}(0, \underline{v}, \underline{w}) = 0 \qquad f_{0,0}(t+1, \underline{v}, \underline{w}) = \underline{w}(t)$$

$$f_{1,0}(0, \underline{v}, \underline{w}) = 0 \qquad f_{1,0}(t+1, \underline{v}, \underline{w}) = f_{0,0}(t)$$
$$f_{1,1}(0, \underline{v}, \underline{w}) = 0 \qquad f_{1,1}(t+1, \underline{v}, \underline{w}) = f_{0,0}(t) + m_0(t)$$

$$f_{2,0}(0, \underline{v}, \underline{w}) = 0 \qquad f_{2,0}(t+1, \underline{v}, \underline{w}) = f_{1,0}(t)$$
$$f_{2,1}(0, \underline{v}, \underline{w}) = 0 \qquad f_{2,1}(t+1, \underline{v}, \underline{w}) = f_{1,0}(t) + m_1(t)$$

$$f_{2,2}(0, \underline{v}, \underline{w}) = 0 \qquad f_{2,2}(t+1, \underline{v}, \underline{w}) = f_{1,1}(t)$$
$$f_{2,3}(0, \underline{v}, \underline{w}) = 0 \qquad f_{2,3}(t+1, \underline{v}, \underline{w}) = f_{1,1}(t) + m_1(t)$$

$$f_{3,0}(0, \underline{v}, \underline{w}) = 0 \qquad f_{3,0}(t+1, \underline{v}, \underline{w}) = f_{2,0}(t)$$
$$f_{3,1}(0, \underline{v}, \underline{w}) = 0 \qquad f_{3,1}(t+1, \underline{v}, \underline{w}) = f_{2,0}(t) + m_2(t)$$

$$f_{3,2}(0, \underline{v}, \underline{w}) = 0 \qquad f_{3,2}(t+1, \underline{v}, \underline{w}) = f_{2,1}(t)$$
$$f_{3,3}(0, \underline{v}, \underline{w}) = 0 \qquad f_{3,3}(t+1, \underline{v}, \underline{w}) = f_{2,1}(t) + m_2(t)$$

$$f_{3,4}(0, \underline{v}, \underline{w}) = 0 \qquad f_{3,4}(t+1, \underline{v}, \underline{w}) = f_{2,2}(t)$$
$$f_{3,5}(0, \underline{v}, \underline{w}) = 0 \qquad f_{3,5}(t+1, \underline{v}, \underline{w}) = f_{2,2}(t) + m_2(t)$$

$$f_{3,6}(0, \underline{v}, \underline{w}) = 0 \qquad f_{3,6}(t+1, \underline{v}, \underline{w}) = f_{2,3}(t)$$
$$f_{3,7}(0, \underline{v}, \underline{w}) = 0 \qquad f_{3,7}(t+1, \underline{v}, \underline{w}) = f_{2,3}(t) + m_2(t)$$

Since OBJ3 does not support higher order functions we must remove the stream arguments $\underline{v}, \underline{w}$ from the above functions. We simply declare $\underline{v}$ and $\underline{w}$ to be functions from the naturals to our abstract arithmetic data type without giving any equations to define them. They are thus 'unconstrained' functions and behave like constant function symbols.

An alternative would be to define a sort $[\mathbf{T} \to R]$ together with an evaluation operation $eval(\underline{s}, t) : [\mathbf{T} \to R] \times \mathbf{T} \to R$ to compute the value of stream $\underline{s}$ at time t. This approach corresponds to the official algebraic methods of handling streams in the theory of SCAs; see [32, 20, 4]. This approach is not used here as it would complicate the OBJ3 code.

Writing the above equations as an OBJ3 module we get

```
th PP is protecting TIME + LEMMA1 .
        ops v w : Time -> Abs .
        ops q0 q1 : Time -> Abs .
        ops m0 m1 m2 : Time -> Abs .
        ops f00 f10 f11 f20 f21 f22 f23 : Time -> Abs .
```

```
        ops f30 f31 f32 f33 f34 f35 f36 f37 : Time -> Abs .

var T : Time .
        eq q0(0) = 0 .
        eq q0(s T) = v(T) .
        eq q1(0) = 0 .
        eq q1(s T) = q0(T) .

        eq m0(0) = 0 .
        eq m0(s T) = r(2^ (s s 0)) * v(T) .
        eq m1(0) = 0 .
        eq m1(s T) = r(2^ (s 0)) * q0(T) .
        eq m2(0) = 0 .
        eq m2(s T) = r(2^ (0)) * q1(T) .

        eq f00(0) = 0 .
        eq f00(s T) = w(T) .

        eq f10(0) = 0 .
        eq f10(s T) = f00(T) .
        eq f11(0) = 0 .
        eq f11(s T) = f00(T) + m0(T) .

        eq f20(0) = 0 .
        eq f20(s T) = f10(T) .
        eq f21(0) = 0 .
        eq f21(s T) = f10(T) + m1(T) .

        eq f22(0) = 0 .
        eq f22(s T) = f11(T) .
        eq f23(0) = 0 .
        eq f23(s T) = f11(T) + m1(T) .

        eq f30(0) = 0 .
        eq f30(s T) = f20(T) .
        eq f31(0) = 0 .
        eq f31(s T) = f20(T) + m2(T) .

        eq f32(0) = 0 .
        eq f32(s T) = f21(T) .
        eq f33(0) = 0 .
        eq f33(s T) = f21(T) + m2(T) .

        eq f34(0) = 0 .
        eq f34(s T) = f22(T) .
        eq f35(0) = 0 .
        eq f35(s T) = f22(T) + m2(T) .
```

```
      eq f36(0) = 0 .
      eq f36(s T) = f23(T) .
      eq f37(0) = 0 .
      eq f37(s T) = f23(T) + m2(T) .
endth
```

6.4 Verification by rewriting

We now wish to prove Theorem 1, that is, for $j \in \{0, \ldots, 2^n - 1\}$:

$$f_{n,j}(t + n + 1, \underline{v}, \underline{w}) = \underline{w}(t) + r_\alpha(j) \times \underline{v}(t)$$

Since we have chosen $n = 3$ we have to prove that the following eight equations hold:

$$
\begin{aligned}
f_{3,0}(t + 4, \underline{v}, \underline{w}) &= \underline{w}(t) + r(0) * \underline{v}(t) & f_{3,1}(t + 4, \underline{v}, \underline{w}) &= \underline{w}(t) + r(1) * \underline{v}(t) \\
f_{3,2}(t + 4, \underline{v}, \underline{w}) &= \underline{w}(t) + r(2) * \underline{v}(t) & f_{3,3}(t + 4, \underline{v}, \underline{w}) &= \underline{w}(t) + r(3) * \underline{v}(t) \\
f_{3,4}(t + 4, \underline{v}, \underline{w}) &= \underline{w}(t) + r(4) * \underline{v}(t) & f_{3,5}(t + 4, \underline{v}, \underline{w}) &= \underline{w}(t) + r(5) * \underline{v}(t) \\
f_{3,6}(t + 4, \underline{v}, \underline{w}) &= \underline{w}(t) + r(6) * \underline{v}(t) & f_{3,7}(t + 4, \underline{v}, \underline{w}) &= \underline{w}(t) + r(7) * \underline{v}(t)
\end{aligned}
$$

We do this by creating a new module with a unconstrained constant t and reducing each equation in it.

```
th VERIFY is protecting PP .
        op t : -> Time .
endth
```

```
reduce in VERIFY : f30(s s s s t) == w(t) + r(0) * v(t) .
reduce in VERIFY : f31(s s s s t) == w(t) + r(s 0) * v(t) .
reduce in VERIFY : f32(s s s s t) == w(t) + r(s s 0) * v(t) .
reduce in VERIFY : f33(s s s s t) == w(t) + r(s s s 0) * v(t) .
reduce in VERIFY : f34(s s s s t) == w(t) + r(s s s s 0) * v(t) .
reduce in VERIFY : f35(s s s s t) == w(t) + r(s s s s s 0) * v(t) .
reduce in VERIFY : f36(s s s s t) == w(t) + r(s s s s s s 0) * v(t) .
reduce in VERIFY : f37(s s s s t) == w(t) + r(s s s s s s s 0) * v(t) .
```

Notice that we have to write the time $t + 4$ as $s\,s\,s\,s\,t$ and the natural numbers $1, \ldots, 7$ in a similar unary notation.

7 Concluding remarks

By means of a case study of a conventional piece of hardware we have shown how to represent a SCA by primitive recursive equations over algebras and how to map them into OBJ3. Further, the proof of correctness can be performed using equational reasoning in OBJ3. This process is systematic and in principle applies to any SCA. Thus it can be automated by means of an appropriate compiler; this is a subject of current research at R.H.B.N.C. and the University College of Swansea.

Many theoretical and practical problems are involved in the complete mechanisation of this process. The correctness of a SCA may involve scheduling of input and output streams which complicates the logical structure of the formulae to be proved (see [20] for example).

The SCA may not have unit delay and involve complex timing conditions in the network (see [19]).

More obviously we must reconsider the simple proof of SCAs of all sizes n given in [4]. Recall that the proof of correctness of Pixel Planes is uniform for all n. With conventional mathematical precision we choose 'any n' and write out the proof. In this paper we copy this process but must choose arbitarily some particular value such as $n = 3$. This is not satisfactory. However it is important to note that

- in verifying a device it is sufficient to verify a specific design of a known size; and

- this selection makes the verification straight forward.

To improve the situation we must uniformise to definition of SCAs to take account of size explicitly. This can be done in a number of ways, for example:

- Introduce indicies as explicit parameters in the module functions.

- Invent a theory of infinite SCAs that simulate a family of finite SCAs of different sizes.

- Introduce space coordinates into module specifications and develop equational logics that reason about space and time.

We have chosen to postpone the treatment of this problem of size in OBJ3 until we have further investigated the theoretic basis of each of these options.

This verification experiment with OBJ3 has convinced us of the potential of this approach. Equational logic is powerful enough to allow straight forward encoding of SCA specifications, and simple enough to afford relatively painless proofs. This style of proof which is a compromise between automatic proof construction and proof checking is, we believe, desirable.

In the course of this proof we have also felt the need for a number of theorem proving facilities such as controlled rewriting and automatic construction of inductive proof templates which are, at present, missing from OBJ3. The lack of documentation about the operational semantics of some features of the language, such as module combinators was a source of irritation. Those issues are currently the subject of joint work between RHBNC and the Programming Research Group at Oxford University.

References

[1] J. Derrick, G. Lajos, and J. V. Tucker. *Specification and Verification of Synchronous Concurrent Algorithms Using the Nuprl Proof Development System.* Technical Report 30.89, Centre for Theoretical Computer Science, University of Leeds, 1989.

[2] N. Dershowitz and J. P. Jouannaud. Rewrite systems. In *Handbook of Theoretical Computer Science, Volume B*, chapter 15, North-Holland, (to appear).

[3] S. M. Eker. *Formal Foundations for the Design of Rasterization Algorithms and Architectures.* PhD thesis, School of Computer Studies, University of Leeds, (in preparation).

[4] S. M. Eker and J. V. Tucker. Specification and verification of synchronous concurrent algorithms: A case study of the Pixel-Planes architecture. In P. M. Dew, R. A. Earnshaw, and T. R. Heywood, editors, *Parallel Processing for Computer Vision and Display*, pages 16–49, Addison Wesley, Wokingham, England, 1989.

251

[5] H. Fuchs. An introduction to Pixel-Planes and other VLSI intensive graphics systems. In R. A. Earnshaw, editor, *Theoretical Foundations of Computer Graphics and CAD*, pages 675–688, Springer-Verlag, Berlin, 1988.

[6] H. Fuchs, J. Goldfeather, J. P. Hultquist, S. Spach, Jr. F. P. Brooks, J. G. Eyles, and J. Poulton. Fast spheres, shadows, textures, transparencies and image enhancements in Pixel-Planes. *Computer Graphics*, 19(3):169–187, July 1985.

[7] H. Fuchs and J. Poulton. Pixel-Planes: A VLSI-orientated design for a raster graphics engine. *VLSI Design*, 2(3):20–28, 1981.

[8] H. Fuchs, J. Poulton, A. Paeth, and A. Bell. Developing Pixel-Planes, a smart memory-based raster graphics system. In *Proceedings of the 1982 MIT Conference on Advanced Research in VLSI*, pages 137–146, Artech House, Dedham MA, 1982.

[9] R. M. Gallimore, D. Coleman, and V. Stavridou. UMIST OBJ: A Language for Executable Program Specifications. *Computer Journal*, 32(5):413–421, October 1989.

[10] S. Garland and J. Guttag. Inductive Methods for Reasoning About Abstract Data Types. In *Proceedings of 15th Symposium on Principles of Programming Languages*, pages 219–229, ACM, January 1988.

[11] S. Garland and J. Guttag. The Larch Prover. In N. Dershowitz, editor, *Lecture Notes in Computer Science, No 355*, Springer Verlag, 1989.

[12] J. A. Goguen. Abstract Errors for Abstract Data Types. In E. Neuhold, editor, *Proceedings of First IFIP Working Conference on Formal Description of Programming Concepts*, pages 21.1–21.32, MIT, 1977.

[13] J. A. Goguen. OBJ as a Theorem Prover with Applications to Hardware Verification. In *Proceedings of 2nd Banff Workshop on Hardware Verification*, Banff, Canada, June 1988.

[14] J. A. Goguen, C. Kirchner, J. Meseguer, and T. Winkler. OBJ as a Language for Concurrent Programming. In S. Kartashev and S. Kartashev, editors, *Proceedings of 2nd International Supercomputing Conference, Vol 1*, pages 195–198, International Supercomputing Institute, Inc., St. Petersburg, Florida, 1987.

[15] J. A. Goguen and J. Meseguer. Rapid Prototyping in the OBJ Executable Specification Language. *Software Engineering Notes*, 7(5):75–84, December 1982.

[16] J. A. Goguen and T. Winkler. *Introducing OBJ3*. Technical Report SRI–CSL–88–9, Computer Science Laboratory, SRI International, Menlo Park, CA 94025, August 1988.

[17] H. A. Harman and J. V. Tucker. Clocks, retiming and the formal specification of a UART. In G. Milne, editor, *The Fusion of Hardware Design and Verification*, pages 375–396, North-Holland, 1988.

[18] N. A. Harman. *Formal Specification of Digital Systems*. PhD thesis, School of Computer Studies, University of Leeds, 1989.

[19] K. M. Hobley. *Specification and Verification of Synchronous Concurrent Algorithms*. PhD thesis, School of Computer Studies, University of Leeds, (in preparation).

[20] K. M. Hobley, B. C. Thompson, and J. V. Tucker. Specification and verification of synchronous concurrent algorithms: A case study of a convolution algorithm. In G. Milne, editor, *The Fusion of Hardware Design and Verification*, pages 347–374, North-Holland, 1988.

[21] G. Huet and J. M. Hullot. Proof by Induction in Equational Theories with Constructors. *JCCS*, 2(25), 1982.

[22] D. Kapur and D.R. Musser. Proof by Consistency. *Artificial Intelligence*, 31(2):125–157, Februrary 1987.

[23] D. Knuth and P. Bendix. Simple Word Problems in Universal Algebras. In J. Leech, editor, *Computational Problems in Abstract Algebra*, pages 263–297, Pergamon Press, 1970.

[24] A. R. Martin. *Specification and Simulation of Synchronous Concurrent Algorithms*. PhD thesis, School of Computer Studies, University of Leeds, 1989.

[25] K. Meinke. *A Graph Theoretic Model of Synchronous Concurrent Algorithms*. PhD thesis, Department of Computer Studies, University of Leeds, 1988.

[26] K. Meinke and J. V. Tucker. Specification and representation of synchronous concurrent algorithms. In F. H. Vogt, editor, *Proceedings of Concurrency '88*, pages 163–180, Springer-Verlag LNCS 335, 1988.

[27] John Poulton, Henry Fuchs, John D. Austin, John G. Eyles, Justin Heinecke, Cheng-Hong Hsieh, Jack Goldfeather, Jeff P. Hultquist, and Susan Spach. PIXEL-PLANES: Building a VLSI-based graphic system. In H. Fuchs, editor, *Proceedings of the Chapel Hill Conference on VLSI*, pages 35–60, Computer Science Press, Rockville MA, 1985.

[28] S. Purushothaman and P. A. Subrahmanyam. Mechanical certification of systolic algorithms. *Journal of Automated Reasoning*, 5:67–91, 1989.

[29] S. Purushothaman and P. A. Subrahmanyam. Reasoning about systolic algorithms. *Journal of Parallel and Distributed Computing*, 5:669–699, 1988.

[30] V. Stavridou, H. Barringer, and D.A. Edwards. Formal Specification and Verification of Hardware: A Comparative Case Study. In *Proceedings of 25th Design Automation Conference*, pages 197–205, ACM/IEEE, Computer Society Press, Anaheim, California, June 1988.

[31] B. C. Thompson. *A Mathematical Theory of Synchronous Concurrent Algorithms*. PhD thesis, Department of Computer Studies, University of Leeds, 1987.

[32] B. C. Thompson and J. V. Tucker. *Synchronous Concurrent Algorithms*. Technical Report, Department of Mathematics and Computer Science, University College Swansea, 1989.

Use of the OTTER theorem prover for the formal verification of hardware*

Paolo CAMURATI   Tiziana MARGARIA
Paolo PRINETTO †

Abstract

Efficient proof techniques are vital for the success of formal verification of hardware. First-Order Logic theorem provers satisfy this requirement. This paper deals with experiences in applying such a tool, OTTER, to the verification of correctness of combinational logic. Several proof methodologies are here discussed: a rewrite rules and a resolution based approach are compared.

1   Introduction

Formal verification of hardware correctness is gaining a growing interest in academic and industrial environments [2], [3]. It needs tools for automating correctness proofs, and theorem provers can efficiently serve the purpose.

Some provers based on *First-Order Logic* implement a large set of algorithms exploiting the resolution principle for the achievement of automated proofs [4]. A member of this group is OTTER (Other Techniques for Theorem-proving and Effective Research) [11], a resolution-style theorem-proving tool for First-Order Logic with equality, developed at the Argonne National Laboratories IL (USA) and available on the public domain.

This paper presents our experiences in using OTTER to prove the correctness of combinational circuits resorting to various strategies. Two proof methodologies are discussed and compared: a rewrite rules and a resolution based approach. Preliminary results have been already presented in [7]. Experimental results on a subset of the IFIP'89 benchmarks [6] are included.

Section 2 deals with the main points in tackling a problem by means of a resolution-based theorem prover, section 3 presents the *paramodulation* inference rule as a simple and natural way of handling equality. Section 4 briefly introduces

---

*This work is partially supported by the EEC under contract ESPRIT BRA 3216 "CHARME"

†Dipartimento di Automatica e Informatica, Politecnico di Torino, Corso Duca degli Abruzzi 24, I-10129 Turin (Italy); *margaria@itopoli.bitnet*

the *set of support* proof strategy, while section 5 summarizes the main features of the OTTER theorem prover. OTTER's application to the formal verification domain is dealt with in section 6, while the following sections show how to submit a problem for automated reasoning and compare two proof methodologies. Sections 9 and 10 present an application example and some experimental results, respectively.

2 Tackling a problem by means of a resolution-based reasoning program

Whenever a problem must be formalized for an automatic reasoning approach, it is necessary to distinguish among the components of the knowledge the reasoning program must possess in order to successfully solve the puzzle.

A general classification of the knowledge the automatic reasoning tools must be provided with is the following [13]:

- *Assumptions* and *axioms* contain general information and the description of problem domain. They constitute a broad description of the environment, the "context", where reasonment will take place.

- *Special facts* that narrow the search to a specific question provide a precise statement of the characteristics of the particular problem to be dealt with.

- *Special hypotheses* give hints about the way to follow in the reasoning process. They can include partial results, obtained during previous reasoning attempts, that may turn out to be useful as intermediate results on the way towards successive or more complex processing.

In this way, a complete scenary is presented to the automatic reasoning program together with some initial hints on what to do or on what to use in order to solve the specific problem.

The proof is found by *refutation* of the denial of the goal, i.e., by disproving that the conclusion is false. The main kernel of the proof process is based on the application of several *inference rules*, a set of algorithms that, when successfully applied to a set of hypotheses or *premisses*, yield conclusions that follow logically from the premisses, thus allowing to perform the basic reasonment steps. Several basic steps can be composed into a chain of logically sound derivations from two or more initial statements to the final result. Even if the single steps are almost intuitive, the composed reasonment can be quite complex and not so easily reducible to the premisses. The power of a resolution based approach derives from this observation, joint with the fundamental characteristic of the easy automation of the basic reasonment steps.

The prover works on *clauses*, disjunctions with no existential quantifiers and with implicit universal quantifiers.

The basic inference rules are: *binary resolution, hyperresolution, negative hyper-resolution, UR-resolution, factoring, paramodulation.* Binary resolution is the basic inference rule, and constitutes a complete set for clauses containing at most one positive literal. Hyperresolution and Unity Reduction (UR)-resolution can be viewed as a performance improving rules derived from the combination of several binary resolution steps providing that the structure of the set of clauses satisfies some of constraints. Binary resolution is usually sufficient for finding a proof. However, in case of clauses with more than one positive literal, factoring has to be employed.

Resolution techniques are essential and they are employed in the reduction phase, but, given the structure of hardware descriptions, which is based on equalities, they are not sufficient to reduce the complexity of the search. Irrelevant clauses should not be generated, or immediately identified and discarded, thus preventing their further combination and the generation of redundancies.

A set of *pruning* strategies helps to automatically identify and discard non promising clauses and to prevent the number of kept clauses from a combinational growth. They include:

- Inference rules like *paramodulation*, discussed in Section 3.1.

- Intuitive strategies like *subsumption* and *deletion*, essentially based on heuristics, that help to reduce the size of the space of already generated clauses, but do not allow to derive new ones, since no reasoning is performed. They overcome the generation of *copies* of the same clause, or multiple *instances* of existing clauses: only the most general clause is kept, being the most powerful one. Any tautology and any subsumed clause is immediately discarded.

- *Demodulation*, which is a rewrite-based approach. It allows to *simplify* and *canonicalize* existing information by means of *rewrite* rules: *semantically*, although not syntactically, redundant information is purged. In some cases, newly added equality clauses can be tagged as demodulators and be applied to the already retained clauses (*back demodulation*).

  In principle, both *left-to right* and *right-to-left* demodulation is possible, but in practice, only one application is chosen. When the demodulation strategy is applied to a clause, a term is treated with as many demodulation steps as possible, trying to canonicalize it by means of rewrites. Intermediate clauses are then discarded, and only the final demodulant is retained.

3   The Equality Relation

The equality relation is very helpful to formulate theorems. As an example, it is sufficient to employ the *equality* predicate, the *successor* function and the constant 0 to formalize the theory of integers according to Peano's axioms.

Equality has several useful properties: it is

- reflexive : $x = x$,

- symmetric : *if* $x = y$ *then* $y = x$,

- transitive : *if* $x = y$ *and* $y = z$ *then* $x = z$, and

- furthermore, it allows to substitute equals for equals.

When the equality relation is used to formalize a theorem, extra axioms must be introduced that describe its properties. If a set of clauses involving equalities is processed resorting to resolution alone, it is not possible to formally prove that that set is unsatisfiable: it is necessary to explicitly introduce the axioms relative to the properties of equality in order to reach the proof. Such a set of clauses is not simply *unsatisfiable*, but *E-unsatisfiable*, i.e., there is at least an interpretation that does not satisfy the reflexive, symmetric, transitive and substitutive axioms of equality.

Treating equality by means of an explicit input of the axioms implies the need of a larger set of clauses for the formalization of equality-based theorems. Moreover, it leads to the generation of useless resolvents during the deduction phase. One among the approaches to the automatic treatment of equality resorts to the introduction of *paramodulation* [4], a simple and natural way of handling equality. It replaces the axioms concerning the properties of equality and, used in conjunction with resolution, allows to prove theorems on E-unsatisfiable sets of clauses in a natural and efficient way.

3.1 Paramodulation

It is an inference rule that allows to substitute equals for equals, with some specific characteristics:

- it is oriented to *terms*, rather than to *literals*

- it is a generalization of the equality substitution

- it combines in a single step the search of a substitution and the equality substitution itself.

It can be shown that the combination of paramodulation and resolution is *complete* for *E-unsatisfiable* set of clauses [4].

This inference rule plays a role of vital importance in case the proof can not be obtained by means of pure rewrites, in a depth-first derivation from input clauses to the refutation. On the contrary, its application allows a controlled breadth-first generation of the space of kept clauses, such that several lines of reasoning are followed in parallel, and a "cross fertilization" step between them can occur if needed. The importance and the impact on the proof strategy of this additional possibility will be discussed in Section 9 on an application example.

3.2 Demodulation vs. Paramodulation

The two most powerful and less immediate approaches to simplification are often easily confused. The differences are nevertheless fundamental [13]:

- with demodulation, unification makes nontrivial variable replacements only in the analogue of the "from" clause, whereas paramodulation, when applied in an unrestrained way, allows sophisticated substitutions in both "from" and "into" clauses;

- for demodulation, the equality literal must be in a (positive) unit clause, while paramodulation does not restrict its application to any particular set of clauses;

- demodulation discards the "into" clause, being essentially a semantic rewrite, while paramodulation retains the clauses before and after substitution, since it embodies the concept of cross fertilization, for which the resulting clause has an original content with respect to each of the parent clauses;

- demodulation can cause loss of refutation completeness, since it involves a deletion or discarding step, while paramodulation still ensures the same degree of completeness that characterized the original set of clauses.

Rewrite rules based automatic reasoning tools like REVE and OBJ [10] rely heavily or entirely on demodulation style approaches. Their limitation appears to be due to the difficulty or impossibility of dealing with more complex proofs, such as the ones requiring more advanced reasonment issues. The choice in OBJ is the introduction of a form of *inductionless induction*, that allows to mimic the true proof by induction procedure. OTTER offers rewrite rules based proof techniques essentially as a partial support to much more sophisticated reasoning capabilities: a powerful set of inference rules including paramodulation, i.e., built-in features for efficient handling of equality.

4 The *Set Of Support* proof strategy

A strategy embodies the way for guiding an automated reasoning program to deal with a problem. Several strategies focus on different aspects of the reasoning process:

- *ordering strategies* direct a reasoning program in the choice of the best clause to focus on,

- *restriction strategies* avoid even taking into consideration certain clauses or combinations of clauses that appear to be non promising for the attack to the problem. In this broad classification it is possible to further distinguish between

- *pruning strategies*, like subsumption and deletion, and

- *canonicalization strategies*, like demodulation.

The *Set Of Support strategy* allows the application of an inference rule to a set of clauses only if at least one of them *has support*, i.e., if it is an input clause and it is designated as having support, or if it is derived by application of an inference rule to a set of clauses, at least one of which has support.

The property of support is in a certain sense inherited, and heavily depends on the user's attribution of the support property to a subset of the input clauses, the *set of support*. Generally recommended choices for the set of support are either the set of clauses that constitute the special hypotheses plus the denial, or simply the clauses of the denial. Either of these choices has the property that the complementary set of input clauses is expected to be consistent, i.e., *satisfiable*. The set of support strategy is a restriction strategy: it prevents the reasoning program from simply expanding a set of consistent clauses, by requiring that at least one of the clauses involved in each allowed reasoning step be tightly related to the specific problem to be solved. Should the set of support be chosen unwisely, the proof might be never reached. The effectiveness of the strategy thus is heavily influenced by the initial choices of the user.

5   The OTTER theorem prover

OTTER is a resolution-based theorem prover with equality for First-Order Logic. It is coded in C and is portable on a large variety of computers. We have it currently running on SUN 4/60 *SPARCstations-1* under UNIX and on PC under MS-DOS.

The inference rules it supports are *binary resolution, hyperresolution, UR-resolution, binary paramodulation*, and *factoring*. They constitute a small but totally general-purpose and redundant set of elementary operations in the resolution-style reasonment approach to automatic proof, which enables a user to perform automatically and efficiently all the checks of logical derivation of any statement from the general and special premises describing an environment of his choice. Their application is preceded by a *unification* step, and is based on the *resolution principle*.

As a last-generation product, it is also capable of factoring, weighting, and term ordering. It includes built-in evaluable functions and predicates, as well as forward and back subsumption and demodulation. The proof is found by *refutation*, by working on *clauses*. The input can be given either as a set of First-Order Logic formulæ or as a set of clauses. In the former case universal quantification on variables must be explicitly stated. The translation of formulæ into clauses is automatically performed: after being put in negative normal form, *Skolemization* follows. They are eventually rewritten in CNF (Conjunctive Normal Form) [11].

OTTER uses the *"given clause"* proof algorithm, derived from the *set of support* strategy [4]. It maintains three lists of clauses:

- the **axioms** list, containing the postulates,

- the **sos** list, containing the set of support,

- the **demodulators** list, containing all the needed equalities under the form of rewriting rules.

The choice of the proof methodology is left to the user. A wide selection of options concern the basic inference rules already mentioned, not only with respect to their enforcement, but also to control the modalities of their application to the given clause.

Another rich set of options controls the strategies that enable the theorem prover to limit the search space, trying to discard as rapidly as possible all non promising branches.

Evaluable functions and predicates for integer arithmetic, boolean operations, conditional expressions, and lexical comparison enable the user to "program" some aspects of the deduction process.

The notation for lists is very close to the Prolog [5] style. All the usual operators on lists can be easily defined by means of equalities that become theorems of the underlying theory.

Several parameters help the user in limiting the resources the prover can use: memory capacity to be dynamically allocated, running time, as well as the number of given, kept, and generated clauses. An upper bound on the demodulation steps limits the number of rewrites that can be performed on a single clause. Weighting and lexical ordering, in fact, do not guarantee termination.

Statistics are output at the end of the processing, together with a listing of the proof. Very detailed figures concerning runtime, memory allocation, and clauses management may be easily obtained.

6   Application of OTTER to formal verification

In our approach, consistent with [8], the formal system is a "theory", given by First-Order Logic plus a set of description-specific non-logical axioms.

The First-Order Logic embedded in OTTER already groups the three basic building blocks of the formal system: a first-order language, a set of logical axioms, and a set of inference rules, but to define the specific properties of the application domain, First-Order Logic is augmented with specific non-logical axioms by introducing new function and predicate symbols. This enlarged formal system constitutes a first-order theory, or simply a "theory".

The non-logical axioms of the theory associated with hardware descriptions are essentially *description-specific* axioms, aimed to capturing the semantics of hardware descriptions.

In our approach, they are based on a set of postulates and theorems of switching algebra. However, it is not immediate to decide a priori which postulates and which theorems should be selected for inclusion into the basic set. Practical experiences here show that the composition of this set, in fact, heavily influences the efficiency of the prover, in terms of both speed and memory usage. In [7] alternative strategies have been outlined for ensuring the consistency of the basic set of theorems.

In the application of OTTER to formal verification, we have concentrated on several specific domains:

- proof of equivalence of multilevel boolean expressions,

- verification of hardware circuits, at two different levels:

    - *implementation vs. implementation,* useful in the correctness proof of transformational design rules derived from experience, as heuristics, and for correctness check of automatically synthesized circuits [6],
    - *specification vs. implementation,* allowing to proofcheck several possible realizations with respect to higher-level requirements.

    The *specification* description is at the functional level, while the *implementation* is described at the gate level, for both combinational and synchronous sequential circuits.

In the following, the attention is concentrated on the *implementation vs. implementation* verification of combinational circuits. Our work aims at drawing a first comparison of two general proof methodologies: a rewrite rules based approach and a resolution based strategy, whose application is not mutually exclusive.

7 Submitting a problem in OTTER

At the structural level, verification is performed starting from the circuit topology. According to a *definitional* method ([9], [12]), descriptions specify input variables, internal connection lines, and one or more output variables. From our experience, translation into a First-Order Logic form suitable for the OTTER theorem prover requires that:

1. the set of postulates and proven theorems of switching theory and of integers either form the set of axioms in a resolution based approach or be included in the set of demodulators for a rewrite rules based proof technique,

2. input variables be mapped into variables,

3. internal nodes be transformed in functions with explicit dependency on free variables,

4. the circuit structure be expressed in terms of equalities to be included in the set of demodulators,

5. the statement to be proven constitute the set of support and be written as a formula that negates the goal, with universally quantified free variables.

A first preprocessing phase is left to the user. Several transformation steps are required in order to render the formulation of the problem suitable for processing.

OTTER works on clauses, even if two input formulations are accepted: clauses and formulas.

Starting from already formalized specification and/or implementation descriptions given in one of the standard formats for the benchmark sets [6] [1], or from plain boolean expressions for the multilevel expressions equivalence proof, the most natural choice has led us to express fundamental postulates, useful theorems, and the circuit description in clausal form, but to submit the goal as a formula with all input variables universally quantified.

The set of axioms and of demodulators is constituted entirely by clauses input by the user, while the set of support (usually a single expression) is input as a formula and then automatically clausified.

An example of description translation in the OTTER format is reported in Section 9.

A modular design style is based on several instances of functional blocks that can be verified separately. Whenever possible, verification is performed resorting to a "divide et impera" approach, by separately proving the equivalence of corresponding internal nodes that only depend on primary inputs, then reducing the complexity of the remaining circuit by transforming those nodes into primary inputs. This *proof and substitution* step is performed iteratively until primary outputs are reached. In some cases the complexity of the proof can be kept linear with the parallelism of the circuit.

8   Proof methodology

The equivalence proof can be reached following several strategies: by enumeration, by means of theorems, by means of theorems after elimination of redundant axioms, and by resorting to rewrite rules. A discussion and some results concerning the first three approaches are given in [7], but the most promising proof methodologies supported by OTTER are essentially a *resolution based method*, that heavily relies on the paramodulation inference rule, and a *rewrite rules based one*, consisting on the preferential application of the demodulation strategy.

8.1   Proof by resolution

Implementing resolution based strategies, OTTER's proofs are reached by refutation.

The reasoning consists of the preferential repeated application of the binary paramodulation inference rule, i.e., of the substitution of equals for equals, in a chain of derived lemmas and theorems. Demodulation is used for reconstructing the overall structure of the circuit from the description, while the contradiction is found and evidenced by means of a binary resolution step that generates the empty clause.

By means of initial settings binary resolution and paramodulation inference rules are enforced, demodulation is specified to be regarded as an additional rule, thus enabling rewrites, and some directions must be given on how to use paramodulation: substitutions are applied only to variables, in a left-to-right application of theorems and lemmas, and occur only into the given clause.

Obviously, the complementary choice can be made, that reverses the direction of the application for equality substitution. The enforcement of the two strategies simultaneously is generally not recommended, since an infinite loop of substitutions could derive.

Substitution is to be applied on all occurrences of a variable at a time, since the effect of the application of a given value on a fan-out stem affects simultaneously all the fan-out branches.

8.2 Proof by means of rewrite rules

This methodology looks for a proof exclusively by means of rewrite techniques. In a pure rewrite rules based approach no paramodulation is allowed. Demodulation is handled as if it were an inference rule. Only the final step is due to binary resolution. Description of operator properties and formulation of the problem are in the demodulator list, while the negated goal to be disproved is the only clause with support. The sole axiom $x = x$ is added, to detect contradictions.

In some simple cases the proof is easily reached by repeated application of demodulation steps, until the contradiction is evidenced by binary resolution. More generally, some nontrivial substitutions must be carried out through paramodulation, even though the bulk of the reasonment is constituted by rewrites. Inference rules like binary resolution and paramodulation are therefore still enforced, but the proof is mainly (if not exclusively) carried out by means of rewrite rules, resorting to a demodulation-based approach.

9 Example of application

As a simple complete example, aimed at showing our methodology, we include the correctness proof of the transformation function that maps the C499 circuit of the ISCAS'85 benchmark set for combinational ATPG [1] into the C1355 is considered. Its three-level logic expression is:

$$exor(x, y) = nand(nand(x, nand(x, y)), nand(nand(x, y), y))$$

The application environment is described through a list of useful theorems and lemmas. In this example, the set contains the postulates and basic theorems of switching algebra.

In a resolution based approach the set of theorems constitutes the list of axioms. In general it is redundant, since it is difficult to exactly know "a priori" what properties will be involved in a complex proof.

In a rewrite rules based proof, useful theorems are regarded as transformation rules, therefore they are included in the set of demodulators.

The problem under consideration is submitted by means of clauses containing a structural description of the two circuits. It is formalized by the following set of rewrite rules:

```
list(demodulators).
57 (o1(x,y) = nand(a1(x,y),a2(x,y))).
58 (a1(x,y) = nand(x,a3(x,y))).
59 (a2(x,y) = nand(a3(x,y),y)).
60 (a3(x,y) = nand(x,y)).
61 (o2(x,y) = exor(x,y)).
end_of_list.
```

The formula representing the negation of the thesis constitutes the set of support:

```
formula_list(sos).
   -(all x all y (o1(x,y) = o2(x,y))).
end_of_list.
```

and it is automatically clausified as

```
list(sos).
   (o1(c1,c2) != o2(c1,c2)).
end_of_list.
```

The need to explicitly state every function's dependency from free variables is due to the need for correct propagation of Skolem's constants.

The equivalence proof can be reached through several strategies. In general, both proof methodologies outlined here rely on the enforcement of the same set of inference rules and options. However, in case of quite small or simple circuits, as in the example under consideration, demodulation would suffice to obtain the proof by rewrite.

Listings of the proofs obtained by means of theorems and of rewrite rules are given in appendix A.

Tabs. 1-3 report the most significant statistics that allow to evaluate the different approaches: proof by enumeration, by resolution, and by means of rewrite rules. The results and statistics on enumeration are reported only for completeness, but the strategy is clearly not applicable: any proof reached by means of theorem application is 3 to 4 times faster on small circuits with only few inputs and avoids the quasi-exponential explosion in the number of generated clauses. The rows of the following tables correspond to the parameters for which statistics are automatically output by OTTER at the end of a proof session.

	strategy		
	enumeration	resolution	rewrite rules
total CPU time (s)	4.71	1.36	0.07
total # of clauses	970	279	18
last step	binary res.	binary res.	binary res.
# of mallocs	15	4	1
malloc size (Kbytes)	32.7	32.7	32.7
memory used (Kbytes)	480	128	32

Table 1 – Overall results and statistics

	strategy		
	enumeration	resolution	rewrite rules
clauses input	62	47	16
clauses given	51	51	1
clauses generated	1683	511	1
demod & eval rewrites	78	6	33
tautologies deleted	0	0	0
clauses forward subsumed	777	281	0
(subsumed by sos)	638	142	0
clauses kept	907	231	2
empty clauses	1	1	1
clauses back subsumed	0	0	0
clauses not processed	19	3	0

Table 2 – Detailed statistics on clauses management

	strategy		
	enumeration	resolution	rewrite rules
run time	5.74	1.58	0.08
input time	0.14	0.12	0.04
clausify time	0.01	0.00	0.00
binary_res time	0.05	0.02	0.00
para_into time	0.73	0.16	0.01
pre_process time	2.68	0.66	0.01
demod time	0.40	0.09	0.00
for_sub time	0.47	0.09	0.00
cl integrate	0.28	0.07	0.00
print_cl time	0.72	0.25	0.01
post_process time	0.96	0.34	0.00
conflict time	0.22	0.19	0.00
back_sub time	0.58	0.08	0.00
FPA build time	0.40	0.17	0.00
IS build time	0.16	0.01	0.00
weigh cl time	0.09	0.02	0.00

Table 3 – Detailed time statistics

10   Results and conclusions

Verified multiple output circuits include some ripple carry adders and multipliers of different parallelism [6], whose sets of expressions represent the function extracted from layout and a translation of the behavioral description. Tab. 4 contains some preliminary results on the IFIP'89 benchmarks set, obtained resorting to a resolution based proof methodology, while in Tab. 5 are reported the results obtained on the same benchmarks in a rewrite based approach. The circuits under consideration are ripple carry adders, *rip02* has a two bit parallelism, while *rip04* has a four bit parallelism. This *implementation vs. implementation* verification requires the proof of equivalence of two different gate-level realizations, and it has been carried out for each output separately. The rows of the table contain the results relative to the correctness proof of each output: sum outputs are listed LSB first, then the carry output follows. Notice that the circuits generating the outputs labelled with ** have an identical structure, therefore it would be sufficient to verify the correctness of the generic n_{th} output bit, $n > 1$. CPU times are expressed in seconds, the size of a malloc is 32.7 Kbytes, and the proof length is measured with the number of clauses it contains, including those relative to the circuit description.

Ripple carry adders					
circuit	total t.	input t.	reas. t.	mallocs	clauses	proof cl.
rip02_1	1.27	0.19	0.91	4	376	16
rip02_2	2.16	0.22	1.71	5	462	22
rip02_cout	3.37	0.16	2.85	5	860	17
rip02	6.80	0.57	5.47	14	1698	55
rip04_1	1.31	0.19	0.94	4	376	16
rip04_2	2.15	0.19	1.73	5	462	22
rip04_3	8.89	0.19	7.56	11	2483	15
rip04_4	8.78	0.20	7.45	11	2483	15
rip04_cout	74.44	0.22	62.40	31	9436	22
rip04	95.57	0.99	80.08	62	15240	90

Table 4 – Preliminary results on IFIP'89 benchmarks with resolution

Ripple carry adders					
circuit	total t.	input t.	reas. t.	mallocs	clauses	proof cl.
rip02_1	0.19	0.18	0.06	2	1	7
rip02_2	0.20	0.19	0.08	2	1	12
rip02_cout	0.19	0.19	0.09	2	1	11
rip02	0.58	0.56	0.23	6	3	30
rip04_1	0.20	0.19	0.07	2	1	7
rip04_2**	0.20	0.18	0.08	2	1	12
rip04_3**	0.27	0.25	0.09	2	1	17
rip04_4**	0.29	0.26	0.10	3	1	19
rip04_cout	0.28	0.24	0.12	3	1	16
rip04	1.24	1.12	0.46	10	5	71

Table 5 – Preliminary results on IFIP'89 benchmarks with rewrite rules

In general, paramodulation plays a role of vital importance in case the proof can not be obtained by means of pure rewrites, in a depth-first derivation from input clauses to the refutation. On the contrary, its application allows a controlled breadth-first generation of the space of kept clauses, such that several lines of reasoning are followed in parallel, and a "cross fertilization" step between them can occur if needed.

Due to the depth-first derivation of clauses, a demodulation based approach is by far faster and more efficient in terms of memory requirements. Nevertheless, the pure rewrite rules methodology is immediately applicable only on the proof of equivalence of structurally identical circuits.

In case of circuits with the same behavior, but different gate-level structure, some resolution steps may be required to perform substitutions that imply the application of properties of the equality relation. Even very simple circuits, like the transformation function examined, are often naturally translated into an *E-satisfiable* set of clauses. Demodulation alone is not powerful enough, additional rules must be added in order to simplify the substitution steps, and at least one paramodulation step still has to be employed: the two methodologies therefore are complementary, rather than mutually exclusive.

Rewrite rules are efficient in terms of performance, therefore their application is to be encouraged. When they fail in reaching the goal, in order to avoid inference steps, it is necessary to expand the set of rewrite rules by adding some "special purpose" transformations that simplify the substitution phase, introducing a series of intermediate steps. Unfortunately, looking for the "ad hoc" rules can be quite expensive in terms of designer's time, and is not always justified by the improved performance of the theorem prover.

Finding the most effective compromise between the two strategies in order to minimize the overal verification effort is clearly a matter of experience.

An advantage of the OTTER theorem prover seems to be its wide range of applicability, including in the same resolution-style proof framework issues currently preferably addressed by means of different tools.

References

[1] F. Brglez, H. Fujiwara: "*A neutral netlist of 10 combinational benchmark circuits and a target translator in Fortran*," ISCAS-85: IEEE International Symposium on Circuits And Systems, Vol. 3 of 3, Kyoto (Japan), June 1985

[2] P. Camurati, P. Prinetto: "*Formal verification of hardware correctness: introduction and survey of current research*," IEEE COMPUTER, Vol. 21, n. 7, July 1988, pp. 8-19

[3] P.Camurati, M. Fourman, C. Pixley, P. Prinetto, S-K. Chin, H. Takahara: "*Formal verification: is it practical for real-world design?*," IEEE Design & Test of Computers, December 1989, pp. 50-58 (D&T roundtable)

[4] C.L. Chang, R.C. Lee: *"Symbolic logic and mechanical theorem proving,"* Academic Press, Inc., 1973

[5] W.F. Clocksin, C.S. Mellish *"Programming in Prolog,"* Springer-Verlag, 1981.

[6] L. Claesen, D. Verkest: *Special session on benchmarks,* IMEC-IFIP Workshop on "Applied Formal Methods For Correct VLSI Design", Leuven (Belgium), November 1989.

[7] P. Camurati, T. Margaria, and P. Prinetto: *"The* OTTER *environment for resolution-based proof of hardware correctness,"* Microprocessing and Microprogramming, The Euromicro Journal, Vol. 30, n. 1-5, August 1990, pp. 413-419.

[8] H. Eveking: *"The application of CHDL's to the abstract specification of hardware,"* CHDL '85: IFIP 7th Int. Symposium on Computer Hardware Description Languages and their Applications, Tokyo (Japan), August 1985, pp. 167-177

[9] M.J.C. Gordon: *"LCF-LSM: a system for specifying and verifying hardware,"* Technical Report 41, Computer Laboratory, University of Cambridge, UK, 1984

[10] J. Goguen, T. Winkler: *"Introducing OBJ3,"* Technical Report SRI-CSL-88-9, SRI International, Computer Science Lab, August 1988

[11] W.W. McCune: *"OTTER 1.0 User's Guide,"* Rep. ANL-88-44 Mathematics and Computer Science Division, Argonne National Laboratory, Argonne, IL (USA)

[12] B. Moszkowski *"A Temporal Logic for multi-level reasoning about hardware,"* CHDL '83: IFIP 6th Int. Symposium on Computer Hardware Description Languages and their Applications, Pittsburgh, PA (USA), May 1983, pp.79-90

[13] L. Wos, R. Overbeek, E. Lusk, J. Boyle: *"Automated reasoning: introduction and applications,"* Prentice-Hall, Englewood Cliffs, NJ (USA), 1984.

A   Proof listings

The following listings show two equivalent derivations of the proof of correctness of the transformation function that maps the C499 circuit of the ISCAS'85 benchmark set for combinational ATPG [1] into the C1355.

A.1   Paramodulation

In this first case the proof is reached by means of theorems and equality substitution, thus resorting to a paramodulation based approach.

```
---------------- PROOF ----------------
34 (nand(x,y) = nand(y,x)).
35 (nand(x,y) = or(not(x),not(y))).
36 (nand(nand(x,y),nand(w,z)) = or(and(x,y),and(w,z))).
42 (exor(x,y) = or(and(x,not(y)),and(not(x),y))).
45 (and(x,y) = and(y,x)).
49 (and(or(x,y),or(not(x),z)) = or(and(x,z),and(not(x),y))).
53 (or(and(x,y),and(x,z)) = and(x,or(y,z))).
56 (o1(c1,c2) != o2(c1,c2)).
57 (o1(x,y) = nand(a1(x,y),a2(x,y))).
58 (a1(x,y) = nand(x,a3(x,y))).
59 (a2(x,y) = nand(a3(x,y),y)).
60 (a3(x,y) = nand(x,y)).
61 (o2(x,y) = exor(x,y)).
62 [56,demod,57,58,60,59,60,61]
   (nand(nand(c1,nand(c1,c2)),nand(nand(c1,c2),c2)) != exor(c1,c2)).
67 [para_into,34,62]
   (nand(nand(nand(c1,c2),c1),nand(nand(c1,c2),c2)) != exor(c1,c2)).
99 [para_into,36,67]
   (or(and(nand(c1,c2),c1),and(nand(c1,c2),c2)) != exor(c1,c2)).
204 [para_into,53,99] (and(nand(c1,c2),or(c1,c2)) != exor(c1,c2)).
212 [para_into,45,204] (and(or(c1,c2),nand(c1,c2)) != exor(c1,c2)).
226 [para_into,35,212]
   (and(or(c1,c2),or(not(c1),not(c2))) != exor(c1,c2)).
291 [para_into,42,226]
   (and(or(c1,c2),or(not(c1),not(c2))) !=
or(and(c1,not(c2)),and(not(c1),c2))).
292 [binary,291,49] .

------------ end of proof -------------
```

A.2 Demodulation

The following listing contains an equivalent proof of correctness, achieved by means of a rewrite rules based approach, thus mainly resorting to a demodulation strategy.

```
---------------- PROOF ----------------

1 (x = x).
2 (o1(x,y) = nand(a1(x,y),a2(x,y))).
3 (a1(x,y) = nand(x,a3(x,y))).
4 (a2(x,y) = nand(a3(x,y),y)).
5 (a3(x,y) = nand(x,y)).
6 (o2(x,y) = exor(x,y)).
7 (nand(x,y) = or(not(x),not(y))).
8 (not(or(x,y)) = and(not(x),not(y))).
9 (not(not(x)) = x).
10 (or(x,y) = or(y,x)).
11 (not(and(x,y)) = or(not(x),not(y))).
12 (and(x,y) = and(y,x)).
13 (and(or(x,not(y)),y) = and(x,y)).
14 (and(or(not(x),not(y)),x) = and(x,not(y))).
15 (exor(x,y) = or(and(x,not(y)),and(not(x),y))).
16 (o1(c1,c2) != o2(c1,c2)).
17 [16,demod,2,3,5,7,7,8,9,9,4,5,7,7,8,9,9,10,7,8,9,11,12,
   14,12,8,9,11,12,13,10,6,15,12,10]
   (or(and(not(c1),c2),and(not(c2),c1)) !=
    or(and(not(c1),c2),and(not(c2),c1))).
18 [binary,17,1] .

------------ end of proof ------------
```

Proof-based transformation of formal hardware models

Holger Busch *

Abstract

Formal design and verification of realistic hardware are still limited by the complexity of interactive proofs and logical formulæ. Hierarchy helps to overcome complexity. In many designs, however, optimisation reorganises hierarchy, even at late stages of a design process. Consequently, the partitions of the implementation structure do not always match the functional units of the specification. Instead of hierarchical modularisation, we therefore transform a specification to an implementation by a series of rule applications to a complete circuit model. Contrary to other approaches, we not only specify equations, but also implications for performing component-level reasoning without unfolding definitions.

In this paper we mainly address constrained data refinement in parameterised structures as part of our transformational design strategy. We define pseudo-components to express constraints on signals and for data conversion. Inserted into generic hardware models, the pseudo-components support modular data refinement of circuit descriptions and constraint propagation.

Our methodology has been applied to the formal verification of a complex FIR-filter design using the proof system LAMDBA.

1 Introduction

In recent years, a lot of experience with formal hardware verification has been gathered. Theorem provers are successfully applied to many designs, some of them having considerable complexity [7, 3, 10]. Currently, there are efforts to apply formal methods directly for synthesis of hardware, thus integrating design and verification [1, 6]. The results are promising, but they also show that interactive hardware proofs are still quite tedious for non-trivial examples and require experts. Further research is needed to manage the complexity of industrial applications. This research should address advanced verification and modelling strategies, but also proof-engineering and convenient user-interfaces.

To cope with the complexity-problem, hardware proofs are usually modularised by exploiting an existing hierarchy or introducing a new one. Specifications are implemented by hardware structures consisting of components that are refined independently at the next level of hierarchy. This procedure is applicable to many hardware designs. Sometimes, however, a design step changes the hierarchical decomposition. Consequently, the implementation structure does not directly reflect the functional units of the top level specification. In addition, there are interrelations between different components that cannot be captured adequately by a separate consideration of the components.

---

*SIEMENS AG, Corporate Applied Computer Sciences, Munich, Germany
holger%sun11b@ztivax.siemens.com

We developed a proof-based methodology addressing such design problems. We transform an abstract structure model, our specification, into an implementation model represented by one coherent logical formula. The corresponding implementation proof has to be modularised into manageable subproofs. Therefore, we gradually transform the circuit model by a series of rule applications. The transformation rules are equations or implications, some with additional preconditions. The rules are proved separately and focussed on subparts of the circuit. Equations are reduced with respect to signal variables, thus allowing for algebraic reasoning at function-level, i.e., without unfolding the function definitions representing hardware models. We design tactics and meta-rules that also allow us to perform implicational transformations at function-level. Those parts of the circuit that are irrelevant for a specific transformation are replaced by most-general free function or context variables in the transformation rule. This allows us to keep the rule expressions much smaller than the parts of the circuit model with which they are unified. The proofs of these abstract transformation rules are more concise, the rules themselves are more robust with respect to later changes of specifications, and the rules are applicable to different instances of the same basic problem.

Often, hardware components at lower levels of abstraction only implement corresponding specifications or high-level components if specific abstraction constraints imposed on the signals are satisfied. For instance, the integer domain of input signals must be compatible with the internal word-length of a two's-complement component. Usually, hand-calculations and simulations are performed to test whether design parameters have been sufficiently dimensioned. Therefore, a formal treatment of abstraction constraints is an essential element of our methodology. We prove separate refinement rules for each component and apply them to the complete circuit structure. Signal constraints and conversion between different abstraction levels are formalised in pseudo-blocks and form parts of an implementation referring to an abstract subcomponent. In the next step the pseudo-blocks are eliminated or propagated to the borders of the circuit. Hence, the auxiliary components are only temporarily inserted in the inner parts of the circuit to bridge different abstraction levels. In the scope of this paper, we deal with data refinement and constraints on signal values. We have defined similar pseudo-components to perform temporal refinement.

Parameterisable hardware models support the formulation of generic transformation rules. We formalise basic structures that are parameterised with (also parameterisable) primitive and pseudo-components to represent specific circuits. In the top-down process of implementing an abstract specification, new parameters are introduced. Parameter restrictions are imposed incrementally with transformations that are only valid for a subset of all parameter instances. That way, design decisions are postponed as much as possible to offer more flexibility for realising design alternatives. A parameter-oriented modelling and design-strategy greatly improves the reusability of proof components and hardware specifications. Higher-order logic is very well suited for implementing parameters describing many different objects, e.g., word-lengths, latency and hardware-structures.

We tested our methodology on an existing sophisticated FIR-filter design. Starting from a simple integer-level structure, we derived a model of the complex implementation at full-adder-level. The original design is described in [13] and was manufactured as a VLSI-chip. Our implementation model is very general and also covers variations that have been produced later. Due to space limitations, this paper only summarizes parts of our work.

M. Sheeran was the first researcher to extend higher-order functional programming concepts for the design and transformation of regular hardware [14]. In the specification language Ruby, she introduced relational models [15]. Although basically not machine-

supported, the approach is successfully being applied in industrial projects for the design
of digital signal processing circuits. W. Luk uses heterogeneous combinators to model
regular array circuits with differing components [12]. J. Joyce has defined and verified
generic ROMs, reasoning about a 'personalisation function' to create instances according
to functional specifications [11]. He did this work with the proof-system HOL. D. Verkest verifies parameterisable module generators of the silicon compiler Cathedral-II with
the Boyer-Moore theorem prover [16]. J. Herbert has studied temporal abstraction under
symbolic lower level timing constraints with the HOL system [9]. Chin has also used the
HOL system to verify synthesis functions creating functional representations of negabinary
array-multipliers of arbitrary size [2]. All these works show the power of parameterisation
in the context of hardware design and verification.

The LAMBDA proof system [4] has been conceived as a core system for CAD environments to develop digital circuits, integrating design and verification. It implements a constructive higher-order logic. Unlike similar systems that are based on theorems, LAMBDA
processes rules with one conclusion and an arbitrary number of premises. Together with
meta-functions to transform between equivalent rule representations, rules provide more
flexibility for programming ML-tactics that reduce the number of elementary proof steps.
The concept of contexts and syntactic functions is essential for formulating generic rules.
Another useful feature is the 'flexibilisation' of hypothesis lists allowing for posterior introduction of new hypotheses. For synthesis, this facility can be used to introduce hardware
components satisfying parts of a specification. In our approach, we will introduce restrictions instead, as is shown in the next section. The system allows for the ML-like definition of
recursive datatypes and functions. The close similarity between the formal LAMBDA logic
and the functional programming language ML, which is also the implementation language
of LAMBDA, eases the animation of user-defined functional LAMBDA-specifications. This
helps one to detect specification errors before starting the actual proof sessions.

2 Transformational design with the proof system LAMBDA

A hierarchical approach to hardware design with a proof system has been described in [5].
The synthesis starts with a tautological rule saying that if the predicate representing a
specification is true then the predicate is trivially true.

$\vdash SPEC$
—————————
$\vdash SPEC$

Then components satisfying individual parts of the top level specification $SPEC$ are introduced and the premise is simplified and finally discharged. The resulting rule is

—————————
$IMPL \vdash SPEC$

where $IMPL$ represents the netlist with all components.

In our transformational approach, we start with the same trivial rule. Then we also apply
a series of rule applications, but instead of simplifying the specification in the premise's
assertion, we generate the implementation by transforming the specification with rules like

—————————
$\vdash SPEC_i === SPEC_{i+1}$

or

$$\overline{\hspace{3cm}}$$
$$\vdash spec_{ij} === spec_{(i+1)j}$$

where the second rule only rewrites parts of $SPEC_i$[1].

Some of the transformation rules are conditional. As far as the conditions cannot be derived from existing hypotheses, we generate them as new hypotheses in the top rule's conclusion and premise.

$$\vdash SPEC_i(...,spec_{ij},...)$$
$$\overline{\hspace{3cm}}$$
$$\vdash SPEC$$

is transformed to

$$R \vdash SPEC_{(i+1)}(...,spec_{(i+1)j},...)$$
$$\overline{\hspace{3cm}}$$
$$R \vdash SPEC$$

with a conditional equation of the form

$$\overline{\hspace{3cm}}$$
$$R \vdash spec_{ij} === spec_{(i+1)j}$$

The new hypothesis could impose restrictions on parameters that are contained in both $spec_{ij}$ and $spec_{(i+1)j}$ or only in $spec_{(i+1)j}$. In the second case, the transformation would introduce a new parameter in the top rule and a corresponding new hypothesis would state the parameter to be a defined object and impose constraints on the parameter.

Equations can be considered reversible transformations. They are particularly appropriate for situations, where we temporarily need a representation to ease a specific transformation and re-establish the original basic structure afterwards. Many of the basic transformation rules are used in both directions. While keeping the transformation rules in a variable-free form, we are able to algebraically apply these rules without having to unfold the complete circuit description[2].

Alternatively, an implicational transformation rule could be applied by substituting the implication's hypothesis for the top rule's assertion together with logical transitivity.

$$\overline{\hspace{3cm}}$$
$$R, SPEC_{(i+1)} \vdash SPEC_i$$

transforms

---

[1] '===' is the equivalence that is TRUE, iff the objects on both sides are identical or UNDEFINED.

[2] The proofs of reduced transformation equations start with the same scheme. Rules for function extension and eta-expansion are applied to create parameter versions of the equations,

$$\vdash forall\ x,y.\ spec_{ij}\ x\ y === spec_{(i+1)j}\ x\ y$$
$$\overline{\hspace{3cm}}$$
$$\vdash spec_{ij} === spec_{(i+1)j}$$

then the equations are transformed into propositional bi-implications and both directions are separately proved. For changing an equivalence to a bi-implication, the objects must be of type om (TRUE or FALSE) and exist under the same preconditions.

$$\vdash SPEC_i$$
$$\overline{}$$
$$\vdash SPEC$$

to

$$\vdash SPEC_{(i+1)}$$
$$\overline{\phantom{\vdash SPEC_{(i+1)}}}$$
$$R \vdash SPEC$$

Implications transforming subcomponents can also be applied without unfolding function definitions as will be demonstrated in the next section.

We consider a limitation to purely equational reasoning as inappropriate for capturing all steps of an arbitrary top-down design process. Partial specifications cannot always be related by reversed implications to implementations that typically have a lot of additional properties not stated in the specification. Additionally, implicational reasoning provides more facilities to work with relational models. At an intermediate design stage, we sometimes take advantage of predicates that do not embed unique functional relations between inputs and outputs of a circuit component. On the other hand, implicational reasoning is exposed to the false-implies-everything problem. Therefore, the implementation model must be carefully checked to represent meaningful hardware.

3 Generic functions for hardware description

In this section, we give an impression of how we specify basic structure components and prove properties within the proof system LAMBDA. We do not present a comprehensive library of combining forms and corresponding rules, but only those entities that appear in the examples discussed in this paper. In our definitions and proofs, we make extensive use of higher-order parameterisation[3].

Contrary to M. Sheeran, we specify combining forms and primitives as prefix functions, because we have additional parameters for expressing irregularities besides those for signal objects. Another reason is that we want to be able to reason about partial applications in LAMBDA. Our implicational transformation concept gives us more freedom for designing the top-down implementation process resulting in an enhanced repertoire of transformations. Due to the strong typing of LAMBDA expressions, we have to be more precise about the types of signal objects than the RUBY language does. For instance, functions to convert signal lists into list signals or to relate signal tuples and signal lists must be explicitly inserted. The LAMBDA logic is constructive. Therefore we have to consider the existence of objects while reasoning about them. Although we have to pay a price for higher precision, getting machine-assistence is certainly advantageous for proving and performing transformations, and for managing assumptions that restrict the applicability of transformations.

A basic combining form is the polymorphic composition function, simply specified as

fun com COMP1 COMP2 x y =
        exists z. COMP1 x z $\wedge$ COMP2 z y

---

[3]For reasons of succinctness, e.g., for not having to introduce definitions that are unessential for the understanding of this paper, we slightly modify some of the definitions and expressions. This also applies for subsequent sections.

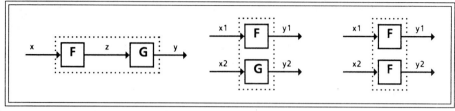

Figure 1: *com F G x y, comb2 (F,G) (x1,x2) (y1,y2), c2comb F (x1,x2) (y1,y2)*

Its most important property is the associativity, stated by:

$$\text{——————}$$
$$\vdash com\ F\ (com\ G\ H)\ ===\ com\ (com\ F\ G)\ H \tag{R3.1}$$

This law is often used to prepare the complete structure model for the application of a particular transformation rule.

    With the definition of *com*, we now demonstrate the use of implications for the transformation of compound stuctures. If we have proved the theorem

$$\text{——————}$$
$$com\ P\ (com\ F\ Q)\ x\ y \vdash com\ P\ (com\ G\ Q)\ x\ y \tag{R3.2}$$

where *P* and *Q* are implicitly all-quantified and *F* and *G* denote particular components, we can apply *(R3.1,R3.2)* to the assertion of the rule

... ⊢ *com P1 (com P2 (com G P3)) x y*
$$\text{————————}$$
... ⊢ ...

and get

... ⊢ *com (com P1 P2) (com F P3) x y*
$$\text{————————}$$
... ⊢ ...

with the unifications *P:= com P1 P2* and *Q:=P3*, not having unfolded the model of the compound structure. The same transformation could have been performed by simple term rewriting instead of unification with

$$\text{——————}\qquad\qquad\text{if available.}$$
$$\vdash G\ ===\ F$$

    Two combinators define parallel relations for pairs of input and output signals:

fun comb2 (COMP1,COMP2) (x1,x2) (y1,y2) =
        COMP1 x1 y1 ∧ COMP2 x2 y2

and

fun c2comb COMP (x1,x2) (y1,y2) =
        COMP x1 y1 ∧ COMP x2 y2

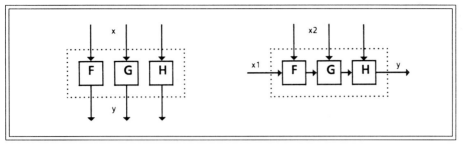

Figure 2: *cmapL [F,G,H] x y, cfoldL [F,G,H] (x1,x2) y*

Figure 1 illustrates these basic combinators.

There are a lot of components that define a functional relation between one input and one output signal. For building generic tactics it is quite useful to standardise these components by using the basic building block:

fun cF f x y =
        forall t. y t === f (x t)

A collection of combining forms are defined to describe higher-order structures. A list combinator that applies component lists to signal lists is defined[4]:

fun cmapL COMPs xs ys =
        length xs == length COMPs ∧
        length ys == length COMPs ∧
        andL (map (fn i ⇒(el i COMPs)(el i xs)(el i ys)) (indsL COMPs))

The length predicates exclude the incompatibility of components and ports. Note also, that in variable-free (with respect to the ports) expressions the length information is implicitly contained in the component lists.

A homogeneous version, where all components are identical, is given by:

fun cmap COMP xs ys =
        length xs == length ys ∧
        andL (map (fn i ⇒COMP (el i xs)(el i ys)) (indsL xs))

This time, the width of the parameterisable component is only defined by the lengths of the signal arguments, i.e., the actual dimension is determined by the environment in a compound structure containing some explicitly dimensioned components. For specifying reduced transformation equations focussed on subparts, we introduce a function making widths explicit where necessary:

fun sdim w x y = length x == w ∧ x == y

---

[4]*length, map* and *el* correspond to the common list functions. *andL* is the conjunction of a list of predicates and *indsL* is a function to generate a sorted list with all legal indices for a list.
In a system with dependent data types, e.g. VERITAS [8], the length information could be a data type attribute. From our practical experience, the equal-length condition can be handled quite well with our definitions and appropriate rules.
The second logical operator for expressing equality in LAMBDA: *x == y* requires identity and existence of both objects.

278

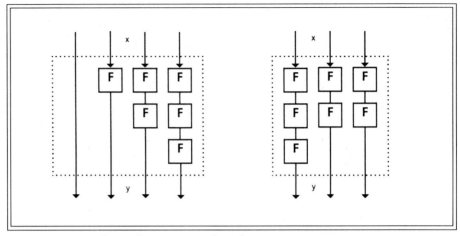

Figure 3: *crepL F [0,1,2,3] x y, crepL F [3,2,2] x y*

With this definition, we are able to relate identical structures of parallel components specified with *cmapL* and *cmap*, for instance in[5]:

$$\underline{\quad\quad\quad\quad\quad}$$

$$\vdash cmapL \ [F,F,F] === com \ (sdim \ 3) \ (cmap \ F) \qquad\qquad (R3.3)$$

Further examples are the local function:

fun cfoldL' [] (cin,[]) y =
      y == cin
| cfoldL' (COMP::COMPS) (cin,h::t) y =
            exists z. COMP (cin,h) z ∧
                  cfoldL' COMPS (z,t) y

and the corresponding external function

fun cfoldL COMPS (cin,x) y =
      length COMPS == length x ∧ cfoldL' COMPS (cin,x) y

cfoldL is a basic definition for cascade structures. We use this definition for the specification of cascaded adders with varying parameterisations, e.g., the internal word-length of the individual adders. The local function *cfoldL'* is partial, for the result is undefined in those cases, where the lengths of component and signal lists are not identical, whereas *cfoldL* is total. *cfold* is a homogeneous version of *cfoldL*.

---

[5]Of course, we could provide an explicit length parameter for *cmap*, but there are some transformations, where we do not need the length information. For this reason, we decided to only generate the explicit length information if necessary.

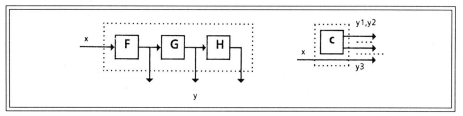

Figure 4: *cforkL [F,G,H] x y, c2fst c x ((y1,y2),y3)*

crep describes parameterised repetition of a particular component, e.g., a register chain, whereas *crepL* applies repeated components with individual repetition factors[6]:

fun crep 0 COMP x y =
      x == y
| *crep (S m) COMP x y =*
      exists z. COMP x z ∧ crep m COMP z y

fun crepL COMP dl =
      cmapL (map (fn m ⇒crep m COMP) dl)

We can specify an upper triangular matrix of registers as

crepL D [0,1,2,...,n].

Arbitrary register structures may be created by just parameterising with corresponding number generating functions as is illustrated in Figure 3.
    Another structure is defined for the distribution of an input signal through components of a fork structure:

fun cforkL' [COMP] x [y] = COMP x y
| *cforkL' (COMP::COMP1::COMPs) x (h::h1::t) =*
      COMP x h ∧ cforkL' (COMP1::COMPs) h (h1::t)

fun cforkL COMPs x y =
      length COMPs == length y ∧ 0<length y ∧ cforkL' COMPs x y

    Constants are generated with

fun const c (t:time) = c

and

fun c2fst c x ((y1,y2),y3) =
      y3 == x ∧ y1 == const c ∧ y2 == const c

    We also define combinators to restructure signal objects[7].

fun sflat x y =
      y == flat x

---

[6] $S :=$ successor of a natural number.
[7] The identifiers for combinators that take hardware components as parameters begin with *c*, all the others with *s*.

280

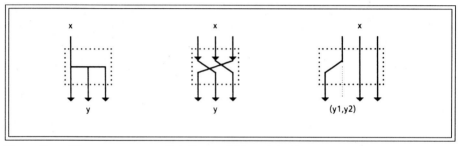

Figure 5: *smklist x y, spermute [2,0,1] x y, shdfst x (y1,y2)*

with *flat* recursively transforming a list of lists into a list of all list elements.

fun shdfst (x::xs) (y,ys) =
$\quad\quad$ *y == x ∧ ys == xs*

is used to prepare a list of input signals for cascade structures.
$\quad$ A combinator for distributing input signals is

fun smklist x y =
$\quad\quad$ *y == mklist (length y) x*

where *mklist n x* is a function to generate a list containing *n* times the element *x* . Again, the structure's size is implicitly defined by the signal argument *y*.
$\quad$ The permutation of signals in a list is performed by

fun spermute il x y =
$\quad\quad$ *eqm il (indsL x) ∧ y == permute il x*

where *permute il x* reorders the elements of *x* according to the index list *il* whose elements must be a permutation of all legal indices for *x*. This definition has been used for the reordering of coefficient bits in our FIR-filter example[8].

4   The specification and propagation of constraints

If we want a bitstring signal of limited word-length to implement an integer signal, we must restrict the integer values. In reduced equations constraints must be expressed without reference to explicit signals. We therefore define pseudo-components for signal constraints. These blocks can be used exactly like ordinary hardware models and inserted into the generic hardware structures. The pseudo-components are parameterisable with restriction functions that are applied to all valid signal values at all time instants.

fun sR rst x y =
$\quad\quad$ *forall t. rst(x t) ∧ x == y*

The component *sR* tests whether an atomic signal fulfils some boolean restriction *rst*. We also force the second port of *sR* to be identical to the first one.

---

[8]The corresponding proofs are too lengthy to be given in this paper.

We illustrate constraint propagation by a simple example. Let *rst10* and *rst19* be functions checking whether signal values are smaller than 10 or 19, respectively and *CMULTI* a component performing multiplication of a signal by a constant coefficient. The following equivalence is to be proved[9]:

$\vdash com (sR\ rst10)\ (CMULTI\ 2) === com\ (CMULTI\ 2)\ (sR\ rst19)$

After generation of signal arguments we split the goal into

$com\ (sR\ rst10)\ (CMULTI\ 2)\ x\ y \vdash com\ (CMULTI\ 2)\ (sR\ rst19)\ x\ y\quad (G4.1)$

and

$com\ (CMULTI\ 2)\ (rst19)\ x\ y \vdash com\ (sR\ rst10)\ (CMULTI\ 2)\ x\ y\quad (G4.2)$

Due to the identity between both signal arguments of *sR*, two general rules can be proved:

$$\overline{\qquad\qquad}\qquad\qquad\qquad\qquad\qquad\qquad\qquad (R4.1)$$
$$\vdash com\ F\ (sR\ rst)\ x\ y === (F\ x\ y \wedge sR\ rst\ y\ y)$$

$$\overline{\qquad\qquad}\qquad\qquad\qquad\qquad\qquad\qquad\qquad (R4.2)$$
$$\vdash com\ (sR\ rst)\ F\ x\ y === (sR\ rst\ x\ x \wedge F\ x\ y)$$

We apply these rules here just considering goal (*G4.2*):

$sR\ rst10\ x\ x,\ CMULTI\ 2\ x\ y \vdash CMULTI\ 2\ x\ y \wedge sR\ rst19\ y\ y$

and consequently get

$sR\ rst10\ x\ x,\ CMULTI\ 2\ x\ y \vdash sR\ rst19\ y\ y$

Unfolding the component definitions and application of some basic rules directly discharge the goal. In this way, the constraint on the input of the multiplier has been transformed to a constraint on the output.

In practical proof situations, constraints sometimes have to be combined or restructured as sketched in another simple example. Let a rule for the combination of some special constraints *r1* and *r3* be given:

$$\overline{\qquad\qquad}\qquad\qquad\qquad\qquad\qquad\qquad\qquad (R4.3)$$
$$\vdash com\ (sR\ r1)(sR\ r3) === sR\ rstX$$

We want to apply this equivalence to a specification like

$\vdash com\ F\ (com\ (sR\ rst1)\ (com\ (sR\ rst2)(com\ (sR\ rst3)\ G)))$

to get

$\vdash com\ F\ (com\ (sR\ rstX)\ (com\ (sR\ rst2)G))$

The transformation can easily be performed with the commutativity law for arbitrary constraints *rst1* and *rst2* (and the associativity of *com*):

---

[9]In all cases, where we do not print the horizontal line that usually separates conclusion and premises of a rule, the sequent corresponds to the premise we are currently working on, and the conclusion is suppressed in our abbreviated notation. Those rules without premise are theorems, they are always assumed to have already been proved.

$$\frac{\text{—— —— ——}}{\vdash com \ (sR \ rst1) \ (sR \ rst2) === com \ (sR \ rst2) \ (sR \ rst1)} \quad (R4.4)$$

Let us now call a constraint being introduced with a refinement transformation *secondary*. We can impose parameterisable primary constraints on the inputs of arbitrary circuits. The parameters then have to be instantiated or restricted in such a way that the internal secondary constraints are satisfied. But the different locations of primary and secondary constraints do not directly allow to relate the constraints. We have the choice of performing the proof to eliminate the secondary constraint including the intermediate circuit components, or of propagating the secondary or primary constraint in order to join both. We favour the propagation method in order to modularise the proof. Again we consider an example which principally shows the elimination of secondary constraints.

$$\vdash com \ (sR \ (rstp \ a))(sR \ rst10) === sR \ (rstp \ a)$$

Here, *rstp a* is a parameterisable function for the restriction of signals to values smaller than *a*. The secondary constraint *(sR rst10)* can easily be eliminated, if *a* is chosen smaller than *11*. Hence we introduce an appropriate parameter restriction and get a sequent that can be reduced to *TRUE*:

$$a < 11 \vdash com \ (sR \ (rstp \ a))(sR \ rst10) === sR \ (rstp \ a)$$

If we think of more complicated constraints with several parameters, the choice of the parameter instances and restrictions can take into account different trade-offs. The examples are very simple, but the constraints formalised in that way can be quite complex.

Two derivations from *(R4.2)* are useful when reasoning about constraints:

$$\frac{\text{—— —— ——}}{sR \ rst \ x \ y \vdash y == x} \quad (R4.5)$$

$$\frac{COMP \ x \ y \vdash sR \ rst \ y \ y}{COMP \ x \ y \vdash com \ COMP \ (sR \ rst) \ x \ y} \quad (R4.6)$$

Given a hardware structure with one signal input, we impose a global input constraint by means of the implication:

$$\frac{\text{—— —— ——}}{com \ (sR \ rst) \ COMP \ x \ y \vdash COMP \ x \ y} \quad (R4.6)$$

that transforms

$$com \ COMP \ (...) \ x \ y$$

to

$$\vdash com \ (sR \ rst) \ (com \ COMP \ (...)) \ x \ y$$

This constraint may be propagated to satisfy constraints appearing in inner parts of the hardware structure. The following functions support specification and propagation of value constraints:

fun rgInt (xmin,xmax) x =
  (xmin <= x) $\wedge$ (x <= xmax)

fun rgfLInt f ((xmin, xmax) :: t) x =
  rgInt (xmin, xmax) (f x) $\vee$
  rgfLInt f t x
| *rgfLInt f [] x == FALSE*

rgfLInt accepts a list of intervals denoting the range of legal values for the application of function *f* to the value *x* .

For invertible component functions, we now specify a generic rule to propagate value constraints:

———————   (R4.7)

forall x. h (g x) === x
$\vdash$ *com (sR (rgfLInt f bds)) (cF g)*
 ===
  com (cF g)(sR (rgfLInt (fn x $\Rightarrow$ f(h x)) bds))

For example, the function $g := fn\ x \Rightarrow c * x$ only matches the rule with $c \neq 0$. The advantage of having the function parameter in *rgfLInt* is that the transformation of the value intervals according to the functionality of the components may be postponed. When the propagated constraints can directly be related to the internal constraints, the latter ones have to be satisfied by a proper selection of *bds* and *f*.

5 Data abstraction

Abstraction is closely linked to the consideration of value constraints. Therefore, this section also deals with constraints. The complexity of these constraints for compound circuits forces us to perform a stepwise refinement of components. Introducing pseudo-components for data abstraction and refinement allows us to introduce and propagate these constraints at the most convenient datalevel.

  We define the following pseudo-components for data abstraction and refinement.

fun sI2 n x y =
  forall t:time. E(x t) $\rightarrow$ isInt n (x t) $\wedge$ y t === intToList n (x t)

fun s2I n x y =
  forall t:time. (E(x t) $\rightarrow$ length (x t) === S n) $\wedge$ y t === listToInt (x t)

intToList and *listToInt* are library functions for the transformation between integer and two's-complement representation of numbers.

We now discuss a trivial example for the refinement of a composed structure:

$\vdash$ *com F G x y*

Supposed, we have already proved the implementation theorems:

————————   (R5.1)

com (sR rstF) (com (sI2 w) (com F' (s2I w))) x y $\vdash$ F x y

284

and

$$\frac{}{com \ (sR \ rstG) \ (com \ (sI2 \ w) \ (com \ G' \ (s2I \ w))) \ x \ y \vdash G \ x \ y} \tag{R5.2}$$

with the abstraction constraints *rstF* and *rstG* and the implementation level blocks *F'* and *G'*. We want to derive the compound implementation theorem

$$\frac{}{\begin{array}{l}com \ (sR \ rstX) \ (com \ (sI2 \ w) \ (com \ F' \ (com \ G' \ (s2I \ w)))) \ x \ y \\ \vdash com \ F \ G \ x \ y\end{array}} \tag{R5.3}$$

with some constraint *rstX* both satisfying *rstF* and the internal constraint *rstG* . In general, the determination of the global constraint *rstX* cannot be automated. But during the proof process parameter restrictions can be derived and simplified that allow one to trade off between different combinations of parameter instances.

In our simple example we start by joining the two implementation theorems:

$$\frac{}{\begin{array}{l}com \ (sR \ rstF) \ (com \ (sI2 \ w) \ (com \ F' \ (com \ (s2I \ w) \\ (com(sR \ rstG) \ (com \ (sI2 \ w) \ (com \ G' \ (s2I \ w))))))) \ x \ y \\ \vdash com \ F \ G \ x \ y\end{array}} \tag{R5.4}$$

The global constraint *rstX* now has to be chosen in such a way that it satisfies:

$$\frac{}{Cf\#(rstX), \ sR \ rstX \ x \ x \vdash sR \ rstF \ x \ x} \tag{R5.5}$$

and

$$\frac{}{\begin{array}{l}Cg\#(rstX), \\ com \ (sR \ rstX) \ (com \ (sI2 \ w) \ (com \ F' \ (s2I \ w))) \ x \ y \ \vdash sR \ rstG \ y \ y\end{array}} \tag{R5.6}$$

$Cf\#(rstX)$ is some condition on *rstX* making *R5.5* a provable theorem[10]. An appropriate choice for $Cg\#(rstX)$ with respect to *R5.6* is derived by symbolically propagating *rstX* to the output of the substructure. But for this task, the two's complement component *F'* may be replaced in the hypothesis using the implementation theorem *(R5.1)* and *(R5.5)* . The resulting propagation rule reads:

$$\frac{}{com \ (sR \ rstX) \ F \ x \ y \vdash com \ F \ (sR \ rstX') \ x \ y} \tag{R5.7}$$

We now impose the constraint $Cg\#(rstX)$ on *rstX/rstX'* to satisfy *rstG*. The composition of the dual data converters between *F'* and *G'* is eliminated with two theorems:

$$\frac{}{\vdash com \ (s2I \ w) \ (sI2 \ w) \ === \ sR \ (iswlen \ w)} \tag{R5.8}$$

[10]Generally, $B\#(x)$ denotes some context with free occurrences of *x*. In this paper, such an expression could also contain more free variables we want to hide to keep formulæ small. According to the original LAMBDA syntax, *B* could represent a syntactic context function allowing for second-order resolution as well as a defined abbreviation. In the latter case, each free variable of the abbreviated expression would have to appear in the parameter list.

and

$$\frac{}{\vdash com\ (sI2\ w)\ (com\ F'\ (sR\ (iswlen\ w))) === com\ (sI2\ w)\ F'}\qquad (R5.9)$$

R5.9 makes the length preserving property *F'* must satisfy explicit. With these preliminaries, the complete metamorphosis of our trivial circuit is:

$\vdash$ *com F G x y*

$\vdash$ *com (sR rstF) (com (sI2 w) (com F' (com (s2I w)*
         (com (sR rstG) (com (sI2 w) (com G' (s2I w))))))) x y

Cf#(rstX)
$\vdash$ *com (sR rstX) (com (sI2 w) (com F' (com (s2I w)*
         (com (sR rstG) (com (sI2 w) (com G' (s2I w))))))) x y

Cf#(rstX),Cg#(rstX)
$\vdash$ *com (sR rstX) (com (sI2 w) (com F' (s2I w)*
         (com (sI2 w) (com G' (s2I w)))))) x y

Cf#(rstX),Cg#(rstX)
$\vdash$ *com (sR rstX) (com (sI2 w) (com F' (com (sR (iswlen w))*
         (com G' (s2I w)))))) x y

Cf#(rstX),Cg#(rstX)
$\vdash$ *com (sR rstX) (com (sI2 w) (com F' (com G' (s2I w)))) x y*

The scheme has been presented to illustrate transformational refinement of compound structures. More complex structures are treated in a similar way. By means of separate refinement theorems for each component, we are able to propagate constraints at the abstract level, which is in most cases easier than at the two's-complement level. By different propagation rules, constraints could also be handled at the lower level.

6   Applications

All the above concepts contribute to the proof for the FIR-filter design mentioned in the introduction. The proof-tree is constructed top-down, where circuit models and rules are always kept as general as possible to capture design alternatives. The remainder of this paper will demonstrate fragments of our proofs.

Retiming of the input structure With the combining forms introduced in section 3, an integer-level structure of a FIR filter in serial-in-/parallel-out form can be described as:

com   *(cforkL(map (fn d ⇒crep d D) (alpha::mklist n 1)))*
(com   *(cmapL (map CMULTI cs))*
(com   *shdfst*
      (cfold ADDI)))

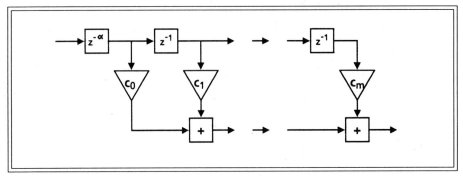

Figure 6: Serial-in/parallel-out transversal filter structure at integer level

alpha is some latency, which may stay unspecified at the beginning, but will later be restricted when specific transformations are performed distributing the latency among combinational components. We only constrain n to be the decremented length of the coefficient list. D represents a register, in Figure 6 marked by 'Z'.

We first prove a generic transformation rule:

$$\overline{} \qquad\qquad\qquad (R6.1)$$

acL $F1s$ $G1s$ $==$ acL $F2s$ $G2s$
$\vdash com\ (cforkL\ F1s)(cmapL\ G1s) === com\ (cforkL\ F2s)(cmapL\ G2s)$

where acL is a function producing a list of all component chains, the input signal runs through on its way to each output of the fork structure. Informally the theorem states that two fork structures are functionally equivalent if the chains for all possible paths between input and outputs are functionally equivalent, i.e., the component chains may be transformed to equivalent chains. Considering the input part of our FIR filter structure, we can now apply this general transformation rule to prove the special theorem[11]:

$$\overline{} \qquad\qquad\qquad (R6.2)$$

$\vdash \quad com\ (cforkL\ (map\ (fn\ d \Rightarrow crep\ d\ D)\ (alpha::mklist\ n\ 1)))$
$\qquad (cmapL\ (mklist\ (n+1)\ id))$

$\quad ===$

$\quad com\ (cforkL\ (mklist\ (n+1)\ id))$
$\qquad (cmapL\ (map\ (fn\ d \Rightarrow crep\ d\ D)\ (iter\ alpha\ (alpha + n))))$

We only have to satisfy the hypothesis with:

$$\overline{} \qquad\qquad\qquad (R6.3)$$

$\vdash \quad acL\ (map\ (fn\ d \Rightarrow crep\ d\ D)\ (alpha::mklist\ n\ 1))(mklist\ (n+1)\ id)$

$\quad ===$

$\quad acL\ (mklist\ (n+1)\ id)(map\ (fn\ d \Rightarrow crep\ d\ D)\ (iter\ alpha\ (alpha + n)))$

which is proved by induction on n.

At first sight, it might appear disappointing that we have to prove a quite complicated hypothesis in order to apply a generic rule. But in fact the induction on chains is much

---

[11]*iter n m* produces a list of natural numbers from n to $(m-1)$, *id* is the neutral element of composition

more pleasant than proofs on fork structures. It happens quite often that very general rules can only be applied, if complex hypotheses are satisfied. We must trade off the proof complexity of an instantiated generalisation hypothesis for the advantage of applying a general rule instead of proving simpler instances of it wherever they occur. In the FIR-filter proof this theorem is used to push all registers of the initial serial-in/parallel-out structure into the coefficient branches, where they are not considered until the combinational function has been refined and the final latch structure is set up.

Flattening of functional units Instead of separate refinement of the coefficient multipliers, the multiplications have been split and reordered into modified bitplanes in order to reduce the wiring complexity of the final layout. We decompose the multiplication by digitising the coefficients with:

$$(R6.4)$$

$$
\vdash \quad CMULTI\ c
$$
$$
===
$$
$$
com\ smklist
$$
$$
(com\ (cmapL\ (map\ CMULTI\ (intToDigits\ n\ c)))
$$
$$
(com\ shdfst
$$
$$
(cfold\ ADDI)))
$$

The function *intToDigits* creates a list with $n+1$ weighted (integer) bits of the coefficient c. This allows us to reason about two's complement multiplication at the integer level. The multiplication of two's complement numbers can be represented as the following term:

$$
x \times c = x \times \left(\sum_{i=0}^{n-1} c_i \times 2^i \right) - x \times c_n \times 2^n
$$

where c_i are the integer versions of the coefficients' bits at two's complement level; thus the factors $c_i \times 2^i$ are the elements of the list generated by the function *intToDigits*. The coefficient c must be restricted according to $-2^n <= c < 2^n$. The multiplier substructure of the FIR filter is transformed with:

$$(R6.4')$$

$$
\vdash \quad cmapL\ (map\ CMULTI\ cs)
$$
$$
===
$$
$$
cmapL\ (map\ (fn\ i \Rightarrow
$$
$$
com\ smklist
$$
$$
(com(cmapL\ (map\ CMULTI\ (intToDigits\ (el\ i\ ns)(el\ i\ cs)))))
$$
$$
(com\ shdfst
$$
$$
(cfold\ ADDI)))))\ (indsL\ cs))
$$

To prepare the structure for the next steps, the sub-hierarchy is transformed with the following generic rule:

$$(R6.5)$$

$$
\vdash \quad cmapL\ (map\ (fn\ i \Rightarrow com\ F\#(i)\ G\#(i))\ il)
$$
$$
===
$$
$$
com\ (cmapL\ (map\ (fn\ i \Rightarrow F\#(i))\ il))
$$
$$
(cmapL\ (map\ (fn\ i \Rightarrow G\#(i))\ il))
$$

288

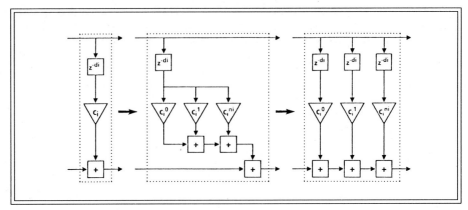

Figure 7: *Decomposition of coefficient multipication*

where $F/G\#(i)$ denote arbitrary (but well-typed) terms, containing i as a free variable.

Concentrating on the adder structure, we use the combinator *sflat* to flatten the list of input signal lists down to a non-hierarchical signal list and write:

$$\begin{array}{ll}
\overline{} & (R6.6)\\
\vdash \quad com\ (cmap\ (com\ shdfst & \\
\qquad\qquad (cfold\ ADDI)) & \\
\quad (com\ shdfst & \\
\qquad (cfold\ ADDI)) & \\
\quad === & \\
\quad com\ sflat & \\
\quad (com\ shdfst & \\
\qquad (cfold\ ADDI)) &
\end{array}$$

The proof is performed by nested induction along the dimensions of the two levels of hierarchy.

In the FIR-filter proof we then perform permutation of the flattened structure. After this, we could use the inverse transformation to generate the bitplane-hierarchy. In the actual proof, we postpone this step to a later stage, because we prefer working on the flat and thus more regular structure.

Refinement of adders This paragraph is supposed to convey to the interested reader some idea of what the actual data refinement proofs looks like.

In the FIR-filter design, carry-save arithmetic has been chosen to implement the addition of the partial products. Splitting of intermediate sums into carry and sum words causes one problem: carry and sum words may diverge. Therefore, at each addition stage, the provided word-length would have to be incremented, even if the results could easily be represented with a smaller number of bits. To overcome this problem, in the FIR-filter example an overflow correction has been installed, distributing overflowing carry-word values between sum and corrected carry word. In the data refinement proof we temporarily separate carry-save adder and overflow correction. We specify an ideal carry-save adder producing an output carry-word, whose word-length is incremented by one with respect to the input carry-word.

Hence, the implementation can directly be related to its integer version. The constraint on the data inputs is trivially satisfied by the environment of the addition unit, where the bus size automatically restricts the intermediate inputs. This constraint is handled implicitly in the conversion blocks. The results of the carry-save units are fed into the overflow correction units, which try to produce an equivalent two's complement representation with reduced carry-word lengths. The overflow correction works under the condition:

$-2^w <= c + s < 2^w$

where c and s are the abstracted input words, $w+1$ the size of the outputs of the overflow correction unit. This condition must be satisfied in every single stage of the complete addition structure. A more detailed description is given in [13].

Before giving a sketch of the procedure for deriving an implementation with global input constraints for the addition structure, we informally introduce some abbreviated notation:

CSA#(i) ((ci,si),d) (co,so):
carry-save-adder for bitstring signals, where the word-lengths vary with the parameter i,
OVC (co,so) (co',so'):
over-flow-correction for bit-string signals, function as described above,
CSAI#(i) ((ci,si),d) (co,so):
integer relation corresponding to an abstraction of *CSA*, where i controls different scaling factors of the individual stages,
id2 (a,b) (x,y):
fun id2 (a,b) (x,y) = forall t:time. x t ++ y t === a t ++ b t
corresponds to the abstraction of the overflow correction *OVC*, and
sR2 (isInt2 w) (x1,x2) (y1,y2):
states that the pairs of signals are identical and the sum of signal values can be represented on busses of width $w+1$. First we prove the implementation theorems for the single components[12]

———————— (R6.7)

com (comb2 (c2comb(sI2 win#(i)),sI2 wd#(i))
(com CSA#(i)
    (comb2(s2I (w#(i)+1),s2I w#(i)))) x y
⊢   *CSAI#(i) x y*

abbreviated:

———————— (R6.7')

CSAimp#(i) x y ⊢ CSAI#(i) x y

and[13]

———————— (R6.8)

com (sR2 (isInt2 w#(i)))
(com (comb2 (sI2 (w#(i)+1), sI2 w#(i)))
(com OVC
    (c2comb (s2I (w#(i)+1))))))) x y
⊢ *id2 x y*

---

[12] $w...(i)$ denote individual word-lengths for different interface signals.

[13] Here we have an example of a one-directional transformation-rule that greatly simplifies the proof effort. In proving the other direction, we would have to consider the context defining the functionality of the interface signals at the abstract level.

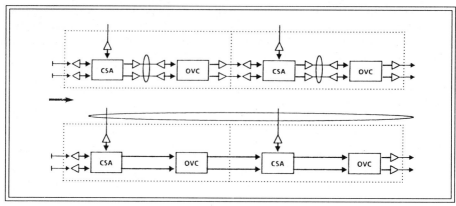

Figure 8: Propagation of secondary constraints

abbreviated:

$$\frac{\text{————————}}{\textit{com (sR2 (isInt2 w\#(i))) OVCimp\#(i) x y} \vdash \textit{id2 x y}} \qquad (R6.8')$$

Our goal is to implement the integer level substructure

$$\vdash \qquad \textit{com (c2fst 0)(cfoldL (map (fn i} \Rightarrow \textit{com CSAI(i) id2) itl)) x y}$$

Analogous to the implementation scheme presented in section 5, we start with combining the implementation theorems *(R6.7,R6.8)* to

$$\frac{\text{————————}}{\begin{array}{l}\textit{com CSAimp\#(i) (com (sR2 (isInt2 w\#(i))) OVCimp\#(i)) x y} \\ \vdash \textit{com CSAI\#(i) id2 x y}\end{array}} \qquad (R6.9)$$

and insert the modules in a cascade structure with the generic rule:

$$\frac{\text{————————}}{\begin{array}{l}\textit{forall x,y. andL (map (fn i} \Rightarrow \textit{COMP1\#(i) x y} \rightarrow \textit{COMP2\#(i) x y) itl)} \\ \vdash \textit{cfoldL (map (fn i} \Rightarrow \textit{COMP1\#(i)) itl) x y} \rightarrow \\ \qquad \textit{cfoldL (map (fn i} \Rightarrow \textit{COMP2\#(i)) itl) x y}\end{array}} \qquad (R6.10)$$

We are now going to replace the internal constraint *(sR2 (isInt2 w#(i)))* in each stage by some global constraint on the inputs of the cascade structure and later eliminate the internal data-converters:

com (sRL rstp)
(com (c2fst 0)
 (cfoldL (map (fn i ⇒*com CSAimp#(i) OVCimp#(i)) itl)) x z*
⊢ *com (c2fst 0)*
 (cfoldL (map (fn i ⇒*com CSAimp#(i)*
  (com (sR2 (isInt2 w#(i))) OVCimp#(i))) itl)) x z

which is transformed to:

sRL rstp x x ∧
c2fst 0 x ((y ,y),x) ∧
cfoldL (map (fn i ⇒com CSAimp#(i) OVCimp#(i)) itl) ((y ,y),x) z
⊢   *cfoldL (map (fn i ⇒com CSAimp#(i)*
                    (com (sR2 (isInt2 w#(i))) OVCimp#(i))) itl)) ((y ,y),x) z

rstp is some restriction function to be specified later, *sRL* is a restriction component for lists. The proof process starts with a right induction on the index list *itl* . The base case is trivial, for both cascade structures are identical without any constraint. The induction step is described in the sequent:

[(sRL rstp x x ∧
c2fst 0 x ((y ,y),x) ∧
cfoldL (map (fn i ⇒com CSAimp#(i) OVCimp#(i)) itl) ((y ,y),x) z1
→
cfoldL (map (fn i ⇒com CSAimp#(i)
                (com (sR2 (isInt2 w#(i))) OVCimp#(i))) itl) ((y ,y),x) z1] ∧
sRL rstp (x@[x1]) (x @[x1]) ∧
c2fst 0 (x@[x1]) ((y ,y),x@[x1]) ∧
cfoldL (map (fn i ⇒com CSAimp#(i) OVCimp#(i)) (itl@[i1])) ((y,y),x@[x1]) z
⊢   *cfoldL (map (fn i ⇒com CSAimp#(i)*
                    (com (sR2 (isInt2 w#(i))) OVCimp#(i))) (itl@[i1])) ((y,y),x@[x1]) z

The induction hypothesis is satisfied with the rules (and some more):

——————   *(R6.11)*
cfoldL (map (fn i ⇒COMP#(i)) (itl@[i1])) (a,b@[c]) d
⊢   *exists e. cfoldL (map (fn i ⇒COMP#(i)) itl) (a,b) e* ∧ *COMP#(i1) (e,c) d*

and

——————   *(R6.12)*
sRL rstp (a@[b]) (a@[b]) ⊢ *sRL rstp a a*

After some rewriting and instantiation of flexible variables the induction premise becomes:

sRL rstp (x@[x1]) (x @[x1]) ∧
c2fst 0 (x@[x1]) ((y ,y),x@[x1])
cfoldL (map (fn i ⇒com CSAimp#(i)
                (com (sR2 (isInt2 w#(i))) OVCimp#(i))) itl) ((y,y),x) z2,
CSAimp#(i1) (z2,x1) z3 ⊢ *sR2 (isInt2 w#(i1)) z3 z3*

    The different implementation theorems are now applied to derive a pure integer representation of the characterising premise for the restriction function *rstp*:

sRL rstp (x@[x1]) (x@[x1]) ∧
c2fst 0 (x@[x1]) ((y,y),x@[x1]) ∧
cfoldL (map (fn i ⇒com CSAI#(i) id2) itl) ((y,y),x) z2 ∧
CSAI#(i1) (z2,x1) z3
⊢   *sR2 (isInt2 w#(i1)) z3 z3*

    The instantiation of *rstp* to a function that discharges the premise takes into account the function of the integer adder cascade as well as word-lengths of the different busses for each stage.

Propagation of input constraints The principle of constraint propagation is demonstrated with a simplified version of a FIR-filter structure. A symbolic input constraint will be propagated towards the secondary constraint's location.

The structure has one data input. We impose an unspecified symbolic restriction on this integer type signal. This primary constraint is now going to be propagated by the application of separate transformation rules.

$$\frac{\text{—————}}{com \ (sR \ (rgfLInt \ fid \ bds)) \ smklist \ x \ y \vdash smklist \ x \ y} \hspace{3em} (R4.6')$$

The introduction rule for the value constraint is a specialisation of *R4.6*. Propagation into the individual coefficient branches of the FIR filter is performed with

$$\frac{\text{—————}}{\vdash com \ COMP \ smklist === com \ smklist \ (cmap \ COMP)} \hspace{3em} (R6.13)$$

Due to the retimability of the restriction component

$$\frac{\text{—————}}{\vdash com \ (sR \ rst) \ D === com \ D \ (sR \ rst)} \hspace{3em} (R6.14)$$

the retiming rule for the register field holds:

$$\frac{\text{—————}}{\begin{array}{l} \vdash \quad com \ (cmap \ (sR \ rst)) \ (crepL \ D \ dflp) \\ \quad === \\ \quad com \ (crepL \ D \ dflp) \ (cmap \ (sR \ rst)) \end{array}} \hspace{3em} (R6.14')$$

We already showed propagation of *rgfLInt* for a special type of components. All components in the coefficient branches belong to this type[14] except the parameterisable (bit-)multiplier that does not satisfy the invertability condition. Here we specify the propagation rule:

$$\frac{\text{—————}}{\begin{array}{l} \vdash \quad com \ (sR(rgfLInt \ f \ bds)) \ (CMULTI(Int \ (bitvalue \ c,0))) \\ \quad === \\ \quad com \ (sR(rgfLInt \ f \ bds)) \\ \quad (com \ (CMULTI(Int \ (bitvalue \ c,0))) \\ \quad\quad (sR(if \ c \ then \ (rgfLInt \ f \ bds) \ else \ (fn \ a \Rightarrow a==0)))) \end{array}}$$

Having performed all propagation operations, primary and secondary constraints are now connected in the model of the complete circuit at this design stage:

$$\begin{array}{l} \vdash \quad com \ (...) \\ \quad (com \ (cmapL \ (map \ (fn \ i \Rightarrow sR \ (...)) \ itl)) \\ \quad (com \ (sRL \ rstp) \\ \quad\quad (...))) \ x \ y \end{array}$$

Elimination of the secondary constraint Figure 9 illustrates the propagation of the primary constraints[15]. The lower ellipse in the right picture represents the secondary constraint, which is going to be eliminated with appropriate instantiations and restrictions of free parameters.

---

[14]They do not appear in Figure 9

[15]Mixed level representation: the triangles represent data conversion. dashed ellipse: additional primary constraint in 4.

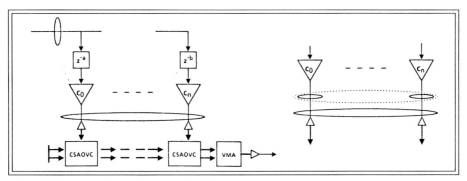

Figure 9: Propagation of input constraint

Essentially we want to transform the following sequent to a list of restrictions on the parameters *cbls, bds* without any reference to signals[16].

cmapL (map (fn i ⇒if (el i cbls) then
$\qquad$ *(sR (rgfLInt (fn a ⇒a quot (2 ˆ (el i sfs))) bds)) else*
$\qquad$ *(sR (fn a ⇒a == 0))) itl)) x y*
⊢ $\qquad$ *sRL rstp x y*

We first select *bds* to be *[(Int(0,2 ˆ win),Int(2 ˆ win - 1,0))]*, hence there shall be no other value restriction on the input data signal than the one imposed by the bus size, reduced with

—————— $\hfill$ (R6.15)

⊢ *rgfLInt f [(Int(0,2 ˆ win),Int(2 ˆ win - 1,0))] x === isInt win (f x)*

After several more steps we get[17]:

andL (map (fn i ⇒if (el i cbls)
$\qquad$ *then isInt win (el i z) quot (2 ˆ (el i sfs))*
$\qquad$ *else (el i z == 0) itl)*
⊢ $\qquad$ *andL (map (fn i ⇒isInt (el i ws) (sumIntL (before (S i) z))) itl)*

We now prove and apply the first approximation by excluding *(el i cbls == FALSE)* in the hypothesis:

—————— $\hfill$ (R6.16)

andL (map (fn i ⇒if (el i cbls)
$\qquad$ *then*
$\qquad\qquad$ *isInt win (el i z) quot (2 ˆ (el i sfs)))*
$\qquad$ *else*
$\qquad\qquad$ *(el i z ==0) itl)*
⊢ *andL (map (fn i ⇒isInt win (el i z) quot (2ˆ (el i sfs))) itl)*

---

[16]The expressions have been simplified with respect to the integer coefficients' sign processing. *quot* denotes integer division, *2 ˆ* produces powers of 2, and *isInt* is a restriction function referring to powers of 2. *sfs* is a list of scaling factors for the individual adders.

[17]The assertion has been derived from the instantiated restriction function *rstp*. *sumIntL* produces the sum of a list of integers.

leading to

andL (map (fn i ⇒isInt win (el i z) quot (2 ˆ (el i sfs))) itl)
⊢   *andL (map (fn i ⇒isInt (el i ws) (sumIntL (before (S i) z))) itl)*

A second approximation is proved to get rid of the variable z that still represents a signal value:

$$\overline{} \qquad\qquad\qquad\qquad\qquad\qquad\qquad (R6.17)$$

andL (map (fn i ⇒isInt win (el i z) quot (2 ˆ (el i sfs))) itl)∧
andL (map (fn i ⇒isInt (el i ws)(sumIntL (before (S i)
               (map (fn j ⇒Int (0,2ˆ (el j sfs + win))) itl))))
    itl)
⊢ *andL (map (fn i ⇒isInt (el i ws) (sumIntL (before (S i) z))) itl)*

With *R6.17* we get a sequent that defines a pure restriction on parameters:

⊢   *andL (map (fn i ⇒isInt (el i ws)*
               (sumIntL (before (S i) (map (fn j ⇒Int (0,2 ˆ (el j sfs + win))) itl)))) itl)

The definition of *sfs:= permute (flat (map (fn n ⇒iter 0 (S n)) (rev ns))) il* now leads to the final parameter restriction that relates *ws* : internal adder word lengths, *ns* : coefficient word-lengths, *win*: input data word length, and *il* : permutation parameter (e.g., to reorder calculations to modified bitplanes). This restriction is contained in the hypothesis list of the final parameterisable design. To create a special circuit, the parameters have to be selected satisfying all hypotheses. The restrictions on the parameters can be chosen according to external requirements. For instance, if the circuit is to implement a low pass filter, the filter's coefficients interpolate a *si*-function ($sinx/x$). This function is symmetric and its global maximum is 1.0 whereas the next local maxima of its absolute values are $|si(3/2\pi)|$ and $|si(-3/2\pi)| < 2/9$. Hence the peripheral coefficients can be represented as two's complement numbers with reduced word-lengths. Such information can be exploited to weaken restrictions on other design parameters.

Whereas the interactive proof to create the generic implementation model has been complicated, the satisfaction of the parameter restrictions can be automated, for all restrictions only contain functional expressions that can be evaluated by rewriting with the function definitions. Hence the implementation model may serve as a basis for a generator to create verified instances for a class of circuits. User-defined parameters may be specified within a restricted solution space. ML-heuristics can be programmed to explore the design space. For large design spaces, the checks of parameter instances could be performed with pure ML-versions of the parameter constraints. Finally the found optimal solution could then be checked by rewriting in the prover.

7   Conclusion

We have presented a method for transforming a circuit at a higher level of abstraction to a lower-level implementation without dividing the model of the complete circuit. Equations as well as implications were specified in a most general way to provide a basis of universally applicable transformation rules. For this purpose, basic regularities were exploited. Polymorphic higher-order functions were defined to embed individual components or compound structures. Parameterisation turned out to be valuable for a flexible handling of proofs and specifications.

The bridging between two abstraction levels is done by gradual transformation of compound hardware structures. Parameterisable auxiliary blocks for data conversion and signal constraints in connection with propagation rules allow for separate refinement of integer components and for dealing with constraints at the most convenient abstraction level. Our definitions support propagation, commutation, and elimination of constraints in compound hardware structures. Using this methodology in hardware design, the parameters for the primary constraints can be traded off with the parameters of the secondary constraints according to specific optimisation requirements.

In the context of temporal abstraction, J. Herbert formulated a principle [9] which can be summarized as

input conditions →
  (low-level behaviour →
  (high-level behaviour ∧ *output conditions))*

We explicitly define parameterisable pseudo-components to state the similar theorem

————————

strong input constraint ∧ *low level behaviour* ∧ *data conversion*
⊢ *high-level behaviour (*∧ *weak abstraction constraint)*

The FIR-filter example is still a semi-regular design. Our components inserted into polymorphic generic definitions have to be of the same basic type with respect to the signal ports. The transformational approach would also apply for irregular structures, if we specified hardware with less rigid predicates. With existentially-quantified internal signal variables, combinator-based specifications could be combined with free-style specifications of random logic to take as much advantage as possible of inherent regularities.

The transformation principle we successfully applied to design our overall proof can be characterised as an interplay of the four questions: what is the next state of a design to be achieved? what transformation rule is needed for this purpose? how can the validity of the transformation be justified with existing or derivable knowledge? and what is the most-general formulation of the transformation rule, i.e., what irrelevant information can be neglected in a specific design step? In most cases, the single transformation steps are still smaller than those performed by hardware designers for reasons of provability. But with powerful special-purpose heuristics embedded in the prover environment, this statement may at least partially be discharged in future.

Acknowledgements   The author would like to thank the members of the system synthesis group in the design automation department at SIEMENS Munich for their helpful comments on drafts of this paper, especially M.J. Kaelbling, H. Nusser and T. Rössel. The LAMBDA system and the advice I received from the people of Abstract Hardware Limited have also been invaluable for my work.

References

[1] B.C. Brock and W.A. Hunt Jr. The formalization of a simple hardware description language. In L. Claesen, editor, *Proc. of IMEC-IFIP Int. Workshop on Applied Formal Methods for Correct VLSI Design*, 1989.

[2] S.-K. Chin. Verified synthesis functions for negabinary arithmetic hardware. In L. Claesen, editor, *Proc. of IMEC-IFIP Int. Workshop on Applied Formal Methods for Correct VLSI Design*. North Holland, 1990.

[3] A. Cohn. A proof of correctness of the Viper microprocessor: The first level. In G. Birtwistle and P.A. Subrahmanyam, editors, *VLSI Specification, Verification and Synthesis*, pages 27–72. Kluwer Acad. Publ., 1989.

[4] S. Finn, M. Fourman, M. Francis, and R.Harris. Formally based system design - interactive synthesis based on computer-assisted formal reasoning. In L. Claesen, editor, *Proc. of IMEC-IFIP Int. Workshop on Applied Formal Methods for Correct VLSI Design*, 1989.

[5] M.P. Fourman, R.C. Holte, W.J. Palmer, and R.M. Zimmer. Top-down design as bottom-up proof. In *Proc. of Electronic Design Automation Conf., Wembley*, 1987.

[6] M.P. Fourman and E. Mayger. Formally based system design - interactive hardware scheduling. In G. Musgrave and U. Lauther, editors, *Proc. of Int. Conf. on VLSI*, 1989.

[7] B.T. Graham. SECD: The design and verification of a functional microprocessor. Master's thesis, Dep. of Comp. Science, Calgary, Alberta, 1990.

[8] F.K. Hanna, N. Daeche, and M. Longley. VERITAS+: A specification language based on type theory. In M. Leeser and G. Brown, editors, *Hardware Specification, Verification and Synthesis: Mathematical Aspects*. Springer, LNCS408, 1989.

[9] J. Herbert. Temporal abstraction of digital designs. In G.J. Milne, editor, *The Fusion of Hardware Design and Verification*. North Holland, 1989.

[10] W.A. Hunt Jr. *FM8501: A Verified Microprocessor*. PhD thesis, The University of Texas at Austin, 1985.

[11] J.J. Joyce. Generic structures in the formal specification and verification of digital circuits. In G.J. Milne, editor, *The Fusion of Hardware Design and Verification*. North Holland, 1988.

[12] W. Luk and G. Jones. Specifying and developing regular heterogeneous designs. In L. Claesen, editor, *Proc. of IMEC-IFIP Int. Workshop on Applied Formal Methods for Correct VLSI Design*, 1989.

[13] T. Noll. Semi-systolic maximum rate transversal filters with programmable coefficients. In W. Moore, A. McCabe, and R. Urquhart, editors, *Proc. of the 1st Int. Workshop on Systolic Arrays, Oxford*. Adam Hilger, 1986.

[14] M. Sheeran. *uFP, a Language for VLSI Design*. PhD thesis, Progamming Research Group, Oxford University, 1983.

[15] M. Sheeran. Retiming and slowdown in Ruby. In G.J. Milne, editor, *The Fusion of Hardware Design and Verification*. North Holland, 1988.

[16] D. Verkest, L. Claesen, and H. De Man. On the use of the Boyer-Moore theorem prover for correctness proofs of parameterized hardware modules. In L. Claesen, editor, *Proc. of IMEC-IFIP Int. Workshop on Applied Formal Methods for Correct VLSI Design*, 1989.

Ruby algebra *

Lars Rossen[†]

Abstract

An axiomatic definition of the specification language Ruby, suitable for implementing in a theorem prover, is presented. The implementation of this definition in the Isabelle theorem prover is sketched, and examples of its use are shown.

Introduction

The Ruby language is a language of relations where the relations represent circuits. The language is proposed in [12] and is suitable for specification and synthesis of Digital Signal Processing circuits. In [11] Ruby was used for reasoning about systolic circuits, and in [14] butterfly networks and FFT circuits were developed. It is our goal to build a general framework for reasoning with Ruby relation. In this framework the system designer should capture the circuit specification as a relation, and through stepwise refinement construct a circuit suitable for automatic layout generation. Each step in this process should be provably correct, thereby making the circuit correct by construction.

One essential thing in this framework will be a theorem prover. The theorem prover should be used for proving correctness of equivalences used in the synthesis process. Using a theorem prover in this way will eliminate the possibility of using wrong transformations in the synthesis process.

We will investigate how to formalise the Ruby design language in a way that is suitable for implementing in a theorem prover. This work is based on results from a similar approach described in [9, 10]. After introducing the Ruby language we define a minimal subset of Ruby suitable for axiomatisation. We then show how to define the rest of the Ruby language within this axiomatisation. Finally we describe how to implement this in a theorem prover, and we show how to use the system for proving some equivalence relations. The theorem prover we have selected is Isabelle [5].

---

*This work was supported by the Danish Research Academy.

[†]Technical University of Denmark, 2800 Lyngby, Denmark; *lr1@iddth.dk*

Notation

We will be using the notation commonly used in standard mathematical texts. $\exists, \forall, \in, \wedge, \vee$ etc. have their usual meanings. A typed expressions we will be written as $F\colon \alpha$ denoting that F has type α. For integers, natural numbers and booleans we use the type symbols $\mathbf{Z}, \mathbf{N}$ and $\mathbf{B}$.

Usually we will write relations as infix e.g. $a\,R\,b$ denotes a is related to b through the relation R. When defining relations in the Isabelle theorem prover we will use lambda abstractions, meaning that a relation between object of type α and β (a $\alpha \sim \beta$ relation) can be defined as a function (predicate) of type $\alpha \to \beta \to \mathbf{B}$. This means that relations can be defined through lambda abstractions. For example the identity relation can be defined as $\lambda\,a\,b\cdot\ a = b$.

The notation of proofs is inspired by [4], and should be straightforward to read.

Ruby

In this section we will give a short introduction to the original definition of Ruby. It should be noted that this is only a brief and incomplete description of the Ruby language. For a more detailed description, and examples of the use of the language see [12]. If the reader is already familiar with Ruby, skip to the next section.

Signals

A Ruby description of a circuit is a relation between the signals at the left (domain) and the right (range) of the circuit. In the Ruby style of reasoning about circuits the signals we relate are streams of data values, or rather functions from time to data. Furthermore Ruby relations are always binary relations, i.e. relations between two signals.

As we usually reason about circuits that have more than two wires, and as we want to model the circuit as a relation between the wires on the left side and the wires on the right side, the concept of streams of tuples is introduced. if a b and c are signals then $\langle a, b, c \rangle$, $\langle \langle a, b \rangle, c \rangle$ and $\langle c, \langle a, b \rangle \rangle$ are examples of different signals. More formally a signal constructed by grouping other signals in tuples should still be considered a single stream of data, where the data have a corresponding structure.

Spreads

There exists a number of different ways to construct Ruby relations. A simple way is to take a relation between data values and then to "spread" it out over the time e.g. if f is a relation, then

$$F \;=\; \mathsf{spread}\ f$$

means that F is a stream relation, that for any point in the streams relates the data as f would do:
$$a\,F\,b \;=\; \forall t\cdot\; a(t)\,f\,b(t)$$

If **add** is the addition relation ($\{a,b\}\text{add}\,c \;=_{\text{def}}\; c = a + b$) then we can define an adder circuit ADD:

Definition ADD: ADD $=_{\text{def}}$ spread add
Theorem ADD: $\langle a,b\rangle\,\text{ADD}\,c \;=\; \forall t\cdot\; c(t) = a(t) + b(t)$

Wiring relations

A set of relations that are often used when constructing circuits are wiring relations. These relations correspond to some kind of rearranging, duplicating, or deletion of signals. If we use $\wedge$ as an operator for appending two signals, we get the following definitions:

Append–right	$\langle a,b\rangle$ apl $c =_{\text{def}} c = a^\wedge\langle b\rangle$
Append–left	$\langle a,b\rangle$ apr $c =_{\text{def}} c = \langle a\rangle^\wedge b$
Join	$\langle a,a\rangle$ join $c=_{\text{def}} c = \langle a,a\rangle$
First	$\langle a,b\rangle\,\pi_1\,c =_{\text{def}} c = a$
Second	$\langle a,b\rangle\,\pi_2\,c =_{\text{def}} c = b$

Append–left and –right do a regrouping of a signal structure, **Join** wires together 4 signals, and **first, second** throws away one of the components in a signal pair.

Delay

Through **spread** and wiring relations it is possible to define combinational circuits. When we want to make sequential circuits, it is necessary to introduce circuits elements with some kind of state. In Ruby the delay element ($\mathcal{D}$) is defined. This element relates two streams of equal structure, and defines the domain stream to be a one time unit delayed version of the range signal.

Definition Delay: $a\,\mathcal{D}\,b =_{\text{def}} \forall t\cdot\; a(t-1) = b(t)$

Combining forms

The next step in the process of defining a language for describing circuits, is to introduce a way of combining primitive circuits into more complex circuits. In Ruby these primitives are called *combining forms* and many are defined. Some examples are:

Definition

Composition	$a\,R;S\,b$	$=_{\text{def}}$	$\exists c\cdot\; a\,R\,c\;\wedge\;c\,S\,b$
Inverse	$a\,R^{-1}b$	$=_{\text{def}}$	$b\,R\,a$
Conjugation[1]	$R\,/\,S$	$=_{\text{def}}$	$S;R;S^{-1}$
Parallel	$\langle a_1 a_2\rangle[R,S]\langle b_1 b_2\rangle$	$=_{\text{def}}$	$a_1\,R\,b_1\;\wedge\;a_2\,S\,b_2$
Map	$\langle\rangle$ map $F\langle\rangle$		
	$\langle a_h\rangle^{\wedge}a_t$ map F $\langle b_h\rangle^{\wedge}b_t$	$=_{\text{def}}$	$a_h\,F\,b_h\;\wedge\;a_t$ map $F\,b_t$

Composition is traditional relational (serial) composition. Inverse corresponds to mirroring a circuit; this operation is always well defined as we operate with relations. Conjugation is a operation that can be used to pack a relation in between another relation and its inverse. Parallel composition corresponds to stacking two circuits above each other. Map is a generic combining form that lays out a row of relations in parallel, the number of relations is determined through the lenght of the applied signal tuples.

Equivalences

When designing circuits with Ruby it is common to use equational rewriting. You start with a circuit description that is either inefficient or it is impossible to implement it, and then it is transformed into a better circuit through rewriting with Ruby equations.

A large number of Ruby equations has been proven in [12, 11, 13], here are some examples.

Conjugate-Inverse	$\vdash\;(R\,/\,S)^{-1}\;=\;(R^{-1})\,/\,S$
Conjugate-Par	$\vdash\;[R,S]\,/\,[T,V]\;=\;[R\,/\,T,\,S\,/\,V]$
Map-Inverse	$\vdash\;(\text{map}\,F)^{-1}\;=\;\text{map}\,(F^{-1})$

The above equations and many others are obvious when looking at the graphical representation of the expressions, but it is essential in a formal framework to be able to prove the same equations. Below is a proof of the **Conjugate-Inverse** equation:

Proof

From

1	$a(R\,/\,S)^{-1}b\;=\;a(R\,/\,S)^{-1}b$	= Refl.
2	$a(R\,/\,S)^{-1}b\;=\;b(R\,/\,S)a$	Inv-Def.
3	$a(R\,/\,S)^{-1}b\;=\;b(S;R;S^{-1})a$	Conj-Def.
4	$a(R\,/\,S)^{-1}b\;=\;\exists cd\cdot\; b\,S\,c\wedge c\,R\,d\wedge d\,S^{-1}a$	Comp-Def.
5	$a(R\,/\,S)^{-1}b\;=\;\exists cd\cdot\; c\,S^{-1}b\wedge d\,R^{-1}c\wedge a\,S\,d$	Inv-Def.
6	$a(R\,/\,S)^{-1}b\;=\;\exists cd\cdot\; a\,S\,d\wedge d\,R^{-1}c\wedge c\,S^{-1}b$	$\wedge$-Comm.
7	$a(R\,/\,S)^{-1}b\;=\;a(S;R^{-1};S^{-1})b$	Comp-Def.
Infer	$a(R\,/\,S)^{-1}b\;=\;a((R^{-1})\,/\,S)b$	Conj-Def.

Formalisation of Ruby

We will now redefine the Ruby language in a formal way suitable for implementation in a theorem prover.

Strong typing

In the definition of Ruby in the previous section and in [12, 11] there is no type system. This is perfectly all right for reasoning with pen and paper, but when one has to reason in a formal framework like a theorem prover then it is necessary to introduce strong typing. In [13] a strongly typed Ruby was introduced. It was based on a categorical definition of Ruby and that work describes a system similar to the work we present here. We will not focus on the categorical aspect of a type system, but instead we will show how we can use strong types when implementing the ruby algebra.

We first introduce the type of signals. The signals that Ruby expressions relate are functions from time to data. Time is modelled as integers. This means that the signal type can be expressed as:

$$\text{sig}(\alpha) \ = \ \mathbf{Z} \to \alpha$$

The α in the above expression is a general type variable, thus we do not place any restriction on the type of data in a signal. When reasoning about Ruby expressions we are however interested in making a distinction between three kinds of data types; *primitive data, pairs of data* and *lists of data*. This gives us the following data type domain:

$$
\begin{aligned}
datatype \ = \ & primitive\ datatype \\
| \ & (datatype \times datatype) \\
| \ & \text{list}_n(datatype)
\end{aligned}
$$

The *primitive datatype* can typically be integers, naturals, booleans but in general it can be anything.

Notice that we have chosen not to let *tuples* be the basic data type when reasoning with Ruby relations. We shall see that pairs (a primitive form of tuples) and lists (with a length indicator) are a natural set of data constructors when defining Ruby formally.

As mentioned above Ruby expressions relate signals, and signals are functions from time to data. Normally it is convenient to be able to reason about the structure of the data in the signals. To do so without unpacking the data from the signals we introduce a set of higher order functions on signals, that correspond to the operations on the underlying data. Furthermore we introduce abbreviations for the type of signals over lists.

$$
\begin{aligned}
\text{sig}(datatype) \ &= \ \mathbf{Z} \to datatype \\
\text{List}_n(datatype) \ &= \ \text{sig}(\text{list}_n(datatype))
\end{aligned}
$$

The syntax for the type expressions, element construction, and destruction of the data and signal forms can be summarised in the following table:

Description	Type	Element constructor	Destructor
List with length n	$\mathsf{list}_n(\alpha)$	nil $\mathsf{cons}_n(a, b)$	$\mathsf{hd}_n()\ \mathsf{tl}_n()$
Signal–list	$\mathsf{List}_n(\alpha)$	Nil $\mathsf{Cons}_n(a, b)$	$\mathsf{Hd}_n()\ \mathsf{Tl}_n()$
Pair (binary tuples)	$(\alpha \times \beta)$	(a, b)	$\mathsf{fst}()\ \mathsf{snd}()$
Signal–pair	$\mathsf{sig}((\alpha \times \beta))$	$[a, b]$	$\mathsf{Fst}()\ \mathsf{Snd}()$

The following abbreviations are also used:

Lists: $\qquad\qquad \{a_n, \cdots, a_0\}_{n+1} = \mathsf{cons}_n(a_n, \cdots \mathsf{cons}_0(a_0, \mathsf{nil}))$

Signal concatenation: $a :_n b = \mathsf{Cons}_n(a, b)$

Empty signal lists: $\quad \langle\rangle = \mathsf{Nil}$

Signal–lists: $\qquad\quad \langle a_n, \cdots, a_0 \rangle_{n+1} = a_n :_n \cdots a_0 :_0 \langle\rangle$

It is possible to define the above types as a definitional extension to (standard) higher order logic. We will not do that in these notes.

Pure Ruby

A Ruby relation is in general a relation between signals ($\mathsf{sig}(\alpha) \sim \mathsf{sig}(\beta)$). However there are a lot of mathematically well defined relations over signals that we don't accept as Ruby relations. Therefore we want to make a precise statement of what a Ruby relation is.

In [12, 11] a lot of Ruby relations are defined. It is easy to see that some of these relations can be or are defined in terms of other Ruby relations. For example beside ($\leftrightarrow$) is defined in terms of below ($\updownarrow$). To make an axiomatisation of Ruby easy, we will select a small set of primitive Ruby constructs, define them in the logic, and then define the rest of the Ruby language in terms of these primitives. Later we will see how a small set of primitives helps us prove general things about Ruby expressions.

In this axiomatisation of Ruby we will use a syntactic domain for Ruby relations which permits four basic constructs. The language defined by this syntax will be called Pure Ruby. The domain is defined by:

$$
\begin{aligned}
ruby = \quad &\mathsf{spread}(f) \\
\mid \quad &\mathcal{D} \\
\mid \quad &ruby; ruby \\
\mid \quad &[ruby, ruby]
\end{aligned}
$$

These primitives correspond to *combinational circuits, delay element, serial composition* and *parallel composition* (notice that we have redefined **spread** to be a (higher order) function from relation to stream relation). A large selection of primitives and combining forms from [12, 11] can be defined in terms of Pure Ruby. Examples of primitives that can't be defined in terms of Pure Ruby are **pair** and **slow**. These primitives are used when reasoning about circuits with more than one time base. We have deliberately chosen not to include these in Pure Ruby as they don't conform to some nice algebraic properties. It is important to note that though these primitives are not part of Pure Ruby, it is perfectly all right to include them in a specification, and in our proof system, as we will see in a later example.

It remains to be proved that Pure Ruby is a minimal set of Ruby constructs i.e. that it is not possible to define one of the constructs in terms of the others. We will not be concerned about that here.

Ruby type

The above informal Ruby domain equation doesn't include information about the type of the Ruby constructs, but from an axiomatic definition of the Ruby constructs it is possible to infer the type information.

The definitions of the constructors of Pure Ruby are:

Axiom

Spread:	$a\colon \mathsf{sig}(\alpha)$ $\mathsf{spread}(f\colon \alpha \sim \beta)$ $b\colon \mathsf{sig}(\beta) =_{\text{def}}$	$\forall t \cdot\ a(t) f\, b(t)$
Delay:	$a\colon \mathsf{sig}(\alpha)$ $\mathcal{D}\, b\colon \mathsf{sig}(\alpha)$ $=_{\text{def}}$	$\forall t \cdot\ a(t-1) = b(t)$
Ser.:	$a\colon \mathsf{sig}(\alpha)$ $F\mathbf{;}G\, b\colon \mathsf{sig}(\beta)$ $=_{\text{def}}$	$\exists c\colon \mathsf{sig}(\gamma) \cdot\ aFc\ \wedge\ c\,G\,b$
Par:	$a\colon \mathsf{sig}((\alpha_1 \times \alpha_2))[F,G]\, b\colon \mathsf{sig}((\beta_1 \times \beta_2))$ $=_{\text{def}}$	$\mathsf{Fst}(a)\,F\,\mathsf{Fst}(b)\ \wedge\ \mathsf{Snd}(a)\,G\,\mathsf{Snd}(b)$

The above definitions only classify the four constructs as being signal relations. If we want to close the set of Ruby relations under these 4 construct then it is necessary to introduce a Ruby type. This type is a restriction on the type domain of signal relations. If we use the syntactic notation $\alpha \overset{Pure}{\sim} \beta$ to denote Ruby relations, then we have the following domain law:

$$R\colon \alpha \overset{Pure}{\sim} \beta \ \Rightarrow\ R\colon \mathsf{sig}(\alpha) \sim \mathsf{sig}(\beta)$$

This law simply states that the domain of Pure (Ruby) relations is a subset of the domain of signal relations in general, see figure 1.

To give the $\overset{Pure}{\sim}$ symbol a constructive definition we state the following type axioms about Pure Ruby.

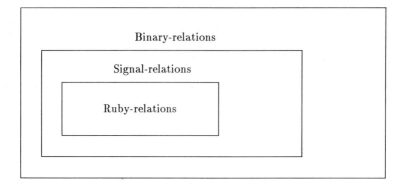

Figure 1: A illustration of how the ruby relations are a subset of the signal relations and signal relation are a subset of binary relations

Axiom

Spread-type	$f: \alpha \sim \beta$	$\vdash$ spread$(f): \alpha \overset{Pure}{\sim} \beta$
Delay-type		$\vdash \; \mathcal{D}: \alpha \overset{Pure}{\sim} \alpha$
Composition-type	$F: \alpha \overset{Pure}{\sim} \beta, \; G: \beta \overset{Pure}{\sim} \gamma$	$\vdash \; F;G: \alpha \overset{Pure}{\sim} \gamma$
Par-type	$F: \alpha_1 \overset{Pure}{\sim} \beta_1, \; G: \alpha_2 \overset{Pure}{\sim} \beta_2$	$\vdash \; [F,G]: (\alpha_1 \times \alpha_2) \overset{Pure}{\sim} (\beta_1 \times \beta_2)$

From this Ruby type definition we can see that **Spread** and **Delay** $(\mathcal{D})$ are the primitive relations when constructing Ruby expressions and the other two construct Ruby expressions from other Ruby expressions.

This observation leads to the definition of a Ruby induction theorem and a recursion theorem.

Ruby Induction

$$\forall f: \alpha \sim \beta \cdot \text{P}(\text{spread}(f)) \land$$
$$\text{P}(\mathcal{D}) \land$$
$$\forall F: \alpha \overset{Pure}{\sim} \beta \; G: \beta \overset{Pure}{\sim} \gamma \cdot \text{P}(F) \land \text{P}(G) \Rightarrow \text{P}(F;G) \land$$
$$\forall F: \alpha_1 \overset{Pure}{\sim} \beta_1 \; G: \alpha_2 \overset{Pure}{\sim} \beta_2 \cdot \text{P}(F) \land \text{P}(G) \Rightarrow \text{P}([F,G])$$

$$\overline{\forall R: \alpha \overset{Pure}{\sim} \beta \cdot \text{P}(R)}$$

Recursive functions are defined through the Ruby_Prim_Rec constant. Its meaning is captured in the following theorem.

Ruby Recursion

$\forall\, S\,D\,C\,P \cdot$
$\forall f \cdot$ Ruby_Prim_Rec $S\,D\,C\,P$ spread$(f)\; =\; S\,f\;\wedge$
Ruby_Prim_Rec $S\,D\,C\,P\,\mathcal{D}\; =\; D\;\wedge$
$\forall F\,G\cdot$ Ruby_Prim_Rec $S\,D\,C\,P\,(F;G)\; =$
$\quad C(\text{Ruby\_Prim\_Rec }S\,D\,C\,P\,F)(\text{Ruby\_Prim\_Rec }S\,D\,C\,P\,G)\,F\,G\;\wedge$
$\forall F\,G\cdot$ Ruby_Prim_Rec $S\,D\,C\,P\,([F,G])\; =$
$\quad P(\text{Ruby\_Prim\_Rec }S\,D\,C\,P\,F)(\text{Ruby\_Prim\_Rec}S\,D\,C\,P\,G)\,F\,G$

If we want a function F to be defined recursively on Ruby relations, we make the following definition:

$$\mathcal{F} \;=_{\text{def}}\; \text{Ruby\_Prim\_Rec }S\,D\,C\,P$$

Where S,D,C,P are functions that defines what the $\mathcal{F}$ evaluates to in the four Ruby cases. By instantiating the **Ruby Recursion** theorem we can derive a useful theorem about F:

$\forall f \cdot \mathcal{F}$ spread$(f)\; =\; S\,f\;\wedge$
$\mathcal{F}\,\mathcal{D}\; =\; D\;\wedge$
$\forall G\,H\cdot \mathcal{F}\,(G;H)\; =\; C(\mathcal{F}\,G)(\mathcal{F}\,H)\,G\,H\;\wedge$
$\forall G\,H\cdot \mathcal{F}\,([G,H])\; =\; P(\mathcal{F}\,G)(\mathcal{F}\,H)\,G\,H$

Ruby–extension

The next step in the process of making a Ruby system is to define the rest of the standard Ruby combining forms. It is not within the scope of these notes to define all the forms from [12, 11]; instead we will concentrate on some illustrative examples.

The first is the definition of relational inverse. If we use the normal definition we could not use the Ruby type axioms on expressions involving inverse without extending Pure Ruby with that form. Instead we define inverse through Pure Ruby. First we define three spreads $\mathcal{R}$, $\mathcal{L}$ and ID:

Definitions.
L-def. $\quad \mathcal{L} =_{\text{def}}$ spread$(\lambda ab\cdot\; \exists c\cdot b = (a,(c,c)))$
R-def. $\quad \mathcal{R} =_{\text{def}}$ spread$(\lambda ab\cdot\; \exists c\cdot a = (c,(c,b)))$
ID-def. $\quad$ID$=_{\text{def}}$ spread$(\lambda ab\cdot\; a = b)$

If we look at figure 2 its seem reasonable to define Inverse as:

Definition: Inverse $\quad F^{-1} =_{\text{def}} \mathcal{L};[\text{ID},[F,\text{ID}]];\mathcal{R}$

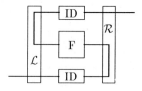

Figure 2: Inverse definition

To complete this definition one has to prove that the normal meaning of inverse is true from the definition. The proof is trivial so we have not included it.

The combining form **map** is usually defined recursively on the length of its arguments, as we saw in the introduction to Ruby.

In our new definition of map we still will still define it recursively on the length of the signal lists, but we make the body of the definition a proper Ruby definition. To do so we need some relations and combining forms to help us:

Definition

Conjugate	$R \, / \, S =_{\text{def}}$	$S; R; S^{-1}$
NIL	$\text{NIL} =_{\text{def}}$	$\text{spread}(\lambda ab \cdot \ (a = b = \text{nil}))$
App Left	$\text{apl}_n =_{\text{def}}$	$\text{spread}(\lambda ab \cdot \ (a = \text{cons}_n(\text{fst}(b), \text{snd}(b))))$

There is nothing new to the **Conjugate** definition. **NIL** is a relation between empty list streams. **App Left**, the definition that relates an element and a list to the list with the element appended to the left, is now defined through **spread**.

We can now make a definition of **map** in terms of the above definitions.

Definition Map:
$$\text{map}_0(F) \quad =_{\text{def}} \text{NIL}$$
$$\text{map}_{n+1}(F) \quad =_{\text{def}} [F, \text{map}_n(F)] \, / \, \text{apl}_n$$

The step case definition can be seen in figure 3.

Of course it is much easier to use the first definition, but we must remember that we have not lost anything by defining map in terms of Pure Ruby. All we have to do is to derive two theorems, one that states that **map F** has a pure Ruby type whenever F has, and one stating that map has the properties of the original definition. With these two theorems one can reason about expressions with map as if it had its original definition.

The two theorems called **Map-type** and **Map** are:

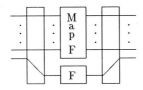

Figure 3: map definition

Theorem
Map-type: $F: \alpha \overset{Pure}{\sim} \beta \vdash \mathsf{map}_n(F): \mathsf{list}_n(\alpha) \overset{Pure}{\sim} \mathsf{list}_n(\beta)$

Map: $\quad$ Nil $\mathsf{map}_0(F)$ Nil

$\qquad a:_n b\ \mathsf{map}_{n+1}(F)\ c:_n d\ =\ aFc\ \wedge\ b\,\mathsf{map}_n(F)d$

A proof for Map-type and the base case of Map is elementary. Before we show a simple proof for the inductive case we state the theorem that captures the usual interpretation of apl.

Theorem: Apl $\vdash\ a:_n b\ \mathsf{apl}_n\ [a, b]$

The proof of **map** is:

Proof
From $n \in \mathbf{N}$

1	$a:_n b\ \mathsf{map}_{n+1}(F)\ c:_n d\ =\ a:_n b\ \mathsf{map}_{n+1}(F)\ c:_n d$	=-Refl.
2	$a:_n b\ \mathsf{map}_{n+1}(F)\ c:_n d\ =\ a:_n b\ [F, \mathsf{map}_n(F)]\ /\ \mathsf{apl}_n\ c:_n d$	map-def.
3	$a:_n b\ \mathsf{map}_{n+1}(F)\ c:_n d\ =\ a:_n b\ \mathsf{apl}_n; [F, \mathsf{map}_n(F)]; \mathsf{apl}_n^{-1}\ c:_n d$	conj-def.
4	$a:_n b\ \mathsf{map}_{n+1}(F)\ c:_n d\ =$	Inv.,;-def
	$\exists e_1 e_2 \cdot\ (a:_n b \mathsf{apl}_n e_1)\ \wedge\ (e_1 [F, \mathsf{map}_n(F)] e_2)\ \wedge\ (c:_n d \mathsf{apl}_n e_2)$	
5	$a:_n b\ \mathsf{map}_{n+1}(F)\ c:_n d\ =\ [a, b][F, \mathsf{map}_n(F)][c, d]$	apl_n–def
Infer	$a:_n b\ \mathsf{map}_{n+1}(F)\ c:_n d\ =\ aFc\ \wedge\ b\,\mathsf{map}_n(F)\ d$	Par-def.

Implementation

The goal of the formal definition of Ruby is to implement the Ruby algebra in a computer system to support formal reasoning. The system we have chosen is the Isabelle theorem prover. The Isabelle theorem prover is a very flexible, and it supports a wide variety of logics. The theorem prover is described in [5, 7, 8]. Isabelle defines a simple Meta-Logic, object logics are then defined in this (meta-) logic. The prover supports backwards proofs, higher order resolution, and easily extensible parser and printer functions. For more information see the references.

One of the object logics distributed with Isabelle is a Higher Order Logic (HOL) and the Ruby system is defined as an extension to this logic. This logic is a many sorted logic similar to the logic in the HOL88 system [1, 2]. A main difference is that in HOL88 the typing of expressions is decideable and the typing is done automatically by the term parser. In Isabelle/HOL the type information is part of the algebra and one has to reason about the types of terms. This concept is related to the idea of "Propositions as type" and gives Isabelle/HOL a more advanced type system. It also makes the proof obligation bigger, as one has to prove theorems about types. Refer to [6] for a discussion of Isabelle types.

The implementation of Ruby is straightforward. First the list with a length indicator is implemented. This can be done as with ordinary lists with an extension of length information. Next a theory of signals is introduced. This is just a collection of higher order functions, and some simple theorems about them. All this can be done as a definitional extension to the logic. Finally the four constructs of Pure Ruby are defined, and the theory of the Ruby type is implemented.

On top of this it is possible to define the rest of the Ruby language, and to prove theorems to assist a designer. Below is an example of some useful theorems.

Examples

We will now illustrate how to use the proposed proof system. Our first example shows how to use the Pure Ruby induction for proving general property about Ruby expressions. After that we show that it can be useful to step out of the pure Ruby world, but still using part of the pure Ruby system.

Retiming

The *retiming* theorem is a good example of a theorem that is essential in the synthesis process of systolic circuits [11]. The retiming theorem states that the relational behaviour of a circuit is preserved when surrounding it with delay elements (fig. 4). There are some kinds of circuits that don't have this property, but one of the nice features of Pure Ruby is that it always have the retiming property:

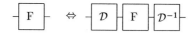

Figure 4: **Retime** definition

Definition Retime: $\vdash$ Retime F =$_{\text{def}}$ $(P(F) \Rightarrow P(\mathcal{D};F;\mathcal{D}^{-1}))$

Theorem Retime: $\vdash \forall F : \alpha \overset{Pure}{\sim} \beta \cdot$ Retime F

To prove this theorem we prove the corresponding theorem for each of the four forms of Pure Ruby and then we use the Ruby–Induction rule. The four theorems are:

Theorem
Retime Spread $\vdash \forall f \cdot$ (Retime (spread(f)))
Retime Delay $\vdash$ (Retime $\mathcal{D}$)
Retime Comp $\vdash$ ((Retime F $\wedge$ Retime G) $\Rightarrow$ Retime $(F;G)$)
Retime Par $\vdash$ ((Retime F $\wedge$ Retime G) $\Rightarrow$ Retime $[F,G]$)

By defining all Ruby constructs in terms of Pure Ruby it is possible to prove general rules in an easy way. To use the above retiming rule the only thing to do before rewriting a sub–expression with a retimed form is to prove that the expression has a type instance of $\alpha \overset{Pure}{\sim} \beta$.

We have proven this in the Isabelle system, but we will not present the proof here, instead we will turn our attention to another interesting property of Pure Ruby expressions.

Slow

One of the transformations the system designer of DSP processors often performs to improve speed is to have duplicate circuits work in parallel. A relation that describe the process of transforming a stream of data into 2 parallel streams (with half the speed) is **pair**.

Definition: pair–def a pair b $=_{\text{def}}$ $\forall t \cdot b(t) = (a(2t), a(2t+1))$

This relation is not part of the Pure Ruby language, and it would not be reasonable to include it as a primitive, as it does not have some of the nice properties that are a characteristic of the Pure Ruby language. For instance it does not have the retiming property.

Not being a part of the Pure Ruby language should not stop us from using it. A way to use a slow circuit as part of a fast circuit is to make two copies and pack them together with **pair**. A combining form that will do this is **slow**:

Definition: slow–def slow R $=_{\text{def}}$ $[R, R]$ / pair

An interesting question to ask is; will 2 copies of a slow circuit behave in the same way as a fast version of the same circuit e.g. is slow R = R. This is not true in general, but if it is a combinational circuit then the behaviour is preserved:

Theorem: slow–Spread $\forall f \cdot$ slow(spread(f)) = spread(f)

A proof for this is:

Proof

From $a \, \mathsf{spread}(f) \, b = a \, \mathsf{spread}(f) \, b$

1	$a \, \mathsf{spread}(f) \, b = \forall t \cdot a(t) f \, b(t)$	Spread–def.
2	$a \, \mathsf{spread}(f) \, b = \forall t \cdot a(2t) f \, b(2t) \ \wedge \ \forall t \cdot a(2t+1) f \, b(2t+1)$	Int.–rew.
3	$a \, \mathsf{spread}(f) \, b = \forall t \cdot \mathsf{fst}\,(a(2t), a(2t+1)) f \, \mathsf{fst}\,(b(2t), b(2t+1))$	fst,snd–intr.
	$\qquad \wedge \ \forall t \cdot \mathsf{snd}\,(a(2t), a(2t+1)) f \, \mathsf{snd}\,(b(2t), b(2t+1))$	
4	$a \, \mathsf{spread}(f) \, b = \exists cd \cdot \ \forall t \cdot \mathsf{fst}\, c(t) f \, \mathsf{fst}\, d(t) \ \wedge \ \forall t \cdot \mathsf{snd}\, c(t) f \, \mathsf{snd}\, d(t)$	$\exists$–intr.
	$\qquad \wedge \ c = \lambda t \cdot (a(2t), a(2t+1)) \ \wedge \ d = \lambda t \cdot (b(2t), b(2t+1))$	
5	$a \, \mathsf{spread}(f) \, b = \exists cd \cdot \ \forall t \cdot \mathsf{fst}\, c(t) f \, \mathsf{fst}\, d(t) \ \wedge \ \forall t \cdot \mathsf{snd}\, c(t) f \, \mathsf{snd}\, d(t)$	$\forall$–intr.
	$\qquad \wedge \ \forall t \cdot c(t) = (a(2t), a(2t+1)) \ \wedge \ \forall t \cdot d(t) = (b(2t), b(2t+1))$	
6	$a \, \mathsf{spread}(f) \, b = \exists cd \cdot \ \mathsf{Fst}(c)\mathsf{spread}(f)\mathsf{Fst}(d) \ \wedge \ \mathsf{Snd}(c)\mathsf{spread}(f)\mathsf{Snd}(d)$	Spread–def.
	$\qquad \wedge \ \forall t \cdot c(t) = (a(2t), a(2t+1)) \ \wedge \ \forall t \cdot d(t) = (b(2t), b(2t+1))$	
7	$a \, \mathsf{spread}(f) \, b = \exists cd \cdot \ a \, \mathsf{pair} \ c \ \wedge \ c \, [\mathsf{spread}(f), \mathsf{spread}(f)] \, d \ b \, \mathsf{pair} \ d$	pair,Par–def.
8	$a \, \mathsf{spread}(f) \, b = a \, \mathsf{pair}; [\mathsf{spread}(f), \mathsf{spread}(f)]; \mathsf{pair}^{-1} \, b$	Comp,inv–def.
9	$a \, \mathsf{spread}(f) \, b = a \, [\mathsf{spread}(f), \mathsf{spread}(f)] \, / \, \mathsf{pair} \, b$	Conj–def
Infer	$a \, \mathsf{spread}(f) \, b = a \, \mathsf{slow}(\mathsf{spread}(f)) \, b$	slow–def

It turns out that the circuit $\mathsf{slow}R$ is equivalent to a circuit R' where R' is similar to R except all delays ($\mathcal{D}$) has been replaced by 2 delays ($\mathcal{D};\mathcal{D}$).

If we want to express this formally we have to define a function that will transform any circuit R into its corresponding R'. This function can be defined through Ruby_Prim_Rec:

Definition: Delay-subst

$$\text{D\_Sub} =_{\text{def}} \text{Ruby\_Prim\_Rec}(\lambda f \cdot \mathsf{spread}(f))(\mathcal{D};\mathcal{D})(\lambda RSrs \cdot R;S)(\lambda RSrs \cdot [R, S])$$

By using the definition of the Ruby_Prim_Rec constant we can derive the following theorem:

Theorem: Delay-subst

$$\forall f \cdot \text{D\_Sub} \, \mathsf{spread}(f) \ = \ \mathsf{spread}(f) \ \wedge$$
$$\text{D\_Sub} \, \mathcal{D} \ = \ \mathcal{D};\mathcal{D} \ \wedge$$
$$\forall F \ G \cdot \text{D\_Sub}(f;G) \ = \ \text{D\_Sub} \, F; \text{D\_Sub} \, G \ \wedge$$
$$\forall F \ G \cdot \text{D\_Sub}([f, G]) \ = \ [\text{D\_Sub} \, F, \text{D\_Sub} \, G]$$

We are now ready to formulate a law about slow:

Theorem: Slow_Delay $\quad \forall R{:}\alpha \overset{Pure}{\sim} \beta \cdot \ \mathsf{slow}R \ = \ \text{D\_Sub}R$

To prove this we (again) use structural induction on R. This gives us 4 subgoals to prove (rewritten with D_Sub and assumptions):

Theorem

Slow_Delay Spread $\vdash \forall f \cdot \text{slow}(\text{spread}(f)) = \text{spread}(f)$

Slow_Delay Delay $\vdash \text{slow}\mathcal{D} = \mathcal{D};\mathcal{D}$

Slow_Delay Comp $\vdash \forall RS \cdot \text{slow}R;S = \text{slow}F;\text{slow}G$

Slow_Delay Par. $\vdash \forall RS \cdot \text{slow}[R, S] = [\text{slow}F, \text{slow}G]$

We have already shown the proof of the first case, and the proofs of the 3 other cases are similar.

Conclusion

The design language Ruby has been presented and a formulation suitable for implementing it in a theorem prover was given.

This formulation was based on a small number of primitives. Structural induction and recursive definitions were defined over these primitives, and it was shown how this could be used for proving general properties about Ruby expressions.

It was also shown how to reason about circuit components that could not be described in terms of the primitives of Pure Ruby. The **pair** primitive was an example of a primitive that could not be described in terms of Pure Ruby, and in fact it does not have some of the nice properties that are a characteristic of the Pure Ruby language. Our framework allowed us to reason about it anyway.

A lot of work lies in front of us now. The implementation in the Isabelle prover can be much improved. If the system should have any practical use an extended set of preproven theorems has to be supplyed, and the proof strategies (tactics) has to be improved. The parsing and printing function could also be improved.

Furthermore this theorem prover should only be seen as a part of a general framework for working with Ruby relations. Two other research projects are currently going on at the Technical University of Denmark. One is the implementation of a transformation system from Ruby expressions to their corresponding graphical interpretation; this is a continuation of the work described in [3]. The other research project is flow analysis of Ruby expressions.

There are other problems in designing a Ruby framework for example designing an interface to a layout systems. We hope to be able to address the other problems in the future.

312

Acknowledgements

Many thanks to Robin Sharp for helpful discussions about my axiomatisation of Ruby and for proof reading an early draft of this paper. Part of the paper was done during my visit to Glasgow University and I am graceful for the help I received there. I wish to thank Mary Sheeran, Geraint Jones and Graham Hutton for some interesting discussions about the type system, and Tom Melham for giving hints about how to implement it in a HOL system.

References

[1] Mike Gordon. Hol a machine oriented formulation of higher order logic. Technical Report 68, University of Cambridge, 1986.

[2] Mike Gordon. Hol a proof generating system for higher-order logic. *VLSI Specificacion, Verification and Synthesis*, 1987.

[3] Bent Warming Hansen and Jesper Jørgensen. Graphical and relational algebra for the synthesis of vlsi. Master's thesis, Technical University of Denmark, August 1989.

[4] Cliff B. Jones. *Systematic Software Development Using VDM*. Prentice/Hall International, 1986.

[5] Lawrence C. Paulson. Natural deduction as higher-order resulution. *The Journal of Logic Programming*, 3, 1986.

[6] Lawrence C. Paulson. A formulation of the simple theory of types. Technical report, Computer Laboratory, University of Cambridge, 1989.

[7] Lawrence C. Paulson. The foundation of a generic theorem prover. *Journal of Automated Reasoning*, 5, 1989.

[8] Lawrence C. Paulson and Tobias Nipkow. *Isabelle Tutorial and User's Manual*, 1990.

[9] Lars Rossen. Hol formalisation of ruby. Technical Report ID-TR:1989-61, Dept. of Computer science Technical University of Denmark, 1989.

[10] Lars Rossen. Relationsbaseret specifikation af vlsi. Master's thesis, Technical University of Denmark, Januar 1989. In Danish.

[11] Mary Sheeran. Retiming and slowdown in ruby. In G. Milner, editor, *The Fusion of Hardware Design and Verification*. North Holland, 1986.

[12] Mary Sheeran. Describing and reasoning about circuits using relations. In *Proceedings, Leeds workshop on theoretical aspects of VLSI design*. Cambridge University Press, 1988.

[13] Mary Sheeran. Categories for the working hardware language designer. *Proceedings, MSI workshop on Hardware Specification, Verification and Synthesis: Matematical Aspects*, 1989.

[14] Mary Sheeran and Geraint Jones. Circuit design in ruby. In J. Staunstrup, editor, *Formal Metods for VLSI Design*. Elsevier, 1990.

Using the Declarative Language LUSTRE for Circuit Verification

Ghislaine THUAU*, Daniel PILAUD•

Abstract

LUSTRE is a synchronous declarative language designed for programming real-time systems. LUSTRE manipulates flows that are sequences of values with an associated clock. This paper explains how the language LUSTRE can be used to describe synchronous digital circuits at different levels of abstraction. Then, it presents the associated verification tool LESAR. This tool automatically proves the correctness of a circuit, i.e. that a circuit implementation and the circuit specification are equivalent with respect to some observation criteria.

Introduction

Due to economic constraints, it becomes very important to provide circuit designers with tools that will help them to produce correct circuits in very short times. Prototyping as a means of debugging circuits has become too expensive, so it is necessary to detect and to rectify all the errors made by the designers before circuits are fabricated. This motivates current efforts on verification techniques, and more particularly on formal verification. The idea here is to *prove formally* that a circuit described at some abstraction level is correct with respect to its specification given at a higher level.

The first problem is to choose a description language. Two main approaches appear : on the one hand the use of programming languages, and on the other hand the use of mathematical formalisms. In the first approach, the programming languages that take into account notion of time [BFM 84, She 84, BGLMOR 85] are used as description languages (Hardware Description Languages) and simulation languages. These languages are easy for designers to learn, but they allow only a partial verification or simulation because formal manipulation of these languages is quite difficult. The second approach based on mathematical formalisms offers unified frameworks for the description and the verification of circuits. Many different formalisms have been proposed and these can be classified according to their underlying calculi [CP 88], for instance first-order logic [Bar 84], higher-order logic [Gor 85], temporal logic [MC 85, BC 86, Mos 85, Boc 82], lambda calculus [Hun 86, BPP 88] and specific calculi [ACH 86, Lar 87]. The verification methods based on such formalisms require that circuit designers become experts in abstract formalisms because in many cases, proofs cannot be performed automatically. Moreover formal circuit

---

* Laboratoire de Génie Informatique (IMAG) INPG - 38031 Grenoble Cedex-FRANCE - gthuau @imag.fr
• VERILOG/CERA 38031 GRENOBLE Cedex-FRANCE

314

descriptions cannot be executed directly so these methods do not offer any alternative in the case where a circuit is too complex to be handled by the proof system.

The verification method proposed here is based on the programming language LUSTRE [CHPP 87]. LUSTRE is a synchronous declarative language that has been developed for the programming of real-time systems. Inputs and outputs of a LUSTRE program are *flows,* which are sequences of values together with a clock that specifies when these values appear. A LUSTRE program is made up of mathematical equations that express identities between flows. LUSTRE offers operators that manipulate clocks. These operators give a powerful means for describing circuits [HLP 86] at different abstraction levels ; LUSTRE can therefore be used to write behavioural specifications as well as to describe circuits at the gate level. This possibility has been raised by other authors [BAR 84, BOC 82, PAI 86]. It has been shown [HPOG 89] that LUSTRE can also be used to specify *safety properties* of the systems, which allows a unified framework for describing the circuits and for writing their specifications.

The second problem is to prove the correctness of a circuit. Formal verification methods will play a part in CAD frameworks only if they are automatic. Most of the verification methods referenced above require some highly skilled user to help the proof system to perform the proof by providing it with well chosen lemmas. This comes from their underlying logics that have great expressive power but do not have decision procedures. This means that the proofs are in most cases quite long, which is not compatible with very short design times. A possible solution to the automation problem is to resort to logics with less expressive power but which support efficient decision procedures, for instance Propositional Logic [CBM 89] or Computation Tree Logic [BC 86].

The compilation of a LUSTRE program that describes a circuit produces a finite automaton. Several techniques have been proposed to check automatically properties of finite automata. The most widely used is *Model Checking* [MC 85][RRSV 87] for the verification of Computation Tree Logic (CTL) formulas. Here, we intend to verify safety properties [MP 81], which can be done without building the state-transition graph. The verification tool LESAR has been developed to check automatically whether some automaton produced by the LUSTRE compiler satisfies some Boolean properties. LESAR traverses this automaton without building it. During the traversal, as soon as it detects that some state does not verify the expected property, LESAR stops the traversal and performs a diagnosis.

The paper is divided in four parts. Part 1 presents the language LUSTRE and shows how circuits can be described in LUSTRE. Part 2 explains how a LUSTRE program is compiled. Part 3 then describes the verification tool LESAR and shows how it can be used to prove a circuit correct with respect to its behavioural specification. Part 4 explains how the circuit's environment can be described with LUSTRE *assertions* and how these assertions are used by the verification tool.

1 The Language LUSTRE

LUSTRE is a synchronous data flow language. A LUSTRE program is made of equations that specify identities between *flows*. A flow is a sequence of values together with a *clock* specifying the sequence of instants when these values appear.

The main features of the language LUSTRE are the following :
- Each variable denotes an infinite sequence of values, that will hereafter be called a *sequence.*

- LUSTRE is a declarative language. All operators and programs are functions that map sequences onto sequences. A LUSTRE program can be seen as a network of nodes, each being a data-flow operator.
- LUSTRE is a synchronous language. Each variable has an associated clock, and takes the nth value of its sequence at the nth tick or cycle of its clock. All the clocks are subclocks of a main clock.

The following sections present the different characteristics of the language, and some circuit descriptions are given to illustrate them. A more detailed presentation of the language can be found in [CHPP 87, PH 87, Pla 88].

1.1 Variables, Equations and Data Operators

As indicated above, any variable denotes a sequence of values. Variables are defined by means of equations : if X is a variable and E is an expression, the equation "X = E" defines X to be the sequence of values $(x_0 = e_0, x_1 = e_1, ..., x_n = e_n, ...)$ where $(e_0, e_1, ..., e_n, ...)$ is the sequence denoted by the expression E.

Expressions are build up from variables, constants (considered as constant sequences) and operators. The usual operators, e.g. the arithmetic, the Boolean and the conditional operators are extended to operate over sequences. They will hereafter be referred to as *data operators*.

Consider for instance a one to two line decoder (active low). An implementation of this combinatorial circuit is given in Figure 1.

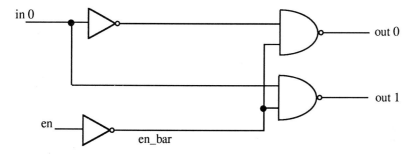

Figure 1 : Two line decoder

This decoder can be described in LUSTRE as follows :

```
let
    en_bar = not en ;
    out 0 = not ( not in 0 and en_bar) ;
    out 1 = not ( in 0 and en_bar) ;
tel.
```

316

1.2 The "pre" and "→" Operators

In addition to the data operators, LUSTRE offers four *sequence operators* that explicitly manipulate sequences. This section presents the "pre" and "→" operators, that can be used to combine sequences having the same clock. The two other operators called "when" and "current" are used to define expressions with different clocks. They will be presented in Section 1.4.

The **pre** ("previous") operator shifts a sequence, one cycle into the future. If $X = (x_0, x_1, ..., x_n, ...)$ then the expression "pre(X)" defines the sequence $(nil, x_0, x_1, ..., x_{n-1}, ...)$. The nil constant is used to represent the undefined value. The "pre" operator can be used to describe delay elements in a circuit. It is necessary for taking into account the delay times of the circuit blocks.

The → ("followed by") operator enables the variables to be initialized. If $X = (x_0, x_1, ..., x_n, ...)$ and $Y = (y_0, y_1, ..., y_n, ...)$ are two variables (or expressions) of the same type, then the expression "$X \to Y$" denotes the sequence $(x_0, y_1, y_2, ..., y_n, ...)$. The expression "$X \to Y$" is equal to Y except at the first instant.

The LUSTRE description of the BCD code checker, whose diagram is given in Figure 2, illustrates the use of these operators. The "pre" operator is necessary to describe the delay elements symbolized by "Δt" in the figure. The "→" operator is necessary to assign initial values to the variables, since the "nil" value is forbidden in the output values.

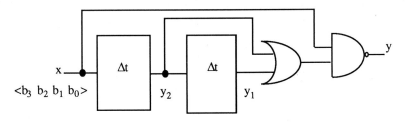

Figure 2 : BCD code checker

The description is the following :
```
    let
        y2 = false → pre (x) ;
        y1 = false → pre (y2) ;
        y = not ((y1 or y2) and x) ;
    tel.
```

1.3 Nodes

Equations can be grouped to form entities called *nodes*. A node is a LUSTRE subprogram. It receives input variables and, by means of a system of equations, it computes output variables, and possibly local variables.

For instance, the LUSTRE node BCD_SPEC describes the BCD code checker at the behavioural level. The equation which defines the output of the node BCD expresses that the sequence $<b_3\ b_2\ b_1\ b_0>$ is a correct BCD code if and only if $b_3 = 0$, or b_2 and b_1 are both equal to 0.

```
node BCD_SPEC (x : bool) returns (y : bool) ;
let
    y = not (Pre (Pre (x))) or Pre(x)) and x) ;
tel.
```

where the node Pre is defined as follows :

```
node Pre (x : bool) returns (Pre : bool) ;
let
    Pre = false → pre(x) ;
tel.
```

1.4 The "when" and "current" Operators

The "when" and "current" operators are used to manipulate clocks. The "when" operator is used to create new clocks and the "current" operator is used to synchronize expressions that have different clocks. The **when** operator allows us to take samples from a sequence. The expression "E when C", where E is an expression and C is a Boolean expression that has the same clock as E, denotes the sequence of values taken by E, when C is true.

E = (	e_0	e_1	e_2	e_3	e_4	e_5	e_6	e_7	...
C = (	true	false	true	true	false	false	true	false	...
X=E when C = (	$x_0 = e_0$		$x_1=e_2$	$x_2=e_3$			$x_3=e_6$		...

```
    0       1   2    3    4    5    6    7
----------------------------------------------------- time of E and C
    0           1    2              3
----------------------------------------------------- time of X
```

Table 1 : The "when" Operator

Remarks
The sequence denoted by "E when C" has not the same clock as E and C, as shown in Table 1. The "when" operator gives a natural means to describe circuits that have several clocks. Subclocks can be obtained from a main clock by providing a sampling expression for each of them.

The last operator of the language is the **current** operator. The "current" operator is a projection operator. If E is an expression whose clock C is different from the basic clock, then "current (E)" is an expression whose clock is the clock of C, and whose values are, at each cycle, the value of E at the last cycle when C was true. Table 2 shows the effect of the "when" and "current" operators.

E = (	e_0	e_1	e_2	e_3	e_4	e_5	e_6	e_7	...
C = (	true	false	true	true	false	false	true	false	...
X = E **when** C = (	e_0		e_2	e_3			e_6		...
Y = **current**(X) = (	e_0	e_0	e_2	e_3	e_3	e_3	e_6	e_6	...

Table 2 : The "when" and "current" Operators

The "current" operator gives a means to combine variables that have different clocks. If E and E' are expressions whose clocks are C and C' respectively, and if C and C' have the same clock C", then the expression "current (E) op current (E')" defines a sequence whose clock is C".

1.5 A Circuit Description

This section gives the complete LUSTRE description of an implementation of the BCD code checker shown in Figure 3.

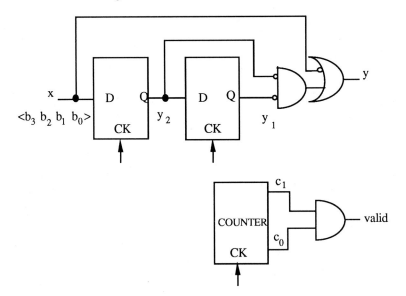

Figure 3 : Implementation of the BCD code checker

The LUSTRE node that describes this circuit can be directly obtained by combining the nodes that describe its subparts. This node BCD_REAL is the following :

```
node BCD_REAL (x, edge : bool) returns (y, valid : bool) ;
var y2, y1 : bool ;
let
    y2 = FLIP_FLOP (x, edge) ;
    y1 = FLIP_FLOP (y2, edge) ;
    y = ((not y2) and (not y1) or (not x) ;
    (c0, c1) = current (COUNT (true when edge)) ;
    valid = c0 and c1 ;
tel.
```

We consider here that the combinatorial gates compute their outputs instantaneously. The storage elements are rising edge D flip-flops. The D flip-flop samples the input value on the rising edge of the clock "d when edge", and stores it till the next rising edge : "current(d when edge)". We consider that the flip-flop has a unit delay. The LUSTRE nodes describing both the rising edge of the clock and the D flip-flop are given below. Table 3 illustrates their behaviours.

```
node FLIP_FLOP (d, edge : bool) returns (q : bool) ;
let
    q = false → pre (current(d when edge)) ;
tel.
```

```
node EDGE (ck : bool) returns (edge : bool) ;
let
    edge = true → ck and pre (not ck) ;
tel.
```

d = (true	true	false	false	false	false	true	true	true	true	false	...
ck = (true	true	false	false	true	true	false	false	true	true	false	...
edge = (true	false	false	false	true	false	false	false	true	false	false	...
d when edge = (true				false				true			...
current(d when edge) =											
(true	true	true	true	false	false	false	false	true	true	true	...
q = (false	true	true	true	true	false	false	false	false	true	true	...

Table 3 : Rising edge D flip-flop

Initializing the variable edge to "true" is necessary to avoid the "nil" value in the sequence it denotes. This initial value defines the initial value of the expression "d when edge", which in turn defines the one of the expression "current(d when edge)". Table 3 illustrates the necessity to initialize the output variable to "true" or "false" and the clock ck to "true" to avoid the "nil" value in the output and clock sequences.

The BCD code checker returns a correct BCD code every four-bit sequence, so a two-bit counter is necessary. The node COUNT is the following :

```
node COUNT ( ) returns (c0, c1 : bool) ;
let
    c0 = false → not pre (c0) ;
    c1 = false → if (not c0 and pre(c0)) then not pre (c1) else pre (c1) ;
tel.
```

2 The LUSTRE Compiler

The language LUSTRE is a programming language so LUSTRE programs can be compiled. Among the compilation modes offered by the LUSTRE compiler, we consider here the compilation which results in finite automata. The result of such a compilation for a given program has two parts : a finite automaton that corresponds to the control part of the program, and a table that contains the code of the program's actions [PH 87, Pla 88].

Digital circuits have characteristics that generally real-time systems have not : at first all the variables that occur in a LUSTRE description of a circuit have finite domain e.g. Boolean variables or n-bit integers ; secondly circuits do not perform any actions in the external world. This means that the compilation of a LUSTRE circuit description would only generate the control automaton.

The compilation of a LUSTRE program is made up of two steps. The first step consists in expanding all the nodes that compose the source program in order to obtain a single system of equations. This system of equations is itself a LUSTRE program. During this expansion, the compiler introduces auxiliary variables prefixed by the character " _ ".

For the D flip-flop whose LUSTRE description is given in Section 1.4, the LUSTRE program generated through this step is the following :

```
node FLIP_FLOP (d : bool ; ck : bool) returns (q : bool) ;
var
    _V4:bool ;
    edge : bool ;
    _V6 : bool ;
let
    q = (false → (pre _V4)) ;
    _V4 = (current _V6) ;
    edge = (true → (ck and (not (pre ck)))) ;
    _V6 = (d when edge) ;
tel.
```

The second step of the compilation consists in generating a finite automaton. The compiler first determines the state variables of this automaton. These state variables are chosen between the Boolean expressions which contain a "pre" or a "current" operator, and the initial state is distinguished in order to evaluate the "→" operators. For the D flip-flop, the compiler introduces three state variables : init, pre(ck) and pre(_V4). Once the state variables are chosen, the generation of the state-transition graph of the automaton is straightforward. A state of this graph is completely defined by the values taken by the state variables. Starting from the initial state of the system defined by the initial values of the state variables, the graph generator performs an exhaustive simulation of the program. The state-transition graph obtained for the D flip-flop is given in Figure 4. The values of the state variables for the five different states of this graph are given below :

	init	pre(ck)	pre(_V4)
state 0	true	nil	nil
state 1	false	true	true
state 2	false	true	false
state 3	false	false	true
state 4	false	false	false

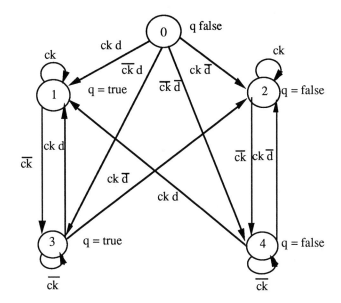

Figure 4 : State-transition graph (rising edge D flip-flop)

3   Circuit verification

This section explains how the verification tool LESAR is used for verifying circuits. Section 3.1 presents the verification tool LESAR, in which the generation of the automaton is replaced by the traversal procedure. Section 3.2 describes how LESAR is effectively used to verify circuits and how this technique is applied to the verification on the BCD code checker.

3.1   The Verification Tool LESAR

LESAR is a tool that has been developed to check whether the finite automaton produced by the LUSTRE compiler satisfies some properties. Several techniques have been proposed to automatically check properties of finite automata. The most widely used is Model Checking, [MC 85] [RRSV 87], for the verification of properties expressed in Computation Tree Logic (CTL). This method consists in building the state-transition graph of the automaton and then, for each property, in traversing this graph to decide if the property holds in some specified states. The problem is that this graph can be very large, so it can be very expensive to build. In this paper, we consider only safety properties, that can be verified without building the state-transition graph of the automaton : it is sufficient to traverse the graph from the initial state, as LESAR does, and for each reachable state, to verify that this state has the required property. If it does not, the traversal will stop immediately.

LESAR is a post-processor of the LUSTRE compiler. It uses this compiler to obtain a single system of equations from the LUSTRE source program to be verified. Then LESAR replaces the building of the state-transition graph of the automaton by a simple enumeration of the states of this graph. Starting from the initial state of the system, LESAR performs an exhaustive simulation of the program but only memorizes the states, and as soon as one of these states does not satisfy the required property, the traversal is stopped.

3.2   Verification Method

This section describes how we use LESAR to verify circuits. We show how the correctness of a circuit realization with respects to its specification can be established automatically by LESAR. The circuit specification and a circuit implementation are described by two LUSTRE nodes called SPEC and REAL respectively. The nodes SPEC and REAL describe the circuit at different levels, in particular their clocks can be different. This means that these LUSTRE nodes are often compared according to some observation criteria. The idea is to build, from the nodes SPEC and REAL and the observation criteria, a third node called VERIF on which a property will be verified. The node VERIF, shown in Figure 5, takes as inputs the inputs of SPEC and REAL, and has only one output named "ok". According to the observation criteria the node VERIF builds the sequences of inputs for which the behaviours of SPEC and REAL must be equivalent ; it then collects the output sequences generated by these nodes and uses them to compute the variable "ok". This node VERIF is given directly to LESAR.

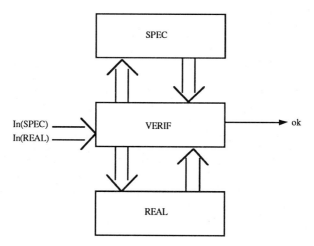

Figure 5 : Verification Method

This verification method is applied on the previous BCD code checker. Its realization diagram is given in Figure 3. The specification and the realization of the BCD are described by the nodes BCD_SPEC and BCD_REAL, given in Sections 1.3 and 1.5 respectively.

The verification is done by comparing the "BCD_SPEC" and "BCD_REAL" descriptions of the BCD code checker. The verification criterion is the following : on the rising edge "edge" of the clock "ck", the input of the specification is sampled on "edge" and at every four-bit sequence identified by the signal "valid", then the output of BCD_SPEC and BCD_REAL are equal. In LUSTRE, we express this criterion by means of the node IMPLIES :

```
node IMPLIES  (a, b) returns (implies:bool) ;
let
     implies = not a or b ;
tel.
```

The verification will consist in traversing the state-transition graph of the following program "BCD_VERIF" and in checking that the variable "ok" is true in each state. The state-transition graph of this program contains 74 states. The example is simple, so the answer is instantaneous.

```
node BCD_VERIF(x, ck : bool) returns (ok : bool) ;
var edge, valid, y_REAL, y_SPEC : bool ;
let
     edge = EDGE (ck) ;
     (y_REAL, valid = BCD_REAL(x, edge) ;
      y_SPEC        = current (BCD_SPEC (x when edge)) ;
     ok = IMPLIES  (edge and valid, (y_REAL  = y_SPEC)) ;
tel.
```

4   Verification in a Constrained Environment

A circuit is usually designed to be integrated in a given environment. This environment imposes constraints on the values of the circuit's inputs as well as on its outputs. These constraints can be static, e.g. only one of a set of inputs can be true at every cycle, or dynamic, e.g. a multi-phase clock has nonoverlapping and cyclic phases. Note that dynamic constraints, that are constraints that involve time, depend on the abstraction level of the circuit description.

This section explains how the constraints imposed by the environment on some circuit's inputs are used in the verification process to avoid declaring a good circuit incorrect. Section 4.1 presents how the circuit designer can describe its circuit's environment in LUSTRE by means of "assertions". Section 4.2 then shows how these assertions are taken into account in the state-transition graph traversal procedure of LESAR. It then explains how the assertions can reduce proof times by reducing the number of states LESAR has to analyze. Section 4.3 illustrates the verification in a constrained environment on the example of the two-phase D flip-flop.

4.1 LUSTRE Assertions

Assertions have been introduced in the LUSTRE language to describe some known properties of the program environment. The idea was that these assertions could be used by the LUSTRE compiler to reduce the size of the program's control automaton. Assertions are Boolean expressions whose value is *invariably* true. They are given in the form :

assert [Boolean expression] ;

LUSTRE assertions can be used to describe both static and dynamic properties of the circuit's environment. For instance the assertion, specifying that the inputs in1 and in2 of a circuit cannot be true at the same time, will be written :

assert not (in1 and in2) ;

The assertion, stating that the initial value of the clock ck is true, will be written :

assert ck → true ;

Finally, the assertion :

assert true → (in1 = pre in1) or (in2 = pre in2) ;

specifies that, at each cycle, either the variable in1 or the variable in2 has the same value that it had at the previous cycle, which means that the values of these two variables never change at the same time. Initializing the expression to "true" is necessary to avoid the "nil" value, forbidden in the assertion values. This is forbidden in the output and clock values too, as noticed in section 1.2.

Complex dynamic assertions can be made of several equations. These equations can be put together into a LUSTRE node, which is then "asserted". Consider for instance the node ALTERNATE which states that the two phases "ph1" and "ph2" of a two-phase clock alternate without overlapping :

```
node ALTERNATE (ph₁, ph₂ : bool) returns (ok: bool) ;
var ph₁b, ph₂b : bool ;
let
    ph₁b = false → if edge (not ph₁) then true
                           else if edge (not ph₂) then false
                                        else pre(ph₁b) ;
    ph₂b = true  → if edge (not ph₂) then true
                           else if edge(not ph₁) then false
                                        else pre(ph₂b) ;
    ok = not (ph₁ and ph₁b) and not (ph₂ and ph₂b) ;
tel.
```

where edge(not ph₁) and edge(not ph₂) define the falling edges of the clocks "ph₁" and "ph₂". The node EDGE, defining the rising edge of a clock "ck" is given in section 1.5.

Table 4 illustrates the behaviour of the node ALTERNATE : the output variable "ok" is "true" if the phases "ph_1" and "ph_2" are alternated and nonoverlapping.

ph_1	true	false	false	false	false	true	true	false	false	false	false	...
ph_2	false	false	true	true	false	false	false	false	true	true	false	...
ph_1b	false	true	true	true	false	false	false	true	true	true	false	...
ph_2b	true	false	false	false	true	true	true	false	false	false	true	...
ok	true	true	true	true	true	true	true	true	true	true	true	...

Table 4 : Behaviour of the ALTERNATE node

Thus, the following assertion defines the two-phase nonoverlapping clock of the circuit :

   assert ALTERNATE (ph_1, ph_2) ;

4.2   State-transition Graph with regards to the Assertions

As mentioned above, assertions have been introduced in LUSTRE to help the compiler to optimize the state-transition graph of the automaton it produces. The idea is that assertions can eliminate some transitions in the state-transition graph, and consequently some states of this graph. Assertions can reduce the size of this state-transition graph, so the explosion of the graph can be avoided on complex examples.

   Figure 6 shows the state-transition graph with 4 states and 10 transitions which would be generated by the LUSTRE compiler without the assertion "not(e1 and e2)" given in the following node EXAMPLE. Figure 7 shows the state-transition graph actually produced by the compiler with only 3 states and 6 transitions. All the transitions labelled with the Boolean expression (e1 and e2) are eliminated and so is the state (3) which can only be reached with such a transition.

```
node EXAMPLE (e₁, e₂ : bool) returns (q₁, q₂ : bool) ;
let
    assert not (e₁ and e₂) ;
    q₁ = false → pre(e₁ or e₂);
    q₂ = false → pre(e₁ and e₂) ;
tel.
```

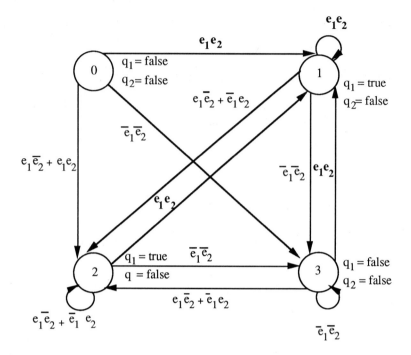

Figure 6 : State-transition graph without assertion

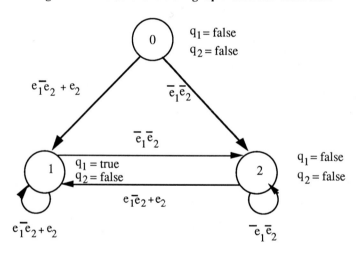

Figure 7 : State-transition graph with assertion

LESAR uses assertions in the same way as the compiler. During the traversal of the state diagram, each time an input pattern that labels a transition is invalidated by the assertions, the transition is not taken into account. This means that if some state in the graph can be reached only with such transitions, this state will never be considered during the traversal.

Note that assertions do not necessarily reduce the number of states that will be examined by LESAR during the verification of a LUSTRE program. In particular this number of states can be larger if the environment imposes dynamic constraints on the inputs. In this case the assertions that describe these constraints contain "pre" or "current" operators, so the compiler associates *new* state variables to these expressions. This means that the number of state variables associated to the program with the assertions is larger than the one associated to the program alone. This implies that the automaton obtained for the program with the assertions can have a larger number of states than the one for the program alone.

4.3 Example of the Two-phase D Flip-flop

Let us illustrate this approach with the example of a two-phase static register (master-slave flip-flop). The realization diagram of the one bit register or D flip-flop is given in Figure 8 (logical and electrical levels). The simple one bit register or latch, whose diagram is shown in Figure 9, gives the LUSTRE description of the D flip-flop.

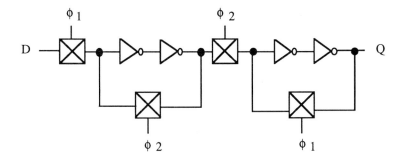

Figure 8 : D flip-flop (realization)

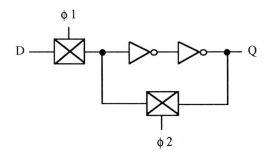

Figure 9 : Latch

328

The LUSTRE node of the latch is the following :

```
node LATCH (d, ph1, ph2 : bool ) returns (q : bool) ;
var x, y, z : bool ;
let
    x = d when ph1 ;
    y = q when ph2 ;
    z = if ph1 then current (x) else if ph2 then current (y) else pre (z) ;
    q = false → pre (z) ;
tel.
```

The LUSTRE description of the D flip-flop is directly obtained from the node LATCH, where the assertion of the ALTERNATE node defines the two-phase nonoverlapping clock (section 4.1) :

```
node FLIP_FLOP_REAL (d, ph1, ph2 : bool) returns (q : bool) ;
var q1 : bool ;
let
    q1 = LATCH (d, ph1, ph2) ;
    q = LATCH(q1, ph2, ph1) ;
    assert ALTERNATE (ph1, ph2) ;
tel.
```

The LUSTRE specification of the D flip-flop (architectural level) is given below :

```
node FLIP_FLOP_SPEC (d, ph1, ph2 : bool) returns (q : bool) ;
var q1 : bool ;
let
    q1 = false → pre (current (d when ph1)) ;
    q  = false → pre (current (q1 when ph2)) ;
tel.
```

The validation is directly performed by the comparison between the realization and the specification of the D flip-flop, with the following program. The compilation of this program gives a state-transition graph with 21 states ; the output variable "ok" is true in each state of the graph. The answer is instantaneous on this simple example.

```
node FLIP_FLOP_VERIF (d, ph1, ph2 : bool) returns (ok : bool) ;
var q_descr, q_spec : bool ;
let
    q_descr = FLIP_FLOP_REAL (d, ph1, ph2) ;
    q_spec = FLIP_FLOP_SPEC (d, ph1, ph2) ;
    ok = (q_descr = q_spec) ;
tel.
```

Conclusion

This paper has presented a verification method of circuits based on the synchronous declarative language LUSTRE. It has shown that LUSTRE can be used to describe circuits at the different abstraction levels used during their designs, i.e. from the behavioural level down to the gate level, and that LUSTRE can also be used to describe the environment of a circuit, by means of assertions. This means that the environment of a circuit is naturally taken into account during its verification.

The verification method proposed here allows us to verify that a circuit implementation is correct with respect to its high level specification. It could also be used to check that a circuit satisfies some safety properties. This other kind of verification, complementary and critical in the field of circuit design, will be very similar. In fact, it has been shown that these safety properties can be expressed in LUSTRE [HPOG 89] so that the circuit designer would not have to learn another language. This finally gives a natural way of making modular proofs : once a subpart of a circuit has been verified, it can be replaced by some assertions that express the properties of this subpart useful for the remainder of the proof. The use of modular verification will allow us to check complex circuits by reducing the size of the automaton that must be considered.

Both kinds of verification consist in proving that every state of some finite automaton satisfies a property, for instance that the value of some output is always equal to true. This verification is made by a tool called LESAR that takes as input the description of the automaton, i.e. its state variables and some equations, and traverses the state-transition graph of the automaton without building it. As soon as LESAR finds some state of the automaton where the property does not hold, the traversal is stopped and a diagnosis is performed.

The current version of LESAR uses state enumeration to traverse the state-transition graph of the automaton. It has been shown in [CBM 89] that this traversal procedure can be replaced by a traversal procedure that manipulates sets of states represented by their characteristic functions. This symbolic traversal procedure seems to be, in some cases but not in all, more efficient than the procedure used in LESAR. Some research is still necessary to determine the domains of applications of these procedures.

References

[ACH 86]   Amblard P., Caspi P., Halbwachs N. : *Use of time functions to describe and explain circuit behaviour* , IEE Proceedings-E, vol. 133, n° 5, September 1986.

[Bar 84]   Barrow H.G. : *Proving the Correctness of Digital Hardware Designs*, VLSI System Design, vol.5, n°7, July 1984.

[BC 86]   Browne M.C., Clarke E.M., : *Automatic Circuit Verification Using Temporal Logic : Two New Examples*, Formal Aspects of VLSI design, Edinburgh, 1985

[BFM 84]   Babiker S.A., Fleming R.A., Milne R.E. : *A tutorial for LTS* , R.R. 225 84 1, Standard Telecomunication Laboratories, 1984.

[BGLMOR 85]   Barbacci M.R., Grout S., Lindstrom G., Maloney M.P., Organick E.I., RudisilL D. : *ADA as a hardware description language : an initial report*, CHDL 85 : 7th International Conference on Computer Hardware Description Languages, Tokyo, August 1985.

[Boc 82]   Bochmann G.V. : *Hardware Specification with Temporal Logic : An Example*, IEEE Transactions on Computers , vol.c-31,n°3, March 1982.

[BPP 88]   Borrione D., Paillet J.L., Pierre L. : *Formal Verification of CASCADE descriptions*, Proc. IFIP WG 10.2 Internation Working Conference on "The fusion hardware design and verification", Glasgow (UK), 3-6 July 1988.

[BT 89]   Bronstein A., Talcott C.L. : *Formal Verification of Synchronous Circuits Based on String-Functional Semantics*, The 7th Paillet Circuits in Boyer-Moore, In Proc. Workshop on Automatic Verif. Methods for Finite State Systems, Grenoble, 1989.

[CBM 89]   Coudert O., Berthet C., Madre J.C. : *Verification of Sequential Machines Based on Symbolic Execution*, Proc. on Automatic Verifi. Methods for Finite State Systems, Grenoble, 1989.

[CHPP 87]   Caspi P., Halbwachs N., Pilaud D., Plaice J.A. : *LUSTRE, a declarative language for programming synchronous systems* , 14th ACM Symposium on principles of programming languages, Munich, January 1987.

[CP 88]   Camurati P., Prinetto P. : *Formal verification of hardware correctness : introduction and survey of current research*, IEEE Computer, vol.21,n°7, July 1988.

[Gor 85]   Gordon M. : *Why higher-order logic is a good formalism for specifying and verifying hardware*, Formal Aspects of VLSI design, Edinburgh, 1985.

[HLP 86]   Halbwachs N., Longchampt A., Pilaud D. : *Describing and designing circuits by means of a synchronous declarative language* , IFIP W.G. 10.2 Working Conference, Grenoble, September 1986.

[HPOG 89]   Halbwachs N., Pilaud D., Ouabdesselam F., Glory A.C. : *Specifying, Programming and Verifying Real-Time Systems, Using a Synchronous Declarative Language*, In Workshop on Automatic Verif. Methods for Finite State Systems, Grenoble, 1989.

[Hun 86]   Hunt W.A. : *FM8501 : A verified microprocessor*, Institute for Computing Science, University of Texas, Austin (USA), Technical report n°47, February 1986.

[Lar 87]   Larsson T. : *Specification and Verification of VLSI Systems Actional Behaviour*, CHDL 87 : 8th International Conference on Computer Hardware Description Languages, Amsterdam, April 1987.

[MC 85]   Mishra B., Clarke E. : *Hierarchical verification of asynchronous circuits using temporal logic*, TCS 38 (1985).

[Mos 85]   Moszkowski B. : *A Temporal Logic for Multilevel Reasonning about Hardware*, IEEE Computer, vol.18,n°2, February 1985.

[MP 81]   Manna Z., Pnueli A. : *Vérification of concurrent programs : the temporal framework*, In the Correctness Problem in Computer Science (R.S Boyer and J.S. Moore, eds), International Lecture Series in Computer Science, Academic Press, London, 1981.

[Pai 86]   Paillet J.L. : *A functional Model for Descriptions and Specifications of Digital Devices*, Proc. IFIP International Working Conference "From HDL descriptions to guaranteed correct circuit designs", Grenoble, September 1986.

[PH 87]   Plaice J.A., Halbwachs N. : *LUSTRE-V2 user's guide and reference manual*, October 1987.

[Pla 88]   Plaice J.A. : *Sémantique et compilation de LUSTRE, un langage déclaratif synchrone*, PhD Thesis, Institut National Polytechnique de Grenoble, May 1988.

[RRSV 87] Richier J.L., Rodriguez C., Sifakis J., Voiron J. : *Verification in Xesar of the sliding window protocol,* in IFIP W.G.-6.1 7th International Conference on Protocol Specification, Testing and Verification, North Holland, Zurich, 1987.

[She 84]   Sheeran M. : *muFP, a language for VLSI design* , ACM Symposium on Lisp and Functional Programming, Austin (Texas), 1984.

Optimising designs by transposition

Wayne Luk[*]

The purpose of this paper is fourfold: first, to describe some observations about how array-based designs can be optimised by transposition – a method of rearranging components and their interconnections; second, to provide concise parametric representations of such designs; third, to present simple equations that correspond to correctness-preserving transformations of these parametric representations; and finally, to suggest quantitative measures of design trade-offs involved in this kind of transformation.

Motivation

Consider the two designs in Figure 1. Notice that despite the structural differences of the circuits, the relative positions of the external connections are the same. This is achieved by the interleaving wires at the top and bottom of Design B. Transposition is the name for this kind of interleaving and also for the subsequent structure of components, since the rearrangement is similar to transposing matrices. It is clear that the functional behaviour (but not timing characteristics) of the two designs is indistinguishable; we shall show later how this situation can be expressed mathematically as a correctness-preserving transformation.

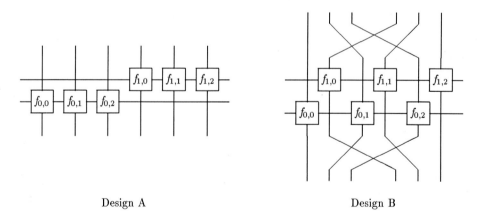

Design A   Design B

Figure 1: An example of transposing designs.

[*]Programming Research Group, Oxford University Computing Laboratory, 11 Keble Road, Oxford, England OX1 3QD; *wayne@prg.oxford.ac.uk*

Why are these designs interesting? In our experience Design A is a generic pattern that arises frequently in the development of circuits. For instance in developing an arithmetic and logic unit, it is more convenient to specify separately the arithmetic and logic operations: $f_{0,0}, f_{0,1}$ and $f_{0,2}$ may represent full adders that process interleaved representations of integers, and $f_{1,0}, f_{1,1}$ and $f_{1,2}$ may perform a specific logic operation, depending on the horizontal input, on their vertical inputs. Figure 2(a) shows a typical configuration in which the outputs of the full adders and the logic circuits are interleaved – transposed – before feeding into an array of multiplexers that select either output. It is, however, more advantageous to perform the transposition at the outset using the transformation described in Figure 1, since we would then be able to form a single array of composite cells each consisting of a full adder, a logic circuit and a multiplexer as shown in Figure 2(b). It is the aim of the circuit designer to use as few types of cell as possible in order to reduce the design and validation effort, because attention can be focused on optimising and testing the basic units which can then be replicated with confidence.

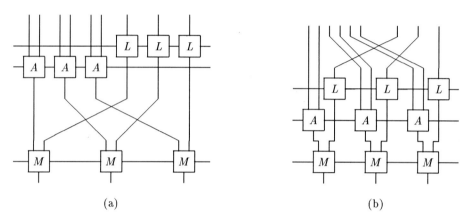

(a)   (b)

Figure 2: Two implementations of an ALU. A, L and M correspond respectively to a full adder, a logic circuit, and a multiplexer.

Another situation in which Design B in Figure 1 offers an improvement over Design A is as follows. Suppose that every component in Design A is latched. However, instead of depending on the propagation delay of the components, the clock speed of the system may be restricted by the propagation delay associated with the two long horizontal wires. In Design B the components are more evenly distributed and the problem of propagation delay is transferred to the wires implementing the transpositions. We shall see later the circumstances in which these peripheral transpositions can be eliminated to produce an efficient layout.

A further benefit of transposing components can be derived from altering the aspect ratio of a design. Given that one can overlay a wire on a component and that the connections of a component can be shifted as long as their direction and order are maintained, the configuration in Figure 3(a) can be implemented as described in Figure 3(b) or Figure 3(c). Hence if every component in Figure 1 has the same height h and the same width w, and

334

ignoring the contribution of the peripheral interleaving wires, then Design B may have an aspect ratio of either $2h \times 3w$ or $h \times 6w$. Design A is not as flexible; the same assumptions will result in an aspect ratio of $h \times 6w$.

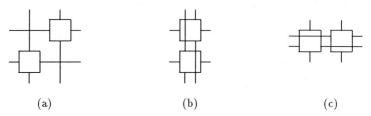

$\quad$(a) $\qquad\qquad\qquad\qquad$ (b) $\qquad\qquad\qquad\qquad$ (c)

Figure 3: Implementing transposition.

So much for motivation. The rest of the paper will describe a framework for expressing transposition parametrically, and will present a catalogue of such transformations together with quantitative measures of the trade-offs involved.

Notation

The formalism we use is based on Sheeran's relational framework and the author's heterogeneous combinators. The background and the details of this approach have been described elsewhere (see [2], [3]), and only the definitions and concepts relevant to our discussion will be introduced here.

A design will be described by a binary relation of the form $x\, f\, y \stackrel{\text{def}}{=} \mathcal{P}(x, y)$ where x, y represent the interface signals and belong to $dom(f)$ and $rng(f)$ (domain and range of f) respectively, and $\mathcal{P}$ is a predicate describing the intended behaviour. For example, an inverter can be specified as $x\, inv\, y \stackrel{\text{def}}{=} x = -y$.

The converse f^{-1} of a relation f is defined by $x\, (f^{-1})\, y \stackrel{\text{def}}{=} y\, f\, x$, and the identity relation is given by $x\, id\, y \stackrel{\text{def}}{=} x = y$. If f is a function, then $f\, x$ represents the value of f for the argument x.

Objects in our notation are either atoms (such as numbers or relations) or tuples of objects: for instance the object $\langle 0, \langle 1, 2 \rangle \rangle$ is a 2-tuple containing the number 0 and the tuple $\langle 1, 2 \rangle$. A tuple is an ordered collection of elements, with the empty tuple denoted by $\langle\, \rangle$. Tuples are concatenated by '$\hat{\ }$' (pronounced 'append'), so that

$$\langle a \rangle \hat{\ } \langle b, c, d \rangle = \langle a, b, c \rangle \hat{\ } \langle d \rangle = \langle a, b, c, d \rangle.$$

Given that x is a tuple, $\#x$ represents the number of elements in it, and x_i (where $0 \le i < \#x$) is its i-th element. Let us call a tuple of tuples a two-level tuple, a tuple of tuples of tuples a three-level tuple and so on. If x is a tuple with two or more levels, then $x_{i,j} \stackrel{\text{def}}{=} (x_i)_j$. Some operations on tuples are given below:

$$x\, \pi_{n+1}\, z \stackrel{\text{def}}{=} z = x_n \qquad \text{(select n-th x, $0 \le n < \#x$)},$$
$$\langle x, y \rangle\, swap\, z \stackrel{\text{def}}{=} z = \langle y, x \rangle, \quad \text{(swap components of 2-tuple)},$$

$$x \ tran \ z \ \overset{\text{def}}{=} \ \forall i, j : 0 \leq i < \#x, 0 \leq j < \#z. \quad \text{(transpose } x \text{, given that}$$
$$(\#x_i = \#z) \wedge (z_{j,i} = x_{i,j}) \qquad x \text{ is a tuple of tuples).}$$

For example, $tran \ \langle\langle 1,2,3\rangle, \langle 4,5,6\rangle\rangle = \langle\langle 1,4\rangle, \langle 2,5\rangle, \langle 3,6\rangle\rangle$. Notice that $tran$ is only defined for rectangular tuples – tuples in which all sub-tuples have the same length.

A rectangular circuit with connections on every side is modelled by a relation that relates 2-tuples, with the components in the domain corresponding to signals for the west and north side and those in the range corresponding to signals for the south and east side. In general, composite signals are represented as tuples with the position of a particular signal corresponding to its relative position, and with its structure – the grouping of signals – reflecting the logical organisation of adjacent signals.

Given a circuit f with connections on all four sides, we can use the generic reverse function $recrev$ which recursively reverses a tuple and all its component tuples

$$recrev \ x \ \overset{\text{def}}{=} \ x \text{ if } x = \langle\,\rangle \text{ or if } x \text{ is an atom,}$$
$$recrev \ (\langle x \rangle\char`^xs) \ \overset{\text{def}}{=} \ (recrev \ xs)\char`^\langle recrev \ x \rangle \text{ otherwise,}$$

to define $f^{\mathcal{V}}$ and $f^{\mathcal{H}}$ which denote respectively the reflection of f in a vertical and in a horizontal axis, and $f^{\mathcal{VH}}$ which denotes the reflection of f both vertically and horizontally:

$$\langle x, y \rangle \ f^{\mathcal{V}} \ \langle x', y' \rangle \ \overset{\text{def}}{=} \ \langle y', recrev \ y \rangle \ f \ \langle recrev \ x', x \rangle,$$
$$\langle x, y \rangle \ f^{\mathcal{H}} \ \langle x', y' \rangle \ \overset{\text{def}}{=} \ \langle recrev \ x, x' \rangle \ f \ \langle y, recrev \ y' \rangle,$$
$$\langle x, y \rangle \ f^{\mathcal{VH}} \ \langle x', y' \rangle \ \overset{\text{def}}{=} \ \langle recrev \ y', recrev \ x' \rangle \ f \ \langle recrev \ y, recrev \ x \rangle.$$

To deal with sequential circuits an expression is considered as relating a stream (an infinite tuple of data) in its domain to a stream in its range. In most cases, such as in the absence of conditionals, the same algebraic theorems can be applied to expressions representing both combinational and sequential systems [1].

Combinators

Combinators are higher-order functions that capture common patterns of computation as parametrised expressions. These patterns can represent behaviour, in which case the behaviour of a composite device is expressed in terms of the behaviour of its components; or they can represent the spatial organisation of a circuit, in which case they describe the connection of components to form the composite device. The following binary combinators are adapted from Ruby [2] to define various ways that two components can be connected together:

$$x \ (f ; g) \ z \ \overset{\text{def}}{=} \ \exists y. \ (x \ f \ y) \wedge (y \ g \ z) \qquad \text{(relational composition),}$$
$$\langle x, y \rangle \ (f \parallel g) \ \langle x', y' \rangle \ \overset{\text{def}}{=} \ (x \ f \ x') \wedge (y \ g \ y') \qquad \text{(parallel composition),}$$
$$\langle a, \langle b, c \rangle\rangle \ (f \mathbin{+\!\!\!+} g) \ \langle\langle p, q\rangle, r\rangle \ \overset{\text{def}}{=} \ \exists s. \ \langle a, b \rangle \ f \ \langle p, s \rangle \wedge \langle s, c \rangle \ g \ \langle q, r \rangle \quad \text{(beside),}$$
$$\langle\langle a, b\rangle, c\rangle \ (f \mathbin{\mp} g) \ \langle p, \langle q, r \rangle\rangle \ \overset{\text{def}}{=} \ \exists s. \ \langle a, s \rangle \ f \ \langle p, q \rangle \wedge \langle b, c \rangle \ g \ \langle s, r \rangle \quad \text{(below).}$$

Since $(f \mathbin{\mp} g)^{-1} = f^{-1} \mathbin{+\!\!\!+} g^{-1}$, we only need to work out the properties of either *beside* or *below*.

We shall use the abbreviations $\text{fst} \ f \overset{\text{def}}{=} f \parallel id, \text{snd} \ f \overset{\text{def}}{=} id \parallel f, \text{fsth} \ f \overset{\text{def}}{=} f \mathbin{+\!\!\!+} id, \text{sndh} \ f \overset{\text{def}}{=} id \mathbin{+\!\!\!+} f, \text{fstv} \ f \overset{\text{def}}{=} f \mathbin{\mp} id, \text{sndv} \ f \overset{\text{def}}{=} id \mathbin{\mp} f, f \backslash g \overset{\text{def}}{=} g^{-1} ; f ; g$ and $f \backslash\!\backslash g \overset{\text{def}}{=} g^{-1} \backslash swap; f; g$. These

Figure 4: Relational and parallel composition.

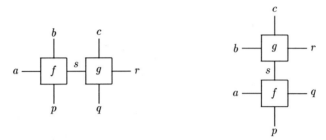

Figure 5: Beside and below.

abbreviations have interesting properties like $\mathsf{fst}f;\mathsf{fst}g = \mathsf{fst}(f;g)$, $\mathsf{fsth}(\mathsf{sndv}f) = \mathsf{sndv}(\mathsf{fsth}f)$, $(f\backslash g)\backslash h = f\backslash(g;h)$, $\mathsf{snd}f = (\mathsf{fst}f)\backslash swap$, and $\mathsf{snd}f^{-1};g;\mathsf{fst}f = g\backslash\backslash(\mathsf{fst}f)$. Note that prefix combinators have a higher precedence than infix ones, and that relational composition has the lowest precedence. The combinators $\backslash$, $\backslash\backslash$ have a lower precedence than all other binary combinators except relational composition.

One can check that in general none of the above binary combinators is commutative, and that only relational composition is associative. For instance, since $\langle\langle x,y\rangle,z\rangle$ and $\langle x,\langle y,z\rangle\rangle$ are distinct tuples, $(f \parallel g) \parallel h \neq f \parallel (g \parallel h)$. We now introduce a class of prefix combinators, called heterogeneous combinators, each of which takes a tuple of components and returns a binary relation corresponding to the composite circuit; and the components that are wired together can be different from one another. For instance, the parallel composition of three distinct components can be expressed as $(\parallel \langle f,g,h\rangle)$ which relates signals of the form $\langle x,y,z\rangle$. Given that $\#f = \#x = \#y = N$, the four common flavours of heterogeneous combinators are described below:

$$a \left(\overset{\circ}{9}\, f \right) b \;\equiv\; \exists s.\,(s_0 = a) \wedge (s_N = b) \wedge \forall i : 0 \leq i < N\,.\,s_i\, f_i\, s_{i+1} \quad \text{(het. chain)},$$

$$\overset{\circ}{9}\;\langle f_0, f_1, f_2, f_3\rangle$$

Figure 6: Heterogeneous chain.

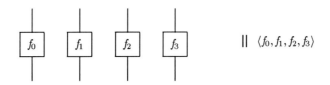

Figure 7: Heterogeneous map.

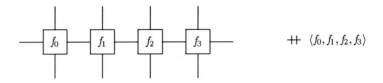

Figure 8: Heterogeneous row.

$$x \left(\; \| \; f \; \right) y$$
$$\equiv \; \forall i : 0 \leq i < N . \, x_i \, f_i \, y_i \qquad\qquad\qquad \text{(het. map)},$$

$$\langle a, x \rangle \left(\; + \!\!\!+ \; f \; \right) \langle y, b \rangle$$
$$\equiv \; \exists s . \, (s_0 = a) \wedge (s_N = b) \wedge \forall i : 0 \leq i < N . \, \langle s_i, x_i \rangle \, f_i \, \langle y_i, s_{i+1} \rangle \quad \text{(het. row)},$$

$$\langle x, a \rangle \left(\; \ddagger \; f \; \right) \langle b, y \rangle$$
$$\equiv \; \exists s . \, (s_0 = b) \wedge (s_N = a) \wedge \forall i : 0 \leq i < N . \, \langle x_i, s_{i+1} \rangle \, f_i \, \langle s_i, y_i \rangle \quad \text{(het. column)}.$$

Given $\Psi \in \left\{ \; \mathring{\!\!\;,}\; , \; \| \; , \; +\!\!\!+ \; , \; \ddagger \; \right\}$ and $0 \leq N \leq \# f$, we shall adopt the abbreviation

$$\underset{i < N}{\Psi} f_i \;\overset{\text{def}}{=}\; \Psi \langle f_i \mid 0 \leq i < N \rangle.$$

The following combinator will be used to describe a rectangular grid of heterogeneous components:

$$\underset{i,j < M,N}{\#} f_{i,j} \;\overset{\text{def}}{=}\; \underset{i < M}{\ddagger} \left(\underset{j < N}{+\!\!\!+} f_{i,j} \right).$$

For many applications the generality of heterogeneous combinators is not required. If f does not depend on i, then the following homogeneous combinators [2] can be used to describe arrays of identical components.

$$f^N \quad \overset{\text{def}}{=} \quad \underset{i<N}{\overset{\circ}{9}} f \qquad \text{(chain)}, \qquad (1)$$

$$\propto_N f \quad \overset{\text{def}}{=} \quad \underset{i<N}{\|} f \qquad \text{(map)}, \qquad (2)$$

$$\text{row}_N f \quad \overset{\text{def}}{=} \quad \underset{i<N}{+\!\!+} f \qquad \text{(row)}, \qquad (3)$$

$$\text{col}_N f \quad \overset{\text{def}}{=} \quad \underset{i<N}{\pm} f \qquad \text{(column)}, \qquad (4)$$

$$\text{grid}_{M,N} f \quad \overset{\text{def}}{=} \quad \text{col}_M \left(\text{row}_N f \right) \qquad \text{(rectangular grid)}. \qquad (5)$$

The subscripts associated with these combinators correspond to the size of the arrays, often omitted when they can be deduced from context.

Properties of transposition

Let us look at some properties of *tran* that will prove useful. If we write $\langle x_i | 0 \leq i < \#x \rangle$ as $\langle x_i | i \in I \rangle$ where I is the set of subscripts $\{i | 0 \leq i < \#x\}$, then the previous definition of *tran* can be rewritten as

$$tran \, \langle \langle x_{i,j} \, | \, j \in J \rangle \, | \, i \in I \rangle \;\; = \;\; \langle \langle x_{i,j} \, | \, i \in I \rangle \, | \, j \in J \rangle. \qquad (6)$$

This shows that transposing a tuple with two or more levels corresponds to permuting the positions of the two subscript generators $i \in I$ and $j \in J$.

From Equation 6 we can conclude that transposing an expression twice leaves it unchanged:

$$tran^2 \;\; = \;\; id_2, \qquad (7)$$

since permuting the positions of the subscript generators $i \in I$ and $j \in J$ twice will return the original expression. Here id_n is the identity relation on n-level rectangular tuples. Equation 7 also shows that $tran^{-1} = tran$.

Now consider the effect of the function $(tran; \propto tran)^3$ on tuples with three or more levels:

$$
\begin{aligned}
&((tran; \propto tran)^3) \, \langle\langle\langle x_{i,j,k} \, | \, k \in K \rangle \, | \, j \in J \rangle \, | \, i \in I \rangle \\
&= \; (\propto tran; (tran; \propto tran)^2) \, \langle\langle\langle x_{i,j,k} \, | \, k \in K \rangle \, | \, i \in I \rangle \, | \, j \in J \rangle \\
&= \; ((tran; \propto tran)^2) \, \langle\langle\langle x_{i,j,k} \, | \, i \in I \rangle \, | \, k \in K \rangle \, | \, j \in J \rangle \\
&= \; (\propto tran; (tran; \propto tran)) \, \langle\langle\langle x_{i,j,k} \, | \, i \in I \rangle \, | \, j \in J \rangle \, | \, k \in K \rangle \\
&= \; ((tran; \propto tran)) \, \langle\langle\langle x_{i,j,k} \, | \, j \in J \rangle \, | \, i \in I \rangle \, | \, k \in K \rangle \\
&= \; (\propto tran) \, \langle\langle\langle x_{i,j,k} \, | \, j \in J \rangle \, | \, k \in K \rangle \, | \, i \in I \rangle \\
&= \; \langle\langle\langle x_{i,j,k} \, | \, k \in K \rangle \, | \, j \in J \rangle \, | \, i \in I \rangle,
\end{aligned}
$$

so we obtain

$$(tran; \propto tran)^3 \;\; = \;\; id_3. \qquad (8)$$

Notice that at each step of the above derivation, the positions of two of the subscript generators are permuted. One can generalise this result for an M-level tuple where $M > N$ by applying a cyclic permutation to the first $N + 1$ subscript generators, so that

$$(tran\,;\,\alpha\,tran\,;\,\alpha^2\,tran\,;\,\ldots\,;\,\alpha^{N-1}\,tran)^{N+1} \;=\; id_{N+1}.$$

In other words,

$$\left(\,\mathop{\overset{\circ}{9}}_{i<N}\,\alpha^i\,tran\right)^{N+1} \;=\; id_{N+1}.$$

With $N = 1$ we obtain Equation 7, and with $N = 2$ we obtain Equation 8.

Next, we shall present three ways of eliminating $tran$ from an expression. The purpose is to remove unnecessary transpositions which are wasteful of area, or to make the description more uniform so that further optimisations can be applied.

Theorems with preconditions

The first method of eliminating $tran$ involves using theorems with preconditions. For example, with the precondition $h;g = id$, it can be shown that

$$\mathop{\overset{\circ}{9}}_{i<N}\,(g\,;\,f_i\,;\,h) \;=\; g\,;\left(\,\mathop{\overset{\circ}{9}}_{i<N}\,f_i\right);\,h,$$

$$\mathop{+\!\!\!+}_{i<N}\,(\mathsf{fst}\,g\,;\,f_i\,;\,\mathsf{snd}\,h) \;=\; \mathsf{fst}\,g\,;\left(\,\mathop{+\!\!\!+}_{i<N}\,f_i\right);\,\mathsf{snd}\,h,$$

$$\mathop{\#}_{i,j<M,N}\,(g\,\|\,g\,;\,f_{i,j}\,;\,h\,\|\,h) \;=\; \alpha g\,\|\,\alpha g\,;\,\mathop{\#}_{i,j<M,N}\,f_{i,j}\,;\,\alpha h\,\|\,\alpha h,$$

since the g's and h's within the array cancel one another. Instances of these theorems include

$$(g\,;\,f\,;\,h)^N \;=\; g\,;\,f^N\,;\,h,$$
$$\mathsf{row}\,(\mathsf{fst}\,g\,;\,f\,;\,\mathsf{snd}\,h) \;=\; \mathsf{fst}\,g\,;\,\mathsf{row}\,f\,;\,\mathsf{snd}\,h,$$
$$\mathsf{grid}\,(g\,\|\,g\,;\,f\,;\,h\,\|\,h) \;=\; \alpha g\,\|\,\alpha g\,;\,\mathsf{grid}\,f\,;\,\alpha h\,\|\,\alpha h.$$

Now we can use the result obtained in the last section: the above theorems will be applicable for $g = tran$ and $h = tran$, or $g = (tran\,;\,\alpha tran)$ and $h = (tran\,;\,\alpha tran)^2$, and so on. In this way transpositions in the wiring between adjacent cells can be eliminated.

Array of wiring cells

The second method of eliminating $tran$ involves developing an array of wiring cells that corresponds to an expression involving $tran$. For instance, given that

$$
\begin{aligned}
x\ fork\ y &\overset{\text{def}}{=} y = \langle x, x\rangle &&\text{(duplication)},\\
\langle x, xs\rangle\ apl\ y &\overset{\text{def}}{=} y = \langle x\rangle\hat{}\,xs &&\text{(append left)},\\
\langle xs, x\rangle\ apr\ y &\overset{\text{def}}{=} y = xs\hat{}\,\langle x\rangle &&\text{(append right)},\\
\langle\langle x\rangle\hat{}\,xs, y\rangle\ shl\ u &\overset{\text{def}}{=} u = \langle x, xs\hat{}\,\langle y\rangle\rangle &&\text{(shift left)},\\
\langle x, xs\hat{}\,\langle y\rangle\rangle\ shr\ u &\overset{\text{def}}{=} u = \langle\langle x\rangle\hat{}\,xs, y\rangle &&\text{(shift right)},
\end{aligned}
$$

340

it can be shown that

$$fork\,; (apr^{-1};\pi_1) \parallel (apl^{-1};\pi_2)\,; tran \;=\; apl^{-1}\,; \mathsf{row}\,(\mathsf{snd}\,fork;\,shr)\,;\pi_1,$$

$\mathsf{row}_4\,(\mathsf{snd}\,fork;\,shr)$

Figure 9: A row of wiring cells.

The right-hand side of the above equation is in the form of a row (Figure 9) and can be optimised further, such as combining its components with those of adjacent arrays. Other examples include

$$(f \parallel g \,\backslash\; tran) \,\backslash\backslash\, \mathsf{snd}\,swap \;=\; (\mathsf{snd}v\,f) + (\mathsf{fst}v\,g),$$
$$f \parallel g \,\backslash\; tran \;=\; (\mathsf{fst}v\,f) + (\mathsf{snd}v\,g).$$

Duplication and truncation

A further possibility of eliminating *tran* arises when signals are being duplicated or discarded. For instance, given the function dup_N which duplicates its argument N times,

$$x\,dup_N\,y \;\stackrel{\mathrm{def}}{=}\; (\#y = N) \wedge (\forall i : 0 \le i < N.\ y_i = x),$$

it can be shown that

$$dup_N\,; tran \;=\; \propto dup_N.$$

Similarly, for rectangular tuples of length less than or equal to i, we have

$$tran\,; \pi_i \;=\; \propto \pi_i.$$

Transposition theorems

Transposition theorems belong to one of several classes of theorems useful for circuit optimisation [4]. They relate circuits interleaved in different ways. In this section we give a number of transposing theorems that have been found useful in developing designs. Theorems involving columns can be derived from the corresponding theorems for rows, since $\mathsf{col}\,f \;=\; (\mathsf{row}\,(f^{-1}))^{-1}$.

Linear structures will be discussed first. The theorems obtained will then be extended to cover rectangular structures.

Linear arrays

First, let us consider a linear array that can be described as a map of maps. The components of the array can be transposed if the domain and the range signals are transposed accordingly

(Figure 10):

$$\underset{i<M}{\|} \left(\underset{j<N}{\|} f_{i,j} \right) = \underset{j<N}{\|} \left(\underset{i<M}{\|} f_{i,j} \right) \setminus \mathit{tran}. \tag{9}$$

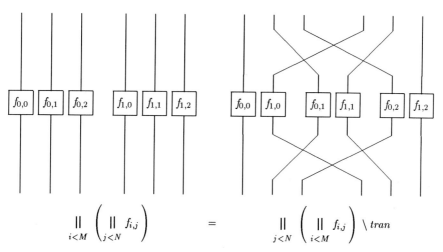

$$\underset{i<M}{\|} \left(\underset{j<N}{\|} f_{i,j} \right) \qquad = \qquad \underset{j<N}{\|} \left(\underset{i<M}{\|} f_{i,j} \right) \setminus \mathit{tran}$$

Figure 10: A theorem for transposing a map of maps ($M = 2$, $N = 3$).

A common special case of this theorem is

$$\propto (f \parallel g) = (\propto f \parallel \propto g) \setminus \mathit{tran}.$$

Next, we consider a collection of rows displaced horizontally and vertically from each other. They can be combined into a single row with the displacement transferred to the components; this usually results in a more compact layout as described in the introductory section:

$$\underset{i<M}{\|} \left(\underset{j<N}{+\!\!+} f_{i,j} \right) \setminus \mathit{tran} = \underset{j<N}{+\!\!+} \left(\underset{i<M}{\|} f_{i,j} \setminus \mathit{tran} \right) \setminus\!\!\setminus \mathsf{fst}\ \mathit{tran}. \tag{10}$$

An example of the circuits represented by this equation, with $M = 2$ and $N = 3$, is given in Figure 1.

Special cases of Equation 10 include

$$\propto (f +\!\!+ g) \setminus \mathit{tran} = (\propto f \setminus \mathit{tran}) +\!\!+ (\propto g \setminus \mathit{tran}) \setminus\!\!\setminus \mathsf{fst}\ \mathit{tran},$$
$$(\mathsf{row} f \parallel \mathsf{row} g) \setminus \mathit{tran} = \mathsf{row}\,(f \parallel g \setminus \mathit{tran}) \setminus\!\!\setminus \mathsf{fst}\ \mathit{tran}.$$

Rectangular arrays

The theorem for transposing linear arrays can be extended to deal with rectangular arrays:

$$\underset{k<K}{\|}\left(\underset{i,j<M,N}{\#} f_{k,i,j}\right) \backslash tran = \underset{i,j<M,N}{\#}\left(\underset{k<K}{\|} f_{k,i,j} \backslash tran\right) \backslash (tran \| tran). \quad (11)$$

Special cases of this theorem include

$$\propto (\operatorname{grid} f) \backslash tran = \operatorname{grid}(\propto f \backslash tran) \backslash (tran \| tran),$$
$$(\operatorname{grid} f \| \operatorname{grid} g) \backslash tran = \operatorname{grid}(f \| g \backslash tran) \backslash (tran \| tran).$$

Distributing components in arrays with bends

In this section we present some theorems for reasoning about arrays with bends in them. The idea is to distribute the components as evenly as possible throughout the network. The circuit *bend* is a piece of wire that bends backwards:

$$\langle x, y \rangle \ bend \ z \quad \overset{\mathrm{def}}{=} \quad x = y.$$

Note that x and y can themselves be tuples. In such cases cross-overs are needed to maintain the order of the signals (Figure 11). z is a dummy signal that corresponds to an unused connection.

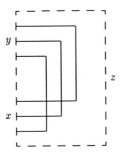

Figure 11: A vertical instance of the circuit *bend*.

We shall start by looking at how components can be distributed in linear arrays with a single bend. The results will then be extended to include linear and rectangular arrays with multiple bends.

Linear arrays with a single bend

A bend can be added to a chain of N components (Figure 12):

$$x \left(\underset{i<N}{\overset{\circ}{9}} f_i\right) y \equiv \langle x, y \rangle \left(\mathsf{fst} \ \underset{i<N}{\overset{\circ}{9}} f_i \ ; \ bend\right) z.$$

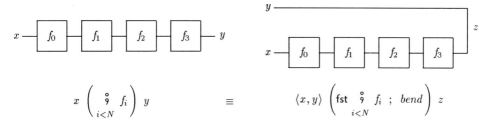

$$x \left(\underset{i<N}{\overset{\circ}{9}} f_i \right) y \qquad \equiv \qquad \langle x, y \rangle \left(\text{fst } \underset{i<N}{\overset{\circ}{9}} f_i \ ; \ bend \right) z$$

Figure 12: Adding a vertical bend to a chain ($N = 4$).

We can now move some of the components from the lower branch to the upper branch (Figure 13):

$$\text{fst} \left(\underset{i<N}{\overset{\circ}{9}} f_i \ ; \ \underset{i<N}{\overset{\circ}{9}} g_i \right) ; \ bend \ = \ \left(\underset{i<N}{\overset{\circ}{9}} f_i \right) \| \left(\underset{i<N}{\overset{\circ}{9}} g_{N-i-1}^{-1} \right) ; \ bend$$

$$= \ \underset{i<N}{\overset{\circ}{9}} (f_i \| g_{N-i-1}^{-1}) ; \ bend. \qquad (12)$$

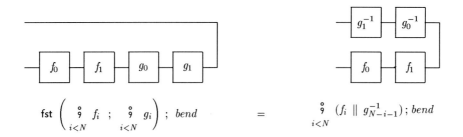

$$\text{fst} \left(\underset{i<N}{\overset{\circ}{9}} f_i \ ; \ \underset{i<N}{\overset{\circ}{9}} g_i \right) ; \ bend \qquad = \qquad \underset{i<N}{\overset{\circ}{9}} (f_i \| g_{N-i-1}^{-1}) ; \ bend$$

Figure 13: Transforming a chain with a vertical bend ($N = 2$).

For homogeneous arrays Equation 12 becomes

$$\text{fst} \, (f^N \ ; \ g^N) ; \ bend \ = \ (f \| g^{-1})^N ; \ bend.$$

Similarly, a bend can be added to a component with connections on every side:

$$\langle x, y \rangle \ f \ \langle u, v \rangle \ \equiv \ \langle \langle x, v \rangle, y \rangle \ (\text{fstv} \, f \ ; \ \text{snd} \, bend \ ; \ \pi_1) \ u.$$

One can move the component to the upper branch provided that it is reflected vertically,

$$\text{fstv} \, f \ ; \ \text{snd} \, bend \ = \ (\text{sndv} \, f^V) \, \backslash\!\backslash \, (\text{fst} \, recrev) \ ; \ \text{snd} \, bend.$$

From this, it is easy to derive an equation which introduces transposition to a circuit with two components:

$$\mathsf{fstv}\,(f \mathbin{+\!\!\!+} g)\ ;\ \mathsf{snd}\ bend\ =\ (f \parallel g^{\vee} \setminus tran)\ \backslash\!\backslash\ \mathsf{fst}\,(\mathsf{snd}\,recrev)\ ;\ \mathsf{snd}\ bend.$$

If both components are themselves rows of N components, then we can move half of the components from the lower branch to the upper branch and transpose the resulting circuit (Figure 14):

$$\mathsf{fstv}\left(\mathbin{\underset{i<N}{+\!\!\!+}} f_i \mathbin{+\!\!\!+} \mathbin{\underset{i<N}{+\!\!\!+}} g_i\right)\ ;\ \mathsf{snd}\ bend$$

$$=\ \left(\left(\mathbin{\underset{i<N}{+\!\!\!+}} f_i \parallel \mathbin{\underset{i<N}{+\!\!\!+}} g^{\vee}_{N-i-1}\right)\setminus tran\right)\ \backslash\!\backslash\ \mathsf{fst}\,(\mathsf{snd}\,recrev)\ ;\ \mathsf{snd}\ bend$$

$$=\ \mathbin{\underset{i<N}{+\!\!\!+}}\ (f_i \parallel g^{\vee}_{N-i-1} \setminus tran)\ \backslash\!\backslash\ \mathsf{fst}\ transrev\ ;\ \mathsf{snd}\ bend, \tag{13}$$

where

$$transrev\ \overset{\text{def}}{=}\ tran\ ;\ \mathsf{snd}\ recrev.$$

If the two arrays are homogeneous then Equation 13 becomes

$$\mathsf{fstv}\,(\mathsf{row}\,f \mathbin{+\!\!\!+} \mathsf{row}\,g)\,;\,\mathsf{snd}\ bend\ =\ \mathsf{row}(f \parallel g^{\vee} \setminus tran)\ \backslash\!\backslash\ \mathsf{fst}\ transrev\ ;\ \mathsf{snd}\ bend.$$

Linear arrays with multiple bends

We now explore how multiple bends can be introduced in linear arrays. First, observe that a bend can be twisted to form a zig-zag piece of wire containing three bends:

$$bend\ =\ \mathsf{snd}\,(\pi_2^{-1}\ ;\ shl\ \backslash\!\backslash\ (\mathsf{snd}\ bend)\ ;\ \pi_1)\ ;\ bend$$

This process can be continued so that a single bend can be twisted to form a piece of wire containing an odd number of bends:

$$bend\ =\ \mathsf{snd}\,(\pi_2^{-1}\ ;\ (\mathsf{col}_N\ shl)\ \backslash\!\backslash\ \mathsf{snd}\,(\propto_N bend)\ ;\ \pi_1)\ ;\ bend.$$

In the same vein one can add $2N-1$ bends to a chain of $2N$ components by the following theorem:

$$\mathsf{fst}\left(\mathbin{\underset{i<2N}{\overset{\circ}{9}}} f_i\right)\ ;\ bend\ =\ sndbends_N\ ;\ \mathsf{fst}\left(\mathsf{fst}\ \mathbin{\underset{i<2N}{\overset{\circ}{9}}} f_i\right)\setminus apl\ ;\ \propto_N bend$$

where

$$sndbends_N\ \overset{\text{def}}{=}\ \mathsf{snd}\,(\pi_2^{-1}\ ;\ \mathsf{fst}\,(\propto_{N-1} bend^{-1})\ ;\ \mathsf{col}_{N-1}\ shl)\ ;\ shr\ ;\ apl.$$

345

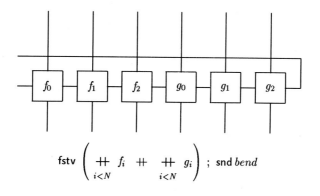

$$\mathsf{fstv}\left(\underset{i<N}{+\!\!\!+}\ f_i\ +\!\!\!+\ \underset{i<N}{+\!\!\!+}\ g_i\right)\ ;\ \mathsf{snd}\ bend$$

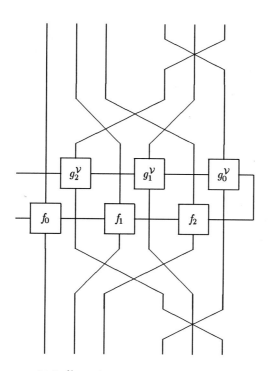

$$=\qquad \underset{i<N}{+\!\!\!+}\ (f_i\ \|\ g^{\mathcal{V}}_{N-i-1}\ \backslash\ tran)\ \backslash\!\backslash\ \mathsf{fst}\ transrev\ ;\ \mathsf{snd}\ bend$$

Figure 14: Transforming a row with a vertical bend ($N = 3$).

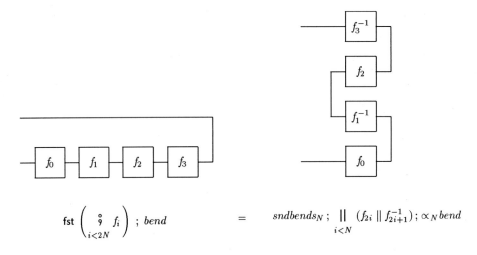

$$\textbf{fst}\left(\begin{smallmatrix}\circ\\9\\i<2N\end{smallmatrix} f_i\right)\; ; \; bend \qquad = \qquad sndbends_N\; ; \; \underset{i<N}{\|}\; (f_{2i}\;\|\; f_{2i+1}^{-1})\; ; \propto_N bend$$

Figure 15: Adding multiple bends to a chain ($N = 2$).

We then move some components from the bottom branch onto the other branches (Figure 15):

$$\textbf{fst}\left(\begin{smallmatrix}\circ\\9\\i<2N\end{smallmatrix} f_i\right)\; ; \; bend \;=\; sndbends_N\; ; \; \underset{i<N}{\|}\; (f_{2i}\;\|\; f_{2i+1}^{-1})\; ; \propto_N bend. \tag{14}$$

The same procedure can be applied to a row of components (Figure 16):

$$\textbf{fstv}\left(\underset{i<N}{+\!\!+}\; (f_{2i}+\!\!+ f_{2i+1})\right)\; ; \; \textsf{snd}\; bend \;=\; \textbf{fst}\; sndbends_N\; ; \; \Phi_N\; ; \; \textsf{snd}\propto_N bend$$

where

$$\Phi_N \;\overset{\text{def}}{=}\; \left(\underset{i<N}{\|}\; (f_{2i}\;\|\; f_{2i+1}^\nu \setminus tran)\setminus tran\right)\;\backslash\!\backslash\; \textbf{fst}\propto(\textsf{snd}\,recrev). \tag{15}$$

The above two theorems can be specialised to deal with homogeneous arrays:

$$\textbf{fst}\; f^{2N}\; ; \; bend$$
$$=\; sndbends_N\; ; \propto_N (f\;\|\; f^{-1})\; ; \propto_N bend,$$

$$\textbf{fstv}\; (row_N\; (f+\!\!+ f))\; ; \; \textsf{snd}\; bend$$
$$=\; \textbf{fst}\; sndbends_N\; ; \; (\propto_N (f\;\|\; f^\nu \setminus tran)\setminus tran)\;\backslash\!\backslash\; \textbf{fst}\propto(\textsf{snd}\,recrev)\; ; \; \textsf{snd}\propto bend_N.$$

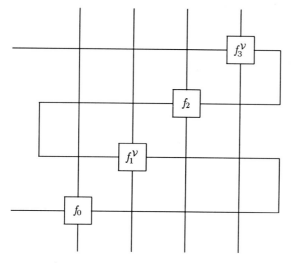

$$\text{fst } sndbends_N \text{ ; } \left(\underset{i<N}{\|\|} \ (f_{2i} \ \|\ f_{2i+1}^{\nu} \setminus tran) \setminus tran \right) \ \|\| \ \text{fst } \propto (snd\,recrev) \text{ ; } snd \propto_N bend$$

Figure 16: Adding multiple bends to a row of components ($N = 2$).

Rectangular arrays with multiple bends

In this section we extend the results for linear arrays to cover rectangular arrays. First, let us state two theorems for rearranging vertical bends in rectangular arrays:

$$\text{fstv} \left(\underset{i,j<M,N}{\#\#} f_{i,j} \ + \!\!\!+ \ \underset{i,j<M,N}{\#\#} g_{i,j} \right) \text{ ; } snd \ bend$$

$$= \ \text{fst } tran \text{ ; } \underset{i,j<M,N}{\#\#} \ (\text{fstv } f_{i,j}) \ + \!\!\!+ \ \underset{i,j<M,N}{\#\#} \ (\text{fstv } g_{i,j}) \text{ ; } snd \ (\propto bend) \tag{16}$$

$$= \ \text{fst } tran \text{ ; } \underset{i,j<M,N}{\#\#} \ (f_{i,j} \ \|\ g_{i,N-j-1}^{\nu} \setminus tran) \ \|\| \ \text{fst } transrev \text{ ; } snd \ (\propto bend) \tag{17}$$

where $transrev \overset{\text{def}}{=} tran \text{ ; } snd\,recrev$ as before. Equation 16 corresponds to implementing the feedback paths as internal wiring cells, and Equation 17 corresponds to a transposition forming composite cells each consisting of an $f_{i,j}$ and a reflected version of $g_{i,N-j-1}$ (Figure 17).

Again these can be specialised for homogeneous grids, for example:

$$\text{fstv } (\text{grid} f \ + \!\!\!+ \ \text{grid} g) \text{ ; } snd \ bend$$
$$= \ \text{fst } tran \text{ ; } \text{grid} (f \ \|\ g^{\nu} \setminus tran) \ \|\| \ \text{fst } transrev \text{ ; } snd \ (\propto bend).$$

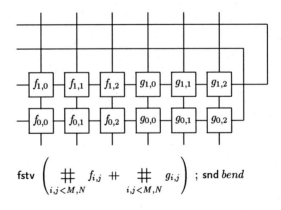

$$\mathsf{fstv} \left(\underset{i,j<M,N}{\#} f_{i,j} \; +\!+ \; \underset{i,j<M,N}{\#} g_{i,j} \right) \; ; \; \mathsf{snd} \; \textit{bend}$$

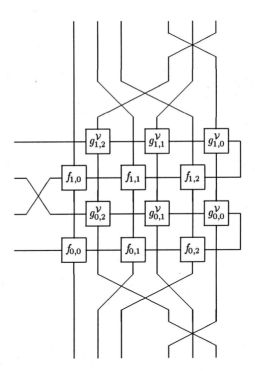

$$= \quad \mathsf{fst} \; \textit{tran} \; ; \quad \underset{i,j<M,N}{\#} \; (f_{i,j} \; \| \; g^{\nu}_{i,N-j-1} \; \backslash \; \textit{tran}) \; \backslash\!\backslash \; \mathsf{fst} \; \textit{transrev} \; ; \; \mathsf{snd} \, (\propto \textit{bend})$$

Figure 17: Rectangular arrays with multiple vertical bends ($M = 2$, $N = 3$).

Next, consider a grid consisting of four heterogeneous arrays:

$$grid4\,\langle p,q,r,s\rangle \quad \overset{\text{def}}{=} \quad \left(\underset{i,j<M,N}{\#}p_{i,j} \,+\!\!+\, \underset{i,j<M,N}{\#}q_{i,j}\right) \ddagger \left(\underset{i,j<M,N}{\#}r_{i,j} \,+\!\!+\, \underset{i,j<M,N}{\#}s_{i,j}\right).$$

A rectangular array with vertical and horizontal bends (the top diagram of Figure 19) can be described by

$$grid4bends\,\langle p,q,r,s\rangle \quad \overset{\text{def}}{=} \quad \mathsf{fsth}\,(\mathsf{fstv}(grid4\,\langle p,q,r,s\rangle));\,bend\,\|\,bend.$$

The first optimisation, as before, is to implement the feedback paths as wiring cells within the array. This is captured by the following theorem:

$$grid4bends\,\langle p,q,r,s\rangle \quad = \quad map2tran\,;\,grid4\,\langle \Omega\,p,\,\Omega\,q,\,\Omega\,r,\,\Omega\,s\rangle\,;\,map2bend \qquad (18)$$

where

$$\Omega\,f \quad \overset{\text{def}}{=} \quad \underset{i,j<M,N}{\#}\,(\mathsf{fsth}\,(\mathsf{fstv}\,f_{i,j})),$$

$$map2tran \quad \overset{\text{def}}{=} \quad (tran\,;\,\propto tran)\,\|\,(tran\,;\,\propto tran),$$

$$map2bend \quad \overset{\text{def}}{=} \quad (\propto bend\,\|\,\propto bend)\,\|\,(\propto bend\,\|\,\propto bend).$$

However, there are still long combinational paths in the circuit which can be eliminated by a further rearrangement of components. Before doing that, let us define the combinator representing the wiring pattern that will be required (Figure 18):

$$transwap\,\langle a,b,c,d\rangle \quad \overset{\text{def}}{=} \quad ((\mathsf{sndh}\,a\,\|\,\mathsf{sndh}\,b)\setminus tran) \ddagger ((\mathsf{fsth}\,c\,\|\,\mathsf{fsth}\,d)\setminus tran).$$

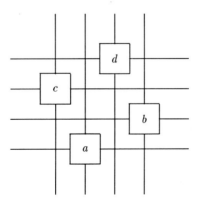

Figure 18: $transwap\,\langle a,b,c,d\rangle$.

350

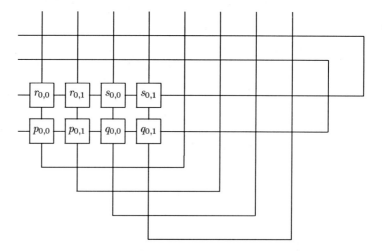

$$\mathbf{fsth}\left(\mathbf{fstv}(grid4\,\langle p,q,r,s\rangle)\right);\; bend \parallel bend$$

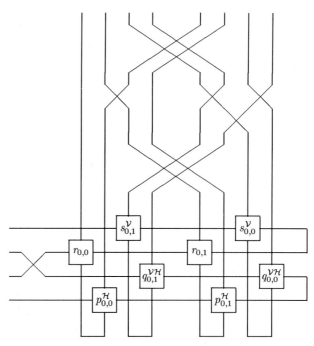

$$= \; maprevs\,;\; \underset{i,j<M,N}{\#}\left(transwap\,\langle p^{\mathcal{H}}_{M-i-1,j},\, q^{\mathcal{VH}}_{M-i-1,N-j-1},\, r_{i,j},\, s^{\mathcal{V}}_{i,N-j-1}\rangle\right);\; mapbend2$$

Figure 19: Rectangular arrays with vertical and horizontal bends ($M=1$, $N=2$).

A useful result concerning *transwap* is

$$\textsf{fstv}\,(\textsf{fsth}\ \#\ \langle\langle a,b\rangle,\langle c,d\rangle\rangle)\,;\,bend\parallel bend\ =\ revs\,;\,transwap\,\langle a^{\mathcal{H}},b^{\mathcal{VH}},c,d^{\mathcal{V}}\rangle\,;\,parbend2,$$

where

$$revs \overset{\text{def}}{=} (tran;\textsf{fst}\,(recrev\parallel recrev))\parallel(tran;\textsf{snd}\,(recrev\parallel recrev)),$$
$$parbend2 \overset{\text{def}}{=} (bend\parallel bend)\parallel(bend\parallel bend).$$

Using this we can obtain a theorem that produces a more even distribution of components for $grid4bends\,\langle p,q,r,s\rangle$, an instance of which is depicted in Figure 19:

$$grid4bends\,\langle p,q,r,s\rangle$$

$$=\ maprevs\,;\ \underset{i,j<M,N}{\#}\left(transwap\,\langle p^{\mathcal{H}}_{M-i-1,j},q^{\mathcal{VH}}_{M-i-1,N-j-1},r_{i,j},s^{\mathcal{V}}_{i,N-j-1}\rangle\right)\,;$$

$$mapbend2 \tag{19}$$

where

$$maprevs \overset{\text{def}}{=} (tran\,;\,\textsf{fst}\propto recrev\,;\propto tran\,;\,tran)\parallel(tran\,;\,\textsf{snd}\propto recrev\,;\propto tran\,;\,tran),$$
$$mapbend2 \overset{\text{def}}{=} \propto(bend\parallel bend)\parallel\propto(bend\parallel bend).$$

These theorems can be specialised for homogeneous networks as well; for instance one can show that

$$\textsf{fstv}\,(\textsf{fsth}\,(\textsf{grid}_{2,2}\,(\textsf{grid}_{M,N}\,f)))\,;\,bend\parallel bend$$
$$=\ maprevs\,;\,\textsf{grid}_{M,N}\,(transwap\,\langle f^{\mathcal{H}},f^{\mathcal{VH}},f,f^{\mathcal{V}}\rangle)\,;\,mapbend2.$$

Trade-off analysis

This section suggests some quantitative measures of the trade-offs involved in the transformations discussed in the preceding sections. As explained in the introductory section, transposition usually results in a more uniform distribution of components in the array at the expense of increasing the complexity of the interface. In the following estimation of size and performance the contribution of the interface will not be included since it is usually application- or implementation-dependent. Hence the reader must check for the particular situation whether the improvement brought by the transformation is offset by the increased complexity of the interface.

Table 1 summarises the effects of various transposition strategies introduced earlier. The calculation is based on the simplified case in which all components have the same aspect ratio $h \times w$. We also assume, as explained in the introductory section, that wires can be overlaid on components in assessing the alteration of aspect ratio, and that all components are latched in estimating the reduction of long combinational paths.

Table 1: Summary of trade-offs in transposition strategies, showing the features of the designs represented by the left- and the right-hand side of a given equation in the text.

Equation	LHS aspect ratio	RHS aspect ratio	LHS longest path	RHS longest path
9	$h \times MNw$	$h \times MNw$ or $Mh \times Nw$	0	h or 0
10	$h \times MNw$	$h \times MNw$ or $Mh \times Nw$	h or Nw	h or w
11	$KMh \times KNw$	$KMh \times Nw$ or $Mh \times KNw$	$(K-1)Mh$ or $(K-1)Nw$	$(K-1)h$ or $(K-1)w$
14	$h \times 2Nw$	$2Nh \times w$	$2Nw$	0
15	$h \times 2Nw$	$2Nh \times w$	$2Nw$	$(2N-1)h$
16	$Mh \times 2Nw$	$Mh \times 2Nw$	$(M-1)h + 2Nw$	$2Nw$
17	$Mh \times 2Nw$	$Mh \times 2Nw$ or $2Mh \times Nw$	$(M-1)h + 2Nw$	h or w
18	$2Mh \times 2Nw$	$2Mh \times 2Nw$	$2(M-1)h + 2Nw$ or $2Mh + 2(N-1)w$	$2Mh$ or $2Nw$
19	$2Mh \times 2Nw$	$4Mh \times Nw$ or $Mh \times 4Nw$	$2(M-1)h + 2Nw$ or $2Mh + 2(N-1)w$	$4h$ or $4w$

Concluding remarks

We have developed a number of techniques for optimising array-based designs by component transposition. The major innovations include the description of properties of *tran* that are useful for design optimisation and the collection of theorems for transforming expressions with *tran* and *bend*. Let us summarise the main features of our work and examine its design implications.

Summary

A principal challenge in providing a theory for transforming designs is to find useful design abstractions. We have identified the parametrised building blocks *tran* and *bend* and showed how they correspond to common ways of interconnecting components. These generic building blocks allow concise descriptions of complex wiring patterns.

The use of *tran* and *bend* also enables us to follow a simple equational style of presenting transformations. Several schemes for transposing components of regular array circuits have been discussed. Although the more refined versions require a higher degree of sophistication in interface arrangements, they can still be captured succinctly using the appropriate combinators and primitives. These transformations form a valuable part of a coherent framework for developing and optimising designs (see [2], [3], [4], [6], [7]).

Design implications

The increase in performance brought by transposing components comes mainly from localising interconnections by wiring cells. The elimination of long wires reduces the area and power required for a circuit. We have also indicated how further improvements can be obtained by wiring over the computational blocks, a technique which is eased by the adoption of multi-layer interconnections in some CMOS technologies. An advantage of our approach is that the transformations preserve the regularity of the architecture. This simplifies both the implementation of regular array circuits and the comparison of alternative designs.

Our work, however, is not restricted to custom integrated circuit designs; for instance, transposition can also be applied to vary the array dimensions of programmable cellular structures in order to maximise cell utilisation.

The introduction of bends provides a further opportunity for meeting design constraints, such as satisfying requirements for an array to conform to a given aspect ratio or for the input and output ports to be arranged in a specific manner. In particular, our work provides a possible optimisation for systolic implementations involving long feedback paths [5]. The optimised design can be achieved with little additional effort as the transformations only involve the reflection of components. A more complicated interface may be required, however, although this may not be an issue if the data come in the right format or if the resulting increase in performance justifies the complication.

Further work is needed in three areas. First, a deeper understanding of the scope and the value of transposition requires the application of this method to circuits of greater complexity than those discussed in this paper. Second, it is important to study how transposition fits in with other techniques – such as pipelining – in order to provide an overall strategy for optimising designs. Third, the implementation of transposition should be facilitated by appropriate computer-based tools which are compatible with other circuit design aids and cell libraries.

354

Acknowledgements. I thank Geraint Jones for contributing the bottom array in Figure 19 and for providing useful suggestions. I also thank Michael Jampel, Mary Sheeran and the referees of this paper for their comments. The support of the UK Alvey Programme (Project ARCH 013), the Croucher Foundation and Rank Xerox (UK) Limited is gratefully acknowledged.

References

[1] G. Jones and M. Sheeran, *Timeless truths about sequential circuits*, in S. K. Tewksbury, B. W. Dickinson and S. C. Schwartz (eds.), *Concurrent computations: algorithms, architectures and technology*, pp. 245–259, Plenum Press, 1988.

[2] G. Jones and M. Sheeran, *Circuit design in Ruby*, in J. Staunstrup (ed.), *Formal methods for VLSI design*, North-Holland, 1990.

[3] W. Luk, *Specifying and developing regular heterogeneous designs*, in L. Claesen (ed.), *Formal VLSI specification and synthesis*, pp. 391–409, North-Holland, 1990.

[4] W. Luk and G. Jones, *The derivation of regular synchronous circuits*, in K. Bromley, S. Y. Kung and E. Swartzlander (eds.), *Proceedings of International Conference on systolic arrays*, pp. 305–314, IEEE Computer Society Press, 1988.

[5] J. Moreno and T. Lang, *On partitioning the Faddeev algorithm*, in K. Bromley, S. Y. Kung and E. Swartzlander (eds.), *Proceedings of International Conference on systolic arrays*, pp. 125–134, IEEE Computer Society Press, 1988.

[6] L. Rossen, *HOL formalisation of Ruby*, Technical Report ID-TR 1989–61, Department of Computer Science, Technical University of Denmark, 1989.

[7] S. Singh, *An application of non-standard interpretation: testability*, in L. Claesen (ed.), *Formal VLSI correctness verification*, pp. 235–244, North-Holland, 1990.

Author Index

Aagaard, Mark 171
Akella, Venkatesh 99
Borrione, Dominique 153
Brown, Geoffrey M. 120
Busch, Holger 271
Camurati, Paolo 253
Collavizza, Hélène 153
Delgado Kloos, Carlos 212
Dosch, Walter 212
Eker, S. M. 231
Gopalakrishnan, Ganesh 99
Hoare, C. A. R. 196
Hughes, John 92
Johnson, Steven D. 50
Josephs, Mark B. 132
Joyce, Jeffrey J. 68
Leeser, Miriam 171
Luk, Wayne 332
Margaria, Tiziana 253
Mendler, Michael 1
Pilaud, Daniel 313
Prinetto, Paolo 253
Rossen, Lars 297
Stavridou, V. 231
Suk, Dany 29
Thuau, Ghislaine 313
Tucker, J. V. 231
Udding, Jan Tijmen 132
Zhou, Chaochen 196
Zhu, Zheng 50